SELLING HITLER

NICHOLAS O'SHAUGHNESSY

Selling Hitler

Propaganda and the Nazi Brand

HURST & COMPANY, LONDON

First published in the United Kingdom in 2016 by
C. Hurst & Co. (Publishers) Ltd.,
41 Great Russell Street, London, WC1B 3PL
© Nicholas O'Shaughnessy, 2016
All rights reserved.
Printed in India

Distributed in the United States, Canada and Latin America by
Oxford University Press, 198 Madison Avenue, New York, NY 10016,
United States of America.

The right of Nicholas O'Shaughnessy to be identified as the author
of this publication is asserted by him in accordance with the
Copyright, Designs and Patents Act, 1988.

A Cataloguing-in-Publication data record for this book
is available from the British Library.

ISBN: 9781849043526 *hardback*

This book is printed using paper from registered sustainable
and managed sources.

www.hurstpublishers.com

CONTENTS

PREFACE

Democracy is a relatively new political form in the grand sweep of history, sufficiently new for questions of its long-term survivability not to have entirely disappeared. That it can be manipulated by those most hostile to it, that talents of persuasion can sabotage debate and turn public opinion into a commodity like any other, that false consciousness can be engendered, is epitomised by the story of Adolf Hitler.

For many years I had studied political persuasion techniques of commercial derivation, subjects discussed at length in my first book, *The Phenomenon of Political Marketing* (1990).[1] It seemed to me then that 'marketing' was no mere metaphor but a relevant and useful perspective and a way of interpreting US politics and government. This focus yielded to a more general interest in political communication, specifically its more polemical forms, and thus an intellectual ambition to revive the now defunct term 'propaganda' both as a concept and a field of study. Such work had broadened within and beyond political marketing to graduate into related territories, with emotion and symbolisation as the underlying constructs. It could, therefore, be only a matter of time before I alighted on history's most destructive display of both marketing and propaganda, as embodied in the Third Reich, a dystopia which I came to believe would have been impossible without the concept that lay at its heart. Mastery of persuasion explains its rise, sustenance and protracted death-pangs, and the enormity of its atrocity. Such engagement then did not arise from any primary interest in Nazism per se, but because the Hitler regime represented the enthronement of both marketing and propaganda not as mere instruments but as the essential core of government. And herein is their uniqueness as a historical context. Nazism, quite simply, was history's ultimate political campaign, and is therefore of perennial interest to students of campaigning.

Hitler was perhaps not the last but the first, the herald of a new epoch of public duplicity. The journalist John Rentoul[2] has criticised the fatuity of my comparisons of Hitler with latter-day politicians. But I repeat the heresy, for while 'Godwin's law' is an obvious truism, Hitler was way ahead of his era in comprehending the 'engineering of consent'—the troubling matter of how public opinion can be manufactured, and governments elected, via the use of sophisticated methodologies of persuasion developed in the consumer economy.

I would argue that, specifically in the case of the Third Reich, there is merit in some external contribution. Hitler cannot be an exclusive historians' monopoly: psychiatry, for example, surely has something to say on the subject of a historical actor as complex as him. Previous studies of German propaganda under the Third Reich, some extremely distinguished, have tended towards richly descriptive, narrative storytelling; however, there is value in seeking to engage intellectual hinterlands in psychology or the social sciences, and in analytic approaches that might illuminate our conceptual understanding of this phenomenon while avoiding the speculative excesses of 'theory'.

There are certainly limitations in the methods chosen here. Reliance on the Calvin College German Propaganda Archive (which effectively opens up this territory to contemporary scholars) has been extensive, but no serious student of the subject could have done otherwise. It is simply there, astonishing in its wealth; it is a compass that enables scholars to navigate the world of Nazi propaganda, a 'real gem' in the words of Aristotle Kallis. I might also have chosen a different, less pictorial writing style. But the significance of the subject matter and the enormity of its consequences for the human race, the misery it inflicted and the new global order it catalysed, surely justifies a more hyperbolic language. Another feature of the book is extensive citation. However, those who write on Reich propaganda are a small group of scholars possessed of rare eloquence of literary expression and are eminently quotable (such as Frederic Spotts or Jay W. Baird or Corey Ross). But there is also a need for confirmatory support and concurrent authority from practising historians since the claims being made here, although not a radical challenge to the conventional historical interpretations of this period, are not the orthodoxy either.

I would like to thank those who have helped me in this task, and those who have simply waited for its completion. My gratitude in particular to

PREFACE

Giles MacDonogh, who advised on the manuscript and bestowed on me the immense benefit of his command of 250 years of German history; to my cousin Mary Manning, whose expertise in languages has been a valuable resource; to my publisher, Michael Dwyer, who has encouraged and guided me from the very beginning of this project; and to Dr Tim Page, my excellent editor at Hurst. To my parents, John and Marjorie, and my brother Andrew. And to all my friends, who have awaited the long-promised emergence of this volume with at least the facsimile of patience.

Nicholas O'Shaughnessy   London, June 2016

INTRODUCTION

The Ubiquity of Propaganda

As the events of the twentieth century recede in time, an emerging perspective, framed by scholars such as Tim Snyder, has begun to focus on the irrational carnage of that historic era, the 'homicidal radicalism'[1] of which owes much to the totalitarian and/or collectivist ideologies of the age. Yet any cogent explanation of the twentieth century and its assorted terrors—Hitler, Stalin, the Khmer Rouge—clearly needs to go beyond ideology; millenarian and utopian schemes had existed for many centuries prior to the twentieth, and they are likely to exist for many more to come. Rather than attributing the mass slaughter of that era to ideology alone, it is important to recognise that the unique nihilism of the century in fact arose from the union of propaganda and ideology, with the two working together, in Harold Lasswell's words, to push millions of human beings 'into one amalgamated mass of hate and will and hope...'[2]

But history is a public activity as well as a scholarly one, and in this popular or collective public memory the Third Reich stands out as the most vivid, and terrible, of all historic phenomena. Part of this public resonance is its apparent inexplicability: how was it possible for a nation as sophisticated as Germany to regress in the way that it did, for Hitler and the Nazis to enlist an entire people, willingly or otherwise, into a crusade of extermination that would kill anonymous millions? It is an enigma, and the thesis of this work is that a necessary part of the explanation lies in the Nazis' mastery of propaganda, and in the ideology–propaganda nexus; the aim of this book is to elucidate both. The internal–rhetorical conquest of mind via propaganda augmented the external–military conquest of land and people

1

via war. The contention of this book is that the Third Reich's success in driving an ostensibly civilised European country towards this outcome can only be understood by re-examining the nature of the regime and the relationship between Nazi ideology and propaganda.

In what follows, the book argues that the Nazi regime should be viewed and understood as the most comprehensive public relations operation in history, one which was conceived by Hitler himself, whose principal appeal was to a form of social idealism, not hatred. The argument is that Hitler and not Goebbels was the conceptualiser of the propaganda realm: he was its ultimate administrator and editor-in-chief. An ideologue of propaganda to the core, he believed this was the best way to gain and retain power.

This introduction sets out the context, argument and conceptual framework of the book, beginning with a brief discussion of propaganda in the broader context of the time before turning to the methods used by the regime. It then goes on to outline the conceptual structure and the implications of the book's argument for the public understanding of the Third Reich.

Context of Reich Propaganda

The Nazi propaganda regime was heavily informed by a (mis)reading of history, according to which the British had won the First World War due to the negative impact of Lord Northcliffe's enemy propaganda department at Crewe House on the morale of the German army. This was never true of course, as the great Allied turnaround in the summer of 1918 was largely due to superior Allied strategy. However, this narrative, which was held by a broad section of German society, featured heavily in the post-war political engagement with public opinion, which was to become the new essence of political leadership in Germany after the extension of the franchise. But whereas the post-war Allied discourse focused on the abuse of propaganda, the German discourse was about its ineffective use[3]—the propaganda of the Allies in the First World War had supposedly been superior to that of Germany owing to its use of 'scientific' methods. This discourse took centre stage under Weimar, and with it the notion that propaganda could be used to 'manipulate the masses at will'.[4] The propaganda credo therefore arose from Hitler's deep chauvinism: his belief that the Imperial German Army could not be vanquished by licit methods but by magic, and that the name of that magic was propaganda—a naive 'magic bullet', or hypodermic, model of persuasion. The success of the British, according to this interpretation, was largely the result of the way in which they treated the general and the journalist as being of equal importance in winning the war.[5]

This belief in the utility of propaganda arose not only from the retrospective diagnoses of German failure in the First World War. It also derived from a pre-existent rhetorical tradition in German and Austrian political culture: a recourse to ethno-nationalist hyperbole which long pre-dated not only the war but even the era of Bismarck. Political polemic was a German custom, beginning with the first assertions of Teutonic exceptionalism in the Napoleonic Wars (1803–15). Hence it was almost inevitable that ethno-nationalist discourse would find fertile soil in Weimar Germany owing to the legacy of rhetoric in the public heritage, from the anti-Semitic diatribes of Karl Lueger, mayor of Vienna, to the nineteenth-century political Tractarians and their books and assorted texts; for it was in this period that the hyper-nationalist creed appears to have first assumed literary and intellectual form. In this culture of polemic, the Reich represented continuity as well as corruption. A peculiar alchemy turned elements of German and European thinking from the previous 100 years into an incendiary mix. In particular, the Nazis' anti-Semitism resonated in the social context, both via an inherited and malodorous vein in European thought, and more recent forms of conceptual development, specifically Social Darwinism. Anti-Semitism was simply something in the air, something breathed.[6]

The inter-war period was a time of great recourse to propaganda, and the Nazi propaganda regime was consequently able to draw inspiration from contemporary, pre-existing models of propaganda-constructed states which emerged within the cultural context of a commercialised world of mass media and marketing. These included the Italian Fascist state of Benito Mussolini, which had existed for ten years prior to the Nazi assumption of power and which represented a working model of how propaganda could be integrated within the everyday business of government, and how the mass of the population could be convinced that it was embarking upon a mystical quest to reach a glorious destiny. Then there was the Soviet model, the empire already governed by Stalin when Hitler came to power, which had made great use of propaganda in consolidating its rule. As was the case with both of these regimes, the Nazi emphasis was also on the importance of actions and images in conveying messages.

The German propaganda regime, like Mussolini's Fascist Italy and Stalin's USSR, was educated within the broader cultural context of a commercialised and commercialising world of mass media and emergent marketing; the learning environment in which these regimes came of age—consumerism, Communism and Americanism—offered a protracted tutorial for the cadet Nazis in the infernal arts of propaganda and persuasion.

Indeed, their propaganda reflected contemporary theorising about psychological 'suggestion' in sophisticated advertising circles (Hitler himself had spoken of 'mass suggestion').[7] Moreover, the Third Reich occurred at a confluence in history when a new generation of technologies converged on a satisficing level of technical quality. Medium now fluently sustained message: films no longer stuttered silently; sound gave them voice. While Hitler does of course stand in a long succession of Caesars, men who ritualised their raj through public symbols, he owned the means of vivid communication necessary to bequeath an imagistic legacy to history like no other. With the advent of new communication technologies, these messages could be conveyed to an ever-wider audience. Hence the regime's efforts to consolidate its power were greatly helped by the new communications revolution and the ascendancy of consumer communications technology—radios, for instance, had become a common consumer item, thereby enabling Nazi propaganda to reach wide sections of German society.

Yet the Nazi propaganda product was always in competition—with that of the Communists before 1933, whose propaganda was orchestrated by their guru Wilhelm 'Willi' Münzenberg, and with international media in the 1930s, as well as the Allied radio broadcasts of the Second World War. It was a competitive realm, and the image of totalitarian (i.e. total control of communications space) is in fact misleading because the propaganda had to function at a certain level of competence, because it faced rivals throughout the life of the Reich.

Methods of Reich Propaganda

The success of the Nazi propaganda regime in propelling the German nation to the iniquities of the 1930s and '40s was dependent upon the Reich's use of a range of propaganda methods, the first and most important of which was the personality of Hitler himself. Although the Nazis never won a majority of seats in the Reichstag—Hitler was simply appointed chancellor by Hindenburg in January 1933—Hitler projected a charisma which impressed, or even mesmerised, a substantial number of German voters. He was able to convince at both the mass and at the individual level, and offer not merely the experience of conviction but of religious conversion. Those who listened to Hitler often described it as being akin to a mystical experience: one of affirmation, or indeed transcendence; he was both the monarch and the high priest of a faith in which the nation was the core article of belief, and death in its imagined cause the highest sacrament.

He was also an image-maker, a professional actor with a vast repertoire of gestures and a ceaseless flow of tumbling ideas and words, a dramaturgy of performance, a physical act.

Moreover, as party men fighting elections, the Nazis were in many ways traditional operators, opportunists, political in the gut sense, all things to all men, possessed of a chameleon-like capacity to address the different needs of different and antithetical groups in the language those groups recognised. Another method the Nazis employed was to manipulate a perceived existential threat. The war was to be a final global reckoning between the great race and the *Untermenschen*, principally the Jews, who would extinguish Germandom unless they were destroyed first. In the view of their putative nemesis, Theodore Kaufman (see Chapter Four), the Nazis—'perverted chanters of a world-dirge composed by a drunkard, written in a brothel and dedicated to a pimp'[8]—promulgated an imagined Jew, one which ascended the scale of infamy until finally becoming the alpha and omega, the enemy behind all other enemies.

A further, and perhaps more surprising, method was to exploit the capacity of people to compartmentalise, to inhabit one cultural world and yet to work and act in another. This was all the more remarkable since in so many ways these worlds were antipathetic; a contemporary Western consciousness was expressed in the music, the films, the commercial products, harbingers even then of an individualistic consumerism. There was the influence of Americanisation, for the Reich played with and structurally incorporated its antithesis. It was a series of contradictions—progressive and reactionary, modern and anti-modern, American and anti-American. The Reich was a paradox of modernity, and it is the duality of these visions, and their ability to run alongside and in various ways to feed off each other, which makes the Third Reich so alarming an experiment in human consciousness.

But there was also another vision, one which was imperial and ethno-nationalist. The advent of international consumer and popular culture and its ephemera did not point to Stalingrad, or to Auschwitz, yet its existence was a necessary precondition of that other world, the fanatical world of the Nazi state. All of this called on people's ability to perform a great deal of selective perception, and to edit out the unpleasant. Yet the demand was not so much to believe as to see selectively: and the confirmatory evidence of an essentially benevolent status quo could always be found.

SELLING HITLER

The Impertinence of the Non-Historian: Why Alternative Perspectives Matter

Some would argue that it is presumptuous, or even futile, for a non-historian to attempt to offer a novel thesis to history. Nevertheless, there is inherent value in the representative of one perspective or conceptual framework surveying another discipline, as it can help to surface connections and patterns which are not immediately apparent to the internal discourse.

There will be those who would criticise the distinctive theory offered in this book, not least because perspective is not in any sense a form of proof. An assertion that propaganda was the central organising process and fulcrum of the Third Reich and the medium it breathed, the very explanation of its strength, is not watertight, and good arguments can be adduced to negate it. It could be claimed, for example, that although propaganda was indeed the organising principle according to Hitler and Goebbels, this was in many ways a post-hoc rationalisation of things which worked for other and more traditionally political factors. Success—in the diplomatic and military realms, for instance—was its own form of propaganda.

Prominent academic authorities and other commentators have denigrated or denied the significance and function of Nazi propaganda as historical determinism, while others say it is certainly possible to exaggerate its impact. One scholar, Richard Bessel, has demonstrated that the Nazis had limited organisation in Neidenburg (East Prussia) until 1931 but managed nevertheless to increase their vote from 2.3 per cent (1928) to nearly 26 per cent by September 1930.[9] Laurence Rees adds that 'the voters of Neidenburg did not vote Nazi because they were entranced by a Hitler or swamped with Nazi propaganda: they supported the Nazis because they wanted fundamental change'.[10] And in the view of the political scientist Franz Neumann, propaganda as an agent of change is subordinate to other more significant factors.[11] In his seminal work, *Behemoth: The Structure and Practice of National Socialism (1933–1944)* (1942), he asserted that 'National Socialist propaganda did not destroy the Weimar democracy.' Another authority, Gerhard Ritter, thought that 'there is no doubt that the majority of educated Germans—that part of the nation which was consciously aware of its historical traditions—was very distrustful of the Hitler propaganda ... And very many felt at the time of Hitler's victory that his political system was foreign to them.'[12]

These points are well argued; but surely desire for fundamental change has to be articulated, to be talked into people, and its possibility demonstrated, although there is no question that incitement is always a co-production—people must also have a latent appetite for the change that is mobilised by the polemic. Events—even the Great Depression, which in Neidenburg is the intervening variable between 1928 and 1930—seldom speak for themselves; they have to be rhetorically illuminated and structured into an explanatory public narrative. And while historians would certainly accept that the Nazis placed propaganda at the conceptual heart of their regime, many would also argue that the Nazis were guilty of the wrong self-diagnosis, and that propaganda was never more than one, and one among many, explanatory factors for their success in terms of political persuasion. But that defence rests on a distinction between event and the public expression of the event, according to which events have a single essentialist construction in the public mind and do not need the intervening variable of articulation. Such a viewpoint, although defensible, is one with which this author disagrees: the event and its projection are inseparable where explanation for political success is concerned. The two are condensed into the same phenomenon.

Other scholars more disposed to stress the role of propaganda have also offered caveats: the scholar Corey Ross dismisses the 'old seduction thesis' of Nazi propaganda—it is 'an untenably simplistic chain of causality between media message and audience response'.[13] He continues:

> but conventional views about its seductive genius have always been exaggerated, partly because many contemporary assessments were penned by publicists with an inflated view of their own importance, but also because of the exculpatory implication that the Nazis tricked the German electorate as a slick salesman dupes an unwitting customer. Recent research has shown that Nazi propaganda before 1933 was neither as systematic nor as effective as is often assumed, and that the party's message of national rejuvenation, social reform and strong-man leadership was popular enough in depression-era Germany to 'sell itself' without much political sorcery. This was even recognized by Nazi officials at the time, some of whom disagreed with the prevailing emphasis on suggestive and emotional appeal. The Strasser (North German) wing of the Nazi Party had claimed that overstress on this methodology would alienate people. Gregor Strasser, for one, emphasised political education more than agitation, and his brother Otto openly criticised Goebbels's campaigning methods as an 'Americanisation of thinking'.[14]

In Ross's view the contemporary discourse on propaganda, ranging from the scientific to the popular, rested on 'a vast overestimation of the power of propaganda' and also an authoritarian understanding of public opinion, and a deafness to the reality of propaganda; the cause, not the methodology, was what mattered.[15]

Critics of the book's approach would further claim that actions speak louder than words and what mattered were the foreign policy triumphs and the battlefield victories. However, that is to assume that these were separate compartments: was the propaganda just the ribbon on the dust jacket, and what really mattered, what worked, was the product? But then, what was the product? The acceptance of the book's argument is part of a larger debate about how historians deal with the role of persuasion in history. All these are valid perspectives but they remain that, a perspective. Scholars who locate the supreme persuasability in the chronicle of events themselves rather than how those events are interpreted and presented, who see events and not the representation of events as invested with all the historical determinism that one needs, will naturally oppose my perspective and stand aloof from the arguments in this book.

Propaganda and the Historians' Debates

There is no finality to this debate, but arguments about the centrality of propaganda also relate to the more general historiography of the Third Reich and the fierce historians' arguments over its essentialist nature. Another alternative perspective, for instance, has been put in cogent form by Christopher Browning in his study of the operations of an Ordnungspolizei police unit in Poland, *Ordinary Men: Reserve Police Battalion 101 and the Final Solution in Poland* (1992), which claims that the implementation of the Holocaust (in particular) should be attributed to Germany's authoritarian political culture. Hierarchical and particularly military authority was simply obeyed, and hence a pre-existing culture of obedience, and peer pressure, explains why the Nazis were able to do what they did. What made this explanation credible was that the soldiers in this police battalion were not a self-selected elite like the SS but 'ordinary' middle-aged men, not front-line fighters: specifically, their commanding officer gave them a choice as to whether they joined in the mass executions of Jews or not. Nearly everyone did, with fewer than twelve out of 500 refusing. This thesis has in turn been challenged by Daniel Goldhagen in a controversial book, *Hitler's Willing Executioners: Ordinary Germans and the Holocaust* (1996), which sought explanation in what Goldhagen claimed was the unique, inherited anti-Semitism of German political culture, which possessed an 'eliminationist anti-Semitism', making common Germans 'willing executioners'.

Is the truth, then, culture or propaganda? In practice, this is a false dichotomy—the propaganda transmits, feeds off the culture; neither of these explanations, therefore, neither the focus on obedience to authority, nor the ingrained anti-Semitism of German culture, specifically excludes a role for propaganda since persuasion can both reinforce the social pressure to obey as well as the cultural pressure to hate. However, both of them place the explanatory centre of gravity elsewhere and any function accorded to propaganda is a subsidiary one.

In contrast, this book will claim that such emphases underestimate the entrepreneurial capacity of propaganda; beliefs and habits are not static through time, they do not exist in a refrigerated state, but can be diminished or amplified by effective persuasion.[16] Propaganda can thus reinterpret and re-imagine the culture in such a way that people believe themselves to be doing what is authentic or moral in ways that would appal predecessor generations. And propaganda lends us the raw materials for self-persuasion. Thus at the crucial point, 1942, the beginning of the Holocaust, Germans had been subject to several years of toxic anti-Semitic propaganda, and, preceding this, an entire decade or more of propaganda-driven celebration of the concept of national exceptionalism, and specifically endorsement of the idea of a master-race.

A further perspective is via the so-called *Historikerstreit*, or the German historians' debate of the 1980s, which offered two different interpretations of Nazism: the one (conservative) placing it within the broader construct of totalitarianism and thus relating it to Communism, the other, left-leaning approach arguing for the unique moral outrage of German Fascism (the so-called 'Sonderweg' view). An earlier work, Hannah Arendt's *Origins of Totalitarianism* (1949), had also invoked the concept of totalitarianism to emphasise underlying structural similarities between Nazi and Soviet states. Italian Fascism in contrast was authoritarian–nationalist but Nazism was generically a manifestation of totalitarian government and in this sense conceptually akin to the Soviet. Neither perspective of course would specifically exclude a role for propaganda, but neither would grant it centrality.

However, although Nazism has features in common with Communism, and the Reich was indeed recognisably totalitarian, the comparability is more one of individual features than an essentiality of type. Under Nazism, the central role allocated to propaganda was present because Germans were a better-educated and more sophisticated people, and internal, energised commitment to the cause could not simply be coerced (a point made by the historian Alan Bullock). The regime's principal energies had to be exerted in the direction of persuasion as well as coercion. This is of course not for one moment to deny the significance of propaganda in Communism;

indeed, the Bolsheviks offered a paradigm to be copied by the Nazis and patented some significant propaganda genres and ideas. However, the USSR was a nation in an earlier stage of development which did not sustain, and did not therefore need to co-opt, an enormous, and relatively educated, middle class.

What made the Nazis special was their pursuit of propaganda not just as a tool, an instrument of government—which had in fact often been the case in history before—but as the totality, the idea through which government itself governed. They saw public opinion as something that could be created, commodified and re-made. Nor was there really a distinction between policy and propaganda: the two were the same instrument, the one unintelligible without the other. The Third Reich was a laboratory. No regime had taken persuasion this far. There were groups to strengthen rumours, groups to spread graffiti, and the breadth of propaganda mediums—from sculpture to weaponry—and the mediatisation of all artefacts were possibilities that had never been realised before, nor have they been realised since. So the distinction between propaganda and non-propaganda can never be maintained in any analysis of Nazi Germany, and this is what makes the regime unique in history. The Nazis were technological innovators in communication and in the hardware of warfare also, and to some extent these even meant at times the same thing, at least to them. Propaganda was simply one of the things you did in order to function as a paladin of the Third Reich and compete for Hitler's attention: they all possessed their own propaganda cadre, Rosenberg, Himmler and so forth. In the Reich everything could be interrogated for its propaganda potential, every surface inscribed with polemical meaning, every building block of public consciousness from typeface and newsprint to the expression of military communiqués to the architecture to the very design and deployment of weapons themselves. Every medium carried the propaganda, not just art or film. No regime had ever done this before.

Selling Hitler: *The Conceptual Structure*

A question of definition

The term 'propaganda' is generally regarded today as anachronistic, and in modern times the concept has been represented via a surrogate language such as persuasion, communication and so forth. Definitions are of course important, since how we define a concept is an expression in itself of the theories we hold about the concept; and as Edward Bernays pointed out in

Crystallizing Public Opinion (1923), 'the advocacy of what we believe in is education. The advocacy of what we don't believe in is propaganda.'[17] Certainly propaganda is no mere synonym for persuasion but informs much broader ideas of polemical mobilisation (the arguments over the meaning of the term are explored in earlier works by this author, as below, where its various definitions are elaborated, as well as a recent four-volume edition of key essays).[18]

The current book is organised around a triadic division which seeks to interpret Nazi propaganda through a conceptual trinity, namely 'myth', 'symbolism' and 'rhetoric' (see my *Politics and Propaganda: Weapons of Mass Seduction* (2004)).[19] This triumvirate is the conceptual anatomy of all propaganda, via which we are able to condense, organise and interpret almost every aspect of polemical communication. This paradigm is derived from the work of George Schöpflin (1997), who argues that myth, symbol and ritual constitute a language that lies deeper than language itself. Verbalisation is underpinned by symbolisation—symbols simplify reality in order for it to make sense to us. Symbolism becomes a cognitive short-cut.[20] Thus I have argued elsewhere that myth, symbol and rhetoric are an associative trinity, the one irrelevant without the other; good propaganda recognises this interdependence.[21]

The function of this taxonomy in expounding the propaganda of the Third Reich can be summarised as follows:

1. Myth. The essence of any culture is mythological. This is as true of sophisticated industrial countries as it is of earlier epochs. Nazi mythologies exploit an idea of Prussianness which they were anxious to claim as their own, a source of historical paternity; they retrieved memory from recent history, Nazified it and placed it on a plinth. Goebbels in particular understood the value of the mythology and the entire narrative was saturated with myths: the November criminals, the stab in the back, the snatched victory, international plutocracy and the Jewish conspiracy, the Jewish Bolshevik, old reaction. But the propaganda construction of the Jew was pure fabrication and myth in the vernacular sense; the imagined Jew who carried much authentic Nazi baggage, was, in fact, a projection. The true, essentialist Nazi was present in the fictional Semite.

2. Symbols. A symbol 'is an image that stands for an idea; it is a form of language'.[22] The Reich used the modish language of symbolism and was a fecund manufactory of symbols. It created symmetry, turning inchoate masses into hard mathematical forms, and possessed an intuitive insight

into the symbolically charged nature of the human experience (there is in fact some scientific evidence for the role of symbols in elucidating meaning; that is, the mind comprehends and remembers via hosting symbolic representations of reality). Nazis understood that the brevity of the public attention span demanded that meaning be condensed (i.e. symbolised, a thoroughly contemporary imperative for economy of perception).

3. Rhetoric. The Third Reich was conducted as one mighty act of advocacy and assertive argument throughout. Their rhetoric was distinguished from that of former years not only by its vulgarity but also by its brevity: a language which, like advertising, contrived to be both banal and yet memorable, an adhesive, and one made visible by its very mediocrity. In this book, however, rhetoric is discussed primarily in relation to one of the most important works on the subject ever written, by Victor Klemperer (1881–1960): *Language of the Third Reich* (see Chapter Six). And if this may seem like reliance on a kind of intellectual Zimmer frame, then I plead guilty to it. For in general Klemperer evokes how the Reich sought the colonisation of the German language, in line with my thesis that 'the names we give to things organise our thoughts, since words are not neutral tools but embody perspectives'.[23]

Hence the focus.

PART ONE

NARRATIVES AND THEORIES

1

A NARRATIVE OF THIRD REICH PROPAGANDA
(1920–39)

IMAGINING THE REICH

Perverted chanters of a world-dirge composed by a drunkard, written in a brothel and dedicated to a pimp.

Theodore Kaufman

Imposing indeed in its granite harshness and yet infinitely squalid with miscellaneous cumber—like some huge barbarian monolith, the expression of giant strength and savage genius, surrounded by a festering heap of refuse, old tins and dead vermin, ashes and eggshells and ordure—the intellectual detritus of centuries.

Hugh Trevor-Roper

Early History

The German state was a different kind of state, subject not to a king, *Koenig*, but to a Caesar, or Kaiser. The Nazis were satisfying appetites already well defined in the public consciousness for a superhuman leader, a visionary patriot free of the normal deadweight of human vice, an epic figure who would stand alongside the epic figures of history, yet one blessed with the common touch, a 'People's Caesar'. This is what the Kaiser, so identified with the juncker (i.e. landowning) social class and its great privileges, had spectacularly failed to be. Such a leader would also turn the life of the nation into a splendid quest enlightened by the moral mission of righting

15

wrong: the everyday would become a transcendent experience. Since the Nazis were careful to disguise their bellicose agenda from the German people, the Germany of the 1930s was a giddy rollercoaster ride whose destiny never seemed to be war. They created a sense of unstoppable momentum, for the Reich was ultimately a moving bandwagon upon which many made a death-defying leap. It was this sense of historical determinism, of Germany's inevitable pre-destiny, which Hitler was able to generate and from which he sought profit.

The Third Reich was the product of two systems of post-Renaissance/ Reformation European thought, namely the Enlightenment and the Romantic counter-reaction to the Enlightenment, for the Nazi regime was the illegitimate child of both and had characteristics of both: co-mingling streams, not inherently toxic but which created a combustible chemistry when blended. Yet the Nazis saw themselves as the enemies of the French Revolution rather than its inheritors. As Goebbels once remarked, 'the year 1789 is hereby eradicated from history'.[1]

Nationalist thinking: the legacy of poisonous ideas and the emergence of Nazism

It was in no way inevitable that the cumulative impact of Germany's previous 150 years would be a phenomenon like Nazism. Yet in retrospect a long chain of causation can be discerned, as National Socialism was not a phenomenon that emerged independently of all the prior forces in German history. The historian and political scientist Karl Dietrich Bracher, for instance, offers several distinct phases which culminated in National Socialism, even though the inner logic of each event might have pointed to a different outcome: (1) the impact of the French Revolution and its consequences for Germans; (2) the revolutions of 1848; (3) Bismarckian nationalism; (4) the drive of the German Empire to global power and its First World War outcome; and (5) the final stage, the reaction to defeat and the Weimar story.[2]

But Nazism and its ideology also inherited a distinctly Germanic ethnonationalist intellectual and populist tradition, one which it coarsened and interpreted in perverse ways, and it was this legacy which provided the intellectual nutrients to the Nazi dream of German hegemony, of a primacy among nations that would validate the greatness of its culture. Thus ideas of national exceptionalism had penetrated German civic discourse from the very beginning of the nineteenth century, and it is these which served as the conceptual foundations of Nazism. In 1808, for instance, Johann Fichte (1762–1814), a founder of the 'German idealist' school of philosophy, had issued his 'Address to the General German People' which proclaimed the uniqueness of Germans as an 'archetypal people' whose destiny was an entirely new kind of civic order, with its notion of organic—exclusionary and patriotic—national community.[3] Similarly, for Hegel, 'the individual's freedom could only be realised within the state', and his endorsement of concepts such as 'world historic leader' clearly foreshadows both the ideology and the language of the Third Reich.[4] In Germany, middle-class mercantile liberalism and the challenges this posed to autocracy—which had been so apparent in the pan-European revolutions of 1848—consequently succumbed to a 'pseudo-constitutional, semi-absolute feudal, military, bureaucratic state', creating a new kind of nationalism, one which was more intoxicating than rational liberal democracy: 'with increasing frequency, the ideology of a nationally-based socialism was being pitted against the Marxist doctrine of the class struggle'.[5]

The Nazis dredged the debris of the past century or more of German intellectual neurosis. They were designers, not thinkers. The rhetoric of reaction, of Teutonic hyper-nationalism, was the lubricant. However, those who look for a Fascist essentialism are doomed to an elusive quest, as what the Nazis felt, thought and said was often an immediate response to contextual pressure. The Nazi credo was often created ad hoc in response to the immediate pressure of political circumstances; ideas were synthesised to deal with transitory purposes, and those who seek a deep reflectiveness will seek in vain. This was the politics of prefabrication, as the Nazis were never ideological in the sense that Marxism or Communism was ideological (i.e. possessed of a coherent text articulating a logical conceptual design underpinned by clearly defined operational and philosophic principles). *Mein Kampf* was not a text in the normal sense of the term but a stream of consciousness: a collation of feelings and impulses.

The First World War in Nazi propaganda

The anticipation of the Third Reich was the German imperial state of 1916–1918, which culminated however briefly in the acquisition of a mighty empire from the French border to European Russia, since the Treaty of Brest-Litovsk—where Germany acquired much of European Russia—profoundly influenced Hitler's Eastern ambitions.[6] In 1917–18, Russia had been defeated on the Eastern Front, and at Brest-Litovsk Germany had gained a new empire. Under that treaty Russia lost over 1 million square miles of land,[7] and 62 million people now fell under the second Reich,[8] which by this stage was effectively a propaganda-enhanced military dictatorship led, de facto if not de jure, by two soldiers, Paul von Hindenburg and Erich Ludendorff. A new chauvinist party, the German Fatherland Party, which was based on an ethno-nationalist credo that anticipated many of the ideas Nazism would subsequently promote, sought to promulgate the imperialism of the state; civic society atrophied.

German triumph in the East was swiftly followed by triumph in the West. Germany was now near to a total victory in a total war, and was close to acquiring a European empire the like of which had not been seen since ancient Rome. On the Western Front, the German breakthrough of March 1918 came with the Ludendorff Offensive of 21 March–5 April, Operation Michael, named in honour of the patron saint of Germany. For the first time in four years the Western Front was broken, and German armies streamed into the land beyond. But all of this was to prove a mirage. By 8 August 1918 the Allies had crushed the German line,[9] and the British Empire struck back, as it were, achieving in August what the Battle of the Somme had so tragically failed to deliver—the destruction of the German front—which was in turn followed by the American triumphs of early October 1918.[10] Despite the efforts of the German press to maintain optimism in the face of this military reversal,[11] German defeat in the First World War was ultimately marked by the mutiny of sailors at Kiel, Hamburg and Bremen; and then, on 7 November, Munich exploded in revolution.[12]

Hitler refused to accept that Britain had won the First World War through military means; there had to be some other reason, for what power on earth could defeat the Imperial German Army? Thus his seeking a non-military explanation was the consequence of his chauvinism, his Teutomania, his faith in the invincibility of the army. In this search, so well articulated in the sixth chapter of *Mein Kampf* (see Chapter Three), lay the genesis of Nazism's propaganda ethos; propaganda was the druidical magic which had enabled a British victory, therefore, let Germans become superior magicians. Such a view was illusionary, self-serving and completely ignored the reality of 1918; it was simply too convenient to locate defeat in British skills of chicanery.

The sense of grievance due to British propaganda

However, although Germany's defeat in the First World War was clearly attributable to superior Allied strategy in the summer of 1918, the British had indeed been effective propagandists:

A NARRATIVE OF THIRD REICH PROPAGANDA (1920-39)

[By] employing such totally new weapons as leaflets dropped from aircraft and trench newspapers, [Britain] had successfully driven a wedge between people and government, hinting that once the Prussian militarists responsible for the war had been ousted Germany would be accepted as an equal partner in the coalition of European nations. This gave rise to certain consequences. The first was that the British propaganda promises which many Germans felt had not been honoured after the war helped to fuel the sense of grievance which brought Hitler to power.[13]

British propaganda consequently played a number of roles in the evolution of Nazism. On the one hand, the promises the British had made fed into the German sense of betrayal. Yet on the other hand, Hitler saw in British propaganda not only the cause of Germany's failure—this was in fact also the conventional German wisdom—but also the formula for its future Nazi success. Thus Hitler's observation of the enemy's polemical war, which had underpinned its physical war, was a protracted tutorial both for him and for Germany as a whole. British propaganda was sensational, infantile even, but it had certainly been effective.

It should also be noted that the German propaganda effort of the First World War had not been invisible either, and this also exerted an important influence on Hitler and Nazism as a movement. Later in the First World War Ludendorff had become almost a dictator, and he assiduously sought to exploit communications to legitimate an anti-democratic military autocracy, energised by the chauvinist vision of an imperial Greater Germany.[14] After the war, Hitler added a specifically Austrian ideology of a greater Germany to these expansionist ideas,[15] thereby imposing a new, even more revisionist notion of Germany's future on these pre-existing strains of German thought.

Thus Nazi propaganda did not evolve out of nothing, as it had many historical roots both remote and recent.[16] While the arrival of Hitler was not foreordained, he can perhaps be seen as divining and acting out a role already scripted for him by the German people. An earlier generation had constructed 500 statues of Bismarck, and there were also other precedents for Hitler worship;[17] hence the people's Kaiser had existed in the German mind long before his actual arrival. The more immediate genesis lay in the various propaganda movements before and during the First World War. German nationalism of a new and more virulent kind had already been spread by the Fatherland Party, founded by the future putschist Wolfgang Kapp. This movement, which was encouraged by Hindenburg and Ludendorff and financed by army and industry, sponsored pro-annexationist, anti-parliamentarian propaganda, and by July 1918 it claimed a mass membership of 1.25 million.[18] It offered 'hallucinations about empire' and advocated dictatorship.[19] Moreover, after the war, nationalist propaganda was both a cause and a consequence of the fighting between right-wing nationalist militias (the Freikorps) and Poles along disputed borders and the undefined Baltic frontier.[20]

Another explanation for Hitler's embrace of propaganda is that he had functioned as a propagandist himself, having been selected for that task by the German army to propagate a nationalist message to the troops. At the end of the war Hitler had attended a course on 'civic thinking' in the army propaganda department[21] and heard lectures which sought to substitute nationalist for socialist sentiment among the Bavarian troops.[22] Lecturers included the conservative historian Karl Alexander von Müller (1882–1964) and the pan-German economic theorist Gottfried Feder (1883–1941). In August 1919 Hitler the pupil became a teacher,[23] joining other education officers charged with the task of stimulating morale by nationalistic incitement in his role as a propaganda functionary of the Munich military area command.[24] Significantly, then, Hitler's first, regularly paid employment in the period after the First World War was as a professional propagandist, initially within the army itself where he worked as a political commissar fighting the propaganda of the socialists and the Communists.

He proved worthy of this role. Hitler's rhetorical form was developed as he sold a visceral nationalism to his military audiences, and when addressing the groups he fed on the excitement he created.[25] The morale of a defeated army must have seemed a mighty burden, and the soldiers looked for the meaning in their sacrifice, for 'explanations for wasted lives'.[26] What Hitler offered at Camp Lechfeld, where the instruction courses were based, was an explanation and a benediction: the blame could be passed elsewhere, away from the soldiers themselves. The stage villains could be lined up to carry the responsibility of the defeat—Jews, Communists, internationalism, internal traitors, the treacherous Allies at Versailles; for had the Allies not hinted, after all, that Germany would be accepted into the community of European nations?[27]

The Versailles Treaty and the politics of victimhood

In the inequitable Versailles Treaty, the humiliations it inflicted and the injustices it created and perpetuated, the Nazis found their *cause célèbre*. While the pursuit of their many chosen (racial, ideological, class) enemies revealed their polemical and increasingly their physical brutality, in their denunciations of Versailles they found a cause that truly united all Germans, one where they could pose as the righteous defenders of the wronged. The treaty provided an inexhaustible supply of rhetorical points for beer hall meetings as the victimhood of Germany was rhetoricised into outrage through the beery haze of tribal sentimentality.

Much of the German anger at the treaty was directed at the Versailles-mandated seizure of territory in which Germany lost over 14 per cent of its former lands. These included the German colonies, but also Eupen and Malmedy to Belgium; Alsace-Lorraine (German for the previous half-century) to France; two-thirds of West Prussia, and Posen, to Poland; areas of East Prussia to Poland and Lithuania; northern Schleswig Holstein to Denmark; and the acceptance of a 'Polish corridor' through German territory for Polish sea access. Danzig was to become a free city united with Poland by a customs union and other provisions. In October 1922 Upper Silesia went to Poland, and the Ruhr was occupied by France in 1923 because of a failure to deliver coal under the terms of Versailles.[28] The iniquities of the treaty further included the leasing of the industrial area of the Saar to France (not re-incorporated for fifteen years) and the creation of the Czech state, with 3 million German speakers incorporated. Under the Polish stipulation, Germany had to surrender territory to Poland without a plebiscite, but also the mining areas and smaller districts of Lower Silesia (via plebiscite this time—but still the richest part); and there was the assignation of the town and hinterland of Memel to Lithuania. The Rhine was also placed under occupation, and although it was returned to Germany in September 1930, the intervening period gave Hitler many years' worth of rhetorical ammunition.

There were also the reparations. In the period between the Armistice and 1931, for instance, Germany paid $3 billion in reparations in addition to the payments it was forced to make to the various nations occupying the Rhineland.[29] While only a moiety of these reparations was paid, the great bill remained and with the bill the ultimate propaganda opportunity since injustice, or perceived injustice, is the incendiary substance of all propaganda. The Nazis lit the fuse; the perception was real enough without the need for Nazi adumbration, but of course they 'managed' the grievance and its nurture; they commodified it with great skill, in fact (reparations were finally paid off on 3 October 2010).[30]

However, while the grievances were principally territorial–economic, they were not exclusively so. The Allied blockade, for example, and the perpetuity of the serious famine that arose in consequence, allegedly continued until nine months after the Armistice, and this, along with the other injustices listed recurrently in Nazi publications, also provided fertile ground for Nazi propaganda. According to The Weekly Free Newsletter of the German Library of Information in New York, *Facts in Review* (1940), a Nazi publication aimed at US opinion:

> during that period alone more than 100,000 Germans, mostly aged people, women and children died of malnutrition and starvation. They had managed to survive the war. They could not endure the war after the war ... this was, perhaps, a *peace without victory*, but with a different meaning for the words than when they were first spoken. For it was no *peace* either. That became clear for the first time at Versailles.[31]

Nazism was, then, a narrative of victimhood with a roll call of loss and humiliation whose elements could be recited as a formal litany on every conceivable occasion. It follows that Nazi propaganda was but an elaboration of this core narrative, this fable of theft and ignominy. German propaganda constantly portrayed Germans as innocents who had actually believed in the integrity of Wilson's Fourteen Points.

The slogans and speeches of the period are an extended essay in the political usage of grievance. The attacks on Versailles and reparations, the confiscations of territory, the occupations of the Saar and Ruhr, the maps of a shrunken Germany—these resonated, and they were not imaginary grievances but real ones. The cry of injustice which the rhetoric, the banners and the posters expressed was answered, however, by a criminal enterprise of unique dimension. Nazi language was the language of victimhood, a psychology incessantly mobilised by propaganda—Germans, for example, were allegedly paying 60 per cent of all Czech taxes.[32] But grievances, like most other social phenomena, can be manufactured: they do not just exist in some aboriginal state, to be excavated by the righteous. This is not of course to deny that they can have an objective reality too, merely that the perception can be synthesised as well. The Second World War was packaged as the final stage—the dénouement—of a narrative, the unravelling of Versailles. The myriad small states it had spawned were 'parasites on Europe's living substance'.[33]

One further consequence of Versailles was the salience of the newly subjugated German minorities. These German communities who now found themselves stuck in new sectarian states dominated by rival ethnicities[34] also provided conflagatory propaganda material: they were substantial minorities in Czechoslovakia, Poland, Hungary and Romania, and constituted a significant presence in the Baltic and Balkan states. Such eastern ('external' or 'folk') Germans were the theme and target of pan-Germanic extremists such as Alfred Rosenberg (himself a Balt) and the 'Ostforschung' or racial science; and a 'National Socialist' Party already existed in Bohemia before the First World War.[35] Beyond this, and more difficult for statesmen of other nations to grasp, was the conceptual problem of Germandom, for it was a pan-European tribe as well as a nation, with franchises, so to speak, all over Europe to the east of the British Isles and the Iberian Peninsula. And this goes to the heart of the matter—that German claims to imperium could be grounded in the fact of the existence of folk communities everywhere. By inference, Germans in all of Europe could precipitate a Europe that was German.

The full reversal of Versailles was not therefore accomplished until the invasion of France and Poland, and these invasions were in a sense mandated by the notion of reversal and retribution as the public basis of Nazi policy. Unsurprisingly, perhaps, the nationalist Polish government under the leadership of Colonel Józef Beck and his colleagues refused to engage in any negotiations with Hitler over territorial arrangements. But of course the concealed, rather than revealed, agenda went much further in seeking a new German imperium of the East, justified by the idea of Lebensraum and by the ideology of anti-Bolshevism. Beyond this lay the invention of an existential threat. Germandom had been destroyed by the chicaneries of the British externally, and internally by the November traitors; it had been re-made by Adolf Hitler, but now faced destruction again mainly in the shape of the internal and external forces represented by international Jewry. In fact, the National Socialist state and the propaganda which was its expression and stimulant, the pith of its organising principle, could not exist without the perpetual construction of such existential danger. In this lay the source of that state's vigour, its urgency, the moral right it claimed to totalitarian control over people's lives. Hence the propaganda was a serial exposition and re-making of that threat; it would be unthinkable without the systemic of external threat creation.

The party and the putsch: 1920-3

When Hitler was discharged from the army in March 1920 he almost immediately found fresh employment. He had first become aware of the miniature and politically irrelevant German Workers' Party (DAP), the entity that he would build into the Nazi Party (NSDAP, Nationalsozialistische Deutsche Arbeiterpartei), after the army had asked him to investigate it.[36] As a loyal

German military political commissar, he was asked to gauge the counter-revolutionary potential of the DAP, one of many such political groups.[37] So Hitler was not the founder of the German Workers' Party, but merely joined the object of his army intelligence mission. The party had been created by Anton Drexler (1884–1942), a locksmith, patriot and former member of the Fatherland Party, and twenty-five railroad workers at a conference in January 1919.[38] There had in fact been a rise of such pseudo-nationalist groups in Germany from the late nineteenth century (like the pan-German movement of 1893), all of which aspired to integrate Germans into a single ethnic body.[39] But while it is true that Prussia, the great unifier of Germany, was 'an army with a state attached' (and anticipated in its militarism the Nazis' model of society), the real historical ancestry of the Nazi party lies in imperial Austria at the turn of the century, in areas characterised by anti-Slav and anti-Semite nationalism which carried over into German political discourse.[40] Hitler joined the party in October 1919,[41] while still under the control of his army handlers,[42] and swiftly became its rhetorical star turn. By March 1920 he had made himself essential.[43]

In early 1920 Hitler became the tiny party's propaganda director and it is clearly significant that he began his trade not as a leader but as a PR man. He delivered, and his supporters in the army, in Munich society, were satisfied. As director of recruitment and propaganda Hitler placed a huge amount of emphasis on advertising the movement's meetings via vivid posters, and these advertising-driven meetings, which were attended by increasingly large numbers of people, were entirely his idea.[44] He brought the skills of a populist: other right groups, the Thule Society, for example (see Chapter Two), had been elitist, whereas the National Socialists sought a broad political base composed of industrial workers, the petty bourgeois, former members of the Freikorps and so on.[45] Hitler was not an originator but a serial plagiarist: his talent lay in the choices he made among the possible methods, and his integration of them at the conceptual and stylistic level. His first real mass rally, heralded by a luminous red poster,[46] was in February 1920 when he announced the new party programme and the change of name to NSDAP ('Nazi'); he ousted Drexler as chairman in the summer of 1921.[47] Numbers grew. Members of the Freikorps were now joining the new party since these nationalist militias were being dissolved, and membership also increased in the aftermath of the French Ruhr occupation and the hyperinflation of the German mark in 1923, thereby transforming this hitherto fringe party—which has been described as little more than a railway workers' drinking club prior to his taking over—into a mass movement.[48] At this stage, however, Hitler still saw himself as the 'drummer' rather than the chosen one, who would be another and greater man.[49] This would only change later, in March 1924, when Hitler delivered his powerful self-justificatory court speech at his trial for leading the 1923 putsch attempt from the Burgerbraukeller in Munich.

Hence Hitler's first attempt at national power was via extra-constitutional means, a natural choice for a self-professed revolutionary party. In the early 1920s the Weimar Republic looked extremely vulnerable; so effective had been the myths of the stab in the back and the November criminals that the humiliated regime struggled to gain legitimacy, let alone respect. Not merely were the ruled alienated from their rulers (the chancellors at this stage were Social Democrats, as well as—in theory—President Friedrich Ebert), but Weimar was even rejected by components of the civic order such as the government of Bavaria, and Ludendorff himself was the figurehead for the coup. At that time a martial grab for power seemed to be a realistic possibility rather than an eccentric gamble; for had Mussolini not just done the same in his stage-managed 'March on Rome'?

However, in the event, Hitler's Beer Hall Putsch of 8–9 November 1923—which followed the earlier Kapp Putsch of March 1920, a monarchist rebellion,[50] and was forever afterwards the founding myth of the Nazi Party and the source of its sacrament and rituals—was opposed by the forces of the state. Illicit force could not prevail against German legalism and constitutionalism. Henceforth persuasion, not coercion, would be Hitler's preferred route to supreme power. Yet even here, ever attentive to his public, Hitler had remembered his medal:[51] 'concerned with his image even in the depths of defeat, he had the officer of the arrest party pin the Iron Cross first class to his lapel before he was led off'.[52]

The subsequent trial graduated Hitler from regional to national celebrity, garlanded with the laurels of martyrdom and victimhood; the court was his pulpit, the rostrum from which he first spoke to the German nation. He rhetorically pulverised the Versailles Treaty and the 'November criminals' (i.e. the treacherous politicians who had pursued the Armistice and then an unjust peace).[53] He was not the inventor of these myths, but he was the vulgarian retailer. As a result, the reasons for the defeat no longer possessed the quality of an abstraction but were made flesh and blood. Hitler called Versailles 'the greatest propaganda weapon for reviving the nation's dormant spirit of survival'.[54] All Germany now heard him.

The choreography of politics: mass meetings

The lesson of 9 November was that power could not arise from the barrel of a gun but via evolution (not revolution) and persuasion (not coercion). Seen in this light, both the perceived instrumentality of mass propaganda and the extent of the Nazis' engagement with it is more explicable. Hitler simply came to believe that 'endless, almost incomprehensible results' could be achieved by manipulation. Thus Hitler's distinguished biographer Joachim Fest suggests that: 'He preposterously considered the movements of history, the rise and decline of nations, classes, or parties largely as the consequence of differing propagandistic abilities.'[55] But how 'preposterous' is this contention? Perhaps he was right?

In fact the future focus was also on entertainment as well as organised outrage, and the numerous party-devised rallies and speaker meetings were not presented as grim duties for the faithful but as exciting events.[56] The mass meeting was Hitler's innovation and people crowded in from the very beginning: 'it is among the crowded congregations of field churches that the believer sustains his faith and the convert is brought over'.[57] The core of his evangelistic methodology was the speech, and this permitted thousands and eventually millions to have a personal experience of Adolf Hitler. It was a matter of articulating the inarticulate popular will. As Hitler wrote in *Mein Kampf*, the great orator should be borne along by the 'masses in such a way that instinctively the very words come to his lips that he needs to speak to the hearts of his audience'.[58] Hitler events were unlike any other in that they were theatrical, entertaining and boosted by garish poster and booming sound.[59] At the first mass meeting canvassed by banner advertising at the Brown House in February 1920 Hitler proclaimed his twenty-five-point programme in imitation of Luther's theses which had been nailed to the church door in Wittenberg.[60] The promise, among other things, was to nationalise the gains of war profiteers, to abolish child labour, to stop immigration, to provide more old-age welfare and to implement land reform. The programme also condemned 'Jewish materialism'. But there was no ideological coherence; this was a potpourri of the policies of left and right—it was ultimately a populist manifesto designed to sell, despite nods to traditional rightist obsessions such as the Jews.

The Nazis strove to self-inflate, using the organised street procession and leaflet and poster distribution as their methods of sensory assault. Borrowing from the left, they sent lorry loads of men trundling down urban Germany's streets: 'but instead of the fist-swinging, Moscow oriented proletarians who had spread terror and hatred in bourgeois residential districts, these trucks were manned by disciplined former soldiers'.[61] Another element of this street dramaturgy was the loudspeaker wagons. Writing in 1932, a Nazi Party organiser, Helmut von Wilucki, described how:

> we began each time with martial music to set the proper atmosphere for the recorded speech by a well-known party member that followed. We closed with the record of a group singing the Horst Wessel Song. Local group leaders repeatedly told us that this propaganda is particularly suited to areas where meetings are not successful.[62]

Yet the sharp, choreographed performances of the 1930s were long in coming, as the development of party ceremonial was slow and amateurish in the early years.[63] Nor were the results great in terms of electoral impact, despite the effort involved (there were 2,400 demonstrations in 1925 alone, for instance).[64] We can speak again of an evolving technique whose mature effects were only the result of trial and error: practice enhanced the overall coherence via a formulaic approach, such as standardising the uniforms of the storm troops. A turning point in the evolution of these rituals was Hitler's great mass rally in Weimar in July 1926, a highly organised performance with a march past of 5,000 men. In 1927, Nuremberg was chosen for the rally, and 'Hitler's touch could be felt in all the proceedings that dramatised the movement's coherence and belligerency'.[65] This first Nuremberg Congress attracted around 15,000 to 20,000 people.[66]

In 1926 Hitler had appointed Joseph Goebbels as the regional party leader (Gauleiter) in Berlin, an appointment which had radical consequences for the future propaganda preferences exercised by the Nazi party and the impact of that propaganda focus. Goebbels had originally been the protégé of Hitler's NSDAP propaganda successor Gregor Strasser,[67] and his appointment was inspired talent spotting; Goebbels was a romantic socialist, as manifest in his novel *Michael* (1929), originally speaking of the tragedy of Communist/Nazi class brothers fighting in the streets.[68] Yet at this point the party remained an obscure fringe grouping, gaining little more than 2.5 per cent of the vote in 1928.[69] Hence, despite the promotion of Goebbels, by the end of the 1920s Nazism appeared to be a defunct enterprise. In the elections of May 1928, they had lost 100,000 votes with a mere twelve deputies being sent into the Reichstag and only 800,000 voters.[70]

Thus it would be an error to imagine that Nazi propaganda was not faced with effective counter-propaganda, or that the great highway to power in the early 1930s was an easy, confident march. Far from it. Indeed, from the late 1920s onwards all of the parties, and not just the Nazis, were producing and broadcasting propaganda films.[71] Hitler, however, was to learn from the competition: for the Communists could only be defeated with their own outrageous methods, as the bourgeois 'would never be brutal enough'.

Message and manoeuvre: the sabotage of Weimar

Weimar was always the target. It was vulnerable because many did not accept its legitimacy, and because it was there: it stood in the way of Nazi power. The Nazis dedicated the years after the First World War to obliterating it, first through coercion, which failed (the putsch), and then through persuasion, which succeeded.

The primordial Nazi motivation was to avenge the sacrifice of party fighters, to return honour to the German battle flag, to extinguish the threat of global Bolshevism 'and to avenge the two million young men who died for the Fatherland in the Great War ... betrayed by the fat and cuddly republic'.[72] Jay Gonen discusses the nature of Hitler's appeal from a psychiatrist's perspective, specifically the issue of unassimilated trauma, that is to say the losses of the Great War which the Germans would neither understand nor reconcile themselves to.[73] Such a claim rests of course on an analogy between the psychosis of the individual and that of the nation. He sees in the emotions exploited by the Nazis an expression of infantile regression, and an inability to interpret confusing signals. The reaction was fury: the primal scream of Fascism. From this perspective, Nazism was ultimately about avenging the defeat of 1918 and its deaths, rhetorically at first and then physically against those very same enemies. The symbolic aspects of the original humiliation were thus re-engineered by Hitler in the very same rail carriage at the very same spot in 1940. The rituals of French surrender in Foch's wagon-lit on 21 June 1940 were an exorcism.

One view of Europe after 1918 is of a crisis of transition into modernity: some countries were late industrialisers and they had specific problems derived from this, for example part-organised labour. Those countries which began to industrialise at a later stage faced higher levels of social turmoil, and this required new forms of control.[74] Germany at this time fitted all of Robert Paxton's causal criteria for the rise of a Fascist state: (1) it was among the last of the major European states to live with a mass electorate; (2) it was the last of the great powers to industrialise; and (3) cultural conservatives felt threatened by 'artistic experiment'.[75]

Much of the focus of National Socialist propaganda was Weimar or 'the system' (their pejorative term for democracy in general). The Nazis characterised the flag of the Republic as the black of the Catholics, the red of the socialists and the gold of the Jews; the National Socialist students chanted 'we shit on freedom'.[76] A fundamental problem was Weimar's inability to sustain legitimacy or believability—the Reichstag was awash with disparate parties[77]—but, beyond this, hatred of Weimar was ultimately a hatred of the idea of democracy itself and its messy compromises and weaknesses. The idea of a neo-feudal, pseudo-democratic leader had always been around, but because of Weimar's failures the imagined leader's 'anticipatory image move[d] centre right'.[78]

The early targets of Nazi scorn included the Young Plan (1929–30), an American-led proposal to reorganise repayments and limit the total amount of reparations (the plebiscite on this had offered stupendous propaganda opportunities); the League of Nations; Gustav Stresemann's foreign policy between 1923 and 1929, a period in which he pursued reconciliation with the Allied powers and with Russia, and in which Germany joined the League of Nations; but above all Versailles—reparations, they screamed, must cease, signatory ministers be tried for treason: 'the wild campaign it unleashed, together with the farm unrest [stemming from the crisis of over-production], presented the National Socialists with a second great opportunity for the mobilisation of their propaganda and organisational apparatus'.[79]

The great rise of the Nazis began with the Wall Street Crash of 1929 and Hitler's alliance with the media baron Alfred Hugenberg to fight the Young Plan, and industrial funding now seeped in.[80] They had made powerful friends in corporate Germany and were no longer a dissolute, roving band. After joining with Hugenberg—the proprietor of newspapers, a news agency and UFA (formerly Universum Film AG, the biggest German film corporation)—the party suddenly had huge propaganda and organisational resources at its disposal.[81] This new conservative–Fascist coalition had Hitler as its loudest voice, and no one was now able to match the vitriol of Nazi propaganda, nor the resources at their command.[82] The Nazis attributed complex problems to simple causes such as the 'system [i.e. Weimar] parties', the Marxists, the plutocrats, the Jews; above all to Versailles, which performed the happy duty of alibi for the collectivity of disaster, including the economy.[83] Hitler:

> plastered Berlin with flaming red posters. He held Nazi meetings in predominantly communist areas. When fights broke out he mustered wounded stormtroopers on the speaker's platform. He founded a guard of honour consisting of tall, uniformed Aryans and invented ceremonies such as the solemn entrance of flagbearers. He organised marches through poor districts like Red Wedding with its interminable rows of sombre tenements.[84]

The Weimar governments under the chancellorships of Hermann Müller, a Social Democrat (1920, 1928–30) and then Heinrich Brüning of the Centre Party (1930–2) had mere rationality to offer against all this, 'but they underestimated the power of emotional thinking and the growing influence of those who knew how to mobilise this force'.[85] Moreover, the unions could only influence employed workers and not the unemployed. Brüning in particular seemed to have no vision, no answer to the corrosive economic crisis save austerity and its further instalments, no promissory note of a better tomorrow. There were price controls, wage cuts and pensions were slashed; there was a banking crisis; his radical hopes for land reform proved unrealisable.[86]

The public status of propaganda

As elsewhere, both before and since, propaganda was a controversial medium in Germany, and for many of the same reasons: those holding authority resented it, but their challengers deployed it as a tool and advocated it as a function. Propaganda was a stratum of post-war intellectual discourse. Some liberals even endorsed it as a means of managing the demotic chaos of the modern era; hence propaganda was not only self-promotion but 'a means of managing the centrifugal forces of modern society'.[87] In the view of Harold Lasswell, the modern world was fragmented, lacked social cohesion and promoted individual desire before loyalty and tribe: 'propaganda is a reflex of the immensity, the rationality and the wilfulness of the modern world. It is the new dynamic of society, for power is subdivided and diffused.'[88] The study of propaganda became a real concern in Germany and elsewhere, as manifest in the funding of research institutes and universities, and also the interest from official organisations.[89] But there was still antagonism to advertising and to propaganda from members of the civic elite. The post-war labour movement also tended to eschew the rhetorical largely because they were now in power.[90] They could no longer be subversive. Tragically, Chancellor Brüning shrank the state's publicity budget and wanted to terminate the official media machine, remaining aloof despite the pressures to be more publicity-focused.[91]

1930–2

In the two years preceding their assumption of power, the Nazis had become a mighty party but they had not yet sufficiently assuaged popular reservations about their radicalism to win elections. It was propaganda's challenge to answer these fears, to present Hitler as a potential world figure and his acolytes as responsible candidates for government.

It had taken the National Socialists years to break through, but by the beginning of the 1930s they were rivals to the socialists (who had 8 million votes).[92] In the 1930 Reichstag election the Nazis won 107 seats, and by entering into a coalition with Hugenberg's nationalists (who had seventy-three seats), they were the largest single bloc in the Reichstag;[93] they now had 18.3 per cent of the vote.[94] These results were a terrible shock, with centrist and conservative parties flailing; the anti-democratic forces had triumphed with the Communists gaining seventy-seven seats.[95] The NSDAP share of the national vote had increased to 6.4 million, and their percentage of votes in rural constituencies was even greater. As the historian Richard Evans, who speaks of the Nazi 'landslide' of September 1930, points out, the Nazis attained 60 per cent of the vote in one rural seat, 57 per cent in another and 62 per cent in a third.[96] The Nazi rise to power was preceded by the infantilising of democracy, making public opinion more predisposed towards the authoritarian idea. Thus from 1930 and especially from 1932 Germany was increasingly governed by emergency law[97] as per Article 48 of the Weimar Constitution.[98]

Nazi success had been long in coming, but the final rupture was dramatic. In his study of the German town of Northeim, William Sheridan Allen describes a great jump in NSDAP fortunes in the three years before 1933, an outcome he attributes to the ability and effort the Nazis invested in campaigning.[99] This, the 1930 success, was the moment when the Hitler myth went national.[100] In the town of Northeim, three out of five were voting Nazi on the brink of the Third Reich era, and powering this vote was middle-class terror of the Great Depression.[101] But events have to be interpreted, and this is what propaganda does: it defines their meaning, and then it broadcasts this. And the campaigns played a critical role in relaying this specific interpretation of events. During the 'Hitler over Germany' campaigns of April 1932, for instance, when he was standing for the presidency against Hindenburg (an early if not unique example in the world of a politician maximising his presence by taking to the air), Hitler spoke to no fewer than twenty-one meetings in seven days.[102] He even held fourteen simultaneous mass meetings on one day, appearing at every single one of them.[103] It is claimed that Hitler spoke fifty times on the radio in 1933 alone; his prodigies of effort regularly covered three speeches in one day, or such ritual performances as 'maintaining a rigid salute for hours'.[104] He could address each member of his audience separately in understandable language. In the words of Helen Boak, 'a Hitler rally in the early 1930s was no doubt judged well worth the cost of admission, with its singing, marching, flags, military music—and Hitler, portrayed as the one man who could save Germany and lead the Germans to the promised land of the Third Reich.'[105] Yet a casual reading of his speeches suggests a vacuity, an absence of content, and, often, saccharine sentiments which even a liberal would not object to. The process was an emotional cauldron, not a rational seminar.

Why did people vote for Hitler? The old order was notoriously deluded about Hitlerism. According to Franz Neumann, powerful remnants of the establishment 'looked upon the National Socialist Revolution as a new edition of the imperial system, with its basis in the authority of the bureaucracy and the army. Now that it was back in the hands of reliable leaders, the German state would again embody the highest values.'[106] And Nazi propaganda was at its most effective when it resonated with commonly held beliefs, as was the case with the iniquity of Versailles, where it made use of an existing consensus within German society in order to incorporate revolutionary values.[107] But there is a great difference between a conservative and a Fascist, as the latter is a radical and a revolutionary.

The Nazis were first and foremost a mass movement of the middle class, and its leaders had the skills of small tradesmen, with their essential nuggets of practical, real-life knowledge, such as the way to go about buying advertising space.[108] However, the demographics of support varied widely, as the universities were also a ferment of National Socialist sympathy (they were, after all, an organisation with a youthful and radical image). In early 1931, for example, while the party's support among the general electorate stood at around 30 per cent, the comparable figure for the Nazi student organisation among undergraduates was around 60 per cent.[109] There were certainly massive internal Nazi tensions with regard to the sections of society that should be targeted, as manifest in a northern group, which initially included Goebbels, that wanted to attract the industrial proletariat vote.[110] Hitler, however, was bored by socialism—'what is this socialism?! If the people have something to eat and their pleasures, then they have their socialism.'[111] Hence the conflict with the left-leaning Strasser group who attempted dialogue with the unions but 'ran up against the purely propagandistic and utilitarian ideas' of Goebbels and of Hitler[112] (a dissident group of the SA in fact trashed Goebbels's new Berlin office).[113]

Yet the Nazis were not naive ideologues and never lost the central point— it is power that matters, and any method, any hypocrisy, can be used to gain it. Goebbels, for example, even ordered the party and storm troopers to cooperate with the Communists during the Berlin transport workers' strike of 1932.[114]

But it was the Great Depression that proved Germany's nemesis and Nazism's salvation. For all the vigour, the demonic energy, of their self-presentation they would never have arisen from the ranks of murmuring, eccentric minorities but for this. Their skill lay in seizing the moment, in turning a public crisis into a private opportunity via the mystification of propaganda. By the end of 1932, about one-third of the German workforce, or nearly 9 million people, were workless. Writers have well evoked the new and forlorn poverty of Berlin, the shacks, masses of criminalised youth surviving in gangs, the failing small businesses, the suicides; and the Nazis, unlikely as this may seem, turned social workers, feeding the unemployed.[115] The young British poet Stephen Spender thus described Berlin:

> the poverty, the agitation, the propaganda, witnessed by us in the streets and cafes, seemed more and more to represent the whole life of the town, as though there were almost no privacy behind doors. Berlin was the tension, the poverty, the anger, the prostitution, the hope and despair thrown out on to the streets. It was the blatant rich at the smart restaurants, the prostitutes in army top boots at corners, the grim, submerged-looking Communists in processions, and the violent youths who suddenly emerged from nowhere into the Wittenbergplatz and shouted 'Deutschland erwache!'[116]

The novelist Christopher Isherwood recalled how 'hate exploded suddenly, without warning, out of nowhere; at street corners, in restaurants, cinemas, dance halls, swimming baths; at midnight, after breakfast, in the middle of the afternoon'.[117] Erich Kästner's novel Fabian (1931) evokes the same doomed epoch.

Hitler over Germany, 1932

The year prior to Hitler's appointment as chancellor, 1932, was one of perpetual campaigning. There were always elections, and after the end of this great tumult, made vivid by all the arts of film and poster and marketing and airborne campaigning, Adolf Hitler became chancellor of Germany. But his final victory was never a forgone conclusion.

Hitler became a German citizen on 25 February 1932 because the state of Brunswick appointed him state councillor, which therefore gave him citizenship.[118] He then challenged Hindenburg for the presidency: 'Every city, town, village and hamlet was canvassed in a political campaign so violent that it seemed a continuation of war by other means.'[119] But the traditional forces, of the left, of the centre, of old reaction, were soon to be over-whelmed not just by a revolutionary message but by a revolutionary style of evangelism, one which understood persuasion in an urbanised mass economy, and, fatally, had an instinctual grasp of its latest techniques. In the view of Robert Wistrich: 'in the marketing of Adolf Hitler and the creation of his myth they surpass the best that American advertising tech-niques of their time or even today could provide. Already then, they had taken the personalisation of politics to new extremes—rarely if ever equalled.' Hitler was the first political leader:

> to see clearly the similarity between selling a commercial product and marketing a politician to the people; to make a calculated and intense use of mass tech-niques of political education; to understand the value of shock tactics in grabbing media attention; and to perceive that the endless repetition of simple slogans was more important for winning the masses than a consistent doctrine or an inflexible party programme.[120]

The Nazis benefited greatly during these elections from the newspapers of their reactionary ally Hugenberg, including the *Rheinisch-Westfalische Zeitung* (RWZ) he had acquired under the editorship of Otto Dietrich (who became Hitler's press chief); his film company (he had purchased UFA in 1927);[121] and his weekly newsreels.[122]

In 1932 Nazism's positioning strategy was to portray Hindenburg as the immobile status quo and Hitler as the dynamic agent of change.[123] Yet they were not averse to tactical Jacobinism either, as with the above-mentioned 1932 Berlin transport workers' strike. Expediency was their leitmotif. Hitler was quite prepared to play politics, to sacrifice, when opportune, ethno-nationalist conviction as with his refusal to join the other parties in the 'Watch on the Rhine' protest against Allied/French occupation (the occupa-tion only ceased in 1930); his was the only party in fact that did.[124]

Contradiction was never a problem, now or later—Russia could be the propaganda target, then excluded altogether after the Molotov–Ribbentrop pact, then become a target again with the invasion on 22 June 1941.[125] The Nazis even used posters to suggest that good Germans should support Hitler because Hindenburg was the candidate of the Jews (Hindenburg 'extraordinarily, incredibly' being the left-wing candidate supported by Social Democrats, among others).[126] Thus emerged the Iron Front, a liberal–left alliance, which used vehicles for electioneering ('motorised education columns') and supported the local pro-Hindenburg organising committees during the April presidential elections.[127] These committees also used modern propaganda, and vehicles, even aeroplane banners, and huge posters designed to inspire trust.[128] In 1932 there had been a number of signs that the Nazi movement was faltering. But then, suddenly, there was the 'leap to power which relieved the party of all democratic responsibility for its political course. In view of the new upturn in the international economic situation, it was seemingly able to fulfil a number of the promises so magnanimously scattered by its propaganda.'[129] This was a year of permanent election campaigns, with five elections in total, including two for the presidency, one for the state parliament and two for the Reichstag.[130] Hitler was the star of 'Hitler over Germany' and once again an innovator, with four airborne campaigns between April and November 1932: he spoke at nearly 150 massed rallies, with crowds up to 30,000 strong in the cities.[131] Millions of Germans heard him, and millions of Germans therefore had at least some sense of a personal relationship and awareness of the man's physical presence. Hitler's fourth aeroplane campaign was the most vigorous of all, visiting the towns and speaking: 'Against reaction!' was the radical slogan and the full blast of the Nazi propaganda machine was directed at the new Chancellor Franz von Papen and his 'corrupt' camarilla, or clique, of patrician junkers.[132] This was the Nazis' greatest pre-power triumph, their version of a barnstorming American presidential campaign and perhaps the first major political use of aeroplanes anywhere, and with the usual Goebbels-created euphoria via crowds, banners, blazing slogans; the film of the campaign opened in Munich on 23 October 1932. But there were signs of ennui: in the autumn of that year, 2 million fewer voters went to the polls than in July.[133]

The elections of 1932

Hence 1932 was the critical year. In the presidential election Hitler received 37 per cent of the vote but failed to win.[134] Hindenburg was narrowly re-elected on 13 March. The resignation of Chancellor Brüning followed on 30 May 1932 after the Nazi majorities were attained in the Prussian regional elections and the withdrawal of President Hindenburg's support.[135] On 31 May 1932, Hindenburg had asked von Papen to form a non-Nazi administration.[136] This von Papen 'coup' had Hitler again flying across Germany offering 'a vague but potent promise' (i.e. speeches strong on rhetoric, but weak on detail).[137]

This was the 'cabinet of barons' of Nazi propaganda; and the rivals Franz von Papen and Kurt von Schleicher continued their manoeuvring for power.[138] The Nazis had been the second largest party in the Reichstag after the Socialists. But the election of 31 July 1932, while denying Hitler a majority, did make the Nazis the biggest Reichstag party with 230 seats.[139] These elections more than doubled the Nazi vote from 6.4 million to nearly 13.8, and they now had almost 100 more seats than the Social Democrats, the second largest group: 'Left and right now faced each other in the Reichstag, across a centre shrunk to insignificance [since] a combined Social Democrat–Communist vote of 13.4 million confronted a Nazi vote of 13.8 million.'[140] The other parties combined had 9.8 million. Göring became Reichstag president on 30 August and von Papen faced a no-confidence vote.[141] Hitler had insisted that he would only be chancellor, not second-in-command, thereby preserving his mystique.[142] But there was a further election on 6 November, where the Nazis lost seats yet remained the biggest party: 'Nazism seemed in retreat and the Party was exhausted after a year of almost constant elections.'[143]

In the autumn 1932 election there had consequently been a sharp fall in the Nazi vote from 13.8 to 11.7 million, reducing their parliamentary seats from 230 to 196.[144] There were now 100 Communists and 196 Nazis, and both of these parties were intent on destroying the Weimar parliamentary system of which they were part.[145] After the elections von Papen was sacked as chancellor by Hindenburg and replaced by General Kurt von Schleicher, who assured Hindenburg that he could form a non-Nazi majority government.[146] But this ministry was extremely short-lived.[147] The British ambassador now described Germans as overcome by 'an almost oriental lethargy and fatalism'.[148] There then followed an election in the miniature state of Lippe, and all the sinews of the Nazi propaganda machine were stiffened in resolve. In the words of one authority, John Weitz, 'the fate of 70 million Germans was to be decided by 100,000 voters!' The Nazis ultimately won 39.5 per cent of the vote, and subsequently 'trumpeted their "fantastic reversal of fortune"'.[149]

Reassurances were given to President Hindenburg that the cabinet conservatives would control Hitler.[150] Hindenburg reluctantly called Hitler who was finally sworn in on 30 January 1933.[151] Piers Brendon has eloquently evoked the storm troopers' march down the principal Berlin thoroughfares: 'they surged forward in a flood of fire, torches held aloft, boots crashing on asphalt, voices raised as brass bands blared out the HW [Horst Wessel] song, Fredericus Rex and Deutschland über Alles. Onlookers added to the din, cheering wildly and shouting Heil Hitler and Heil, Heil, Sieg Heil.'[152] He also offers an important insight into the motives of the throngs that night:

when the procession reached the chancellery balcony on which Hitler was standing, illuminated by a blaze of searchlights, there were frenzied outbursts of applause ... the people were not cheering the eclipse of democracy so much as the rekindled glow of national pride ... Millions of Germans believed that only this man, framed against the Chancellery window in a dazzling nimbus of light, could lead them out of the depression.[153]

There was a further election in March 1933. However, this campaign was menaced by armed storm troopers and a Nazi–nationalist near-monopoly over the media. The Nazis won just over 50 per cent of the vote in conjunction with their nationalist coalition partners, yet the Nazis by themselves, despite being in power and controlling the media, only managed to secure 43.9 per cent of that vote.[154] The Communists, meanwhile, still managed 12.3 per cent and the Social Democrats 18.3 per cent.[155] Hitler's ascent was completed with the death of President Hindenburg at eighty-seven years old on 2 August 1934; in the plebiscite that followed on 19 August Hitler received nearly 90 per cent of the vote and he was now head of state as well as head of government.[156] In a reflection of the importance the Nazis attached to propaganda, the Ministry for Popular Enlightenment and Propaganda, under the leadership of Dr Joseph Goebbels, was established just six weeks into the life of the regime.[157]

The Reich at Peace

William Shirer evoked, unforgettably, the sight in the Reichstag after the successful Saar Referendum in which the inhabitants of the Saar basin—previously ceded to the French and administered by the League of Nations—voted to re-join Germany on 13 January 1935: the image transmitting the idea that Nazis were first and foremost small men representing a shrivelling of a nation's culture:

> little men with big bodies and bulging necks and cropped hair and pouched bellies and brown uniforms and heavy boots, little men of clay in his fine hands, leap to their feet like automatons, their arms outstretched in the Nazi salute, and scream 'heils', the first two or three wildly, the next twenty-five in unison, like a college yell.[158]

The 1930s, more than any other historical epoch, possess a kind of driven narrative momentum. They offer coherent structure: the shadow of Hitler lengthens ever longer over Europe, over the world, as the decade progresses, and the sound, louder and louder, of the stamp of marching feet. Everything about the decade—its art, its literature, its artefacts—is lit by a kind of fatalism, sometimes congealing into fear or actual hysteria. A long afternoon that became an evening and then a night. A series of terrible, though not accidental, crises now startled the world. Citizen and statesman alike stared in impotent horror, immobile, no longer capable of finding a language to evoke what they saw.

Political regimes usually adopt a responsive function and sometimes a proactive one. They entertain, to a greater or lesser degree, the notion of events as externalities, as things that arise, that happen, and then have to be managed or, *in extremis*, struggled against. But the Nazis, in contrast, perceived time itself as an empty canvas which they and they alone could daub with their fantasies. For the present and future were not things they influenced but things they created. A torrent of events, of manufactured activities, cascaded from the moment they seized power. The Nazi regime began its life with the good fortune of the Reichstag fire in its first year, the Night of the Long Knives in the second, and so it continued on and on and on: the Nuremberg Laws, Kristallnacht and so forth. There was a domestic stage, and then there was a global stage. And upon this global stage was enacted a series of ostensibly inexorable crises deep with symbolic meanings: Abyssinia, Manchuria, the war in Spain and Guernica, the Anschluss, the Czech crisis, all wrought by a remorseless and apparently inescapable pre-destiny. Yet this was also an era of white ocean liners on placid seas, of the artful contrivances of deco furniture, of grand hotels, streamlining in product design, supercharged sports cars and the first airliners, of the mighty, world-roaming flying boats; the playful aesthetic of the age, the teasing frivolities of its material presence, the globe itself now circumscribed by new transport systems as elegant as they were exclusive.

There were three separate elements in the Nazi version of the ideal Fatherland: social integration, rejuvenation by incorporating all those lands of the 'imaginary territorial Fatherland' and, finally, the international mission; this was the framework in which the risk–decision calculus took place.[159] The new or renewed Germany immediately embarked on a policy of global confrontation and the re-writing of the post-1918 political settlement and the Versailles Treaty, beginning with Hitler's announcement of Germany's withdrawal from the League of Nations on 14 October 1933. This was a gesture freighted with symbolism. The international community was no longer relevant to Germany; in fact it was contemptible, and from here on in Nazi Germany would forge its own destiny independent of treaties, pacts and the like. And from the beginning media was an adjunct of government policy. Hence an ostensibly 'spontaneous' 1936 mass media campaign attacked France's negotiation of a treaty with the USSR, thereby enabling Hitler to justify the German reoccupation of the Rhineland in March 1936—with the entry of 30,000 troops and the ancillary propaganda boost[160]—on national security grounds since this was a relationship between an old (national) and new (ideological) enemy.[161] Thus Versailles was unilaterally abrogated. In doing this so recklessly, and apparently disdainful of the consequences, Hitler gained the intermittent love of the German people. Limits on the army, set at 100,000, were discarded and the existence of a secret air force, which had been banned under Versailles, was publicly revealed in March 1935. War reparations ceased. Conscription was also introduced in the same month, while an Anglo-German naval treaty on 18 June 1935 helped secure the neutrality of Britain by regularising the relative sizes of the two navies.[162]

Against the backdrop of delirious crowds there was a further endorsement of the regime in the Saar plebiscite, with the official figure of a 90 per cent vote for Germany under the auspices of the League of Nations on 13 January 1935.[163] The Saar's leader, Max Braun, had urged a 'no' vote, but the Nazi machine destroyed him. Cheap propaganda ministry-distributed radios blared polemic and asserted on the morning of the plebiscite that Braun had fled, and even though he drove open-top through the streets of Saarbrücken it was not enough.[164] The region re-joined the Reich and Germany was whole again (scholars suggest that unlike the later 'referenda' this was an assent freely given, and is therefore an index of public support for the Nazi regime, or at least acquiescence). Such foreign policy dynamism and success stuns the critical faculty: the theatre of foreign affairs was the regime's methodology throughout and a stage for symbolic propaganda.

Hitler's great year of triumph, the *annus mirabilis* of the Third Reich, came in 1938. It was in this year that his audacity, the gathered harvest of his ruthlessness, finally bore fruit in the cost-free creation of a Greater Germany: with the ultimate photo opportunity, the Anschluss, on 14 March 1938, a measure ostensibly designed to 'protect' Germans living outside the Reich.[165] Mass, roaring crowds bellowed their 'obvious' joy at being compulsorily incorporated, forestalling an Austrian plebiscite though 'endorsed' by a subsequent Nazi one on 10 April with, of course, almost 100 per cent support.[166] Austrian Nazis had toiled lovingly for this end, murdering, for example, Engelbert Dollfuss, the Fascist (but nationalist and anti-Nazi) chancellor and dictator of Austria. Hitler entered Vienna in a Roman triumph. The Czech Sudetenland was next to suffer Germany's diplomatically lubricated invasion, with the happy migration of Konrad Henlein and the Sudetendeutsche (i.e. Sudeten Germans) and their entire territory, since the French and British had given Hitler permission at the Munich Conference on 29 September 1938 to dismember Czechoslovakia. This was in turn followed by the German consumption of all Czechoslovakia and German entry into Prague without any international sanctions being imposed in response, the first instalment of Nazi imperialism, and also Germany's military intervention in the Spanish Civil War (1936–9) on the Nationalist (i.e. rebel) side; and thus the glories of the 'Condor Legion' (the Luftwaffe) roaring above the battlegrounds of Spain, raining death from its blazing skies. For many Germans this was an era of perpetual ecstasy, an unbearable lightness of being, a delicious fantasy made real. It was a dream: Germany awoke, and found it true.

In addition to these domestic and foreign policy achievements, Hitler was also able to exploit sexual scandals in order to consolidate his power and war plans. The homosexuality of some members of the SA leadership, for instance, was used as a convenient excuse for them to be purged. There was also the Fritsch–Blomberg crisis of 1938, in which Colonel-General Werner von Fritsch, the commander-in-chief of the army, was forced to confront the fabrications of the male prostitute 'Potsdam Joe' in front of Hitler, while Field Marshal Werner von Blomberg, the defence minister, was forced to resign when it was revealed that he had recently married a prostitute.[167] This crisis, which had been orchestrated via a temporary alliance between Göring, Himmler and Heydrich,[168] permitted the expulsion of the army's top duo, men whose values deviated from the Nazis' and who were uneasy about the path to war. This decapitation of the German army consequently made it much easier to wage aggressive wars of conquest.

These achievements in the years immediately following the seizure of power were ones of which any interwar German leader would have been proud as they transcended party politics. The Nazis had reunited Germany, reignited the economy and reversed Versailles, and while all of this was primarily a triumph of politics, it was also a major achievement of Nazi propaganda; a consequence of their ideology of governance. One by one the humiliations were systematically dismantled, and then out of this re-establishment of the *status quo ante* was constructed the foundation of a new hegemony and a new imperium, a greater Germany—all of these achievements happened with minimal loss of German life or ruinous tax of German treasure. The list of course gives no sense of the generated imagery, a visual–rhetorical journey of the 1930s that left Germans intoxicated: all their problems apparently ceased, unemployment was minimal, and the nation was endowed with a new purpose. But the Reich was always about more than this. The reversals of the verdict of 1918, the conquest of the great depression, were to be followed by a new nirvana, the morphing into empire and superstate.

Institutions and Illusions: The Acclamatory State

The Reich was won by illusion. The Nazis, their fortunes fraying, had produced that magical victory in the miniature state of Lippe by gorging it with their propaganda resources.[169] This had helped persuade Chancellor von Papen to invite the Nazis into government.[170]

An important part of the illusion was to create the sense that some demotic mechanism was substituting for a real democracy: a kind of acclamatory state, government by declamatory rhetoric, which reflected and connected the popular will. In other words, Hitler was to be a medium who divined the deeper thoughts of the masses and embodied them in dynamic action. There was in effect a new discourse, one that involved the shift 'from rational bureaucratic and institutional to charismatic modes of legitimation'.[171] One of the principal ways through which the Nazis engineered this shift was the mass rallies, which served as an alternative concept of synthetic participation. Goebbels claimed they were a persuasive substitute for an actual say in the government, and he even went so far as to argue that participation in rallies was a superior form of voting. Similarly, the various referenda, like the rallies, were used as a form of public legitimacy-seeking. There were in total five referenda before the Second World War, and although these were pseudo-elections and a parody of real ones, they provided a comfort blanket and symbol of civic normality for those who craved one. The entire psychological enterprise relied on the idea of a willing co-partnership in illusion; for example, in the town of Northeim the ballot result was treated as a great Nazi triumph with peeling church bells. As Allen relates: 'the whole electioneering machinery that the Nazis had perfected over the past several years was cranked up again as though this were going to be the real election'.[172]

Gauging public opinion in Nazi Germany is of course difficult but the managed plebiscites of 1934, 1936 and 1938 provide a sliver of evidence, since people were able to refrain from voting. In 1934, for instance, the 'yes' vote was around 75 per cent of turnout in the big cities and lower in some Berlin boroughs such as Aachen, with just 65.7 per cent.[173] There was also the evidence of the shop steward elections of April 1935, in which it was often the case that no more than 30 to 40 per cent of the plant would vote for the single Nazi slate; and yet the majority could no longer resist 'the noise of acclamatory propaganda'.[174]

Leader illusions: the Führer myth

Since Nazism was based on charismatic authority, the image of the leader always had to be the primary thrust of the propaganda. While that image was never static and always evolutionary, at its heart was a permanent idea: the leader's benevolence, honour and civic rectitude.

The greatest illusion was that of Hitler himself and the belief that he was in some way a moderate, restraining the more revolutionary and violent elements of the party; the belief that he and the party were not one, but that he was some kind of benevolent vox populi acting independently of the abuses, mediocrity and corruption of the party lackeys; the notion that he was the loving patriarch, human and humane, caring deeply for the suffering of his tribe and adoring its children and families. All of these were not default imagery, something which happened by chance, but were care-fully calculated and targeted effects achieved by selective use of image integrated with message. The Hitler idea then was the nexus of the illusion, and that message was self-serving for Germans: the idea of a nation wronged, the language of victimhood, framed by a narcissistic conception of all Germans as innately noble and, actually or latently, heroic. This polemic of dispossession, this configuring of his audience as an oppressed people, did contain a core of truth, that of the iniquities of Versailles. Hence this culture of grievance was a shared creation between Hitler and his congregations, in which Hitler would package and retail to these listeners their rage and agitation.

Moreover, beyond this, there was the seeking out of blameworthy groups, the offering to the German people of an alibi for their misfortune and the displacement of causation away from them to enemies within, to traitors to the people. In doing this, Hitler deftly understood and manipulated the psychology of post-First World War Germany: to turn the critical faculty away from self to others he absolved both elites and masses from all blame for defeat. Thus, from the very beginnings of Hitlerite evangelism we see the ability to reinvent truth with self-serving argument. This is not to say that the world Hitler portrayed through his hectoring verbalisations was an entirely fictive one or had no link whatsoever to some objective account. It did, and thus he was a credible figure, but much of it remained locked in a realm of imagining, storytelling and contempt for any kind of candid retrospection on the meaning of the end of the First World War and Germany's defeat. In other words, he led a portion of the nation in a flight from reality. He gave birth to an illusion and he nurtured it and over time it grew, displacing any element in the Nazi narrative that had some kind of defensible rationale.

Ethos: the illusion of the normal

The propaganda of the pre-war years offered a paradox. What *meaning* was the regime seeking to communicate via its propaganda (internally) to the Germans and (externally) to the world? How do we reconcile the grand opera of such stage-managed events as the 1936 Olympics with the demented, and very public, frenzy of the Night of the Long Knives or Kristallnacht; or of the Nuremberg Laws? Where was the coherence of message? Moreover, these terrible events were a form of experiential theatre to be witnessed, or known about, from the anchored certainties of what felt like a Western country fed by the refreshments of a vibrant consumer economy.

Thus, uniforms and public exhortations apart, Nazi Germany resembled a normal Western country. The illusion of normalcy prevailed and it was deliberately fostered by a German government which wanted to project a 'modern' (i.e. pseudo-pluralist) image. Right up until the Second World War, Germany was not a sealed state like the hermit kingdom North Korea; it did not shut out other possibilities. The government did indeed control a huge state propaganda machine and dictated what its media could say, but another objective was to create a facsimile of a contemporary society and hence a permissible level of heterogeneity. Alternative perspectives were available, as Germans were able to read Swiss-German newspapers, listen to international broadcasts or watch Hollywood movies. This was an ideological, but not an ideologically watertight, hemisphere. In 1934, 20 per cent of the new films which premiered in Germany were of American provenance, a figure that increased to 50 per cent in 1935; and they were highly popular with German cinemagoers.[175] It was possible to be both a Nazi and an American movie buff. The contemporary diarist Victor Klemperer, for example, describes attending a cinema where an SA man and his girlfriend were seated next to him, with the young storm trooper both gyrating to the Hollywood rhythm and delighting at the Nazi propaganda.[176]

Germans began to live life in imitation of their propaganda: it caressed and managed an image of a fit and blessed people, who began to resemble the typologies the casting directors had defined. According to the US journalist William Shirer, for instance, members of the Hitler Youth really did seem happy, with children from all walks of life engaging in activities together; they were dynamic, fit. He observed the contrast between the German soldier 'and the weedy English soldiers I saw as prisoners of war in May 1940':[177]

> The young in the Third Reich were growing up to have strong and healthy bodies, faith in the future of their country and in themselves and a sense of fellowship and camaraderie that shattered all class and economic and social barriers. I thought of the latter, in the May days of 1940, when along the road between Aachen and Brussels one saw the contrast between the German soldiers, bronzed and clean-cut from a youth spent in the sunshine on an adequate diet, and the first British war prisoners, with their hollow chests, round shoulders, pasty complexions and bad teeth—tragic examples of the youth that England had neglected so irresponsibly in the years between the wars.[178]

Dualism of image manufacture was part of this illusion: the contrast of Hitlerite imagery and abrasiveness and militarism with the contrary, kind images from a lighter world of journalistic banter, casual curiosity and a pleasure in the exotic. Nazi media was in fact filled with both; it was a visual cornucopia. On 27 April 1939, for instance, *Berliner Illustrierte Zeitung*[179] showcased Hitler's birthday with its rows of goose-stepping ceremonial troops, processions, its great urban caverns of light and darkness and illumination; the parades and the official cars, the mass of standards, the close-ups of the Führer with arms outstretched, the transfixed foreign military attachés, and Hitler rubbing shoulders with old comrades. Little blonde children were shown with bunches of flowers. Yet, following on from this, the paper contains images of Bali: sensuous, oriental, feminine, an exotic world of bareback native women, masks, dancing, temples, parasols and arcane ceremonies. From granite discipline to the sun-kissed tropics within the turning of the page. But that was the Reich, a Nazi world and another world, the object of delight and innocent arousal; it is impossible to understand the success of the one without the other, and it is this polarity of cultural vision which both explains and epitomises the Third Reich. Even altruism was engineered as a component of the appeal, as was the case with the government charity campaign to help the poor, Winter Aid (see Chapter Five), which had been inherited from the Republic but was portrayed as a National Socialist idea.[180]

The regime exhibited a preternatural ability to manufacture enormous and historically resonant events. There was the Reichstag fire on 27 February, for example, one month after Hitler became chancellor on 30 January 1933; the perpetrator, the Dutch Communist Marinus van der Lubbe, had very conveniently emerged from the enemy ranks. The fact that suspicions continued to be aired about this event within German society—namely that Göring had organised it—is a further indication of the relative freedom that still prevailed in this period.[181] Then there were the 'spontaneous' pan-German book incinerations of 10 May 1933, where a bonfire even blazed opposite the Berlin Opera. The works of Voltaire, H.G. Wells, Thomas Mann and countless others were consigned to the flickering pyres,[182] a crematorium of intellectual culture which curiously anticipated another kind of crematorium.

In Germany there was clearly a widespread preparedness to accept arguments based not even on marginal objectivity, but on illusion. The question of course is why there was such willingness to suspend critical judgement, and this conscious myopia was no better displayed than at the start of the regime's life with the Night of the Long Knives, which was no mere deceit but a complete reinvention of reality. This was the night that the party savagely turned on its own: the storm trooper leadership (by 1932 the numbers of SA had increased to 400,000, or four times the size of the Versailles-mandated army).[183] But mystification of the truth was fostered via a public narrative; for the massacre was positioned in general perception as the quelling of a revolutionary threat, and its sordid actuality, that it represented the butchery of the more independent and critical party comrades, was concealed. Many were killed in the Röhm purge of 30 June 1934, including public figures (Franz von Papen was fortunate, and subsequently resurfaced as ambassador to Austria and then Turkey). A conventional estimate suggested the figure of over seventy party members killed,[184] but others have suggested as many as 400.[185] Respectable Germandom had feared mindless storm trooper anarchy, and the popular inference was that Hitler had pre-empted carnage by anticipatory ruthlessness.[186] Yet significant actors from the discarded German elite had quite simply been murdered. This inversion of the moral order, where public men could be liquidated without a murmur of protest from the ranks of most of their peers, was an important moment in the progress of the new order of illusion, even though some members of the social elite did now reject the party.

There was the rhetoric, there was the myth, and then there was the movie. *Triumph of the Will* (1935) is a brilliant fabrication in celluloid. It is a rhapsody of harmony, a Nazi opera celebrating community of purpose and party unity. It is a film of the 1934 Nuremberg rally that followed on from the massacres, but it is also much more, the re-imagining of the new order and the storehouse of Nazi imagery for evermore. The storm troopers, cleansed and sanitised, were presented and resurrected before the German people alongside their nemesis, the SS.

And at the Nuremberg rally in September 1935 were promulgated the infamous Nuremberg Laws, and then there followed the Reich Citizenship Law; Jews, half-Jews and even quarter-Jews were stripped of German citizenship. The Nuremberg Laws also prevented intermarriage between Jews and Germans. Rules so brutal, so crudely racialist, were not without international consequences. The scales dropped from people's eyes. In Britain the Rothermere press now abandoned Hitler, and fellow travellers scuttled into their holes. Germany was in danger of appearing in the global perception as a nation soiled, regressing to a new medievalism and the harbinger of a new dark age.

But then, there were the 1936 Olympics, Nazi Germany's embassy to the world and its attempt at self-packaging and concealment. Berlin became a global focus with society visitors from other countries and as many as 1,200,000 tourists.[187] The Olympics were an astonishing success and caused many wilfully to ignore the evidence via a selective perception much facilitated by the regime's manicured public vistas, its tokenism, its paragons of efficiency; a regime that oozed self-belief and self-congratulatory rhetoric could indeed force other people, foreigners, to see what it wanted them to see.

However, throughout the 1930s, the propaganda 'message' seemed to be inconsistent because its objectives were divergent and even irreconcilable. The Nazis wanted Germany to be admired, of course, which was an aim of the propaganda, but that was never enough. They also wanted to terrorise their actual or potential enemies whether ethnic, political or foreign, and to declare war on the Jews. The pretext for the last of these came on 7 November 1938, when a young Jew, outraged by the treatment of his relatives, assassinated a German diplomat. Herschel Grynszpan's killing of Ernst vom Rath in Paris was the excuse Goebbels used to launch Kristallnacht on 8 November. Kristallnacht embodied in fact a familiar Nazi rhetorical conceit: that the sin of one Jew was the sin of all Jews, and that every crime committed by a member of a race was attributable to all members of that race. Crimes were given the valence of typicality—it was normal for Jews to commit such crimes—but the argument never stopped there: a single crime was always a collective crime. On Kristallnacht 7,500 Jewish businesses in Germany and Austria were destroyed, ninety-one Jews killed and over 30,000 Jewish men sent to concentration camps.[188]

Institutions and illusions: propaganda and the climate of fear

Explicit terror

On 20 March 1933 Dachau, the first Nazi concentration camp, opened, and the terror was now real. The inmates were not specifically Jews but Communists, socialists, liberals and in fact general non-Nazi political activists of the Weimar era, or anyone who was politically suspect. The police state had arrived; this was a regime of civic terror and the perversity of a state that was not your friend but your adversary: the knock in the night, the beatings, the disappearances—where the state existed not to protect you from enemies and criminals but was itself enemy and criminal. There was no ambiguity: while the regime desired belief, not all could be believers, so ideological deviationists had their warning. The Nazis were quite explicit, and there was a vast amount they did not even feel the need to hide. Hence another function of the propaganda was coercive insofar as it sought to send a message to people as to the scale of the brutality they might experience for non-compliance. Neumann remarks that a historian and authority on Catholic England attributed the success of Henry VIII to his use of propaganda, defining propaganda as 'the violence committed against the soul': 'propaganda is not a substitute for violence, but one of its aspects. The two have the identical purposes of making men amenable to control from above. Terror and its display in propaganda go hand in hand.'[189]

The propaganda became part of the terror system. People who were guilty of crimes (such as those who listened to foreign radio broadcasts during the war itself) were lavished with publicity.[190] Yet even then, control was never absolute, as demonstrate the multiple conspiracies against Hitler, or the revels of the anti-Hitler Youth Swing Kids (young jazz enthusiasts) and delinquency of the Edelweiss Pirates (alienated teenage gangs) suggest.[191] There was a need also for civilian informers so the terror did not seem arbitrary, and its victims would be popularly recognised as enemies of the people and saboteurs of popular will as embodied in the regime; it worked, therefore, by portraying regime enemies as truly wicked. Moreover, the Gestapo was a sovereign body: after 1936 its judgements were free of the shackles of juridical restraint and this was fully understood publicly and even popular.[192] Retributive justice always sustains a facile public appeal because we all hate criminals. The government was also candid about the Röhm purge: it could hardly be hidden, so why not turn private murder into public celebration? This legitimated future extrajudicial homicides by helping to precipitate a civic climate accepting of arbitrary coercion.[193] Here, then, was a reversion to an older and pre-rational world, the arbitrary despotism of sadistic men; mercenaries and assorted banditti who appeared to have stepped out of the shadows of history. The atmosphere is well evoked by Ambassador Sir Nevile Henderson's description of an SS camp at Nuremberg:

> as I wrote at the time, 'the camp in the darkness, dimly lit by flares, with the black uniform in the silent background and the skull and crossbones on the drums and trumpets lent to the scene a sinister and menacing impression'. I felt, indeed, as if I were back in the days of Wallenstein and the Thirty Years' War in the seventeenth century.[194]

Mood control

The Nazis were expert at mood control, creating public actualities which were apparently spontaneous or authentic but were in fact completely fabricated. Their success was due partly to popular credulity, a naivety as to the scale of the regime's manipulative apparatus, but people were also willing co-conspirators in their own self-deceit; the false consciousness of which they were simultaneously victim and co-creator. The Nazis possessed various instruments to do this, to create as it were an instant public atmosphere via tools of a corporate methodology, and spontaneous demonstrations were one of these. Thus Speer tells us that:

> in 1939, Karl Hanke [latterly a Gauleiter and SS general] told me of the variants of such demonstrations; which manner of demonstration was wanted depended on political and propagandistic factors. From the gatherings of schoolchildren to cheer a foreign guest all the way to the mobilising of millions of workers to express the will of the people, the Propaganda Ministry had a prepared scenario. Ironically, Hanke spoke of 'cheering levies'. Had the future gone according to plan, it would have taken the ultimate of all 'cheering levies' to fill Adolf Hitler Platz, since it would hold a million people.[195]

Such methodologies were as useful at the regime's end as at its beginning. To celebrate Hitler's 'providential' escape from the July 1944 officers' plot, for instance, Goebbels organised 'spontaneous' demonstrations. This 1944 assassination attempt was exploited by Goebbels as treason and trust was briefly recovered, according to intelligence reports. 'Hitler is victory' was the revived slogan.[196]

There was the purposive creation of a public climate of driven hysteria, which licensed the enormities that happened. Klemperer gives an instance of one way in which this was done: by halting all traffic between 12 o'clock and 12.42 in order to 'facilitate [the] nationwide search for publications hostile to the state'. Surely, Klemperer goes on to record, this was a direct and indirect form of fear in equal measure:

> what I mean by this is that the artificial generation of suspense, copied from American cinema and thrillers, is obviously just as much a premeditated means of propaganda as the direct creation of fear, but that, on the other hand, only those who are themselves afraid do this kind of propaganda ...[197]

At the beginning of the Second World War new laws forbade Germans from listening to foreign radio broadcasts. A new atmosphere of vindictive popular denunciation grew, Orwellian in texture, in which the government was trying to control thought. There was even one case in which a man denounced himself: persuasion and coercion were stages along the same continuum.[198] Scholars have spoken of 'German on German' terror, a new kind of popular participation. People sought to exploit the new regimen, leading to what one might call the policehood of all believers, where every man was a political policeman. Indeed, one study has found that 70 per cent of anonymous denunciations were from private sources.[199] Yet the leadership actually worried about the denunciations, since this undermined folk community.

Concentration camps

During the 1930s the Nazis concocted serial mythologies to create an illusory realm. One of these was the myth of the benevolent concentration camp, even though the truth was perceptible in the oft-reported phrase 'shot while trying to escape'. Such myths were a preamble to the Holocaust, the antechamber and preparatory institution.

That the objective reality of something can be so much at variance with the public's truth, even the antithesis of its public descriptor, is the essence of political fiction. But illusion was the core Nazi methodology.[200] The idea, in particular, that Communist hoodlums were being spiritually repatriated represents the illusion that good, moral work was being done. And the misconception continued; for example, many of the concentration camps were closed down in the mid-1930s and then re-opened.[201] There was reality in the Third Reich, and, at every point, its illusory public symbol and counterpart, inevitably at variance with the truth. The licensed sadism and institutionalised psychopathology of the concentration camps became, under this mythologising, simply re-education. There were 1,300 camps in Germany and we must infer a general knowledge of their existence. Thus the camps themselves were vigorously marketed: 'women's magazines included photographs of the coffee breaks enjoyed by the grateful inmates of concentration camps, amid the racially vetted models and tips on household management'.[202] Himmler claimed they had a re-educative purpose: Gellateley remarks that 'he might have been speaking of an American reformatory in the 1950s'.[203] The true horror was always disguised while, paradoxically, always leaving hints as to its true diabolism. It was both concealed and revealed and this was deliberate; elements were allowed to surface. There was no admission about any Holocaust: 'they did, however, unmistakably keep hitting the same notes, making the same threats, and letting the evidence gather'.[204]

Ideology

But violence without ideology was foredoomed. As Hitler argued in *Mein Kampf*, an idea can only be combatted by another idea: 'any attempt to combat a philosophy with methods of violence will fail in the end, unless the fight takes the form of attack for a new spiritual attitude'. The Nazis did not seek acquiescence or even acceptance. What they craved was a nation of believers in the new order, 'a new consensus of values'[205]—they were not merely exploiting an existing value system but were surreptitiously replacing it. The weight of the ideology even bore down on the minutiae of domestic life; thus a 1939 Nazi article explained how one should, as a National Socialist, decorate one's home:[206] 'if interior decoration falls under the purview of the party, what does not? Totalitarian worldviews suffuse private life within public ideology, leaving few avenues for political apostasy to develop.'[207] Such a totalisation of the communications environment had never been possible before, nor has it been since; Soviet Russia, for example, never really possessed the level of resource necessary, whereas a new Germany did.

2

A NARRATIVE OF THIRD REICH PROPAGANDA

ERSATZ VALHALLA (1939–45)

Duff (Duff Cooper, Minister of Information) has returned. He does not look too well. I took him to a film of the 1938 Nuremberg party rally. I do not think it cheered him up very much. It has all come so damned true. All those Hitler jugend were the men who came down in shoals upon Crete. That battle has, I fear, dealt a very severe blow to our morale.

Harold Nicolson MP, *Diaries,* 5 June 1941

At present the ministry is too decent, educated and intellectual to imitate Goebbels. It cannot live by intelligence alone. We need crooks. Why I hate Hitler so much is that he has coined a new currency of fraudulence which he imposes by force. I am prepared to see the old world of privilege disappear. But as it goes, it will carry with it the old standards of honour.

Harold Nicolson, *Diaries,* 3 August 1940

Early Second World War

Peace deceit

The German people had not wanted another war, so the public Hitler was now edited into a peace image. By the end of the 1930s public proselytisation of living space had ceased and the regime knew it could not turn ecstasy about foreign policy into enthusiasm for a new war. Even within the context of a fear-driven totalitarian system, Goebbels and his agents were still able to discern popular sentiment.[1] An internal report issued during the Czech (Sudeten) crisis of 1938 observed that Germans 'favour maintaining peace at any price' and that the motorised columns roaring through Berlin on 27 September 1938 had been greeted with silence.[2] Research conducted by the Sicherheitsdienst (SD, the intelligence agency of the Nazi Party and the SS) also indicated that people were not ready for war. The inference was that they had to be made ready. The propaganda ministry consequently introduced a new discourse of a nation being forced into a war: the old idea of encirclement disinterred, of the West and Poles and Bolshevists together tightening the noose.[3] Hitler was seen as desiring peace and having struggled to avoid war. This was achieved via Nazi propaganda, which continued to sustain a peace image, as with Hitler's early wartime manoeuvre, the 6 October 1939 'peace offer' to the West, whose inevitable rejection was used by Nazi propagandists as proof of Allied perversity.[4] 'Germany needs peace'—Hitler's speech profoundly affected many who heard it. A subsequent propaganda trick, targeted at world opinion, was his 'final peace offer' of a 'negotiated' peace with Britain on 19 July 1940: this later speech suggested that Germany was about to deliver the final death blow to Britain, and most people believed him.[5]

The Second World War functioned on two levels for its participants: as a raw physical event, but also as a media event—as Ross has remarked, war had never before been so extensively communicated to civilian audiences.[6] The war itself began on 1 September 1939 with Germany's invasion of Poland and the British and French declaration of war on 3 September; and then the full horror, the truth of the Nazi–Soviet pact negotiated by Ribbentrop and Molotov, was made plain on 17 September when the Soviet Union invaded Poland from the East. Warsaw fell on 27 September, with Poland being partitioned on the following day. German newsreels offered a swift juxtaposition—a burning German farm, Hitler screaming for revenge against the supposed Polish 'invaders'; Stukas were depicted attacking Polish soil. The newsreels show the pilot's view of the bombing run as he dives, sirens wailing, his murderous cargo flung on to buildings and moving targets,[7] followed by the consequences of the devastation, the ruined trains and charred remnants of the buildings, the debris of war. Then the Polish surrender, their generals escorted to meet their conquerors as the grey Wehrmacht legions march through Warsaw in customary style, bands playing, regimental banners to the front, three officers at their head, a mounted officer leading.

The Polish invasion was followed by the period of 'phoney war' in which the stasis on the Western Front was occasionally broken by eruptions such as the Battle of the River Plate. But this was to change dramatically in the spring of the following year, when the Allies suddenly seemed to disintegrate: Germany invaded Norway and Denmark in April 1940, Neville Chamberlain fell on 9 May, and Germany attacked the Netherlands and Belgium on 10 May, with the aerial decimation of Rotterdam commencing four days later. This was in turn followed by the Anglo-French retreat to the French coast and Dunkirk, and the defeat at Sedan: 'the German public ... pressed into listening to the radio war reports and reading the daily press coverage of the victories in East and West, became saturated, as if through some giant, highly co-ordinated advertising campaign ...'[8]

There were four phases of the war in Germany: the heroic phase of conquest, the phase of challenge, the phase of retreat and finally the endgame when all was clearly lost. During the war, illusion increasingly began to take centre stage and finally morphed into pure delusion, where the paladins of the state themselves could no longer 'see' in any tangible sense and entertained the most tenuous grasp of reality. Illusion then became a kind of psychological comfort-food, as with the claim that the United States would suddenly awake to the Bolshevik menace and make peace, leaving the Reich to battle with the monster from the East.

But that lay at the end. In the beginning was the rationale for conquest, namely the notion that the conquered had brought conquest upon themselves due to their hatred of Germans. This led to all else: the stunning demoralisation of all critical faculty and the acceptance of the new mythologies which the propaganda ministry would now proceed to conjure, the myths of the Judeo-Bolshevik conspiracy, the myth of violent US imperialism and the arrant lunacy of Germany's claim to some kind of moral superiority over capitalist, individualistic societies. All of these junior myths were successful because the first and greatest myth—i.e. the invincibility of Adolf Hitler—was never interrogated or negated in the minds of the German people. Hyperbole replaced reason, feeling substituted for analysis and visceral emotion saturated popular consciousness.

The Nazi justification for war

After invading Poland, the Reich had a mission to explain and it was determined to expound its defiant truths to the neutral world, which at this stage still included the United States. *Facts in Review* (1940), the German

Library of Information in New York newsletter, was in no doubt about the righteousness of the German cause: 'Divisions—inspired by victory and the restoration, at last, of the wrongs of Versailles—rolled on over the ruins of the defeated French army ... wiped out the iniquity of 1918.'[9] Goebbels's propaganda machine argued for the victimhood of Germans: the war had been forced on them by foreign aggression. 'This is not a war of crown and altar; it is a war for wheat bread, a full table three times a day.'[10] The world, in this view, had declared war on a Germany defending its borders from brutal Polish invaders. This was the demented fantasy Germany presented to the world via newsreel and other mediums of propaganda, and it never deviated from this narrative. Thus Goebbels constantly reminded the media to stress the fact that the enemies in September 1939 'had taken the unilateral decision to declare war on the Reich and had repeatedly scorned Germany's "peace" offers'.[11] The Nazis engaged in the promulgation of 'evidence' of Germany's peaceful intentions, all of which had supposedly been frustrated by an aggressive England. The Blitz against Britain and elsewhere, for instance, was presented as a form of defence rather than an attack.[12] On 1 September 1939 Hitler gave a speech which dwelt on the theme of Danzig and the corridor—arguing that these territories were German and had been confiscated from their rightful owners—while also claiming that 1 million Germans had been forced to leave their homeland after the First World War.[13] Germany, outrageously, also presented itself as a global underdog seeking self-preservation against the oppression of an Anglo-Jewish plutocratic status quo.[14]

Goebbels's methodology

At the start of the war Goebbels had yet to recapture the institutional monopoly over regime self-presentation that he had nearly possessed in 1933 when he was briefly propaganda supremo in fact as well as theory. The war, then, was his great opportunity to command the centre stage as he had once briefly done. Moreover, while propaganda had been a major structuring device for the Nazi civic state, in the military state that followed it was not merely this, an integument of government, but also a major weapon of war: an instrument alongside bombs and guns to beat the enemy. This was Goebbels's opportunity and he took it: via ownership of propaganda he would re-engineer his place in the most important struggle of all in wartime Germany—the struggle for precedence among Hitler's court.

Sensitivity

All was not well in the Reich, however; this was war, after all. Berlin presented a dreary Christmas 1939: 'few presents, spartan food, the menfolk away, the streets blacked out, the shutters and curtains drawn tight ... The Germans feel the difference tonight. They are glum, depressed, sad ...'[15] Yet Goebbels was a supremely sensitive operator who was deeply aware of the factors which affected civilian morale and the public, of the symbolic construction of events and how they resonated with the masses; as is clear, for example, in his description of the visits he made to wounded men. Though very much the domain of his job anyway, this kind of behaviour contrasted with other paladins of the Reich and their crass insensitivity. Goebbels always understood the value of materialised propaganda in all aspects of his work. He would distribute cigarettes and cognac at the front, and even donated 5,000 radios on one occasion.[16] In his diaries he writes of how he gave gifts to 400,000 people in December 1940.[17] Goebbels was also sensitive to the needs of foreign correspondents who, by an astonishing metamorphosis of status, were class-reassigned as 'heavy labourers' and therefore awarded double rations as a form of bribery.[18] He had an incisive understanding of popular culture and the mass mind, the populist perspective, which enabled him to grasp the importance of class resentment. This was something he knew how to mobilise for his own ends, even at the expense of the officer corps, an appeal that (when used) invoked the deepest fractures in old European cultures.

The scale and scope of Goebbels's operations extended also to the tasks of gauleiter of Berlin, which was yet another propaganda opportunity in that it gave him the chance to solve the practical problems of war effectively at the operational level and therefore win the battle for public opinion, as well as changing the balance of power between himself and the other paladins. One of his diary entries from October 1939, for example, records how there was a shortage of salt in Berlin due to difficulties in transportation and how he quickly took measures to ensure relief.[19]

Goebbels will forever be associated with the idea of shamelessness. No trick was too low if it succoured the cause. For him, fear was just another weapon of diplomacy, one which should be used to extract maximum national advantage. Indeed, for the Nazis as a whole, the end always justified the means, and thus on 9 November 1939 Goebbels wrote about what he called his infamous tactic of refusing to deny the rumour floating around the Netherlands and Belgium that Germany was about to attack;[20]

this really does suggest a depth of cynicism and an acuity of tactical manipulation. Similarly, on 12 November, he used neutral circles to foster a rumour about a German invasion, adding that he was 'deliberately letting the pot simmer on this'. He recorded the panic among neutral countries, writing how he intended to 'let them stew'.[21]

Goebbels scoured the adversary's political geography for its points of fragility: since their critique of Germany was primarily a moral critique, it was essential to attack the ethical base of their own society. Something like concentration camps or the persecution of Jews could not be refuted by Goebbels and he did not seek to try. He instead attacked the enemy directly at the most vulnerable points in the public moral edifice it had constructed. With Britain, this was the empire and the iniquities of empire, and every wrong committed in its long history could be mobilised against it rhetorically. Goebbels's maxim was never defend, always attack; his diaries from November 1939, for instance, record how he intended to reply to the attacks on the concentrations camps in the British press with a book detailing English colonial policy.[22] Yet he remained deeply aware of the danger of propaganda regressing to trite and sterile formulae, and discussed the importance of freedom for individual creative work: 'otherwise we shall trip slowly on bureaucracy'.[23] He wanted something bright, hard, avant-garde even, and self–regenerative (but that is not what he got). Hence the nature of the propaganda changed according to political context. Thus on 17 December 1939 Goebbels issued 'instructions that enemy statesmen are no longer to be portrayed as comic figures but rather as cool, vengeful tyrants. This goes for Chamberlain, in particular.'[24] This is an interesting remark: Goebbels was constantly changing the focus and pace of the propaganda in line with the development of events. In evoking a credible enemy, the shift represents a mature, even counterintuitive propaganda appeal.

Realism

The Nazi construction of the British was as cunning enemies, and the construction of the Jew was as an intelligent threat. Goebbels prescribed candour, which is not the sentiment most publicly associated with Nazism and its paladins. On 20 November 1939 he spoke to the heads of the Reich Propaganda Office, instructing them that 'truth is the best propaganda'.[25] Then again, as Baird has noted:

> early in the war Goebbels endeavoured to present accurate reports on the bombing. This brought him into conflict with the strategic high command. He under-

stood that to camouflage the truth would cause credibility problems, because the German people could verify the news for themselves. Subsequent events proved Goebbels correct.[26]

On New Year's Eve 1940 Goebbels wrote that 'it will be a hard year, and it will be well to be prepared for it. Victory will not be given to us as a gift. We must earn it ...'[27] He felt that too much optimism would undermine credibility. After the fall of France in June 1940 he told the Reich Propaganda Office to emphasise to party workers that Britain would not be defeated so quickly, and that the continuation of the war with Britain would be extremely difficult; with the invasion of Greece and Yugoslavia in April 1941 he sounded his customary notes of caution; and in May he spoke against exaggerating the significance of a speech by David Lloyd George since it did not reflect British opinion.[28] Goebbels was circumspect about the invasion of the Soviet Union; it was not to be a time for the trumpet notes of triumphalism: 'there can be no assertion that the Soviets have used up their last reserves. They have enormous numbers of soldiers at their disposal', and, seven weeks later, 'it is now clear to all sober observers of the war that it cannot be won quickly'.[29] He continued to preach against optimism on 18 August 1942 via Propaganda Guideline no. 40, and on 21 September he told Germans that the conquest of Stalingrad was not imminent. He then retrieved a once rejected slogan, 'Life or death.'[30]

The illusion of English perfidy: race and empire

Facts in Review (1940) concludes with a simple fact: 'Only one enemy remains: England.'

Pre-war references to the British were capable of nuance, and Hitler's ambivalence towards Britain is manifest in the residuum of deference discernible in Nazi pre-war filmography. The films about the British are more decorous than those about the Communists, and less visceral than those about Jews.[31] But after the failure of Hitler's offer of a peace deal to Britain following Dunkirk, the hyperbole of enmity went into overdrive. The film *Victory in the West* (1941) argues that a fearful Britain created encirclement policies and was planning for war.[32] Part of the 'oppression' psychosis, the language of victimhood, was the claim that the Allies not only wanted to deny Germany its expansionist rights—rights that exist in nature—but further wanted to confiscate German territory and, beyond even this, to sterilise all Germans. Britain and France were determined to return Germany to the ranks of victims. In the words of the German propaganda magazine *Signal* (modelled on *Life* magazine and published in over twenty-five languages by the Wehrmacht), the British wanted to 'frustrate a sensible revision of Germany's eastern frontier' and the French to deprive 20 million Germans of their nationality.[33] The British had forced war on Germany: do the Allies, the article continues, 'want hell on earth again?' These are 'the criminal minds of those who have thought fit to involve Europe in a fresh massacre ...'[34]

A rhetorical assault on the empire framed this illusionary Britain, and a kernel of truth could make the charge resonate. The aim was to stress the perfidy of British imperialism. The Nazis returned to the nineteenth century to retrieve the right imagery, such as an 1899 cartoon of a claw-like hand stretching over the globe, or various European anti-British cartoons excoriating the evils of British imperialism—starvation, opium, the atrocities of the South African War. The imagery of Anglo-Saxon imperial backwardness was lazily varnished. Newfoundland, for example, which was still a British colony during the war, was described as being so poor that 'many of the children have never in their lives seen a coin'.[35] The British Empire was portrayed as a gigantic act of theft and piracy sustained over hundreds of years. This view was by no means confined to Nazis, but they advocated it with an extraordinary admixture of detail and vindictiveness. In the words of another *Signal* article, Britain was a global pirate: '250 wars in approximately as many years were necessary in order to fund their power'. Yet the argument here and elsewhere in Nazi propaganda was not one of sympathy for the colonised: the emphasis was instead placed on the psychological affront to the hubris of the other empires who had their colonies taken from them.[36] Nazi propaganda, somewhat surprisingly, can often come across as a protracted, brattish whine; the Nazis were masters in the politics of grievance, of finding and packaging grievances both real and imaginary for their mass audience. One such grievance was 'Living Space', the idea that Germans had been granted inadequate quantities of land on which to live and were entitled to take more from peoples more land-rich and culturally poor (this was the essence of the case for invading the USSR). Grievance can be talked into people, a sense of gross injustice created (even where none existed, although Germans did have genuine grievances), and all the by-ways of history pillaged as evidentiary basis for that narrative. Thus *Signal* compared the territorial power of Britain with the sheer numbers of Germans who had so little:

> 46 million Britons control over 40 million square kilometres of land—stolen by brute force (etc.) ... Germans on the other hand, must earn their daily bread from

600,000 square kilometres, and should even have to ask London to keep the permission to do that. We, the German have-nots fight for our food—and what about the British exploiting caste—they fight for dividends at the cost of the blood of the peoples—but for the last time.[37]

The mythology of German impotence, then, articulated in the language of anti-imperial rebellion and a parody of the suffering of an oppressed native people.

British international perfidy was always a theme in Nazi propaganda, as with *Signal*'s pictures of the British destruction of French battleships at Oran (Mers-el-Kébir, 3 July 1940). Vichy France had refused to de-commission them or hand them over, and *Signal* depicted them as though they were the broken toys of some giant child who had smashed them in a fit of frustration; and alongside this contextual imagery there were also pictures of the funeral ceremony for the French dead. *Signal* speaks of 'this unparalleled, monstrous, British crime against an ally of yesteryear'.[38] For once, of course, some objective opinion might have agreed with this Nazi verdict, and this is the key point. Nazi propaganda was never true, but it often contained a truth, a famished particle of right amid the falsehoods. Seldom was it a total lie and this was an intentional and significant part of their ideology of persuasion. Moreover, a new stereotype was never invented when an ancient one could be refreshed, as was the case here, with *Signal*'s image of perfidious Albion, the most cunning of the nations, and a treacherous 'friend' quite prepared to stab old allies in the back in pursuit of national self-interest. According to Goebbels the English were 'the Jews among the Aryans'; his editorials of 1941 even go so far as to attribute genocidal war aims to the British.[39] A leading *Das Reich* article of 5 February 1941, for instance, proclaimed that 'Churchill promises Germany to Jews ... solidarity of world parasite renewed': thus Britain and America were now seen as being ruled by Jews and as serving the Jewish aim of degrading and exterminating non-Jews (as per the Periodical Service Directive of 30 May 1941 and 6 June 1941).[40] Germany, by contrast, had grasped the Jewish danger in time. The directive of 30 May even asserted that Roosevelt had 'Jewish blood'.[41] However, the periodicals were also ordered to 'avoid injuring or mocking non-Jewish USA citizens'.[42]

The war was based on a myth of German victimhood which was mobilised again, the same story Hitler had proclaimed from the earliest days of his activism: Germany was menaced by enemies and the *casus belli* was a Polish attack that the loyal were invited to believe had begun in September 1939. Further conquests were necessary to give the Germans a wider security umbrella. There is a surrealism about this constant manufacture of threats which provided a sustaining rationale of conquest, such that by midsummer 1940 Hitler was master of most of Europe. And all of this was a war of defence, not attack: the confection of illusion had become so much the practice of the Reich that it became habitual, more reflex than strategic choice. An instant empire, in other words, was the riposte to those whose determination had been to humiliate the Reich: the Poles, for example, had attacked Germany first, had they not? The conquered people were constantly portrayed as aggressors with a delinquent hatred of their Teutonic neighbours.

The invasion of France and Poland

The Germans proved willing conscripts in this, an imperium of deceit that underlay a new and very tangible empire: a necromancy of supercharged illusion, licensed by a moribund critical faculty and absolute, blind faith in a messianic leader. The threatened were transformed into the threat by the melding of myth, rhetoric and symbolism into a new synthesis. From this rationale flowed all the other illusions—the belief that the conquered peoples were pleased with their uninvited guests, the wish to view slaves as in some way grateful for their enslavement. Such beliefs truly become credible if people have first made the rupture with sanity by buying into the central and core illusion. Hence Germany claimed that the British were planning to land in Denmark and Norway and that there had to be a pre-emptive invasion, and they made this sound plausible as a rationale. Likewise, the invasion of lands over the Dutch, Belgian and Luxembourg frontiers in May 1940 was anticipatory aggression, necessary to forestall attacks from Britain and France—again, a German invasion was presented as a benevolent defence of the countries who were, in fact, being invaded. The later Soviet invasion was also explained as a pre-emptive strike in which Germany had just managed to forestall the Soviet attack on the Reich; as Kershaw says, people believed Hitler.[43]

The collapse of France, when it began, had been swift. On 21 May Amiens and Arras fell; on 28 May Belgium surrendered; and the Dunkirk evacuation commenced on 26 May and finished on 4 June with the rescue of 340,000 French and British soldiers. On 10 June Italy declared war. With German troops now in Paris, Philippe Pétain replaced Paul Reynaud on 16 June and solicited an armistice the following day.[44]

For the Nazi propagandist France was not a culture but an anti-culture. The Reich defined itself by its multiple antitheses, and it found one in the

French. The French were first among Germany's vanquishers in the First World War, the confiscators of its territory (Alsace-Lorraine), the occupiers of its living space (the Ruhr) and the hangmen of Versailles, and the loudest callers for its draconian demands to be obeyed. It was the French who had acted as the executioners of Albert Schlageter—who had attempted to sabotage the French Ruhr occupation—in May 1923.[45] And they were the racial poisoners of Europe, the leasers of a multi-racial empire whose brown and black soldiers had occupied part of the German heartland. France was a cipher for the polyglot and a contaminant of the ideal of racial purity. Thus in one Nazi newsreel the producers juxtaposed St Joan with 'scenes of escaping Jews, forced to abandon their stylish cars loaded with booty. A nattily dressed black, shown lighting a cigarette on a street in Paris, seemed to symbolise everything that the invaders wanted to liquidate.'[46] *Signal* offered a full-page spread, entitled 'Defenders of French Culture', showing demoralised soldiers as categories of racial types: 'and again today France confronts German soldiers with the coloured troops: Berbers, Moroccans, Arabs, Senegalese and then Negroes'.[47] The war itself was a battle for European civilisation against the forces of Judaism, Communism and liberal degeneracy. France's claim to be the standard bearer of European civilisation was bogus and this trust had now passed to Germany; thus *Victory in the West* shows German soldiers solemnly entering a Gothic church bombed by the enemy. 'An enlisted man strikes up the chords of Bach—the battle of France was a struggle for civilization.' In Baird's words, the film 'picked out familiar themes: blacks in the French army—that is France as European race corrupter, the cathedral of Rouen saved by German soldiers after being set alight by the French; France as a fraud in its civilisation claims.'[48]

Then there were the Poles, hatred of whom was a common property among many Germans and not just the Nazis. Hence it was not difficult for Nazi propaganda to articulate fears of a greater Poland or to present the Polish regime as an actively expansionist power. The Poland of Nazi propaganda was an active predator and an expansionist state, a rival imperium; thus in the film *Return* Warsaw was portrayed as seeking a greater Poland to the Oder or even beyond, and as constantly harassing along the border.[49] To Nazi eyes, Polish ownership of what was perceived as heartland German territory was a mortal sin. Poles were furthermore the brutal oppressors of folk comrades trapped within their synthetic pseudo-state. The 'Polish corridor' awarded after Versailles to give Poland sea access had cut off East Prussia, while the city of Danzig was declared a Free City, or city state, a status that had not only to be revised but also avenged. The

Nazis entered Poland with not just a military strategy but a decapitation one: they would liquidate the ruling classes of this insolent nouveau state, and in the months following on from 1 September 1939 they began to do exactly that.

The role of propaganda was to clarify and refresh this mission. The sub-humanity of the Poles had to be evoked in lurid terms, with their depravities, such as the murder of German-speaking Poles, being sufficient to justify their conquest and where necessary their elimination:

> propaganda spread the conviction that war with Poland was justified in a conflict which had been forced on Germany. General credence was given to reports of persecution of the German minority in Poland, these convince people that armed intervention was the only way to end the provocation of the Poles. Propaganda also dwelt successfully on the danger of encirclement.[50]

Thus the Nazi media vilification of the Poles began in the summer of 1939. The newsreels showed imagery of burning German farms. In *You and Your People*, a publication for youths, readers were told that blind Poland 'committed atrocities of unimaginable depravity on defenceless ethnic Germans ... insane Polish forces marched into German Reich territory', and naturally 'The Führer fights back' so that inevitably 'days later, there is no longer a Polish state ... all these are areas for Germany' (such as West Prussia).[51] Britain thus declared war 'blinded by hatred against ethnic Greater Germany'.

Film and documentary media backed up and underlined the press campaign against the Poles. *Return*, for instance, is a nuance-free piece of crude anti-Polish propaganda. It animates the mythology of German victimhood, and is essentially a cartoon with a checklist of atrocities and insults such as the ripping of a swastika necklace from a German girl and the blinding of an elderly German. Then, as the Germans are about to be murdered, we hear the rumble of Hitler's tanks: as was to be the case throughout the war, the Nazis were once again projecting their own crimes on to their victims.[52] The film *Feldzug in Polen* (The campaign in Poland, 1940), which contains similar themes, features a band of Germans led to safety and secular salvation in the Reich by a Teutonic maiden.[53] Goebbels spoke of 'a bitter racial struggle' against the Poles and visited the graves of what he described as murdered ethnic Germans: 'here they live in their hundreds in long rows. One must see it in order to remain hard and not become sentimental.'[54] The activity of self-persuasion never ceased, even in the mind of one who was actively persuading others every moment of the day.

Images of destruction were offered to German readerships—one article, for example, shows a decimated Rotterdam with every building a shell: 'after Warsaw, it was Rotterdam that, issuing a challenge, learned how hopeless it was to resist ... and paid for the lesson by the destruction of the centre of the city'.[55] Nothing stands intact, even partly. It is a lunar surface. German media were awash with such imagery of war and the instruments of war, with the violence somehow detached from any kind of consideration as to its meaning. *Der grosse Sieg Im Westen* is a photo-chronicle of the nihilism of war; of Dunkirk, of the debris of Britain's war-machine now a junkyard on the beaches.[56] With its screaming Stuka bombers and its gothic scripts, this Reich is often a self-parodic Reich. The images exist on their own account, brutal, stupendous, but any kind of interpretation of them going beyond the merely euphoric is denied. The rhetoric and the imagery are triumphalist. A French soldier is described in one article as having 'left his giant of steel and [walking] towards the German infantry-man with upraised arms. They have silenced his breathing fortress. Human courage is harder than steel—the picture convincingly symbolises this truth.'[57] The image of a towering mortar is said to be 'like some prehistoric monster'. Pictures of ruin are accompanied by the visions of an enemy, beaten, broken.[58] *Signal* could neither contain nor resist the hubris with its pictures of 'the never ending columns of prisoners', or a photograph of an exhausted British soldier, or a view of the Armistice carriage with German soldiers marching around it. This is where, we are told, 'conditions of a humiliating Armistice were dictated to Germany in a most offensive manner' in 1918.[59] Hugh Trevor-Roper would subsequently write of a Reich 'imposing indeed in its granite harshness and yet infinitely squalid with miscellaneous cumber—like some huge barbarian monolith, the expression of giant strength and savage genius, surrounded by a festering heap of refuse—old tins and dead vermin, ashes and eggshells and ordure—the intellectual detritus of centuries'.[60]

German media also displayed a fondness for ephemera—a staple perhaps of the journalistic trade in any era, but thus eluding engagement with context by creating an aura of normality and domestic triviality in situations which represented anything but. Nazi German propagandists also understood the power of narrative. In Nazi propaganda the war was often depicted in terms more akin to a kind of extended trashy novel to be bought at a railway station, using the popular novelist's craft: the creation of pace, drama, shallow characterisation, economic prose and the judicious use of the vernacular. They succeeded in presenting the war itself as a kind of fiction, something going on in a world apart, exciting and breathlessly fast-moving; but tenanting a kind of moral vacuum with no concept of suffering, no sense of a lifetime sentence being imposed on the living, or eternity upon the legions of the dead. The illusion also resided in a quality of shamelessness that characterised all Nazi rhetoric. In evoking the fall of France for example, a *Signal* article talks of: 'these poor old women [who], driven from home by ruthless propaganda, haunt the highways of France'.[61] The full-page monochrome of the two frail women is a bleak and brilliant character study; Nazi media were shocking in their candour about the destruction they had unleashed on Europe, exploring graphically what they had done, and constantly asserting the rectitude of this fate. Blame for destruction was placed securely on the shoulders of the Allies, along with all of the guilt. Thus another *Signal* article features a picture of a plume of smoke with silhouettes of soldiers: 'the roads along which the British retreated towards the Channel ports lined by tall pillars of smoke: towns and villages belonging to their "allies" were pillaged and set on fire'.[62] The human cost was not only admitted but described in detail, yet the causation of that cost was firmly laid elsewhere. *Signal* pictures a refugee child sleeping in a pram, and comments, 'who could look at the scene in a mighty tragedy without feeling deeply[?]'.[63] Indeed—but who caused it?

Illusions: hubris

The Nazis rhapsodised about their new empire; purple prose hailed a gimcrack imperialism, a new realm which incorporated the heritage ancient Europe they claimed to be heirs to, a cultural neo-patrimony. A typical caption in *Signal* proclaims 'the flag of the young victorious German army waves above the centuries-old pillars of the Acropolis' above a two-page spread of three German bombers flying over Athens and the Parthenon:

> the engines of the German machines sweep across the blue skies of Greece. Below them in the landscape we see the red brown earth, the cypress hedges, the white walls and the marble stones. ... a classical land greets them with its coloured walls and temples. The new epic is sounding over the immortal atoms of Pericles ... and far below, the unforgettable panorama unfolds and fades away once more ... an iron will is driving them on.[64]

Nazi media was suffused with vanity during the first, conquest phase of the Second World War; it offered little else. The aesthetic of destruction was material: the charred ruin and smashed tank exerted a compulsive fascination for the celebrants of Nazi conquest, the lifeless corpse rather less so. Magazine images were selected for their symbolic resonance—for example, a German soldier looking at a statue of André Maginot and others gazing at the statue of Joan of Arc; German troops in Paris, and French soldiers as prisoners; black French troops (sarcastically referred to as warriors in the struggle for civilisation); the signing of surrender in Compiègne; the swastika flag draped over the Armistice Memorial in Paris.[65] The function of Nazi rhetoric was to inflate the currency of illusion. A proclamatory vainglory was the official rhetoric, the public poetry of the regime insofar as it had one: 'this reason is what Germany's enemies believed was her weakness: the revolutionary, dynamic character of the Third Reich and the National Socialist leadership. That fighting power can only be explained by the presence of an idea which engaged the entire Nation.'[66] This dynamism was especially represented by the symbolism of the paratroop drop in the invasion of Crete, for example. The Nazis always sought to ensure that their images were state-of-the-art, and thus the reality of the German army—that much of it at this stage was horse-drawn as armies had been for centuries—was obscured by the forceful, techno-centric images of Blitzkrieg. German audiences only saw the hardened edge of the Wehrmacht.

The enemy was usually (though not always) presented as feeble and inept, with Allied armies often depicted as being in retreat before the advancing German war machine. Thus *Signal* offered a two-page colour spread of a Spitfire being hunted by a Messerschmitt, headlined 'In the Cloud Covered Sky over England': 'the RAF pilot dives in an attempt to escape, but the Messerschmitt follows, hurtles towards him, spraying with machine-gun fire and the enemy plane crashes to the ground'.[67] Despite its vividness, such an image gives the impression that the Royal Air Force was easy to beat, giving rise to unfulfilled and unfulfillable expectations. In fact, this kind of bombast only served to help the British since it sustained a claim that they had vanquished an aeronautical goliath.[68] Reichsmarschall Göring (the genial uncle of the Reich and its human face), for example, had said, 'if a single enemy airman gets through, my name is Meyer'; he had proclaimed the fiction of 'a Reich surrounded by a ring of steel through which no enemy bomber could penetrate'.[69] As with other Nazi propaganda material, *Signal* was also strong on lurid pictographic representations; in one article naval losses were represented by a vast sea with dozens of ships being sucked down into a whirlpool: 'according to British admissions twice as many British warships are sunk than can be replaced by new launching'[70] (there is surely some flaw in this logic).

The Germans affected to perceive Chamberlain, and latterly Churchill, in the same way the Allies saw Hitler: as an avenging conqueror determined to build up a European empire. An article in *Signal* describes how 'in April 1940 London prepared an attack on the Scandinavian states with the object of seizing the Swedish ore mines in preparing the advance against the north of Germany', while 'German forces took over the defence of the Balkans against London's ... aggression';[71] and thus also 'Italy was to be attacked from the Mediterranean—with North Africa as the base—and from Greece.'[72] An illustration in the same magazine made the paths of Britain's global retreat look like the tentacles of a flailing octopus. All of this was placed in the context of a Britain that had destroyed all the great empires of the world, including the Spanish, the Portuguese, the Dutch and the French; its malodorous project, we understand, continues.[73]

Illusions of this magnitude can only be fostered on people who wish to believe. The evidence for a false belief can always be found and a logic of causation manufactured. Indeed, one of the functions of propaganda is to facilitate self-persuasion by providing a patina of pseudo-rationality. But we must look at the habit of illusion and its consequences as a Nazi political strategy, in which it increasingly took the place of less extravagant and more credible forms of manipulation. The Nazi media product was characterised by hubris, and then, as nemesis inevitably followed, by self-deceit. Radio excelled in producing both commodities, with the radio star Hans Fritzsche's supercilious tone being excelled by an even more extreme rival, Dr Karl Scharping, who would repeatedly emphasise the supposed dishonesty of the Allies in claiming that Germans had mistreated and exploited those living in the occupied territories.[74]

Illusions: the grateful victim

A part of this illusion, this looking-glass world of Nazi propaganda, was the much-expressed conviction that the victims were grateful for their victimhood. The colonised were supposed to be pleased with their new conquerors and deeply curious about their culture. These sentiments occupied that borderland often seen in Nazi propaganda, the point at which the propagandist and propagandised began to be overwhelmed by their co-creation and actually began to believe in it, not out of political duty alone, but because they had ceased to think analytically. A lazy habit of non-interrogation can quite easily dissolve into the promiscuous acceptance of all statements emanating from the official state, no matter how nonsensical. Thus:

on the 10th of April, one day after the German Army had taken over the defence of Norway against the intended invasion of the Western powers, complete calm reigned in the capital of the country. Life went on in the usual manner, and in the parks, the inhabitants were enjoying the spring sunshine (*Signal*).[75]

The images supplied were of sedate citizens sitting on park benches. But notice the defence of action—the Nazis claim they were acting to stop aggression—as well as the image of tranquillity and acquiescence they attempted to create. Again the fiction was maintained that in some way the Germans were there to help the Norwegians and that they had come in friendship.

The pretence was that German soldiers were greeted happily by the populace of conquered lands. Another article in *Signal*, for instance, describes the situation in Greece after the Nazi invasion: 'at the head of the population, the Greek Orthodox Archbishop and the mayor of a small town greet the commander of the troops just marching in'.[76] Predictably, and typical of regimes of war, there are also interviews with the captured enemy. The propaganda value of these is always dubious since any reader would make the reasonable assumption that the context is coercive. The explicit narrative was that the Germans were decent conquerors and jailers, a claim which, specifically in relation to the captured British, they could probably have sustained. *Signal* introduces one soldier, a Jew, who says he was captured because the British suddenly disappeared,[77] and another who claimed to be a former London policeman. The Germans, he tells *Signal*, are 'fine fellows'. A black soldier is also pictured and he tells the story of how the British ran away: 'I'm better off now than I have ever been. We have no need to work at all. Have you a cigarette, sir?' An Australian prisoner of war, meanwhile, is quoted as saying that 'it was impossible to beat the Germans'.[78] Hence another part of the narrative was to expose the inadequacy of the British fighting machine compared with the Germans, and the universal disillusion of those who had fought for Britain.

Illusions: the grateful enslaved

In Nazi propaganda it was not merely the conquered who were grateful for their new status. So also were the slaves. It was part of the serial illusion of Nazi propaganda that the victims enjoyed their victimhood. The offerings, for example, of Fritz Sauckel, a senior Nazi and labour plenipotentiary who was hanged at Nuremberg, read like a self-parody.[79] In *Europa Arbeitet in Deutschland* (1943) he asks his readers to believe that the foreign worker, that is to say (in most cases) an abductee, was well treated in Germany and enjoyed model labour and housing conditions. Moreover, the author announces himself as a believer in persuasion and education. In other words, the haunted faces and broken bodies of the slaves could actually be succoured into a belief in the ideology that enslaved them. While this does at least contain the ghost of recognition that coercion alone was not enough, it stands as yet another instalment in the great luminous fantasy of the slave loving his enslavement: 'I respectfully believe foreign workers who could see Hitler's picture hanging in the factories ...'[80] It is beyond mockery. Such was the now customary conspiracy of self-deceit, where fiction was inflated to such swaggering proportions that it propelled belief by its sheer rhetorical velocity. There was consequently a point at which the German people just came to accept anything their government told them, however outlandish, on the authority of Hitler's charisma alone. A war of conquest was packaged as a war of defence, with each invasion of a new country justified as necessary to stop further encroachment. Beyond the insanity of defending the Reich against Polish 'invasion', the ultimate illusion the Reich asked Germans to accept was that Soviet Russia, with which Ribbentrop had signed a pact, was about to invade Germany. These illusions would not survive challenge. Their essence was destruction: unlike other empires or putative empires in history, the Nazi one offered no idea of liveability as a colonial subject.[81] All it could promise was life as the most abject serf, or the finality of death.

The illusion of military nobility

The Nazis sought three specific things in their wartime portrayal of their own military. First and most important was the idea of the hero: heroism was the highest of the virtues preached and it was the great classical virtue as well, blessed by history and tradition. Thus heroic-virtue stories were told, offering typologies to be emulated, two-dimensional heroes of dauntless courage, and self-sacrificial. Such stories emphasised communitarian rather than individualist values, yet they were also moral parables that tied in with inherited religious schemata, for the heroes often saved the lives of others and did not just destroy the enemy. It was in this vein that *Adler*, the Luftwaffe photo-journal, chronicled the Knight's Cross-winners: one typical illustrated story tells of an airman who leapt out of a flaming aircraft and stopped a locomotive before escaping aboard the train.[82] However, though the procession of Knight's Cross-winners continued over time, increasingly the smiling images were in fact posthumous.

The second great Nazi military virtue was humanity. For those who would express mild surprise at this, it is important to stress that this was the publicly articulated ideal and not the privately executed real. In Nazi propaganda the German fighter was a decent man who did not pitilessly destroy his enemy but actually saved his life where opportune, even at personal risk. A complete moral exemplum was thereby built up—again the moralising language of the Third Reich. Nazi media was keen to give the impression that Germans were humane and always sought to project the regime as virtuous to its domestic 'market'. Sailors, for example, were depicted as tough, but also as sentimental. Similarly, in the documentary *Baptism of Fire* (1943), it was implied that members of the air force went to great lengths to avoid civilian targets.[83]

The third virtue, namely camaraderie, was expressed as comradeship, pranksterism and derring-do, particularly when depicting the ethos of life in the air force. An *Adler* journalistic essay, for instance, showed photographs of life in the Mölders Squadron, with attention to its key personalities: everyone is smiling, and the rituals of a fighter pilot life are wryly evoked—sick pay, chalk drawings on the mess table, revving up and taking off, the intensely focused gazes of the operational planning meeting.[84] There is a self-conscious manufactory of a jaunty touch, absurdist imagery such as a man in what appear to be underpants standing among parked fighters, shaded by a big umbrella;[85] or a fun feature about the miniature train used to move around airmen—all of its passengers blissfully amused.[86] *Adler* attempted to evoke the cavalier spirit of air force life, something very far removed in fact from our idea of Nazi Germany as a vast labour camp inhabited by heel-clicking automata. One *Adler* cover shows three handsome airmen with the Knight's Cross decoration, full-page, slicked-back hair, all beaming, the approved 'sunny' disposition thus showcased, and within its pages the smiling rosters of the latest winners of the Knight's Cross.[87] Despite the supreme danger to their lives, airmen were in fact presented as merely an animated cliché, as with *Adler*'s 1943 cover of 'sunny' airmen rolling a menacing bomb.[88] Individual portraits celebrated general types, such as a dashing airman sitting atop his cockpit.

The focus in Nazi media was also on leader imagery—for example, on airmen listening to a leader eagerly, all gathered around in a circle with an animated figure of command taking centre stage. They look relaxed, wearing casual dress. None of this was accidental: it was part of the strategic imagistic contrivance of the Third Reich. The leader principle was celebrated as not just the cornerstone of the Nazi state but the foundation principle of everything else, especially the military. Yet the 'leader' was never a Fascist brute, but intelligent and even egalitarian, so the led were happy with their lot. There is, for example, a famous painting, *The Tenth of May 1940* by Paul Mathias Padua,[89] which portrays the forging of a river in dinghies. Raw physical power is evoked by the boat's forward momentum; amid the anonymous mass of steel helmets one face turns backwards to look. Explosions hit the water. In their midst is a standing figure of command, his arm outstretched in gesture, his mouth wide open. He is their leader, and this painting is a celebration of the leader principle at a moment of high German triumph. May 1940 was the absolute victory mark: France had been conquered, Soviet Russia had not yet been invaded and Britain lay prostrate. The figures are cast in shadows, with several faces illuminated, and the sea lit by exploding shells. The men are shown working as one, thereby representing the Nazi military ideal of absolute coordination under the fearless leader.[90]

The soldier or airman was never depicted as working alone, but as fighting with the knowledge of a dedicated retinue behind him, namely the support services whose machines and professionalism would carry him from danger and mend his broken body. Thus the magazines show a medical airlift as a bespoke service; a photo-journalist essay describes how the injured in the desert war were flown back to the comfort and safety of metropolitan Germany: there are vistas of scorched, endless desert, and happy men recuperating, sitting around together presided over by smiling nurses. There are images of the medical plane interior, the kindly attendants. Similarly, in a 1942 *Adler* photo-journal essay on a desert crash-landing, wounded men are shown holding a distress flare and radioing for help.[91] The crisis is resolved when the ever-maternal Storch aircraft arrives to take them away. The message was that the Reich cares for the soldier, ultra-efficiently.

Allied defeat

By all canons of historical precedent, Britain was objectively defeated in 1940; the continuity of the struggle was by no means certain and perhaps in defiance of rational expectations. Few defeats in history were ever more absolute than Dunkirk; but, subjectively, it was not a defeat because the British refused to surrender. War is a state of mind, battle a psychological condition, defeat arises only when we consent to it. After the glories of the Battle of Britain, what actually followed was a *via dolorosa* for the British

Empire, with defeat after weary defeat culminating in the 1941 vote of no confidence motion against Churchill in the House of Commons. The Axis thrust was remorseless even if there were setbacks such as the effective defeat of Italy in North Africa and Greece. This was the context of early German war propaganda, which remained hubristic despite Goebbels's warnings. Nothing seemed to go right for the stubborn British. They had been blitzed at home, U-boated on the high seas and humiliatingly thrashed abroad: Allied forces had been turned back at Dakar in September 1940; Greece had been evacuated and the British defeated in Crete on 20 May– 1 June 1941 (though at great cost to the German paratroop divisions); Tobruk had been surrounded and eventually fell on 21 June 1942; the disastrous Dieppe raid took place on 19 August 1942; and all the while Rommel continued his relentless advance to Cairo. At this stage, Nazi propaganda even had the effect of demoralising the political elites of the Allied powers. Thus in June 1941 Sir Harold Nicolson recorded:

> Duff (Duff Cooper, Minister of Information) has returned. He does not look too well. I took him to a film of the 1938 Nuremberg party rally. I do not think it cheered him up very much. It has all come so damned true. All those Hitler jugend were the men who came down in shoals upon Crete. That battle has, I fear, dealt a very severe blow to our morale.[92]

The world, and important leaders, were increasingly betting on the Axis, including Pierre Laval in France, Amin al-Husseini (the mufti of Jerusalem), Subhas Chandra Bose from India, and the new Iraqi government (which had fought the British at Habbaniyah); Vichy France, meanwhile, was effectively supporting Germany in North Africa, Syria and Madagascar.[93] It is not difficult to see why: the USSR had apparently collapsed and army after army had been crushed and surrounded by the Wehrmacht in classic battles of encirclement on the ancient model of Hannibal at Cannae (Apulia, 216 BC). This was then followed by Pearl Harbor and Hitler's declaration of war on the United States, as well as the loss of the Philippines, Singapore and the Malay Peninsula and Hong Kong to the armies of imperial Japan, along with the French bases in Indo-China. Through Burma, Japan had approached the borders of India, arousing the dark, unthinkable nightmare of an Axis breakthrough so total that German and Japanese forces could link up in Baluchistan. The turning point for the Allies did not come until the second Battle of El-Alamein on 23 October–11 November 1942; before that, as Churchill observed, everything was defeat, but after it, all was victory.

Self-deception: Imperial Japan

German propaganda gloried in the imagery of the destruction of the American fleet at Pearl Harbor as photographed by Japanese pilots themselves. *Signal* informed its readers that 'we reproduce the first photographs from the Japanese war theatre, which we got to Europe by devious routes',[94] and described Pearl Harbor as 'the grave of the US Pacific fleet': 'high fountains of water spurt into the air, the first signs of a work of destruction unprecedented in naval history'.[95] Never does the remarkable contradiction of a white supremacist power creating a new global order in conjunction with a non-white power ever surface, the contradiction at the heart of the Axis conveniently resolved by the 'honorary Aryan' status conferred on the Japanese. Such purple prose raises the question of how far the Nazis actively damaged the forward thrust of their cause both by creating unfulfillable expectations and by believing their own propaganda. Hubris was therefore the universal and definitive characteristic of the Nazi wartime media product. The authors of *Berlin Rom Tokyo* (1942), for example, cannot refrain from humiliating the enemy with a huge picture of defeated British soldiers guarded by the Japanese as they march, prisoners of war.[96]

It could not last, and Nazi propagandists clumsily sought a new tone which would retain the old proud notes while qualifying them with a greater realism. Deceitfulness, however—of others, but also increasingly of self—was also a permanent feature. *Signal* thus issued a salutation to the power of the Japanese navy, and referred to Japan's 'great struggle for the new order of eastern Asia'.[97] The West, as ever, was the tireless aggressor. Japan, too, needed living space, and was presented as being engaged in a parallel struggle to Germany's. The United States, the article maintained, was powerless to prevent 'the fast Japanese aircraft carriers from suddenly appearing for example, on the West Coast of America and there attacking the numerous military objectives'.[98] America, the argument went, would need to keep much of its air fleets to defend the West Coast, frustrating any attempt to defeat Germany from the air. Such *bien pensant* thinking, a Panglossian best in the best of all possible worlds, characterised the Nazi public media output. Although the argument seems tightly reasoned, it is entirely fallacious.

The Middle War

After hubris came nemesis for the Germans. But this did not happen instantaneously. In this second phase, that of challenge, the British Empire fought back, inflicting on Nazi Germany serial reverses in the Battle of Britain, at Alamein and on the high seas. Germany then began to sink in the quagmire of the USSR. A tone of exultant optimism had marked the beginning of the Soviet campaign on 22 June 1941 and the regime's public narrative dripped with vanity. Here then was no mere other-deception but also self-deception. Goebbels wrote that 'Bolshevism would collapse like a house of cards. We stand before an unparalleled victorious campaign.'[99] Though Goebbels's default position was generally antagonistic to excess optimism, he too could fall prey to a public climate that graduated from hubris to denial. Nazi journals were filled with depictions of German men and weapons and military life on the Eastern Front, while the enemy was consistently portrayed as weak, dying, in retreat and so forth. In October 1942, for instance, the front-page headline of *Völkischer Beobachter*, written in big black and red letters, read: 'The Military End of Bolshevism, the Eastern Campaign has been Decided ... Incomparable Masterstroke of Strategy'.[100] The article claimed that the blitz had dealt the Russians a mighty, irrecoverable blow.

War with the USSR

The onset of the war with the USSR enabled the resurrection of an old propaganda trope from street fighting days: the merging of anti-Semitism with anti-Bolshevism. But there had been no propaganda preparation for the attack on the Soviet Union and the Nazis consequently had to seek retrospective justification. There emerged, for example, a pamphlet entitled 'Germany has Entered the Fight to the Finish with the Jewish Bolshevik System of Murder'.[101] It was claimed that Jewish Bolsheviks had been conspiring with the British in a policy of encirclement with the aim of surrounding Germany.[102] This line resurrected the old Weimar conspiracy of Jews, democrats, Communists and reactionaries (a very broad front indeed). As Goebbels wrote in his diary, 'the enemies of 1932 confront us again, and they will collapse now just as they did in January 1933 inside Germany'.[103]

Hence the old internal struggle became the new external one. As before, the aim of Germany's enemies remained the same—to destroy the German state. For the Nazis everything could be explained by the all-purpose anti-Semitic narrative, and this time it was the war with the USSR.[104] However, the fight against the Soviet Union used propaganda material that was more polemical and combustible than that directed against the West:[105] a new press directive was issued instructing Nazi publications to emphasise the alleged unity of Europe against Bolshevism, and Hitler's speech to the Reichstag on 11 December 1941 embodied a discourse on European history as the struggle between civilisation and barbarism.[106] This simple binary idea was easily dramatised via a pictography of Red Army atrocities and such events as the Nazi Party's 1942 exhibition and booklet, *The Soviet Paradise*.[107] Serial fictions were manufactured to justify the war, and this sophistry contrasted with the earlier triumphalism. The new claim was that the Allies wanted to give Europe to Stalin and that Germany was fighting against encirclement by a powerful coalition. The subsequent Soviet counteroffensive was used by Hitler as evidence that Moscow had been preparing to attack Germany and Europe in order to destroy the German essence of Western culture. Hitler thus claimed that the later reversal in Soviet fortunes justified the original Nazi invasion, arguing in a 1943 speech that the war was one against Bolshevism's thrust for world conquest.[108]

War is a visually engrossing activity and the Nazi photo-journals recorded its look, its feel and its hysterical dynamism. In January 1942, for example, an article in *Die Wehrmacht* offered war in the frozen winter; stark shots juxtaposed bright snow with blackness, while its cover artfully captured the image of ski troops.[109] 'Breathless' stories of heroics, initiative and happy endings crowded the Nazi media. The use of the camera as narrative storyteller was a staple of the illustrated magazines, and for many Germans it was the camera which served as the interpreter of the war. The focus was always on action and excitement. Thus a 1943 photo-journalistic essay in *Adler* about an attack on a farm 'bunker' was replete with images of interrogations and searches for arms, along with pictures of the captured *Untermenschen*.[110] Uniformed Russian soldiers, readers were told, are 'bandits' to be hunted with the full blessings of technology—a Fieseler Storch aircraft helps in the hunt. However, readers were also continually reminded that this was a global struggle. As well as much material on the Eastern Front, Nazi publications also contained pictures and illustrations of Pearl Harbor and of the now global fight—in the Crimea, the Arctic, Africa.[111] The news from the long siege of the Libyan port of Tobruk and Rommel's desert war also feature in the propaganda from this period. Yet after 1941 the Soviet campaign was always the principal story, with pictures of the advance into the USSR and enormous illustrative materials detailing everything about the war: the cover of *Die Wehrmacht* in July 1942, for instance, contained a thickly printed section of the geography of the Eastern Front,[112] while later articles contained aerial views of Stalingrad, and many vividly dramatised maps.[113] Images of a large bomber plane and its crew were used to frame a high-altitude view of Leningrad with lines added to illustrate key points. The immense scale of the Eastern Front was made very clear, with yet more huge maps of what *Die Wehrmacht* called 'the nine million front'.[114] The focus of these articles was on the devastation wrought by the Nazi war machine, something they evoke with a merciless eye.[115]

Such images are, however, designed; a sharp aesthetic captures, arranges and condenses the war into a romantic ideal of violence that is visually arresting, for example the blazing buildings and fires, framed by a large church, of the Russian city of Smolensk in August 1941.[116] In addition to the action imagery, the machinery of war was also a theme; the assorted pictures and drawings celebrate German fire-power, as with the massive artillery piece depicted on the front cover of *Die Wehrmacht* in June 1943, for example.[117] The backstage of war was also well represented—there are an article and photographs on altitude testing, and much on the support acts of the Soviet campaign such as the role of horses.[118] A set of colour images in *Signal* magazine, entitled 'The Leader and his Reich Marshal', shows Hitler with a genial Göring, the benevolent president of the destruction of nearly 2,000 Soviet aircraft by the evening of a single day in return for thirty-five German machines.[119] Complacency set in early.

The Nazi media engaged in a kind of war tourism. Thus in July 1943 *Adler* provided a spread, 'Over Leningrad', brand-marked with eagle logo and gothic script, and sights of Soviet ships attacked by dive-bombing Stukas.[120] The overall tone was callous and sardonic: the enemies were presented as a walkover, invariably left as a smouldering pile of rubble, the emphasis being the materiality of his demolition and the imagery that the bonfire yields. Thus an illustrated story from the Eastern Front by an officer, Hauptmann Kiel, shows the destruction of Soviet planes on the ground. Photo sets celebrated the bombing of a British oil tanker off the African coast, and an image in *Die Wehrmacht* shows the shooting down of a plane via the camera of its German assailant.[121] Its resident artist imagines the fate of the aircraft carrier HMS *Eagle*, with British sailors flailing about in the sea; it also pictures the sinking of the American ship SS *President Coolidge*,[122] men tumbling out, and offers a visual/narrative account of the sinking of HMS *Ark Royal*.[123] The amount of self-deception on the Battle of Stalingrad is especially notable as the gap between the reality of German failure and the fantasy of continued success grew ever wider. Realism began to set in with the bombing of Germany, yet the propaganda machine was initially confused with how to deal with this; not to refer to it would be to lose all credibility, while to convey its full horror would raise questions about the efficiency of the German war machine, and broader ones about Germany's self-belief, its by now protracted public narrative of pre-destined victory. Thus on 5 May 1943 *Die Wehrmacht*[124] carried imagery from an Allied 'night of terror', but the article only showed light injury and cosmetic damage, and this is significant. Propaganda continued to exude confidence, with lots of pictures of smiling fire brigade women, for example, something which was a novelty for Germans.[125]

The war was depicted as a human drama and readers were invited to meet its German participants, the fearless, happy warriors. This served to personalise the epic scale of the assault and to make it more accessible, a metallised world of planes and guns and machinery softened into the brave private struggles of individuals. One of *Adler's* photo-journal essays from this period describes the mission of a flying boat to attack enemy shipping, along with the associated dramaturgy:[126] the pilot is pointing, talking excitedly, generating an atmosphere of comradeship and efficiency. An airman is shown lighting a cigarette with a candle: gay in the anachronistic sense of the word.[127] War as pictured here could be sublimely beautiful, and even approaches the condition of surreal art, as with the night pictures of flak over England, their black and white patterns turning the front cover of the magazine into an illuminated exercise in geometric abstraction.[128]

Middle East

The defeat of British forces in Tobruk on 21 June 1942 represented a nadir of Allied fortunes in the Second World War. By this time the Arab world had already emerged as a ripe target for Hitler's propaganda machine. In May of the previous year, Britain's ambassador to Egypt had spoken of a 'rain of anti-British pamphlets' and he would later write that 'the majority of Egyptians still remain convinced of German invincibility'.[129] Nazi propaganda utilised a dual strategy in the Middle East and North Africa, namely to present itself as being anti-imperialist and anti-Zionist, the outer garments of the colonial liberator. Ribbentrop made claims to Hitler about the effect of daily Berlin radio broadcasts on the Middle East, with Arab audiences being targeted by the Zeesen radio broadcasts. Amin al-Husseini, the mufti of Jerusalem, met Hitler, and the photograph of the event was visible around the world: 'a further token of the respect of the Führer for the Mufti and the cause he represents was furnished by the Mufti's being given a place of honour on the occasion of the delivery of

Hitler's speech of December 11 [i.e. the speech in which Hitler declared war on the United States]'.[130]

Final Solution

In the early years the Nazi 'case' against the Jews was that they had undermined Germany after the First World War, and hence a Nazi David was now standing up to the Jewish Goliath.[131] Nor were Jews the original primary enemy. As Robert Gellately reminds us:

anti-semitism had not been a top priority issue for the Nazis in the last elections of the Weimar Republic. On propaganda posters used in the various elections leading up to 1933, the main 'enemy groups' were political parties identified with defeat and revolution in 1918, and with the Weimar system: only 6 of the 124 Nazi posters from these elections pointed to the Jews as the main enemy.[132]

Michael Burleigh has similarly pointed out that anti-Semitism was barely significant in Nazi agitation, especially where there were alternative objects of loathing such as the Danes or Poles, or in areas that had no previous history of anti-Semitism or an indifferent party leader.[133] Hitler did not suggest genocide until 30 January 1939; before that time he had called merely for the removal of the Jews. But between 1939 and 1943, Hitler repeated his prophecy of genocide six times.[134] From the beginning of 1942, the Nazi regime became increasingly fanatical, and this was especially apparent on the Jewish question. As Kallis has observed, this period was characterised by 'the intensification of ideological fanaticism, regardless of the practical implications of policymaking in this direction'.[135] With the war in the East, the SS Einsatzgruppen began their terror through the agency of bullet, pistol and lime pit, but it was the Wannsee conference of 20 January 1942 that mandated and structured the process of ethnic liquidation: beginning with Auschwitz in January, the exterminations continued in the death factories. Industrial process, hitherto associated with material creation, was now devoted to human obliteration: Belzec in March, Sobibor in May, Treblinka in July; by the late autumn of 1943 between 2 and 2.5 million Jews had been murdered in the six Nazi extermination camps in Poland.[136]

For Hitler, the war was, perhaps primarily, a race war between Jew and Aryan. In the early war and pre-war films, Jews are shown as catalysing social discord by alienating worker from state; they also precipitate Polish atrocities. But the first rabidly anti-Semitic films did not appear until 1939— *Robert and Bertram*, and *Linen from Ireland*—and it is these that first caricatured Jews as subhuman.[137] Goebbels then repeated the tripartite formula of 1933, that first year in power when the three political-ideological party films were shown consecutively with short intervals (*SA Mann Brand*, *Hitler Youth Quex* and *Hans Westmar*). So now, in 1940, there was a new trinity whose fable lay not in storm troopers versus Communists but rather (in *The Rothschilds*, *Jud Süss*, *The Eternal Jew*), the serial depravities of the Jew. Goebbels also forbade the term anti-Semitic from being used in Nazi propaganda at the end of the 1930s—it now had to be replaced with things like 'opposition to Jews', since Nazism was seeking global alliances and these included Arabs.[138]

The illusion of American perfidy

A new illusion that had to be created was the image of American perfidy following the US entry into the war, and fresh myths had to be generated to confront the challenge. As with Germany's portrayal of its other enemies, Nazi propaganda reverted to its tried-and-tested technique of attribution, where the Nazis' own ambitions and crimes were projected on to those the Reich was fighting against. Hence the United States was presented not as acting in self-defence—despite the fact that Hitler had declared war on the United States first—but as a dynamic and ruthless empire-builder. According to *Signal*, the United States was simply seeking to take over the old British Empire 'in exchange for 50 obsolete destroyers' while simultaneously creating an empire of its own by asserting its hegemony over South America.[139] The Nazi propaganda 'line' was consistent in this regard, declaring that the aim of American policy was to suppress and supplant the British Empire: in the words of *Signal* 'the collapse of the British Empire began, as it were, within view of the same continent which dealt the first blows'.[140] Like all good propaganda, there was a whisper of truth to this claim, and the Nazi critique in fact anticipated later attacks more often expressed by the international left. But what emerges in Nazi propaganda is the wilful misrepresentation of America's purposes in fighting the war and a caricature of its culture and national hopes. On 24 March 1942, for example, Ribbentrop issued global propaganda guidelines according to which Nazi publications were to emphasise that 'World Jewry' was using America to reclaim the position it had before the coming of the Third Reich in Europe.[141] The Nazis certainly achieved an impressive degree of consistency in their global propaganda output, with the same key messages reiterated in multiple languages to multiple peoples and ethnicities; this was global emission on an industrial scale.

However, in the eyes of Hitler's propagandists, the American order had a different essence to that of the British. In its propaganda targeting the United States, the Reich focused on the supposed American worship of money, something of course that could not happen in Nazi Germany. This was in part configured as an attack on the workings of the market economy with its lavish advertising and its delayed purchase schemes, a critique that has retained its resonance today, and clearly did resonate with contemporary Germans. The United States, in this view, was the harbinger of the world of consumption, one underpinned by an equally sinister world of production, including the ravages of Fordism (i.e. oppressive production line organisation) and the diminution of the worker to a unit of efficiency within some grossly impersonal machine, to be measured, hectored and fired whenever necessary. This critique consequently combined two elements, namely the ruthlessness of capitalism and the manipulated consciousness of the market economy. The citizen was a dual victim, both as producer and as consumer. Nazi polemicists offered clichés about US business civilisation, illuminating what they saw as the nexus of mediocrity and crassness and rebuking Americans for 'the herd instinct of such frightening uniformity', perhaps a case of the pot calling the kettle black.[142] The accusation levelled was one of egalitarian banality. In the words of an August 1944 article in *Das Reich*, entitled the 'Kitschified Mass Soul', 'They used America's freedom to reduce everyone to the same level. Thanks to their untiring efforts, the nation's male hero is the successful businessman, the female hero is the laughing girl one sees everywhere from Florida to Washington who uses the right make-up.'[143] Such criticisms resemble Marxist attacks on the fetishism of commodities; Americans worship consumption and consumables, they are in other words victims of a false consciousness:

> Their glory is to have made the refrigerator into a North American cultural ideal. They have created a state in which people see the hand of God in a good income, and think the biggest Symphony Orchestra is also the best. They used the years of peace to get people to use Camel and Palmolive, to train them to drive Chevrolets and use Kelvinator refrigerators.[144]

The consequence, according to the Nazis, was discontent. The assertion was that Germany and its allies were a 'worldwide coalition of the have-nots', and Goebbels also instructed German propagandists to write pamphlets claiming that America possessed no self-created culture.[145] There was the depravity of action, but also of taste: greed generated fabulous wealth, which was lavished on self-celebration and artefacts of the most hideous vulgarity, such as an effigy of the retail magnate F.W. Woolworth counting his dollars atop the Woolworth building, described as 'grotesque' in one *Signal* article.[146] Corruption in acquisition gave rise to corruption in expression. This was a paradox that appealed to the Nazis: perhaps they again recognised in this their own mirror image, projecting their own persona on to their enemies.

Illusion: 'Europe', the new spin

But by 1942/3 the war had begun to go badly for Germany: Goebbels sponsored a number of major late war campaigns which certainly transgressed the boundary between manipulation and illusion. The first was his great re-branding of the war (although he had doubts about it), in which the war was now a pan-European struggle for the survival of European culture and identity against the twin enemies of Bolshevik barbarism and US consumerism. 'Europe' was the new spin: the inhabitants of Rotterdam, for example, so brutally and pointlessly bombed in 1940, would now know that the Reich was in fact their best protector. As Europe's self-proclaimed culture-state with its martial muscle, Germany was now the altruist. The measure of other-deceit, of self-deceit and of shamelessness embodied in this campaign should not surprise but be seen merely as a representative act of the propaganda of the Third Reich, its method. Hence the Reich did what it always did, it created illusions: new replaced old and the landscape of illusion was now complete, a cognitive empire of false beliefs and false gods in which articulated truth would have been treason.

Nazi Germany was now the self-anointed vanguard of Europe's struggle for freedom against the Jewish–Bolshevik anti-type, a struggle it had itself precipitated. The old illusions had included 'Lebensraum', living space, an idea the Reich had propagated in countless speeches, pamphlets and documentaries; a manufactured delusion that the nation could no longer be self-sustaining, and that it had a moral right to confiscate the territory of other people. The new illusion was equally paranoid. As the situation worsened for Germany, there were fresh illusions to compensate, a synthesised narcotic to prevent glimpses of the truth, that Germany faced a terrible reckoning. Germany was self-portrayed as the guardian of European culture, and this becomes prominent from the summer of 1941. It also provided legitimacy for other kinds of excess such as the conscription of labour from other European countries. The new slogan was 'Europe is Working in Germany', with its associated fables—wonderful working conditions in Germany, happy European workers and rhetoric of 'young peoples of

Europe'; Goebbels spoke of the 'liberation of Europe from the chains of plutocratic England'.[147] The Reich simply inverted truth at this point. But no one seemed unduly concerned: 'Europe' (or 'Fortress Europe', Festung Europa) was a very good slogan in that it dignified what had hitherto been a murderous enterprise and it did in fact persuade a few pathetic European recruits to join the Waffen SS. 'Europe', under Germany's guidance, would ultimately defeat the Anglo-Bolshevist alliance, for in the view of *Signal* the British and Soviets 'cannot stand out alone against Europe, which is defending herself with supreme energy. The small Europe is fighting stubbornly, tenaciously ... against the hideous danger of Bolshevism'[148] and also against the menace of an America that sought to replace the high culture of Europe with her own miscegenated low culture. A consequence of the crusade against Bolshevism in the Nazi view would be 'the extermination of the Jewish bacillus that is at its source', namely Russia.[149] It is of course an important insight into the delusional bubble now inhabited by the Nazis that they could actually believe, or purport to believe, that what had been a cruel war of conquest had become an enlightened war of defence; a metamorphosis into altruism without seemingly even than most tremulous note of embarrassment. The word 'Europe' increasingly replaced the word 'Germany' in this period: Europe in other words was a nascent Teutonic community seeking salvation through the musculature of the greater Reich. Germany now had the opportunity to 'conduct the economy on a continental scale', and Nazi politicians and propagandists hence began to speak of 'the new Central European system', with references to 'Europe's new organisational unity' and conscripted labour 'working for Europe'.[150]

If the Nazis were fabricators of illusions on this scale, the inference of course is that they were the greatest liars history ever produced. The strategic lie was a major propaganda tool, albeit one with the inherent constraint that to be exposed as a liar destroys credibility. Therefore, the Nazis were not universal liars, but selective liars. Assuming they were amoral, but intelligent, this conclusion makes sense. For example, the Nazi accusation that Soviet propaganda (evoking Germans as 'the blonde witch' etc.) deliberately sought to incite rape was a very effective lie, since this fabrication is still accepted by many Western historians.[151] It had a number of merits—first, it could not be disproved by the ordinary Germans who would have had very little exposure to Soviet media before the end of the war, and secondly, again like all good propaganda, it contained not the truth but a truth (i.e. the predilection of Soviet forces for rape). Moreover, what Goebbels was actually doing much of the time was subterfuge, which is conceptually distinct from a lie: it is hiding truth rather than asserting a falsehood. Thus, for example, speaking of the importance of German influence over French film production, he remarked in his diaries that 'we intend to build a camouflage system so that the average Frenchman scarcely notices who is really calling the tune. This is the way the English have always done things. One thing is certain: I shall not relax ... until the entire European film industry belongs to us.'[152] In addition, the strategic lie is not a lie for a true believer, since such is the superiority of the cause that subterfuge in its service is not immoral: an untruth can simply be the deeper truth for the convinced fanatic.

According to Klemperer, the Soviet campaign gave the concept of Europe a new urgency as an entity that had to be protected from Bolshevism; during the campaign, Goebbels wanted everyone to be aware of the danger that Europe would be turned into steppes, Europe as a Russian prairie. A new language arose of pan-European defiance—'un-blockadable', 'economically self-sufficient Europe', 'honourable Continent' (betrayed by Britain and universally threatened under Stalin).[153] In the words of Toni Winkelnkemper, one of the Nazi's leading propagandists, 'All of Europe supports the Führer's effort to build a new order. Blow by blow, the accomplices of World Plutocracy's warmongers are beaten down. England's final fortress on the continent, the Bolshevist Soviet Union, is crumbling.'[154] After Stalingrad, Goebbels banned the term 'allied nations' and instructed Nazi media to use the term 'ancillaries' of the Soviet Union instead.[155] Thus there was an exhibition headlined 'From the Vanguard of the Movement of the Defenders of Europe'. Germany became the 'power which imposes order', what Klemperer calls a euphemistic pretext for the use and abuse of power.[156] In his Total War speech, Goebbels 'resorted to an unprecedentedly explicit language with reference to the Bolshevik menace'.[157] Thus 'the gist of his passionate sermon was that this is no longer a confident, triumphant war, fought in the remote lands of Asia, but a critical defensive war for the survival of the Reich'; the 'Jewish Bolshevik hordes' were presented as 'liquidation squads', and the war would be transformed into a 'campaign of annihilation'.[158]

Later War

Illusions: Stalingrad and Total War

Then there was Stalingrad and 'Total War'. The battle of Stalingrad, which raged from the end of August 1942 to the beginning of February 1943, was the pivot and turning point of the Second World War. The scale of the debacle, and the abrupt end of German optimism, dictated a new kind of propaganda, one that was significantly different in content and tone. One consequence was 'Total War', Goebbels's 1943 propaganda campaign and the weapon he used to try and abolish the residuum of the civilian consumer economy. Yet it was only a rhetorical pause, as the Reich was now moving into the endgame. The effect of Stalingrad was not initially even admitted: the loss of the Sixth Army, most of whom never returned to Germany even if they were taken prisoner, was evoked symbolically by the playing of three days' funereal music over the airwaves. Goebbels fought back with a new media offensive, including the making of the colour epic *Kolberg* (1945) about a city surrounded in the Napoleonic Wars. Then, finally, with the Reich crushed between the armies of West and East, having united the ideologies of capitalism and Communism against it, trapped, with no refuge, no dignified end possible, Goebbels conducted what was in many ways his propaganda swansong: the great creation of the myth of the Folk Storm (Volkssturm). This motley army of old men and youths were incorporated into yet another campaign, the symbol of popular will, the quintessence of demotic rage, the German masses empowered, vengeful.

The fate of the Sixth Army was a defeat so complete, so absolute in its tragedy for the Reich, so unimaginable in its human consequences and so subversive in its destruction of all the hyperbolic imagery the Nazis had ever fashioned that it needed a quite extraordinary level of creative delusion to stifle its truth. Goebbels sought to be equal to the task. This was one of the 'great cover-ups of Western history': Goebbels banned any reference to the battle or even to the southern sector during its final phase; cinemagoers saw Hitler welcoming Romanian Marshal Ion Antonescu and images from the northern sector of the war, but nothing about Stalingrad, not even in the February newsreels.[159] And though newspapers and radio were used in the three days of mourning, the newsreels continued to concentrate on the North Atlantic and the persona of Hitler; they retained the old triumphalism but with an added gravity.[160] The propaganda was growing tired, however, and the people suffered from cognitive as well as physical exhaustion; they were afflicted with political stimuli wherever they looked. Moreover, whatever the attitudes to Hitler still prevailing, antagonism to the Nazi Party (after the fat peace years of its corruption and the lean war years of its incompetence) was now an ingrained popular response; by 1943 the party had even begun to suppress the use of its name in its own publications.[161] Particularly after early 1943, Nazi propaganda assumed a more sober, realistic tone of rationalised hope; indeed it had to, for without that it would have lacked all believability.[162]

Total War

Goebbels's Sports Palace speech of 18 February 1943 was his apotheosis, the moment of re-branding, the entire war conceptually re-positioned as a defence of Europe against Bolshevism with Germany as its heroic shield, necessitating ultra-radical action. The propaganda line about general and grenadier fighting 'shoulder to shoulder' now changed with the Sports Palace rally and the Total War campaign,[163] the high water-mark of Goebbels's supremacy in the Third Reich and his finest hour. Goebbels, the club-footed dandy of the Reich, made his Total War speech on 18 February 1943, soon after the Stalingrad collapse; did they want Total War? This was the question he proclaimed as he goaded the crowd into set-piece mass hysteria. The call to war of 1812 was revived: 'let our war cry be: now the people rise up and storm break loose'.[164] Thus the famous rhetorical tour de force: 'Do you want total war? ... Are you determined to follow the Führer and fight for victory whatever the cost?'[165] This speech was of course packaged with customary banners and symbols, and slogans such as 'A total war is the shortest war'.[166] As Goebbels posed his famous ten questions on Total War, the crowd screamed 'Ja'! And thus, as Burleigh describes it, 'he reached the rhetorical crescendo, a series of challenges and responses. "Do you want total war?" (Loud cries of "Yes!" Loud applause). "Do you want it, if necessary, more total and more radical than we can ever imagine it today?"(Loud cries "Yes!" Applause).'[167] Goebbels exhorted 'therefore let the slogan be from now on: people arise, and the storm, break loose! ...' The shouting and stamping of the audience continued for twenty minutes after the speech had ended.[168]

The speech was strategic; according to Speer it was 'directed not only to the population but also to the leadership which had ignored our proposals', in order to 'create more pressure against some of the leaders'.[169] His target was not only the public, but Hitler, to evangelise the need for a fully war-conscripted, war-driven economy.[170] Speer was overjoyed by the results: 'I had never seen an audience so effectively roused to fanaticism apart from Hitler's most successful public meetings. The effect on the audience, and nation, was electrifying. It was what they wanted to hear.'[171] For Speer it was a revelation—it had been an act of pure dramaturgy, of theatre in fact, a supremely conscious exercise in public manipulation:

back in his home, Goebbels astonished me by analyzing what had seemed to be a purely emotional outburst in terms of its psychological effects—much as an experienced actor might have done. He was also satisfied with his audience that evening. Did you notice? They reacted to the smallest nuance and applauded at just the right moments. It was the politically best-trained audience you can find in Germany.[172]

After the speech Stalingrad was virtually never mentioned by Nazi media, but only alluded to in the abstract, as in the speech Goebbels gave on 5 June 1943 which contained the sentence 'the winter crisis is over'.[173] A campaign of leaflets and slogans spread by the 'White Rose' (a clandestine anti-Nazi student organisation) was murderously suppressed in 1943.[174]

Multiple illusions: a visible Hitler

Hitler himself had become more mythical essence than physical substance, the central illusion in an illusionary world; silence, invisibility where all before had been presence and volubility, his public self an edited image, a censored photograph. He was often away—at the Wolf's Lair in East Prussia, at the Berghof, with field commanders. Yet Goebbels understood how essential was the currency of the Hitler symbol, how it energised and refreshed,[175] and if the real Führer could not be delivered, then a cinema Führer could be. Migrated to a different century, a different costume, re-animated in celluloid, Hitler was transmogrified into the glorious figures of Germany's past. So Hitler's cinema surrogate, King Frederick the Great of Prussia, appeared once more, as did posters and other images:

with final victory proving elusive, propaganda struck a new note of heroic resis-tance, and stoicism, or 'holding out' … [which] replaced the earlier enthusiastic superiority. Out of the distorted shadow of Nazi history a new film on Frederick the Great was released in the spring of 1942, entitled *Der grosse König* (The Great King).[176]

Thus Goebbels worked even more zealously to sustain the myth in the increasing absence of the man himself.[177]

Popular animosity was still not directed at the Führer. Hitler had become the projection of national aspirations to greatness: Kershaw argues that 'a sufficient platform had been constructed by years of propaganda and ideo-logical indoctrination to buttress the transfer of the blame to Germany's external enemies—the Bolsheviks, the Jews, the British, the Americans, or to internal incompetence, naturally, stopping short of the Führer'.[178] Blame for Germany's plight did not transfer to Hitler: wartime failure, like party excess, was the fault of someone else. The end, when it came, was expressed with the familiar corporate formulae; Hitler's death was dignified over the airwaves on 1 May 1945 with strains of Wagner, Bruckner and the Horst Wessel song, melodies that supposedly conveyed a heroic final act.[179]

Illusion: costume drama

The later war, after Stalingrad, was in a sense the externalisation of the internal struggle; the new enemies were really the old enemies, the global shadows of the extinct German socialists, Communists and bourgeois reactionaries and Jews; the same arguments Goebbels had flung at them could be thundered at the Allies. Goebbels was a strategist of illusion, with a further celluloid answer to Germany's dilemma, one long (since 1943) in preparation and which anticipated later conditions. The film *Kolberg* is about the resistance of a German town to the French, a colour epic with thousands of extras on a grand scale, artillery and explosive power; Veit Harlan was commissioned to direct *Kolberg* in the summer of 1943 and it is set in the Napoleonic Wars from 1806 to 1807.[180] The analogy with the Third Reich is omnipresent; a nation surrounded and determined to fight. This was the great epic of the closing months of the regime, a heroic Nazi parable about what guts and initiative can do against overwhelming odds. Hence the thrust of the film is hope. In Robert Herzstein's words, by the end of the war the Nazi elite could not distinguish 'their own drama from the wishful thinking in period dress ideology of *Kolberg*'.[181] How much so is illustrated by the fact that—as in the movie—Goebbels sacked the garrison commander of Kolberg and replaced him with a younger man. He hid the news that Kolberg had fallen to the Russians on 18 March 1945;[182] an astonishing act and emblematic of the role of propaganda as the central organising principle of the Third Reich. 'Hold out' became 'the most overused word in the propaganda lexicon.'[183]

Illusion: the dignity of death

Then there was the matter of how to deal with death and the mortality inflicted on the German people by German wars and German empire. Since this was a regime which was overtly irreligious, what propaganda really sought was the creation of some kind of Roman idea of heroic afterlife: 'heroic images of fallen leaders being saluted for the last time by the titans of the Third Reich often dominated the week's news. The state or party funerals were splendid opportunities for the newsreels to demonstrate the solemn unity of the party, state and army.'[184] This idea was entirely synthetic, a pseudo-religion, inviting us into the palpable illusion that there was in fact a kind of Teutonic hereafter of Nordic heroes. But Goebbels rose to the occasion and recognised the vacuity of the party's sham heroics and ersatz Valhalla. He knew the psychological toll inflicted by mass death, people's need to have something to hang on to, that they, the survivors, should not find these deaths of loved ones bereft of all meaning. So the party bade ritual farewell to its fallen; with visits, letters, books of condolence and ceremonies with classical music and a speaker to affirm the glory of death in battle against an existential threat to the life of Germany and the continuity of Germandom.[185] Again, then, the illusory world of the Third Reich. People were made to feel, or at least the party tried hard to make them feel, that these deaths had value, that the huge loss among German youth was invested with sacerdotal meaning. It was part of the effectiveness of the Reich that it persuaded victims to value their victimhood, to believe in the force that exterminated those closest to them, that the Third Reich was a noble cause and not the most squalid of all the imperialisms ever to afflict the human race.

Illusion: the Folk Storm

The harbingers of doom increasingly appeared, read in every death notice, inscribed on every bomb dropped and heard in the sound of murderous machines droning from beyond the clouds. Germany was fighting for its life: rationally, there could be no good end, and the propagandists had no difficulty in constructing the notion that such an end, if not prevented, would be terrible indeed. But the regime still sought to reassure: what else, indeed, could it do? But in doing this it made the final progress from illusion to delusion. What it offered at the rhetorical level was no longer a world of even make-believe, but a perverse refusal to confront the finality of what was impending. In the final era of their rule, the leaders of the Reich were indeed delusional and dragged some but not all of the German masses into this delusion. The above-mentioned Volkssturm (Folk Storm, a party-organised militia of older men and youth) was the last great propaganda campaign of the Third Reich: the concept of populist uprising, mobilisation of the totality of the social structure, which would succeed where the most efficient army in the world, and in human history, had manifestly failed. It was foredoomed. Thus the Volkssturm was the last great public narrative of Nazi Germany. The aim was to evoke the radical defiance of the early years of the Nazi movement, to invoke a fanatical—their word—will.

On 12 November 1944 the Volkssturm of Greater Berlin took its oath, its members made up of ordinary and ordinary-looking civilians lifted from shops, offices and factories. They marched in winter coats and hats. There were bands, banners, officers and party officials; and the slogans, aggressive, exhortative. Goebbels spoke, compelling, lucid as ever; there was proud music; and yet this was a synthesised fanaticism, the spirit was gone. Defiant imagery could not hide the essential pathos, the unwarrior-ness of these men or the fixity of their expressions: newsreel inadvertently captured the flash of vacancy, that expression of weariness. There is of course a point at which the propaganda regime of the Third Reich swung from illusion to delusion, that is to deny reality and tenant an essentially fictive world. In this delusional order, anything could be asserted, everything believed. The Volkssturm was entirely a part of this imagined world, as by this stage the leaders of the Reich had ceased to connect with any kind of objectivity. The imagery of old men going out to do battle must surely have been a promise of the end, and it was strange to turn it into an index of renewal and military virility. The band was playing 'We're Marching through Greater Berlin', the song of the Volkssturm; posters depicted an old man and a boy and there were new slogans such as: 'Save Our Women and Children from the Red Beasts', 'For Freedom and Life', 'Hard Times, Hard Hearts'.[186] The relevance of the Volkssturm was not to the war itself, 'but it was a vibrant symbol and a new theme for Goebbels's propaganda bureaucracy'.[187] Losing would mean the destruction of the German people, and hence the war was a struggle for national survival, the ultimate message repeated many times in the later expressions of Nazi propaganda. Occasionally indeed their propaganda had conjured a vision of such an end, as imagined by radio director (and SS man) Winkelnkemper in 1942: 'in long, grey columns, the regiments and divisions of the disarmed German Wehrmacht appear. The weapons are broken, the aircraft destroyed, the big guns empty. The glorious flags have been sent to New York, London, and Moscow, there to be mocked by some subhumans.'[188]

Endgame: From Illusion to Delusion

Propaganda attempted to prepare people for the sacrifice of German life in the cause of European domination. Notions of immortality pervade the Nazi media text; the souls of the fallen in the cause are seen to sanctify the living and march at their side. This is the 'immortality' of the pagan, the soul of a fallen warrior watching over his living comrades. There is a need to reconcile people psychologically to massive private as well as material loss and the Nazis thought they knew how to do this. The impact of the propaganda was such that there was no collapse of the home front in Germany in 1945 as there had been in 1918. Street by street, the Reich was defended: partly, it is true, because of the savagery of SS reprisals on waverers, but also because the population had been bludgeoned by huge quantities of propaganda. Even after towns and cities had fallen, menacing Nazi graffiti began to appear and the terrors of a 'werewolf' campaign were promised. The late war saw a recrudescence of techniques from the 'Era of Struggle', when Goebbels's formula was to meld the darkly witty with the elevated appeal. As Herzstein points out, he was now 'Speaker of the nation', and by 1944 he 'was making propaganda as much of himself and the leadership as for the masses';[189] the question now was how far other-manipulation had actually become self-manipulation.

Closing months

The protracted end process of the war, the murderous death throes of the Third Reich, was if anything more thoroughly propaganda-saturated. Context had always dictated content and that content had again altered: the admixture of propaganda with terror, always the default mode of the Nazi regime, was now horribly exaggerated. Consciousness was assaulted with every kind of propaganda medium and message, from the rational (the alliance between Communism and capitalism would collapse), to the fearful (Bolshevik atrocity), to the superstitious (astrology), to the improbable (organised rumours).

The Red Army had reached the Vistula by early August 1944, and the frontiers of East Prussia. Yet this was a teeming area, full of refugees from Anglo-American bombing and retreating armies; as Wiskemann points out, the Eastern people were more credulous of Goebbels's propaganda, and the regime's fear of humiliation meant minimal evacuation measures. Media proceeded to ignore the big picture. On 5 October 1944, *Berliner Morgenpost* now reported a staccato list of 'successes', all minor, such as the damaging of three Soviet PT boats off northern Norway.[190] Late war Germany was a defeated nation. To many intelligent Germans, as well as to foreign enemies, this situation was irretrievable. But there was also no way out. Indeed, Hitler specifically forbade Goebbels from extending any peace feelers to the Allies. In this situation, propaganda had to paint a kind of alternative consciousness, to suggest ground for hope: that the USSR and the West, representing antagonistic ideologies, would quarrel—nor was the idea irrational. But hope, the kernel of the message, had to be conveyed in more tangible forms as well. So there was the Miracle Weapons story—not a campaign exactly, as Goebbels found he could not control when and how this heart-warming information would filter out. And then there was the Endgame, the evanescent stardust of ultimate illusion, where deceit graduated from other-deception to the final act of juvenile loyalty, that is, wilful self-deceit. Nazis sought refuge in the confusion of actual with ideal, and their propaganda represented the enthronement of credulity.

What has mystified many, including Ian Kershaw, is how the regime continued to function to the end, and by extension how the terror continued to work. For example, the judge who sentenced some of the leading anti-Hitler conspirators had arrived at the 'trial' via cargo train and bicycle; Pastor Dietrich Bonhoeffer's death by hanging, along with Admiral Wilhelm Canaris and General Hans Oster, took place within the sound of American guns on 9 April 1945.[191] Yet the German-on-German terror could not be over-sold. Thus *Trial before the People's Court*, a documentary on the fate of the July 1944 conspirators (Count von Stauffenberg, Field Marshal von Witzleben etc.), was never even admitted for general release, even (on Bormann's instructions) for district governments; the victims had 'somehow maintained their Prussian dignity in the face of this madman [i.e. the court's Judge-President Roland Freisler]'.[192]

The Nazi regime also created industrial-scale conventional propaganda in its final year, and leaflets were a favourite form, right until almost the finish. At the end of 1944, more than half a million leaflets were distributed in the Lower Rhine region alone: the message was to fight defeatism and the insidious idea that the British and Americans were better than the Communists, thus undermining the will to resist.[193] Slogans like 'Is It Still Worth It?' were followed by aggressive answers that interrogated popular beliefs about the Anglo-Americans.[194] Much of course was promised: it was announced for example that blitzed German cities were to be rebuilt within three years.[195] Nazi propaganda, Kallis notes, 'portrayed the war on the Eastern front as an apocalyptic struggle that would decide everything—and irreversibly so'.[196] For the regime, the antidote to rising public alienation was the Red Terror and its savage imagery.

The communications problem of the post-Stalingrad era was to arouse a sufficiency of fear without destroying morale, and stimulating resistance through a rhetoric of secular salvation. The new campaign therefore exploited terror of Bolshevism, but the chosen mediums were newsreels and documentaries not feature films (which were assigned a morale-boosting task through the medium of history).[197] Bolshevik Russia was a monstrous enemy because Nazi Germany had conceived it to be so, and turned it via their depravity into the true creature of their false imaginings. Monstrous because it had been so taught, remorseless, implacable. Fiction became truth. Russia was every day a step nearer, the gathered hordes of a brutalised foe: discontent was the problem, and fear the antidote,[198] fear of the mongrelised Bolshevik masses. And then, the Red Army was in Prussia, generating ominous new imagery of terror and destruction.[199] The obverse of celebratory 1940, it was their own destruction which their imagery now chronicled, the great imperial body of Germany itself now invaded, violated. But the unanticipated consequence of the 'red menace' fear strategy, with its emphasis on Soviet atrocity, was the diminution of the will to resist in the areas confronting the Western Allied advance. This undermined attempts at a unitary, integrationist meta-narrative.[200]

Illusion to delusion: rumour

But the regime was now running out of believability. Unsurprisingly, perhaps, its passage from illusion to delusion was not wholeheartedly followed by all of the German people: 'the regime's own smokescreen of lies made almost anything believable, however inaccurate',[201] an example of how propaganda can backfire. In these final months, the regime recognised, however, that the old propaganda mediums, the traditional messages, were bankrupt of credibility. It had not only to invent new messages but also entirely new media to re-engineer the way it sought to manipulate the people. The point about these methods—rumour, graffiti, systematically false information—is that the message was bereft of all official signature. The focus was on ground-level authenticity, and the messages had to appear to have arisen from below. They had to seem real, so the ministry also had its own operation close to the front, 'painting slogans on walls as if they were the spontaneous expression of the civilian population, such as "We believe in victory!", "We will never surrender", "Protect our women and children from the Red beasts!"'[202] P.K. men (military propaganda units) had orders to remain in territory threatened by Allied military even if civilians had fled, and the propaganda continued almost until the Anglo-Americans had arrived.[203] And so the final images of Nazi government were graffiti, the dying breath of propaganda, the regime which began on the streets expired with the protest form of the student rebel. In the end, people succumbed to a complete world of make-believe: 'even as late as April the 29th 1945, the day before Hitler committed suicide in his bunker, a Berlin newspaper was insisting that Hitler would remain steadfast with his people and "wherever the Führer is, there is victory"'.[204]

Illusion to delusion: America against Russia

At this point, Goebbels chose to derive exactly the wrong lessons from history. As Herzstein observes:

> his belief was that now he had authority in waging total war, Germany would salvage the situation, going to the Nazi party history for inspiration. Goebbels built analogy upon analogy. If Germany could hold out—and it was five minutes before midnight in Hitler's melodramatic phrase—the Allies might break up in the West and would allow Germany to destroy the Bolsheviks. Had this not occurred in 1933 when the worried reactionaries came over to Hitler in order to prevent the Reds from coming to power?[205]

Goebbels resurrected the ethos of the era of struggle, apparently convinced that the methodologies which broke the Communists on the streets could sustain him yet. But the wilful misconstruction of the past was another aspect of the delusional endgame: so the function of propaganda was actually, and above all now, to minister to its creators. Through the twin agencies of propaganda and internal terror, Germans fought to the end. Given the objective circumstances of those final years, illusion turned to delusion, wilful, omnivorous, imprisoning the German masses in a false consciousness: 'the victorious peace was not to be, but Goebbels gave Hitler his greatest victory of the war, the final conquest of the German people. There was no "1918". Those who claim that the Germans fought to the end because of the Allied "unconditional surrender" formula have a weak case.'[206]

An example of Nazi wishful thinking was their incredulity that the alliance between Russia and America could possibly persist, and the belief that they could exploit this contradiction. According to Antony Beevor, the Wehrmacht radio station announced that 'the Führer has issued orders from Berlin that units fighting [the] Americans rapidly be transferred east to defend Berlin. Sixteen divisions [are] already moving and can be expected [to] arrive [in] Berlin [at] any hour.'[207] The aim was to 'deceive the population of Berlin into believing that the Americans were now supporting the Germans against the Red Army. By chance, that day American activity over the central Elbe suddenly halted. It was a huge relief for 12th Army soldiers.'[208] Then there was the bogus assurance that General Walther Wenck's 12th Army was about to relieve Berlin: 'Goebbels continued to use all the techniques of whispering campaigns and word of mouth propaganda to get these messages across. The leaflets appealed to Wenck to hurry and relieve the city now that he was at the gates of Berlin. Actually, the leaflets were meant for Berliners, as a way of boosting their morale.'[209] Thus not only were the messages illusional but so also were the channels of communication themselves: no longer just film, print and radio, but whispering campaigns which could mutate and, virus-like, affect huge populations. Hence rumours were just another propaganda channel. Neither sender nor receiver could know they had been conscripted. The completeness of the illusory world which now engulfed the Reich has a curious coherence: fictional messages, fictive mediums. The kinds of things the Nazis had always done, to be sure, but now a core part of operational methodology: graffiti, rumour, great fibs and urban myths were now the order of the day, and then, finally, unbelievably, astrology (see below), the last propaganda medium of the Third Reich. The regime expired as a kind of looking-glass world, where nothing was believed and everything was believed, a manufactory of tall stories told unto itself. Any last vague connection to an objective account or truth simply evaporated. Even by early 1945, film (*Deutsche Wochenschau*, March) showed,[210] or purported to show, tanks and warships, German troops mounting counteroffensives at Königsberg—and interviews with adolescent winners of the Iron Cross; Hitler himself was shown inspecting a detachment of boy-soldiers.[211] We can reasonably speak therefore of a parallel universe of illusion and symbolism which was always a key part of the Third Reich's self-projection, but in war illusions came to dominate and finally to usurp all else.

Illusion to delusion: miracle weapons

Beyond rumour, and the manufacture of rumour, there remained astrology, the ultimate medium and message of the Third Reich. As Speer stated:

> the populace had long since stopped believing the newspapers, and since such ... charts were dependent on the propaganda ministry, for a variety of reasons they were as I learned from Fritzsche at Nuremberg used as a tool for influencing public opinion. Fake horoscopes spoke of valleys of darkness which had to be passed through, foretold surprises, intimated happy outcomes. Only in the astrological charts did the regime still have a future.[212]

The use of horoscopes is extraordinary. No other regime in history has ever taken the manipulation of human consciousness so far. No other regime had Goebbels.

Speer became very conscious of the extent to which the Reich would create a neverland of distortion. Not merely through conventional media, but by pushing beyond anything which has been done before or since, taking persuasion and its illicit derivatives as far as they could possibly go:

> Hitler ... continued to dangle the prospect of the secret weapons ... therefore, I wrote to Goebbels that 'it seems to me unwise to arouse hopes in the public which cannot possibly be fulfilled ... I would therefore request you to take measures so that the daily press and technical journals refrain from alluding to future successes in our armaments production'. Goebbels actually put an end to these reports on new weapons. But strangely enough, the rumours increased. It was only at the Nuremberg Trial that I learned from Hans Fritzsche, one of the Propaganda Minister's foremost associates, that Goebbels had set up a special department for spreading such rumours. Then, too, I realised why these rumours were often so uncannily close to what indeed we projected for the future.[213]

Speer continues:

> how often at our armaments conferences we had sat together in the evening telling each other about the newest technological developments. Even the possibilities of an atom bomb were discussed on such occasions. One of Goebbels's chief assistants had often participated in these meetings as a reporter and thus been present at the evening gatherings.

Speer was of course deeply aware of the non-credibility of all formal mass communication at this stage in the dying of the Third Reich. The people were no longer believers, but that did not restrain the propaganda apparatus. It simply found new ways of penetrating its message into the consciousness of the people, insidious, perverse. But Speer is hardly non-partisan as a witness: 'contrary to impressions given by Speer at his trial and in post-war books, he and his men worked closely with Goebbels ... in armaments propaganda'.[214] They had a significant role in the newsreels.

There was a faith among the Nazis that miracle weapons would snatch victory from the jaws of defeat, and this was at the heart of the miracle weapons campaign, weapons which did indeed define the future of warfare for all time and were the prologue to the space age. Miracle weapons were Goebbels's great campaign, and as with so much propaganda it was neither lie nor truth. Indeed, they really were miraculous, the jets and rockets advanced up an expanding hierarchy of technological ingenuity to climax in the successful prototype of a flying wing. Yet the principal 'miracle

weapons' were weapons of terrorism alone and had no offensive significance. As propaganda, their purpose was vengeance-seeking and nothing
more. But there was a price for that propaganda. The scientist Freeman
Dyson has described his nonchalant reaction on hearing V2s explode in
late-war London. He calculated that each had cost Germany the equivalent
of fifteen of the fighter planes which could have shielded the Reich.[215]

Vengeance

Goebbels, as ever the manipulator, publicly acknowledged the cruelty of
the era: vengeance was his hyperbolic riposte, an England terrorised by 'a
raging daemon', by 'an armada of revenge'.[216] Numerous leaflets sought to
demoralise Allied troops via symbolic representations of the 'flying
meteor', such as the ominous 'V1' superimposed over an image of rubble,
or mighty swarms of V1s over London: England was burning.[217] Ten thousand V1 flying bombs were fired at Britain. V1 signified 'retaliation
weapon' and was thus branded to suggest a long sequence to follow, and
between 12 June and 5 September 1944 nearly 7,000 flying bombs had been
launched (close to half of which were intercepted)—Goebbels bragged
about the imminent incineration of a London allegedly already paralysed.[218]
Indeed, these claims were hardly fantastical since by mid-July 1944 large
parts of London had been laid to waste.[219] And, generally unknown to the
British wartime public, the V3 was being made ready for them. These vast
cannons were to blast London from their concrete encasing in the Pas de
Calais. The V3, according to Squadron Leader Tony Iveson,

> consisted of three bunkers near the village of Mimoyecques buried under a slab
> of reinforced concrete 20 ft ... thick, each bunker with a shaft holding five barrels
> side by side, and each barrel 500 ft ... long. Because of its target it was known
> colloquially as the 'London gun', and the Germans wanted to use it to pour 600
> tons of explosive a day into London.[220]

It was believed that this would have inflicted as much destruction on
London within two weeks as the RAF had on Berlin in the entirety of the
Second World War; but, since it was pulverised by 617 Squadron (the
'Dambusters') of the RAF on 6 July 1944, we shall never know.

Goebbels eventually drew back from this campaign; the miracle weapons
might not after all succeed. They represented an extravagant squandering
of resource, a valorisation of imagery over utility; again, packaging was
essence as well as outward form, substructure as well as superstructure.
The train-borne gun used to bombard Sevastopol (it was the size of a small

apartment block), for example, became in occupied France the image on a poster entitled 'La Puissance de l'Allemagne'[221]—evidence if ever it were needed of the Reich's familiar blend of instrumentality with symbolism. Thus a range of rockets and jets entered, or were entering, war service; the Reich had a great many, principally on the production line or en route to airfields, by war's end. These were the Messerschmitt 262 jet, the Me 163 Komet (a rocket plane), the Arado 234 (a four-engine jet bomber) and the Heinkel 162 *Volksjäger* jet fighter. The Bachem Ba 349 Natter was a manned rocket whose nose, complete with pilot, would detach and descend via parachute (at least in theory)—an astonishing piece of technology for the 1940s. A squadron was about to be launched in formation strength when the airfield was overrun by the Americans[222] (the United States, in contrast, had four jet aircraft in Europe by the end of the war, there solely for propaganda purposes).[223] There was also a flotilla of giant aircraft: the Me 323 six-engine troop carrier; the BV 222 six-engine flying boat; the Me 264 long-range bomber; and the Junkers Ju 390 six-engine transport.[224] A number of the experimental aircraft were actually built, including the Ju 287 V1, a reverse-wing jet, and the Henschel Hs 132 V1 jet fighter; there was also the Fa 223, a large two-engine helicopter;[225] and the revolutionary Gotha Go 229 V2 jet-powered Flying Wing, an anticipation of the stealth bomber, which actually flew.[226] Much else was under development or experiment, and, beyond this, those perennial myths such as the anti-aircraft gun whose magnetic missiles would seek and destroy Allied planes.[227]

Conclusions

No other society that ever existed so placed propaganda at the core of its being, of its political culture. Hitler was perhaps the only politician in history to have seized on the idea that persuasion was not just something, but that it was everything, to anchor the entire regime in the confections of imagery, rhetoric and dramaturgy. The Nazis also understood that war is a branch of the advertising industry: to extend Clausewitz, war was not the continuation of politics by other means but persuasion by other means, a form of creating meaning, murderous, vivid, yet still recognisably a persuasion process. Much in their behaviour both in war and peace flows from this, and hence Nazi propaganda was no mere electioneering device but a serious battlefield weapon, literally. Mortar-fired literature was simply another way of fighting, alongside tanks, flamethrowers and machine guns. Propaganda was a branch of the German artillery. And Hitler might assume command of the Nazi media/propaganda product when he pleased. For him as for no other, persuasion was the main business of governing; all else was driven to the margin. Clearly he was besotted with media because it was a source, and a form, of power, as well as the vehicle for pleasing aesthetics. A final audit, an audit of war, can be made. Germany lost 1,622,600 soldiers; 94,900 air force men; and 149,200 navy. 2,350,000 German civilians were also killed.[228] Of these, 300,000 were murdered by the German state,[229] many of course Jewish. But this latter figure is quite near the total numbers of Britons, civilian and military, killed in the Second World War (or alternatively the total of US deaths)—in other words, the Reich killed almost as many of its own as it did of the British. The Third Reich made all Europe an abattoir: numbers of the Soviet deaths are such that the actual figures, or the search for them, is a quest without a destiny. The genocide of the Poles, a Russo-Germanic enterprise, later emboldened some in the Polish government to seek to represent the weight of their dead citizens via a demand for greater power within the EU at a June 2007 EU summit meeting. While a portion of these horrors is attributable to the reality of high-technology warfare—bombing, shelling, the operation of great armies, the fluid columns of tanks and such like—nothing can diminish the fact that most of the killing of civilians was deliberate. Most of it was genocidal by intent not accident, not a by-product of military conflict but a separate end, in fact an unrelated activity, the consequence of an ethnic nationalism so toxic that it simply extinguished everything it came into contact with.

The original consortium of enemies resolved itself finally into the one enemy, the Jew, the face behind the mask of all the other enemies. Here the Nazis were tapping into an existing emotion which had congealed into a torpid social atmosphere. To Nazi propagandists these imaginary creatures were so consumed by their passions that the other aspects of their humanity had simply petrified or withered. Yet the regime gave primacy to persuasion not terror, as for example with the ubiquity of appeals to altruism and social solidarity, as in the case of the annual state charity campaign, Winter Relief. Hitler had exhibited a great ability to appear the antithesis of what he really was, as in the creation of the peace-loving Hitler image. The projection was of values as well as ideology, and this distinction explains the impact of propaganda, which was in fact a celebration of both. Civic conscience was given a further boost by the war itself which furnished more opportunities to engage with the solidarity appeal; nobody consciously votes for something evil and the Nazis were able to convince of their latent benevolence despite the rituals of aggression. What the Reich actually was, and what its people thought it was, was primarily an achievement of the propaganda.

3

TOWARDS A NAZI THEORY OF PERSUASION

THE PRIMAL SCREAM OF FASCISM

We operate in tune with the principle: constant dripping wears away the stone.

Joseph Goebbels, *Diaries*

No one who has not lived for years in a totalitarian land can possibly conceive how difficult it is to escape the dread consequences of a regime's calculated and incessant propaganda.

William Shirer

How Hitler Did It

Although there is a formidable (and indeed interminable) extant literature dedicated to explaining Hitler and his emotional conquest of Germany, from which the physical conquest of Europe followed, far less work has been invested in resolving the question of 'how' Hitler was able to achieve this. But in order to address this, we need to better comprehend the role of organised persuasion in Hitler's Reich, the enormity of its scale, the rigour of its application, and why exactly the Nazis came to acquire such dogmatic faith in the supremacy of propaganda. What concepts had they picked up from the universe of ideas on persuasion and the psychology of persuasion then extant? How was this ideology of persuasion implemented and in what way was it used? What operational formulae did they manufacture and promulgate to animate the propaganda 'product'? And, in general,

99

what were the conceptual and practical limitations of the particular theories of propaganda Nazis held, and indeed of persuasion itself as the central organising principle of the nation state? Such are the questions that this chapter seeks to answer.

As Goebbels once said:

> there are two ways to make a revolution. You can blast your enemy with machine guns until he acknowledges the superiority of those holding the machine guns. That is one way. Or you can transform the nation through a revolution of the spirit, and instead of destroying your enemy, win him over.[1]

In explaining the Nazi project, Bracher speaks of the success of a conglomerate of ideas—namely a form of socialism liberated from Marxist internationalism and a form of nationalism liberated from capitalism, both of which were welded together: the great 'synthesis' of National Socialism.[2] But he goes on to argue that the success of Nazi ideology can only be understood via the sovereign place of propaganda in the Third Reich, the effects of which were enhanced by the way in which the Nazis used modern techniques of opinion-formation in order to create a 'truly religio-psychological phenomenon'.[3]

This is not to deny the role of coercion in the Nazi regime; this was a totalitarian state after all. Yet while external compliance can be commanded, internal belief is an assent freely given. During the ballot campaign in the spring of 1936, for instance—an 'election' for the Reichstag and referendum on the Rhine re-militarisation—all Germans were instructed to listen to Hitler's speech from the Krupp arms factory at Essen.[4] A typical press announcement of the time read: 'The district party headquarters has ordered that all factory owners, department stores, offices, shops, pubs, and blocks of flats put up loudspeakers before the broadcast of the Führer's speech so that the whole workforce and all national comrades can participate fully in the broadcast.'[5] The near 100 per cent result was of course an entirely manipulated one.

Hitler's strength lay in his command of a methodology of manipulation. In Bracher's words, it:

> overshadowed the banal message attuned to irrationally elaborate visions, which, repeated in endless variations and reduced to terse formulas, [was used] to justify the ruthless virtuosity of the formal-propagandistic means; yet the eclectic historical components of this message proved effective even with portions of the intelligentsia.[6]

Hitler appears to have consciously promulgated a self-merchandising strategy with himself as the offer. Hilmar Hoffmann argues that Hitler:

Like a clever advertising executive, ... had effectively planned a strategy for marketing his product, namely himself, never confusing propaganda with sales promotion. A uniform set of party symbols, a party newspaper (which was founded very early in the history of the movement), and later a Nazified eclectic mass culture were all part of the dramaturgy. The most important component, though, was the perfectly stage-managed public appearance of the Führer, which Hitler had a flair for transforming into gigantic circus-like mass rallies.[7]

But the leadership's ideas on persuasion were never entirely convergent:

For Hitler, as for most Nazi campaigners, this is largely a matter of distilling complex political ideas into catchy, memorable slogans. For Goebbels it was more a matter of style, in forging a subtle union of politics with sensory experience. As one commentator has neatly put it, in Goebbels's view 'the politics of representation was more important than the representation of politics'.[8]

Thus Goebbels emphasised the role of innovation and imagination in propaganda. He consistently sought to employ 'every means available to bring to the masses the new way of thinking in a modern, up-to-date, interesting, and appealing manner ... *That* is the secret of propaganda; *completely* to imbue the targeted person with the ideas of your propaganda without him even realising it.'[9]

Propaganda was the operational method of the Third Reich, the idea that projected the ideology. Speer told the Nuremberg Tribunal 'that what distinguished the Third Reich from all previous dictatorships was its use of all the means of communication to sustain itself and to deprive its objects of the power of independent thought'.[10] Hitler was a magician of illusion. The cultural historian Piers Brendon has described propaganda as the 'Gospel' of Nazism, and notes that Goebbels 'liked to say that Jesus Christ has been a master of propaganda and that the propagandist must be the man with the greatest knowledge of souls'.[11] For Hoffmann 'it seems perfectly justifiable to characterise the National Socialist movement as a "propaganda movement"', and that 'unlike any other politician before or since, Hitler, from the time he began his political activity, had very definite ideas regarding the effectiveness and the methods of modern propaganda'.[12] One youthful observer was John F. Kennedy, who visited Germany briefly in 1937 and attributed Hitler's popularity to his skills as a propagandist.[13] In 1936 Josef Wells, a leading Nazi propaganda theorist, argued that: 'We do not want to distort, confuse or incite, but rather clarify, unify and tell the truth. Political propaganda is the highest responsibility, it is a moral duty, a national duty. We may never think there is too much of it, or that it is superfluous.'[14] Similarly speaking of propaganda, another Nazi theorist and proponent of propaganda, Walther Schulze-Wechsungen, thought that 'we owe our rise to it and will have to depend on it even more in the future. It is a powerful tool in moulding the nature and thinking of the new, the modern man'; politics and propaganda were interdependent—'without politics there is no propaganda and without propaganda there is no politics. Good politics always needs good propaganda.'[15] Hence the Propaganda Committee was an important part of the Nazi Party right from the beginning (Heinrich Himmler was originally vice-chairman of the committee, while the chairman was Gregor Strasser).[16]

Hitler's skill lay in his ability to combine propaganda, ideology and organisation. *Mein Kampf*, particularly in the second volume, 'is truly original only in those parts in which Hitler discusses his crude and effective methods of propaganda, organisation, and mass psychology with cynical frankness'.[17] But as for the rest—'the half-baked ideas of the eternally adolescent charlatan and rootless wastrel of Vienna formed the core of this philosophy, now cast into the mould of a pretentious Weltanschauung and endowed with political effectiveness by the virtuosity of the born demagogue'.[18] Even war itself became, if not a branch of the advertising industry, then certainly a formulaic meld of punch and publicity. Hitler's great insight, which makes him unique among historical actors, was the recognition that violence and propaganda could and should be an integrated phenomenon, the interpenetration of conflict with communication. War and its articulation should not be disentangled since they were interdependent. The Nazis claimed 'we did not lose the war because artillery gave out but because the weapons of our minds did not fire', and thus 'the mobilisation of the mind is as necessary as, possibly even more important than, the material mobilisation of the nation'.[19]

Thus Roger Manvell recounts:

> An anonymous contributor ('a leading figure in the international field of commercial public relations') wrote ... in August 1941 on the high place propaganda occupied in Germany's total war policy: 'one has only to look at the tremendous achievements of the Germans—involving infinitesimal losses, until the present Russian campaign—to realise the part played by propaganda in the German war machine. Practically the whole of Europe has been conquered with losses smaller than those in one major battle in the last war. What clearly emerges is that practically all German military moves may be said to have been timed, if not dictated, by propaganda considerations, no less, and probably often more so, than by military ones. The Russian campaign, whatever other reasons lie behind it, has undoubted propaganda motives ... Propaganda is used by the Germans to prepare and facilitate the way for military action. Conversely, the propaganda

effects of military action are all carefully calculated. The German military tactics themselves have their calculated propaganda effects—intensive violence designed to create panic—deliberate action on the civilian population as demonstrated in Belgium and France to hamper defence, etc.[20]

He contrasted this with the weak position of the British propaganda minister, concluding:

briefly, the Propaganda Minister cannot fulfil his functions unless he is intimately concerned with the shaping of grand strategy. No man can make a greater contribution to the shaping of this strategy if we accept, as accept we must, that this is a war of ideas and ideals—in other words, of human emotions and reactions.

Partners in Wishful Thinking

The Third Reich represents the evolution of a partnership between masses and demagogue, a co-production—for example in the invitation to believe the idea that the Jews had simply been removed to external work camps such as the 'model' Theresienstadt and not murdered. What the Nazis were really saying was that their truth lay deeper than their lies, and that their lies were merely a permissible methodology since the end always justified the means. A 'lie' is thus really a permissible level of suspension of candour in the aid of a great cause. In Kallis's view, propaganda can be defined as the fabrication of truth, but it can also be a blend of consensus, indoctrination, short-term truth and long-term wishful thinking, 'in order to produce a discourse that is both formative and informative'.[21] He regards the identification of propaganda with falsification as misleading: propaganda is a form of truth 'reshaped through the lens of regime intentions ...' In other words, it forms part of a wider discourse 'that links past, present and future in a meaningful, coherent way'.[22] From the perspective of the Reich, the Nazis were selling German truth rather than British falsehood.[23] Subjectivity is deeper than objectivity. As the Nazi propaganda theorist Schulze-Wechsungen argued, 'propaganda is concerned only with its goal, with its justice, its truth. All else is half-truth.'[24]

Although it is an easy assumption to make when contemplating the narrative of the Third Reich, it would be an error to take Hitler's Gustave Le Bon-derived view of the masses, their 'femininity' and suggestibility, at face value. A more accurate representation of the psychology of the process would be to conceive of a partnership in wishful thinking in which the masses were self-deluded as well as other-deluded. I have argued elsewhere that the idea of people willingly misled offends our notion of man as rational, yet this is exactly what polemic often seeks to do. The appeal is not to reason. Persuasion in such cases offers an idea of solidarity and the target of that persuasion is more co-conspirator than victim, an invitation to share in the creation of a hyperbolic fiction.[25] The Third Reich is an essay in the ability of human beings to be persuaded. People will see what they wish to see according to the concepts they possess and the values they hold. But successful persuasion, in business, media or government, does not make the error of asking for belief. It makes no pretence of objectivity. The notion of persuasion as 'manipulative' evokes a passive recipient and a hypodermic or stimulus-response form; but a more sophisticated idea is that of an invocation to partnership.[26] Thus the Third Reich was the emanation of a collective as well as an individual's imagination. Aldous Huxley thought that 'political and religious propaganda is effective, it would seem, only upon those who are already partly or entirely convinced of its truth'.[27]

Thus submersible parts of the ideology, such as the antagonism to religion, the euthanasia campaign, the massacre of Jews, could all have been discovered by the determined enquirer. One theory advanced as an explanation of this is that of group narcissism, which is described by Gonen as one of the most important sources of human aggression: 'in a world that is seen through a narcissistic tunnel vision, only oneself or one's group has any rights'.[28] Theodor Adorno spoke of the need for existential identification with large groups and their protectiveness, and speculated on the 'collective power fantasies' of the powerless who 'considered themselves somebody only in terms of a powerful collectivity'.[29]

Schulze-Wechsungen stressed the need for psychological insight and an understanding of human perception:

> past German politics and war propaganda were based on sentimentality and 'moral' feelings, untroubled by any understanding of the psyche of the masses. ... modern psychology ... supported by psychiatry and neurology, attempts to discover the laws of psychological processes through systematic experimentation and statistical analysis (e.g., logical thinking). These modern methods have led to valuable conclusions, but they are not sufficient by themselves. There are imponderables in the psyche of individuals as well as of the masses that can scarcely be explained.

He also uses the term 'suggestion' ('as an idea transformed into reality through the subconscious') and reminds his Nazi readership of the insight of the philosopher Arthur Schopenhauer: 'when the heart resists, the mind will not accept'.[30]

Methods of Nazi Propaganda

The Nazis methodologised propaganda as well as eulogising it. What they offered was not merely an ideology of propaganda but a formula for implementing it. This distinguishes the Reich from other populist or totalitarian regimes, none of which theorised about propaganda to the same extent as the Nazis.

Ideology plus methodology

Goebbels recognised that the essence of Nazism was ideology plus methodology: the one would be moribund without the other. But violence without ideology was foredoomed. An idea can only be combatted by another idea: 'any attempt to combat a philosophy with methods of violence will fail in the end, unless the fight takes the form of attack for a new spiritual attitude'.[31] The special merit of an ideological system is that it answers all questions from its own internal resources (in the early days at least, all the Nazis appeared to be doing was adding a racial texture to Marxism). As Schulze-Wechsungen argued, the enemy was Marxism:

> Our goal was its annihilation. Our propaganda had to shake the foundations of the core of the Marxist idea in the minds and hearts of the masses, the theory of class struggle. Then we had to replace it with a new theory, which later the organisation or positive power would use to win these same masses to a free state without a theory of class struggle.[32]

Political sectarianism was impelling Germany towards the abyss 'from which we rescued the German people by presenting them with a revolutionary idea that by the help of propaganda became their public opinion'.[33]

Stimulus-response

Goebbels really did see propaganda almost as a kind of stimulus-response exercise, a drug or narcotic: 'nothing is easier than leading the people on a leash. I just [hold] up a dazzling campaign poster and they jump through it.'[34] In his diaries he claimed to have brought the morale situation within Germany during the war under control after a few days ('all one needs is the courage to persist with the right arguments and not to allow oneself to become bogged down').[35]

Subversion

Effective persuasion proceeds by subversion not assault. It does not appear to attack the values of its audience, and recognises that core beliefs do not change immediately but slowly over time, and that the values that succour them hardly change at all.

Baruch Gitlis has argued that: 'wherever the German turned, he met his most "dangerous enemy", the Jew',[36] and that 'while he walked in the street he encountered posters and slogans against the Jews at every square, on every wall and billboard. Even graffiti greeted the German at the entrance to his dwelling: "wake up Germany, Judah must rot!"' He goes on to describe how 'the Street buzzed with trampling marchers, screaming at the top of their lungs the National-Socialist battle cry: "Germany Awake, Judah Rot in the Grave."'

As a metaphor for the public culture of Nazi Germany, this has evocative merit; it does not, however, project the truth, but a truth. The lived, experienced reality was more complex. Indeed, Gitlis himself observes that until 1938 there were no films entirely dedicated to anti-Semitic themes, and that anti-Semitism in Nazi films was often latent (*Rembrandt*, 1942 or *Ohm Krüger*, or the three party films of 1933—*SA Mann Brand, Hans Westmar, Hitler Youth Quex*) and therefore more effective than the polemicism of the three 1940 anti-Semitic films (*Jud Süss, The Eternal Jew, The Rothschilds*).

Hence until the late 1930s anti-Semitism in film was allusive and elusive rather than overt, as for example in the film *Hitler Youth Quex* where anti-Semitism is subtly conveyed: 'this is to be found in the scene in which a sloppily dressed boy, smoking cigarettes and singing bawdy songs written by Jewish composer, is contrasted unfavourably with the healthy, good-looking members of the Hitler Youth group'.[37] Indeed, during the 1930s, a Swedish film about a Jewish business fraudster, *Pettersson and Bendel* (1933), was promulgated but then withdrawn (though it was resurrected after Kristallnacht).[38]

Resonance

Neil Gregor argues that notions of propaganda in relation to National Socialism are much misunderstood. The purpose of Nazi propaganda was not to brainwash ordinary Germans, and it was not intended to deceive the masses even though it did enable the movement to gain new recruits. The principal objective was:

to absorb the individual into a mass of like-minded people, and the purpose of the 'suggestion' was not to deceive but to articulate that which the crowd already believed. The crowd is of one opinion—Hitler speaks of 'the agreement of thousands'. Its experience is of 'intoxication and enthusiasm', of near-hysterical support for the message. The function of propaganda was thus not to dupe, but to mobilise what was already latent. More generally, Hitler saw in the National Socialist movement not merely a means to capturing the state with a few misled supporters, but as a voluntarist mobilisation of healthy national sentiment.[39]

Repetition

The essence of the Nazi propaganda method was repetition; it was an article of faith and everything was reducible to this formula. Goebbels argued that the skill of British propagandists during the Great War resided in the fact that they used just a few powerful slogans and kept repeating them.[40] The British, according to Goebbels, were the Mephistophelian masters of these skills: 'with devilish depravity, they [British lies] were spread systematically throughout the entire world and pounded into the brains of millions of people. At the end, they were helpless victims of mass hypnosis.'[41] Whether or not this was a post-hoc imposition of a simple theory on to complex facts, it is a supreme compliment that, echoing Hitler in *Mein Kampf*, Nazis claimed their core propaganda methodology was plagiarised from the British. It was their conviction that this was how political campaigns, and war, would now be won. The numerous guidelines for propaganda practitioners simply summarise and apply the precepts of Adolf Hitler in *Mein Kampf*, such as how propaganda must limit itself to a few repeated points.

The Nazis believed a formulaic propaganda methodology must be applied even at the cost of alienating the sophisticated:

many a one laughed at the propaganda of the NSDAP in the past from a position of superiority. It is true that we had only one thing to say, and we yelled and screamed and propagandised it again and again with a stubbornness that drove the 'wise' to desperation. We proclaimed it with such simplicity that they thought it absurd and almost childish. They did not understand that repetition is the precursor to success and simplicity is the key to the emotional and mental world of the masses. The masses are mostly extraordinarily forgetful, and their understanding less than that of the learned. Propaganda has to be made not to please the learned, but rather to reach the masses. We wanted to appeal to the intuitive world of the great masses, not the understanding of the intellectuals. The significance of events and facts must be presented over and over again, until after a long time indeed the masses recognize the necessity of a fundamental change ... Scientists, on the other hand, are persuaded by scientific proofs.[42]

Thus Hitlerite evangelism was founded on a notion of the efficacy of repetition;[43] the message penetrated the barriers of inattention through the massive insistence on its replication. The likely success of any political persuasion campaign will thus result from what is now known as the Repeated Exposure Effect.[44] Indeed, some of the most effective advertising campaigns in history have been based on this idea and no other; associations are made to stick, independent of any conscious appraisal. Repetition is one way of dealing with competition for attention. Goebbels was a proponent of this repeated exposure effect, an idea with its roots in behavioural psychology and related to the concept of conditioning. The mass mind was dull and sluggish, and for ideas to take root they had to be constantly re-seeded: recognition, comprehension, retention and conviction are different stages in the cognitive process, and repetition can facilitate them.

It is important to remember, therefore, that what Nazi propaganda also offered was the dubious benefit of sensory exhaustion. The citizen was not a target to be persuaded so much as a victim to be conquered, ravished even. They wanted internal commitment, not just external compliance. Psychological resistance would be demoralised. Through its interpenetration of everything, National Socialism subjected the 'German people to unceasing tensions. The insistence upon activism in place of thinking means that men shall never have the freedom time to think for themselves.'[45] Neumann describes this action as in fact pseudo-action: 'it is not a man who acts but a bureaucratic machine'.[46] Consciousness was beaten into submission and the critical faculty numbed by invasive propaganda, even though oppositional views were indeed available such as foreign news broadcasts.

This colonisation of the German mind represented the first of the Nazi invasions. In this, the ordinary party member was important. G. Stark, a Nazi propaganda theorist, said that 'in such matters, each is his own political propagandist', and that party members were 'fanatic fighters with an unbreakable desire for battle'.[47] For Goebbels, a message had to be coherent since it must be absorbed as well as understood; thus the same limited stock of messages was articulated in a range of formats and media. But the variety lay in the medium, not the message:

> In the long run, propaganda will reach the broad masses of the people only if at every stage it is uniform. Nothing confuses the people more than lack of clarity ... The goal is not to present the common man with as many varied and contradictory theories as possible. The essence of propaganda is not in variety, but rather the

forcefulness and persistence with which one selects ideas from the larger pool and hammers them into the masses using the most varied methods.[48]

The Nazis consequently believed that while method can vary, content cannot. It had to be disciplined and by inference formulaic. As Schulze-Wechsungen argued:

the goal of propaganda is this: to persuade the masses. It ignores everything that wants to make an 'interestingly varied' propaganda, anything that wants to change the fundamental principles and content that propaganda wants to convey. Propaganda methods can, indeed must, vary, but propaganda must be carried out in a unified and disciplined way. Only that brings success, only that leads to the goal.[49]

But whatever the psychological explanation, it is obvious that repeated exposure does affect the retention of information and ultimately both attitudes and the actions which are expressive of those attitudes. Citizens are inadvertent consumers of political information: they rarely seek it, but when the information comes gift-wrapped, or, unsolicited, it captivates consciousness. Complete control of public space was possible and therefore control of the cognitive environment. Repetition ad nauseam was an article of faith for Goebbels: 'it would not be impossible to prove with sufficient repetition and psychological understanding of the people concerned that the square is in fact a circle. They are mere words and words can be moulded ...'[50] At one point early in the war he commented that 'the press is not quite so keen to co-operate, since continual repetition makes them feel uncomfortable ... but it must, it must. From now on I shall keep chewing over the arguments against England ... Then the world will believe them too. This is the essence of propaganda.'[51] Thus he describes Churchill's 'massive fantasy campaign', which he sees as impertinent, adding that 'we shall now initiate an illusions campaign that will strike the English deaf and blind. It will go on until we have it all coming out of our ears. Then every last person in the world will have got the message'[52] (again we note his trust: good propaganda can help the British just as bad propaganda can undermine Germany). Goebbels claimed that propaganda was not a literary genre—the public 'must be thoroughly saturated ... with constant repetition until the message sticks ... Propaganda is repetition, constant repetition.' This is the essence of propaganda, and Goebbels avowed: 'and we intend, in old National Socialist style, not to operate defensively but offensively'. Their enemies—Jew, capitalist, Marxist—'should always be kept on edge and unsettled by propaganda'.[53] Hence the concept of repetition in Hitlerian propaganda meant expressing the same point, but in different ways. As

Randall Bytwerk comments, Hitler realised that in politics as in advertising, consistent effort is necessary to maintain even an established product.[54] Thus a foreign journalist observed late in 1939,

> whether in the press, films, radio, schools, party organisations or industrial organisations, the specific policies that the government is pursuing at a particular moment are constantly paraded before the people in their most liberal favourable light, while opposing views—for example those which one might seek through foreign broadcasts—are buried in an avalanche of positive propaganda or submitted to the type of vilification that is designed to render them false or ridiculous.[55]

There was a universal template and format. On 7 February 1942 the director of the political department in the Foreign Ministry sent a memo to German embassies and consulates and officials on the subject of 'standard propaganda themes that form the basis of all propaganda brought in the near future'.[56] He urges that the same arguments should be repeated through various media including whispering campaigns. They were to be 'learnt by heart like commands and cannot be repeated often enough. The value of effective propaganda lies in constant repetition.' The themes pushed were, for example, that Churchill started the war to expand British power and that Roosevelt and Churchill were working together as exponents of world Jewry.[57]

Entertainment: the propaganda of indirection

Entertainment existed as an important medium of propaganda, independent of its morale-boosting function; but the propaganda message was usually well hidden in Nazi Germany. Effective propaganda was indirect propaganda, and the messaging was implicit rather than explicit. Meaning was to be absorbed unconsciously; it was confectionery not medicine. This explains the Nazis' great emphasis on film, because it was the most discreet as well as the most powerful instrument of persuasion, and thus both Hitler and Goebbels repeatedly affirmed their belief that film propaganda was the best propaganda because it was the most effective means for igniting and directing mass consciousness.[58] Thus, speaking of *Kolberg*, Goebbels remarked that the film had 'the same meaning for the mood of the German people today as a battlefield victory' (1 December 1944).[59] He implemented an orchestral principle where different media performed different roles so that overt propaganda was delegated to newsreel and documentary[60] (the role of the press in opinion-formation was secondary in Bracher's view).[61]

Goebbels grasped an essential truth at the very beginning of the Third Reich, namely that overt propaganda does not work in cinema: 'the conveyor belt brown shirt epics were box office poison—not because of the public's political antipathies, but because of its craving for experiences in cinema which were very different from those outside it'.[62] At the 1943 Reich culture film week, the prizewinning films were conspicuously bereft of swastika flags while the losers were films that invoked party dogma, including *The German Word*; films like *Artists At Work* received the prize from Goebbels.[63] It is a measure of the surface apoliticism of Nazi cinema that so few of these films were actually banned by the victorious Allies. The 1951 catalogue of the Allied High Commission judged only 141 out of 700 adventure films to be politically suspect;[64] 90 per cent of the films produced under the Nazi regime were light entertainment without overt propaganda content.[65] Thus 'generic productions ... constituted 941 of its 1,094 feature films, including 295 melodramas and biopics, 123 detective films and adventure epics. Almost half of all features—to be precise, 523—were comedies and musicals (or what the Nazis termed *heitere*, "cheerful" films)'.[66] Even the Jewish film organisation (the Jewish Filmbühne), to which Jews had been exiled, found little that was objectionable in the bulk of German film productions. Indeed, according to Ross, 'Nazi' films constituted well over two-thirds of the Jewish Filmbühne's entire repertoire.[67]

Nazi imagery was hidden in film. As Rentschler says, 'if one is looking for sinister heavies garbed in SS black, crowds of fanatics saluting their Führer, one does best to turn to Hollywood films of the 1940s'.[68] Heterogeneity was licensed and put there for a purpose: 'films of the Third Reich emanated from Ministry of Illusion, not the Ministry of Fear', and thus the 'decision to eradicate signs of the times and to take flight from present was not made by subversive forces or oppositional artists. The order came from the top.'[69] In 1937 the party's youth journal remarked that:

> one has to look a long time before one finds a cinema programme announcing a film with an obvious political slant ... even the most suspicious filmgoers cannot claim that German films seek to hit them over the head with politics or to impose a worldview. Except for portions of the newsreels, cinema in a newly politicised Germany amounts to an unpolitical oasis.[70]

The SPD (social democrat) intelligence made the same point—'anything one can speak of as a new worldview is entirely absent'.[71] For Goebbels, 'if the masses saw a film and felt that it was mere propaganda, they were misusing the word because such a film was a failure. It could not be propaganda.' His belief was 'that the function of the film was edification, diversion, and relaxation, but in a political sense'.[72] Goebbels remarked that 'the moment one becomes aware of propaganda, it loses its effectiveness'.[73] But Goebbels wanted a mass-internalised ideology, declaiming on 15 March 1933: 'popular enlightenment is essentially something passive; propaganda, on the other hand, is something active. We cannot, therefore, be satisfied with just telling the people what we want and enlightening them as to how we are going to do it.'[74] However, indoctrination had to seduce, not harangue: so popular culture 'often looked so disconcertingly similar to the culture of other times and places. It, too, was based on the tried-and-tested formats of linear narrative, human interest, and storytelling.'[75] Two films, *Request Concert* (1940) and *The Great Love* (1942) (the two most popular films in the Nazi period) are paragons of the Third Reich entertainment ideal, the propaganda of indirection, since they chronicle the relationship 'between the war and the home front, personal fate and forces beyond one's control ... As stories about love, loyalty, and duty, they also carried a distinct political message.'[76] The same themes structure both epics: lovers separated by war, mistakes and misfortune, but who are reunited when duty supersedes desire. The audiences for these films were huge, with *Request Concert* attracting over 26 million, *The Great Love* 20 million. But there were also other films which were almost as popular; cinema was now a basic given of social life.[77]

The situation was similar with radio. The Hinkel Report, an official German government analysis of the effectiveness of wartime radio, had attacked programmes as 'boring, dry and humourless': by mid-war, political information/indoctrination constituted a mere 20 per cent of radio content.[78] Goebbels reproached broadcasters for their 'vigorous politicisation'. Thus the rise of radio entertainment was especially marked during the war years. The information–entertainment ratio had been equal; but it changed to 1:2 by 1939 before reaching 1:4 by 1943–4.[79] Goebbels asserted that 'the primary rule is: just don't be boring. I prioritise this above everything else'; he adds 'do not think that one can best serve the national government by playing thunderous military marches every evening. Rather, you must help to cultivate a nationalistic art and culture that also genuinely matches the modern pace of life and modern sensibilities.'[80] There were exceptions, however: the three 'storm trooper' films of 1933 of course, the three anti-Semitic films of 1940 and, more generally, the film product of the early Second World War; during the first half of the war the overtly political film proportion peaked at 34 per cent in 1941.[81] These were the big budget entertainment-political blockbusters such as *The Great King* or *Ohm*

Krüger, the films usually taken to epitomise the cinema of the Third Reich. *Jud Süss* in particular commanded an audience of over 20 million, about a third of all adults.[82]

Principles of Nazi Propaganda

Conceptual—advertising and propaganda

The worlds of advertising and commerce had an enormous influence on the style, method and tone of Nazi propaganda. Nazism arose within a commercially driven consumerist environment. In 1930 Stark wrote that

> The face of the city, as a centre of production and consumption, is marked by advertising. The concentration of many companies leads to intense competition, which is won not necessarily by the firm with the best product, but rather with the best advertising. Poster pillars, newspapers, billboards and so on hammer incessantly on the victim, until finally he bends to the power of the advertising firm and buys ... This out and out commercial advertising is aimed exclusively at earning money, and appeals only to the billfold. But the most effective advertising is not necessarily for the best product ...[83]

The context was also a German advertising industry, especially the Association of German Advertisers, conscious of its rising power and seeking a concomitant increase in status.[84] The 1929 World Advertising Congress had been in Berlin: there was an embrace of 'science' and experimentation, for example the work of Hugo Munsterberg offered the advertising industry applied techniques based on laboratory investigations of repetition, recognition, memorisation and page placement.[85] Advertising psychology was incorporated into the curricular of colleges and training institutes including that of the University of Cologne.[86] Nazis perceived of course the parallels between consumer advertising and propaganda—how could they not, for advertising was the propaganda of consumption? Yet they were very keen to point up the limitations of the analogy:

> Political propaganda is something entirely different. It uses indeed in part the same methods to reach its goals, but rests on an entirely different set of assumptions. Propaganda is by no means simply commercial advertising applied to the political or spiritual arena. They seek only momentary effect, whereas political propaganda seeks the systematic enlightenment necessary to win supporters to worldview. We recall the many comrades who gave their lives for the movement. They were propagandists of the deed up to the last breath.[87]

They offer an important definition of propaganda, differentiating it from advertising, and that is to say propaganda seeks permanent and not ephemeral change. Its focus is a worldview rather than a transitory appetite. Propaganda is an act not only of the word but also the deed. Yet the Nazis still had to admit that they looked to consumer advertising for lessons on how to conduct political propaganda: 'the task of these propaganda centrals is to study advertising methods and see how we can use them, which requires above all a well organised propaganda organisation'.[88] Josef Wells, a Nazi propaganda activist, dismissed advertising as mere hubbub and hyperbole with no ethical content, unlike the making of propaganda, which is a highly ethical activity:

> Political propaganda may not be confused with advertising. Advertising changes its target as needed. The Americans call it 'ballyhoo'. The word means making a lot of noise about something, whether it is worth it or not. The art of advertising works this way. Advertising agencies push one thing today, another tomorrow, each time making it sound as if nothing else in the world is worth mentioning. There is no thought of moral or national values. 'Ballyhoo' is advertising at any price, with no moral content, no moral thought or responsibility. The Americans made 'ballyhoo' against Germany during the World War until the American public finally believed that the Germans were cannibals whose elimination would be a godly deed. 'Ballyhoo' is unlimited, arbitrary exaggeration. In a political sense, it is incitement, distortion, and it is all immoral.[89]

Other contemporaries, however, such as Schulze-Wechsungen, were more ambivalent about the distinction between advertising and propaganda: 'Advertising experts, historians, scientists, experts and laymen alike have attempted to distinguish the words propagandist and advertising agent by a variety of longer or shorter definitions. No one has really succeeded.'[90] Propaganda was political advertising, political education for the common good; its subject was ideas and not material need, and thus its essence was spiritual.

The propagandist was therefore 'the authorised representative of a political worldview or of a spiritual–religious idea'. However, there are conceptual and methodological commonalities: 'the two have in common an organised set of methods—often different ones—which "result in the acceptance or fulfilment of the needs they present"'. Both use 'agitators'. But the propagandist shoulders a heavy burden: 'he has even greater responsibility to do more, to create more fanatically, for he is a political soldier. Therefore: On with propaganda!' He must become 'as familiar a concept' as the advertising agent, and 'create something necessary: a tradition!'[91]

Emotion

Nazism was an irrational creed promulgated via a view of man as irrational; Nazism felt rather than thought, and therefore the nature of its propaganda appeal was also to feeling rather than thinking. The mobilisation of emotion lay at the heart of everything the Nazis did; propaganda's operational formula.

For Goebbels, the role of the propagandist was to express in words what his audience felt in their hearts.[92] For Hitler 'it [passion] alone gives the words to him whom it has chosen, the hammer blows that open the door to the hearts of the people'.[93] Fascism proclaimed the redundancy of reason; it demanded not scepticism but faith. Unfortunately this insight into the nature of communication rested on well-understood truths about the ability of human beings to be persuaded, comprehending, in other words, the essentially unreasoning nature of humanity. The elemental nature of man was emotional. Schulze-Wechsungen wrote that:

> few people are able to bring the heart and mind into full agreement. Propaganda often has particular importance in that it speaks to the emotions rather than the pure understanding. The individual as well as the masses are subject to 'attitudes'; their emotions determine their condition. The politician may not coldly ignore these emotions; he must recognize and understand them if he is to choose the proper form of propaganda to reach his goals.[94]

Propaganda is emotionally driven. He adds: 'propaganda and passion belong together. Great passion is as rare as great genius is. The greater the passion, the more effective the propaganda.'[95] The clarity with which the Fascists grasped this stands in fact as the basis of their power. But this insight was neither random nor accidental: it was derived from popularisations of some of the nineteenth-century's most original thinkers on psychology, in particular Sigmund Freud and Gustave Le Bon. This thinking, distilled and coarsened via popular pamphlets and books, congealed around the idea of man not as analytic/logical but as visceral/irrational, the restless captive of remorseless drives that lay deeper than consciousness. The works of Freud turned ideas like the unconscious and mass suggestion into general currency: post-Enlightenment notions of politics as 'free people choosing the best policies by the simple exercise of the reason' were now challenged.[96] The new citizen emerged into this world as neither reasoner nor logician, nor utility-maximising economic man deciding according to a rational hierarchy of structured preferences, but as a regressive, a member of the 'bewildered herd', the carrier of ancestral hatreds, both the persecutor and the victim.

Le Bon, for example, who was a major influence on Hitler, acknowledges the role of the unconscious: 'conscious acts are the outcome of an unconscious substratum created in the mind in the main by hereditary influences'.[97] There are secret causes of action of which we are not aware—'the greater part of our daily actions are the result of hidden motives which escape our observation'. Le Bon's ascription of irrationality to the crowd was of course something Hitler strongly shared: they go in a moment 'from the most bloodthirsty ferocity to the most extreme generosity and heroism'. Freud's theory of the group leader foresaw the rise of dictator-manipulated masses, bound by libidinal ties to the leader who becomes a kind of group superego.[98] The Fascist model of man was as an instinctual creature with elemental cravings and intense, tribe-driven passions; intellectually moribund with a complete absence of critical detachment. Reason was not merely secondary but in fact irrelevant to his child-like, needy and emotional nature. His essence was credulity: 'by demonstrating that people care less for their material interests than for some ideological nostrum, and are moved less by rational choice than by irrational forces, [Hitler] challenged the very basis of Western democracy'.[99] George Orwell's insight was that Hitler understood that human beings do not only seek comfort but intermittently want struggle, flags and so forth.[100]

Thus a core part of Nazi grand theory was the dethronement of reason and the celebration of emotion. This in fact was part of its essential modernism. But, critically, the life of the emotions must be praised as superior to the life of reason, and elevated as a quasi-mystical or pseudo-sacerdotal force: 'For example Christ never wrote a party programme, but did preach the sermon on the Mount. He laid the foundations of a new world summarised in the simple phrase. Love your neighbour as yourself' (Goebbels, Nuremberg 1927).[101] In doing this, the Nazis were basing their method not on convenience but calculation, and Hitler and his propaganda subcontractors saw this as superior method. In general, mankind felt rather than thought, and the popular mind was incapable of intellectual abstraction; rather, the enchantments of visuality or sensory experience, or the blandishments of resonant phrases, or the scourge of dogmatic assertion, represented for them the universe of sense-making devices. The important thing was to undermine the individual's ability to resist, and this was a prerequisite of integration: Goebbels defined propaganda's essence as winning people over to an idea so that they succumb 'and can never again escape from it'.[102] The aim was not passive obedience but active conversion. It was an evangelical creed.

Populism: propaganda must speak to the masses

Propaganda must be primitive, appealing to what Hitler in an interview with Sefton Delmer described as man's inner 'Schweinehund'.[103] Typically 'brutally "either- or"', the propaganda appealed to the audience's primitive desire for simplification, thus: 'There are ... only two possibilities: either the victory of the Aryan side or its annihilation and the victory of the Jews.'[104] According to Goebbels, what was distinctive about the Nazis was 'the ability to see into the soul of the people and to speak the language of the man in the street'.[105] The propagandist was an artist who 'sensed the secret vibrations of the people'.[106] What distinguished European Fascism above all was its discovery of new ways, a methodology, of speaking to the working class, something which eluded parties of the conventional right/centre. When speaking about the old school German nationalists, Hitler argued that 'none of them knew how to speak to the people ... the great masses have no mercy, they go straight ahead with the simplicity of innocence'.[107] He saw the essence of German failure in the First World War as the absence of populist leaders.[108] But Fascists, according to Paxton, 'promised access to the crowd through exciting political spectacle and clever publicity techniques; to discipline that crowd through paramilitary organisation and charismatic leadership; and the replacement of chance elections by yes–no plebiscites'.[109]

The Fascists were not ashamed of mass media and marketing, understood the cultures of consumerism and recognised the role these now played in the lives of the masses; media was a new language with which the masses were now familiar, including its styles, forms and assumptions. Fascists were at ease in this exciting new world and recognised that it could be exploited for political purposes, both as a source of methods and as a new kind of culture with a different set of governing assumptions. Goebbels grasped the essence—'most parties today do not know how to speak to the workers'. This is essential, especially where democratic electioneering is new: 'one cannot use white gloved methods to reach them'.[110] Nazi propaganda theorists stressed the need for 'constant touch with the people'.[111] Old conservatives did not proselytise: as Paxton says, 'Fascists quickly profited from the inability of centrists and conservatives to keep control of a mass electorate. Whereas the notable dinosaurs disdained mass politics, fascists showed how to use it for nationalism and against the Left'. The three-class voting system, derived from Prussia and heavily weighted towards the rich and landed, had been abolished in Germany in 1918.[112] Now, politicians had to appeal to the masses to succeed. They did not know how. The parties of the right, centre and left were steeped in an anachronistic paradigm, one stressing the provision of information not persuasion, fact not propaganda; the world had simply moved on, and miraculous new media set the tone. When a nationalist conservative tried to engage with the new challenges mass politics presented by establishing a Propaganda Centre for National Republicans in 1927, 'hidebound conservatives scoffed that his methods were more appropriate for selling a new brand of chocolate than for politics'.[113] Only far right and far left seemed to recognise the need for dramaturgy and that 'the efforts of the bourgeois parties were dragged down by the dead weight of the old-fashioned, hollow ideas from the realm of higher education and suffered from official needs'.[114]

In Ross's view there were in fact many sophisticated contemporaries scornful of the Nazi charade and self-persuaded that a phenomenon so superficial could never endure. Their delusion lay in their perspective, their faith, the premise that reason would ultimately prevail over feeling, objectivity over passion, analysis over hysteria. But it was a perspective that diminished, belittled even, the power of persuasion and the deterministic role of communication in human affairs. This false paradigm amounted to an ideology and its confusion of the desirable with the actual was fatally flawed. Thus Theodor Heuss's book *Hitlers Weg* (1932) was a scorching critique of the Nazi programme and its contradictions. The author argued that National Socialism's effectiveness derived primarily from the persona of Hitler and the propaganda of his party.[115] The book portrayed the Nazis 'as hollow image artists lacking the substance for actual government'. The leading conservative politician Carl Severing was equally dismissive: 'we are well aware how much easier it is to intoxicate hungry and anxious people with the cheap elixir of hollow phrases and empty promises. We condemn this approach.'[116] The *Frankfurter Zeitung* discussed the mystification of the Nazi Party but concluded that 'the realities of life have forced us to return to that which many were so light-heartedly prepared to throw overboard: to reason'.[117] In the view of Neumann, the Nazis' versatility, the 'malleable vagueness of the imagery and the flexibility and adaptability of the terminology',[118] was 'unattainable in a democracy' since 'National Socialist propaganda will always be superior because National Socialist culture is propaganda and nothing else, while a democratic culture is a mixture. National Socialist propaganda cannot be beaten by a democratic super propaganda, but only by a superior Democratic policy that eliminates the soft spots.'[119] Neumann adds, 'worse still, attempts to fight fascism primarily by propaganda methods are almost invariably connected with an abandonment of democratic conventions'. Propaganda was also seen as a way of rectifying the Germans' political naivety: in 1936 Wells stated that 'the average Englander is not nearly as well educated as the German, but he is more mature and sure of his opinions. He therefore does not need the same permanent political schooling as we do.'[120]

Instrumentalism

The Nazi view of propaganda was also ruthlessly instrumental, a means–end rationale, as expounded in Franz J. Huber's *A Propaganda Primer* (1942).[121] For Goebbels, 'propaganda has no principles of its own. It has only one goal, and in politics that goal is always to conquer the masses. Any means to that end is good, and any means that does not serve that end is bad.' And results mattered: 'the propagandist never asks "why?" He needs no justification, but rather only this granite faith: I believe in the Führer, I believe in the Reich, and I believe in victory!'[122] No propaganda opportunity must be disregarded: for the dynamic, cynical Nazi propaganda functionary, even wounded soldiers represented merely another occasion to be exploited: they should for example visit hospitals and mollify the wounded with reading material and entertainment.[123] Goebbels was interested in teaching the methodology of propaganda 'to show practitioners the methods they can use to gradually gain power by winning the souls of the people'.[124] At the same time, this was no Academy of Propaganda. Goebbels said 'the methods of propaganda emerge in a causal sense out of the daily struggle. None of us is a born propagandist.'[125] Propaganda did not exist to vindicate conceptual abstraction: 'the art of politics is far removed from the dry theories of the desktop' and 'the sympathy of the people does not come of itself, it must be won'.[126] So while the emphasis was on pragmatism (National Socialism 'stems not from a desktop, but rather from real life'), Goebbels also believed that '[i]n the long-term, practical work is impossible unless it is supported by a programmatic theory, which in turn can find its methods and goals only from practice.'[127]

Nor was the aim ideological purity, since idealism without power was pointless: 'without power, no political platform will have historic significance'.[128] Ideology and practice were iterative in Goebbels's view insofar as they were mutually reinforcing parts of the same phenomenon. Propaganda translates ideology into popular language:

> Theoreticians found a political movement. Propagandists follow close behind. The theoreticians give a movement its intellectual foundations, the propagandists

put the programmatic content of the movement into the coinage of the people, and spread it to them. It would hardly be worthwhile to argue about who is most important in the struggle for power. The propagandist is nothing without the theorist, but the theorist is also nothing without the propagandist.[129]

Hence, for Goebbels, one of National Socialism's greatest achievements was the synthesis of ideology and propaganda.[130]

Goebbels consequently maintained that the essence was that the movement's message must be comprehended. Effectiveness was the criterion rather than social or intellectual respectability. As he said at Nuremberg in 1927: 'The essential characteristic of propaganda is effectiveness ... The complaints about the National Socialist movement come from bourgeois anxiety. People ... ask if we are not really Bolshevists.'[131]

Ideology is useless without agitation, the essence for example of Communist success: 'Lenin brought Marxism to the masses.' The text and its public exposition are two different things. Thus Goebbels claimed that:

> words were the foundation of the French Revolution, but if an agitator had not stood at his side his theory would have stumbled on the bookshelves. Marx's *Kapital* is the foundation of the Marxist movement. It would have remained book learning had not thousands of educators made it a political force. Lenin gave this philosophy political power, not Marx. Mussolini is both the philosopher and educator of fascist thinking.

Yet a speaker 'who has found a way to connect with the masses' is condemned as a demagogue.

Propaganda was no mere tool, as with other regimes, but an ethos which permeated all activities of life in the Third Reich: 'No other political movement has understood the art of propaganda as well as the National Socialists. From its beginnings, it has put heart and soul into propaganda.'[132] Propaganda had the distinction of being both the means and, in a real sense, the end. Its agenda went beyond securing mere passive acquiescence; it was in fact the production of an entirely new kind of man, National Socialist Man. Goebbels refers 'to an entirely new national way of thinking', his aim being the 'transformation of the character of the broad masses',[133] so the distinction between propaganda and education would in fact be abolished. The regime wanted not mere external compliance but internal fanaticism: it wanted the mind and the soul of its citizens and propaganda was the sorcery that would attain this. 'A world view does not govern the things of life, but rather the relationship of those things. The task of explaining this relationship in the details of public life, of persuading the broad masses of its desirability, is the task of political propaganda.'[134]

All of this of course speaks of great faith in the power of persuasion. Hitler and Goebbels had that faith. If they had not, if they had lacked it, the scale of their ambitions would not have made sense: 'We will gain power only with the people, not against them. They will join us when they feel as we do, when they are persuaded that what we want is correct.'[135] Propaganda 'must convince people of the necessity of our knowledge. It wins new fighters for the movement ... It makes members out of supporters and martyrs out of members.' The task of propaganda is to 'assist in the transformation of the character of the broad masses'.

Means/End

Hitler wrote in *Mein Kampf* that propaganda was a weapon of war, and should therefore be judged with regard to its end.[136] In other words, its content and ethical nature was subordinate to the importance of the objective it served. There was also a failure to distinguish between means and ends in the First World War, when the aim was 'the loftiest, the most overpowering, that men can conceive'—an elemental struggle for national existence. Such a struggle, so heroic but also so necessary, deserved a propaganda worthy of that cause, since it was a potential instrument of victory: 'when the nations on this planet fight for their very existence—when the question of destiny, "to be or not to be", cries out for solution, then all considerations of humanitarianism or ethics crumble into nothingness'. This is especially so if 'they might paralyse the struggling nation's power of self-presentation': that is to say, culture and humanity become a deficiency in time of war. He quotes Helmuth von Moltke, who claimed that in war humanity is brevity, 'and that means that the most aggressive fighting technique is the most humane'.

Influences on Nazi Theories of Persuasion

None of the theories that undergirded the Nazi propaganda ideology originated with Nazis. They came from elsewhere, from history, from revolutionaries and messiahs, pundits and charlatans, even from a local government boss. They borrowed everything and originated nothing. All of these theories were inscribed in *Mein Kampf.*

Mein Kampf

Hitler was enacting a theory of persuasion which he first promulgated in *Mein Kampf.* It is difficult to think of 'great' historical leaders—dictators, war lords, kings and their like—who theorised about the integuments of power or abstracted from this an idea of psychological process. A Caesar might write a *De Bello Gallico*, and though there are also various other memoirists, they offer little in the way of a theory of persuasion per se. Hitler was different. *Mein Kampf* is an incontinent bulk crammed with reflections, ruminations, biographical extracts and frenzied speculations. But, within its seething mass, there is a complete manual of propaganda, one which is focused, concise, harsh and pragmatic. Bracher wrote that:

> The central portions of *Mein Kampf*, and obviously those which interested [Hitler] the most, are devoted to propaganda techniques and mass persuasion; compared to them, the political and ideological portions are nothing but a collection of clichés and catchwords. Hitler doubtlessly owed his rise and the growth of the party to this preoccupation and to his unquestionable genius of mass persuasion. Later, he was able to find a most able assistant in Joseph Goebbels. He was pre-eminent in this area in his own party as well as among other groups of the radical right.[137]

It need hardly be said that Hitler was not an original thinker. He was the collator and organiser of the intellectual spasms of others, the seeker and sorter of myriad ideas, crackpot obsessions and rhetorical flights of fancy: he sorted through the vast debris of nineteenth- and earlier twentieth-century charlatans, thinkers, polemicists, demagogues and failed visionaries. From a tumult of noise he produced a single baleful rhythm: what he added was the coherence of synthesis and system. According to Ross, Hitler's work was 'like most of his supposedly original insights on propaganda, no more than a characteristically brazen way of putting a widely held view'.[138] Hitler was no more than a beachcomber, picking up the ideas around him and forcing them into a coherent structure. He claimed that propaganda had always been his interest ever since he started thinking about politics. For him it was an art form, one which the bourgeois parties rejected out of cultural snobbery. One Teutonic exemplum he cites, however, is the Christian Social movement of Karl Lueger in Vienna, which was successful precisely because it actively propagandised. Elsewhere propaganda was a tool of the left: 'I saw that the socialist Marxist organisations mastered and applied this instrument with outstanding skill.'[139] However, for Hitler, it was the First World War which truly demonstrated the immense potential of propaganda, and the poverty of Germany's propaganda drive outraged him:

There again, unfortunately, all our studying had to be done on the enemy side, that the activity on our side was modest, to say the least. The total miscarriage of the German 'enlightenment' service stared every soldier in the face, and this spurred me to take up the question of propaganda even more deeply than before.[140]

Particularly influential were the writings and practice of Wagner, Lenin, Gobineau, Nietzsche, Ludendorff, Northcliffe, Mussolini, Schopenhauer and Lueger.[141] Goebbels also listed those that he saw as the great propagandists in history, such as Alexander, Caesar, Robespierre, Danton, Mussolini, Lenin, Buddha, Christ and Muhammad.[142] Hitler additionally drew much inspiration from the SPD's mobilisation efforts before and after the war, for in Wilhelmine Germany the Social Democrats had sponsored a vast public literature including an 'aggressive and scandal-mongering' press.[143] But in those early years before the First World War the left by no means enjoyed a monopoly of political evangelism. Among the semi-official organisations fostered by the imperial government were the radical nationalists; for example, the Navy League, a pressure group, offered films from 1901, and by 1905 it had supervised over 1,500 screenings on topics both naval and general.[144]

As well as British wartime propaganda, Hitler attributed his inspiration to post-war Communist agitation propaganda.[145] The early days of the Bolshevik Revolution were very innovative in propaganda terms: parades, effigies, luminous posters, feature films and cinema trains jostled for public attention in a mighty national theatrical struggle, which underpinned the military struggle of the civil war and the economic struggle to sovietise the economy. There were German witnesses to this, latterly also the Germans who saw these things as a result of Soviet–Weimar links (Weimar had bases in Russia and trained its fledgling air force there, as well as Reichswehr General von Seeckt's army). Then there were the German Communists, fraternal visitors to the Soviet Union who borrowed and reinterpreted propaganda techniques from which the Nazis in turn learned, for there in Russia was a working contemporary model of how a state could be run on propaganda lines. There were other recent examples to draw from, including German prototypes; the virulent propaganda of the First World War ultra-nationalist German Fatherland Party and even the derided (but extensive) propaganda machinery of the late imperial Ludendorff–Hindenburg duumvirate and their authoritarian imperial state of 1917–18.

Contribution of Le Bon

While then there were many sources, multiple inspirations, for the idea of founding a regime on the serial production of convulsive emotion, there is one source that stands out. It is (as aforementioned) the late nineteenth-century work by Le Bon, *The Crowd*;[146] in the hands of Hitler it became part of government philosophy. It should first be said that the crowd as Le Bon conceives it is by no means necessarily the physical crowd: 'thousands of isolated individuals may at certain moments, and under the influence of certain violent emotions—such, for example, as a great national event—have the characteristics of a psychological crowd'. He claims that a group of just six men could be considered a psychological crowd. An entire nation can become a crowd. In this work he sometimes appears to believe that the crowd is really the mass body of the nation, our collective consciousness, that is, the flippant, fickle and evanescent public opinion, so cruel in its judgements, so fantastic in its imagining. And while the 'crowd' in the Nazi context was indeed often a physical crowd—the lined streets, the thronged auditoria—inclusion within that crowd was now achieved via projection (i.e. the documentary and the wireless transmission).

Le Bon anticipated the mass embrace of Adolf Hitler when he evoked the psychology of the collective mind. He argued that crowds think, feel and act differently from isolated individuals. Heterogeneity is briefly integrated, and in this process individualism is undermined—'the heterogeneous is swamped by the homogeneous, and the unconscious qualities obtain the upper hand'. Le Bon might have been anticipating the rise of Hitler when he described how the appetite for disorder is replaced by yearning for strong authority: 'abandoned to themselves, they soon weary of disorder, and instinctively turn to servitude. It was the proudest and most untractable of the Jacobins who acclaimed Bonaparte with the greatest energy when he suppressed all liberty and made his hand of iron severely felt.' He would also have understood the Nazi synthetic of tradition. For Le Bon asserted that crowds have a primitive conservatism, 'their fetish-like respect for all traditions is absolute; their unconscious horror of all novelty capable of changing the essential conditions of their existence is very deeply rooted'. The crowd as Le Bon sees it is not necessarily amoral, indeed it can be supermoral; the real point Le Bon makes is that its emotions are extreme, 'feminine', the slaves of impulse: it 'knows neither doubt nor uncertainty' and possesses no sense of responsibility, so that its rages have no limiting mechanism.

Le Bon's work illuminates Hitler's success in constructing an existential threat (Communists, Jews, Anglo-American plutocracy), for while crowds exaggerate, they tend to exaggerate more in a highly negative direction: 'these sentiments are atavistic residuum of the instincts of the primitive man, which the fear of punishment obliges the isolated and responsible individual to curb'. Thus Le Bon had argued that the crowd will reject all discussion, all contrary opinion—crowds react immediately with 'howls of fury and violent invective'. The crowd's beliefs are created by suggestion not reason. Such works as this, and their proclaimed 'science', essentially denied the mass the ability to rationalise (as collectives, rather than individuals); the mass was emotional/regressive/atavistic, so that the rational individual was irrationalised by his crowd membership. This in turn appealed to the despair of the highest social orders about social change, while later authors took this view of an irrational public further, stressing how it could be manipulated through the use of the mass media.[147]

Lessons from the British

Bracher framed the effectiveness of Nazi propaganda in terms of its continuity of First World War tradition. He argues that against a background of turbulent instability Nazi propaganda worked 'precisely because it was a radical continuation and an even more imbalanced exaggeration of the wartime propaganda', and thus 'its arguments, in so far as they did not derive from prewar radicalism, drew largely on the arsenal of war and enemy propaganda'.[148] Hitler's skills lay in hijacking existing models and fabricating a new synthesis:

> It will not do, however, to stress only his oratorical and propaganda talents, to endow them with an almost daemonical quality as some are wont to do. Hitler himself made a point of saying how great a debt he owed to the lessons he learned from the propaganda of World War I. He maintained that the allies, particularly the British, were far superior to the Central Powers in this respect, and that their victory was largely due to that superiority.[149]

This perspective, consistent with Hitler's Teutonic chauvinism, deflects explanation of defeat away from the military. The war memoirs of Ludendorff (1919) fomented this myth: 'before the enemy propaganda we were like a rabbit before a snake ... The propagandists were clever in understanding the effects of such phrases as "a peace without victors or vanquished", "post-war disarmament", "League of Nations", and so on, on the German people.'[150] Hitler's model was Lloyd George, whom he praised for his 'psychological masterpieces in the art of mass propaganda which had made his people serve his will completely'.[151] Lloyd George was successful due to the 'primitiveness of his language, the primordiality of its forms of expression, and the use of easily intelligible examples of the simplest sort'.[152]

Thus in Hitler's view propaganda was more than a mere instrument, more than a battlefield weapon: it was a mystical essence, the route into a nation's soul. In *Mein Kampf* he praises the enemy's effort, as he says, 'for what we failed to do, the enemy did, with amazing skill and really brilliant calculation'. This is an anathema on the negligence of the old regime, its failure in the aspiration to modernity, and all these themes are echoed by Goebbels. The propaganda is quite simply the new medium of leadership, in peace and war: 'there was often more than enough time to think, and the enemy offered practical instruction which, to our sorrow, was only too good'. Among other things, the First World War was for Adolf Hitler a protracted tutorial in the conceptual framework and methodology of aggressive propaganda; 'did we have anything you could call propaganda? I regret that I must answer in the negative.' And yet the Germans did not learn from this: 'the time passed and left no trace in the minds of all those who should have benefitted; partly because they considered themselves too clever ...'[153] There is then this identification of antagonism to propaganda with the cultural snobbery of the German elite of the old order—this is implicit in all Hitler writes about the subject. German efforts could even have the reverse effect to that intended: 'Everything that actually was done in this field was so inadequate and wrong from the very start that it certainly did no good and sometimes did actual harm.'[154] Part of the reason for this substantial error was a failure of insight into the psychology behind mass persuasion, whether of the citizens or indeed of the citizen army. Party loyalists did of course reflect these views. In 1932 the propaganda theorist Hans Thimme argued that 'this breakdown became more profound and widespread and took on the character of a mutiny and of self-lacerations due to the decisive contribution of enemy propaganda'.[155] Eugen Hadamovsky, another Nazi propaganda theorist, writes of the Allies that 'their propaganda succeeded in spreading the fateful belief that by accepting voluntary defeat, by laying down arms', Germans would be justly treated.[156] But German writers forgot the impact of war weariness and social division. It was these factors that made people receptive to the Allied message.

It must also be said that not everyone was as convinced as the future Führer of the ineptitude of German First World War propaganda. Thus a 'neutral' self-consciously informed *The Times*:

> There was not one film showing to give any idea of the work of the British Army or the British Navy. The whole audience looked forward to the antics of one Charlie Chaplin. I could not but compare a similar scene at a great picture theatre in Germany, where prices have lowered and parents are entitled to take their

children free; where all soldiers enter free, and all wounded free, in order that the nation may obtain, from ocular demonstration, information on the one national topic—the war.[157]

The 'neutral' purported to find this contrast 'unpleasant'.[158] In a similar vein, the pro-German paper *Continental Times*, targeted at Americans in Europe, commented about the absence of British sensationalism in Germany:

> it must be remembered that none of the frantic style of advertising which recently took place in England where the entire country was placarded with screaming posters, papers crowded with over-wrought and hyper-sensational advertisements, imploring, admonishing or cajoling the people, and statesmen like Bonar Law even using threats of coercion if people did not subscribe. Here all has been done quietly.[159]

But this is presumably what Hitler was complaining about.

Hitler's two chapters on propaganda in *Mein Kampf* simply reflected the conventional nationalist wisdom.[160] It was not that simple: General Ludendorff in particular had recognised the essential role of propaganda in improving morale. Indeed, he believed that propaganda was so important that it should be treated as a branch of military strategy.[161] His perspective anticipates the fusion of propaganda with military values in the Second World War, for he wrote that 'good propaganda must keep well ahead of actual political events. It must act as pacemaker to policy and mould public opinion without appearing to do so. Before political aims are translated into action, the world has to be convinced of their necessity and moral justification.'[162] He recognised that the army high command was 'losing the battle for public opinion at home', and he 'held the view that official propaganda should be employed more scientifically to uphold morale and exhort the population to fight on'.[163] Thus, according to the propaganda expert David Welch also, the *Mein Kampf* narrative exaggerated the ineptitude of the imperial propaganda effort: 'in fact the second Reich was aware of the need to employ propaganda and established an impressive organisational apparatus that furthered the dissemination of official propaganda. Reich officials lacked, however, a sophisticated appreciation of the relationship between the dissemination of propaganda and its reception by different publics.'[164]

British manipulation and hypocrisy

For Goebbels, the British methodologies in particular were material for outraged public posturing, but they also constituted a prototype to be copied as well as an immoral exemplum to be exposed. Like Hitler he was inspired both by the wartime British and by the post-war Communist agit-prop. As Goebbels presents it, the British were cruel and cunning. It was German high culture which blinded them to the Britons' low guile, fracturing German solidarity by setting the people against the regime. The British were thus seen as the supreme propagandists; the elder Germany was naive, innocents in a harsh world with no antidote to this mesmerism. Goebbels believed that British power rested on an amalgam of ruthlessness and propaganda skill, leavened by hypocrisy. His message was that the Nazis had adopted the same devices but to an even greater extreme. To Goebbels, the British presented a façade: 'they do not only behave as if they were the model of piety and virtue—they really believe that they are. That is both amusing and dangerous'; they perceived their success as a sign of divine providence yet they were fully prepared to land a low blow when necessary. Germans by contrast were a Culture Nation, a benign, philosophical people: 'we were a harmless people who went about our business, giving the world our poets, musicians, and philosophers, never realizing that there were other nations just waiting for the opportunity to knock us flat'.[165]

Global Impact of British First World War Propaganda

The Nazis also believed that the British propaganda campaign in the First World War was not merely impactful, but that it actually succeeded in turning the entire world against Germany. In other words, it was propaganda that had won the war for the British. Schulze-Wechsungen claimed that German 'leaders realised too late the power and effects of this modern weapon, a weapon without limits, that thunders more loudly than cannon fire, that is more destructive than a gas attack'.[166] According to Goebbels: 'Then England got moving. English propaganda turned the whole world against us. One had not thought them capable of it. The experts found its planning and execution brilliant. English propaganda was limited to a few powerful slogans.'[167] These slogans were incendiary: 'There were really only a few slogans that the English spread throughout the world. They spoke of children's hands chopped off, eyes poked out, women raped, and old people tortured.' British propaganda was global in impact: Goebbels said that years of anti-German polemic had convinced the world of German barbarism and of the imperative to obliterate the German entity.[168] The Nazis internalised such lessons about the power of the atrocious image, for example in the illustrated weeklies' exposure, in graphic pictography, of the full horror of the Katyn massacre. Northcliffe, Britain's propaganda minister under Lloyd George, had portrayed Germans as 'child molesting beasts', and he understood the importance of the union of image (e.g. a photograph of a German soldier) with caption ('and then hordes of the Kaiser's child-murderers arrived').[169]

The effect of Allied atrocity propaganda on American opinion in the First World War can be gauged from J.D. Squire's account:

fired by such notions about the behaviour of the enemy and by others equally absurd, the American people launched themselves into the war with an emotional hysteria that can only be understood by realising the power of propaganda in generating common action by a nation under belligerent conditions. Those who did not accept the war ideology were usually few in number and always quite impotent. The almost primitive ecstasy that could sometimes grip the American people has recently been summarised in unforgettable fashion ... We hated with a common hate that was exhilarating. The writer of this review remembers attending a great meeting in New England, held under the auspices of a Christian church—God save the mark! The speaker demanded that the Kaiser, when captured, be boiled in oil, and the entire audience stood on chairs to scream its hysterical approval. This was the mood we were in. This was the kind of madness that had seized us.[170]

Yet Hitler did not see, or refused to see, the obvious truth that the German military's treatment of enemy civilians handed repeated propaganda victories to its adversaries in the First World War; he approved of what the British called 'Prussian frightfulness':

the old Reich knew already how to act with firmness in the occupied areas. That's how attempts to sabotage the railways in Belgium were punished by Count von der Goltz. He had all the villages burnt within a radius of several kilometres, after having had all the mayors shot, the men imprisoned and the women and children evacuated. There were three or four acts of violence in all, then nothing more happened.[171]

One official French report summarised the 'frightfulness' with this claim:

The greater part of the devilry in the Vosges seems to have been the work of Bavarians. At Gerbewiller they proceeded to avenge their losses on the civilian population. They burst into the houses, shooting, stabbing, and capturing the inhabitants—sparing neither age nor sex—and burning and sacking the houses. A woman aged 78 was shot and her body afterwards shamefully profaned.[172]

Insidious Briton and innocent German

Goebbels claimed the British drove a wedge between the German people and their government by advertising their quarrel as with the government alone and not the German people. They repeatedly used this sly trick: 'During the last months of the war, England attempted to hammer into the minds of the German population the idea that it was fighting our government, not us.'[173] It was a case of their lies and German naivety:

> The Allies' only demand was to replace the Kaiser with a republic, after which peace with honour would follow for everyone. These stupid lies were brewed by the English. Wilson was simply the Foreign Office's loudspeaker. And good old Germany believed what England got the Americans to say. We fell into the trap.

Again this demonstrates the German diagnosis of their failure as a failure of propaganda—the orthodox wisdom, not just Goebbels's private opinion. Yet it represents a very incomplete, determinedly naive, understanding of the reasons for their defeat in 1918. But it was a convenient myth, exonerating the military and celebrating the methodology of propaganda that was bringing the Nazis to power.

The continuity of an obsession: German beliefs about British propaganda in the Second World War

The German obsession with the First World War, and the dominant idea that the British had won it through propaganda, continued, and it even seemed to dictate the terms of the Second: the journalist and Nazi propagandist Winkelnkemper observed 'What worsens the guilt of England's leading circle is the fact that it knew how to conduct systematic hate propaganda aimed at Germany's annihilation.'[174] Again the British lie: during the war Goebbels wrote that 'England's swindle today is just as blatant, dirty, and impudent as it was back then. They think we are as dumb today as we were then.'[175] The aim of British propaganda was to sabotage loyalty: 'Today the English newspapers openly write that the task of English propaganda is to drive a wedge between the German people and its leadership.' The British, in this view, were craven and manipulative: 'They want to split Hitler and the nation. Naturally they find hypocritical and smooth-sounding arguments, just as they did during the Kaiser's day.'[176] What is perhaps extraordinary is the latent superstition about British propaganda that such rhetoric demonstrates. Britain, to the Nazis, was always the 'civilisation' which had betrayed them:

> those civilized nations that even after the end of the war allowed millions of mothers and children to starve, that sent Negroes to bring culture to the Rhine, that shot Schlageter, stole our colonies, exploited Germany, and coldly and cyni-

cally broke their most solemn promises to us, the promises the German people had been deceived by.[177]

We defend ourselves

Goebbels was proud of the dynamic aggression of his propaganda war against Britain, for his was a mastery of that art of polemical violence at which the British themselves had once excelled. For him in particular, Britain in the Second World War was a manufactory of propaganda, spitting out its bile from a face flushed with humbug: 'and we now have ways to defend ourselves against London's lies once the English propaganda machine moves into high gear. It floods the public with scare after scare, spreading countless lies with the most pious expression.' The best form of defence was attack: 'We are defending ourselves, even counterattacking as is the National Socialist custom. And how! Our counterattack is powerful, and hits dead center.'[178] The Nazis, Goebbels claimed, were beating the British at their own game. Propaganda was the British weapon which the Nazis had taken and made their own: 'They are being surpassed in an area in which they once were the undisputed master. The National Socialist movement has taught the German nation not only to defend against propaganda, but to use it itself.' Nazi propaganda represented not just a belief system but a blazing faith: 'We defend an idea that fills us with holy conviction, and we wield a propaganda that hits its target, that is experienced and hardened by battle. We use this spiritual weapon with pleasure and enthusiasm.'[179]

Limitations of Nazi Theory

The propagandists did not have it all their own way and we are much mistaken if we imagine Nazi Germany to have been a nation only of fanatics. There were the convinced, the semi-convinced and the doubters; one could in fact have been in all three categories through the lifetime of the Reich. The Nazis were the most electorally successful of all Europe's Fascist parties yet they never garnered more than 37 per cent of the vote.[180] As Allen points out in his scholarly study of the German town of Northeim, despite the arrogant supposition that they could challenge and change the nature of humanity, the Nazi leaders were forced to settle for external compliance rather than internalised commitment.[181]

But they also recognised the limitations of propaganda, in that it is predicated on political results. As Schulze-Wechsungen noted, 'it is clear that even the best propaganda cannot conceal constant political failures'.[182] Even racialist propaganda had its limitations. The masses adored Jesse Owens.[183] Nazi propaganda was always just one competitor in the battle for attention, and there were powerful rivals even during the war. As Paxton has suggested, 'the effect of fascist propaganda also needs to be compared with that of commercial media, which was clearly greater even in fascist countries. Hollywood, Madison Avenue probably gave more trouble to fascist dreams of cultural control than the whole liberal and socialist opposition put together.'[184] Then there was the acknowledged tedium of much of the propaganda. Nazi Germany had inherited (perhaps) the most creative film industry in the world, and yet Shirer for example remembered the hissing of German films. Eric Rentschler, an authority on Nazi cinema, asks, 'but how was one to explain repeated instances of derisive laughter at melodramas and films that hardly set out to be funny?'; in Rentschler's view, out of sync laughter is a potential terrorist in the dark, someone who refuses to let the film cast its spell.[185] Kershaw stresses the fragility of Hitler's charisma, for example the disillusion with him after he rejected the president's offer of the vice chancellorship in August 1932; and that year the Nuremberg auditorium was half empty.[186] And according to the propaganda scholar Robert Edwin Herzstein, Goebbels's early wartime propaganda was not particularly successful; some of it was disastrous.[187]

Morale ultimately deteriorated when victories did not materialise into Victory. Bytwerk describes the experience of one party member during one day in 1943 when he saluted over fifty people with the 'Heil!'; only two returned it.[188] Propaganda, hubristic and exuberant though it was, became part of the problem. Kershaw observes: 'the loss of confidence which set in after Stalingrad was not least a consequence of the totally misleading and frightfully mendacious German propaganda which had preceded the catastrophe'.[189] Kershaw records that party functionaries were heard to say that it would be better if Goebbels stopped writing and speaking altogether, as they 'could not live up to expectations created by propaganda'; its impact was at this stage temporary. Yet around half of the German population was unwilling to even think about unconditional surrender until the very end.[190] Many were still with Hitler right until the end of the war (Germany had to be re-conquered, sometimes street by street), and even beyond the end— there were those guiltless of many war crimes who chose to follow him into the oblivion of suicide. Another criticism, well articulated by Harold Nicolson MP, was that German propaganda brought short-term impact at the cost of long-term credibility:

the German propaganda method is based upon seizing immediate advantages with complete disregard of the truth or of their credit. Our method is the slower and more long-term method of establishing confidence. For the moment, the Goebbels method is the more successful. In the end ours will prove decisive.[191]

And there are more general criticisms of a thesis which endorses the Nazis' own model of hegemonic political control via the enthronement of propaganda. Agnostic perspectives would thus focus on:

The enigma of interpretation. Since interpretation cannot be standardised, the impact of propaganda can never be predicted: in no way does intent foreordain reception, and individuals always possess internal intellectual autonomy even if they offer external compliance. For example, the well-known anti-Semitic film *Jud Süss*, about an insidious adviser (Süss) to a monarch (duke of Württemberg), elicited variable interpretations and many felt the duke equally blameworthy as Süss Oppenheim.[192]

The corrosion of scepticism. The subject cannot be manipulated into persistent irrationality: the perceptual chasm between the edited neo-realities of propaganda and the experiential truths of life as it is lived may be managed but they cannot be concealed. Hence wartime scepticism set in early because of the diminished novelty value of the heroic-polemic but also because of a 'growing sense that the newsreels were far less authentic than they appear'; despite this 'admissions continued at record levels throughout the war'.[193]

Subversion. A message can be spontaneously subverted: even loyalists may be incredulous. There is the example of a newsreel (February 1940) which was 'widely regarded as staged', soldiers in the cinema audience laughed when the camera advanced ahead of a reconnaissance patrol.[194]

User-gratification. German audiences were 'still active, critical users of mass media and could largely take what they wanted' and thus imperatives were in conflict: 'intention and effect were thus difficult to harmonise'.[195] The political gloss when it occurred 'was often little more than pious windowdressing, and indeed was perceived as such by participants and officials alike'—people could plunder the entertainment while ignoring the political message.[196]

Exhaustion. Targets for persuasion can be hectored into indifference; for example after the November 1932 elections even the Nazis realised that 'their propaganda had largely exhausted its possibilities'.[197] And of September 1932 Evans observes that 'many of the meetings [where] Hitler spoke were now half empty, and that the many campaigns of the year had left the party in no financial condition to sustain its propaganda effort at the level of the previous election' (the attacks on von Papen also alienated the middle class, as did the Nazis joining the Berlin transport workers' strike).[198] Moreover, 'the once novel propaganda methods of the party had now become familiar to all. Goebbels had nothing left up his sleeve to startle the electorate with.'[199]

Rejection. There can also be straight rejection, the mere dismissal of the message in its entirety. Ross makes the critical point that *Triumph of the Will*, the most famous propaganda film in history, ran for only three days in Berlin and according to SPD agents managed 'only a very slight attraction'.[200] The grossness of the regime could even provoke rebellion, and thus Goebbels withdrew the Hitler-ordained film of the trial of the conspirators (*Trial Before the People's Court*, summer 1944: see Chapter Two), since it had incited walkouts by the military.[201]

All of this is merely to demonstrate that Nazi propaganda was not invincible and that the Reich could miscalculate because the ideology was, in the end, monstrous. As to whether all this persuasion was causal or merely decorative, I have advocated a perspective: events are seldom inherently deterministic and they have to be 'sold', their meanings made vivid, via all the gathered powers of eloquence or pictography—whether by Marat in the French Revolution, Lenin in the Russian or Churchill in 1940. There is here none of that finality one might seek because this is part of a much greater debate about the role of persuasion in history.

Conclusions

Nazi propaganda was a manual of persuasion, and the influence of the pop psychology of the day such as its notions of 'suggestion' was clearly present: people were assaulted directly but they were also seduced indirectly. Nazism did not ask for belief but for surrender—not through coercion, primarily, but by assaulting consciousness. The essential aim was the extinction of independent thought via images that would now think for you.

Hitler understood, as few others had ever done, the need for the serial creation of enemies. He was a political entrepreneur, possessed of the truly devastating insight that all recent enemies could eventually merge into the one super-enemy, the Jews. Here was an intuitive understanding of how self-definition is achieved through other-rejection, that solidarity, identity and community are in essence gained at the expense of others and appeals based on the brotherhood of man (as, in a sense, even Communism did) would always ultimately fail. This construction of tribal passion could arouse the emotions and therefore render people vulnerable to any kind of visionary persuasion or invocation to epic quest. Yet the seeming ease with which Germans 'went along' with, or ostensibly ignored, the true frauds such as the so-called Polish 'attack' of 1 September 1939 continues to astonish. But such a response is complicated by Germans' powerful need to believe, their faith, which dismissive terms like naivety or credulity do not effectively capture. This belongs in fact to another conceptual domain.

PART TWO

A PROPAGANDA TRINITY

4

MYTHOLOGIES

INVENTING THE THIRD REICH

The Jews are guilty! ... The Jews are guilty!

Joseph Goebbels

A propagandist is a man who canalises an already existing stream. In a land where there is no water, he digs in vain.

Aldous Huxley

The Idea of Myth

This chapter is about the myth system—inherited, reinterpreted or self-created—that underpinned the Nazi propaganda machine. It argues that myth is a core integument of any effective propaganda strategy. The chapter also explains how the Nazis exploited history and tradition as a source of their mythologies, and explores how their myth-making system perverted these ancestral narratives for their own apocalyptic ends.

The Nazis did not necessarily see themselves as Jacobins, or disruptive saboteurs, but instead reached back to an imagined past, a utopian order, which the recent inheritors of power had violated. They restored old truths; they were not true revolutionaries as popularly understood, since theirs was a radicalism of reaction. Revolutionaries such as these promote a concept of the former regime as in itself revolutionary: the overthrown civic order is viewed or publicly portrayed not as traditional and founded in heritage but as itself subversive. This would be true of the English and American Revolutions and perhaps many other revolutions as well. Thus rebellion is presented by its sponsors as regression rather than revolution. For example, England's 'Glorious Revolution' of 1688 may indeed be seen as a reaction against the reforming zealotry of James II, who sought to impose the kind of modern bureaucratic state that existed in the France of Louis XIV.[1] The idea of something lost being retrieved from a mythological past is important for retro-revolutionaries.

The power of myth is the power of narrative. A myth is a story rather than a sequence of ideas or principles, and myths project their truths via narrative rather than by didacticism or exhortation. To understand a society's myths is to understand that society. In Schöpflin's words, 'myth creates an intellectual and cognitive monopoly in that it seeks to establish the sole way of ordering the world and defining world-views'.[2] A myth is 'the master-narrative, the way in which societies achieve self-perpetuation, in fact their mode of reproduction. Powerful myths are more effective than powerful defence. When myths survive, so do [the] societies that successfully incubated them.' In the view of Le Bon, history itself is simply a mythological chronicle since it is 'scarcely capable of preserving the memory of anything except myths'.[3]

Myth is the sound of a culture's dialogue with itself. Myths can be simply rendered and that is part of their charm as well as their political usability; myths do not require a complex system of visual rendition such as sophisticated language—their core essence or meaning can be transmitted by a mere sign. Under the Third Reich, symbols and the mythologies they encoded were often ancient and classic, as in the case of the most important symbol, the swastika, which was of ancient South Asian Buddhist origin. If it was not inappropriate to say this, one could suggest that the myth/symbol systems of Nazism amounted to a postmodernist bricolage.

Sources of Nazi Mythology

History and tradition

The primary sources for the mythologies that so defined the Nazi propaganda culture were history and tradition. There was much else, as we shall see, including the clutter of philosophies, prejudices and pseudo-sciences that nourished the production of myths. The purpose of these myths was to demonstrate the party's legitimacy by anchoring everything it did in the past, in custom, in the national story as re-imagined by the Nazis.

What, then, is a myth? The historian and philosopher Mircea Eliade sees a myth as 'an account of the events which took place in principio, that is, in the beginning, in a primordial and non-temporal instant, a moment of sacred time'.[4] The Nazis plundered the surface of German history and tradition for their mythological symbols and narratives, and what they produced was inauthentic, endowing these with an entirely new and ahistorical meaning. In their revolution there was an appetite for the new, but also a need to connect with the past and return to what previous regimes had shamefully neglected. Part of this involved reclaiming the supposed historic role of the *Volk* in German society. Rebirth was racial, geopolitical, missionary and irredentist; history was both a source of legitimation and an idea of the future.[5] The use of already familiar symbols gave Nazism the comfort blanket of tradition and continuity, despite the fact that it was actually the antithesis of a conservative movement. Things looked familiar, or they seemed so because they bore a familial resemblance. As Schöpflin once observed, 'the past is not therefore an escape from the present but legitimates it by showing the ostensibly unchanging nature of people and by illuminating antecedent causes'.[6] For Duncan Webster, populist movements tend to employ rhetoric as part of their strategic mobilisation of the past, and it should be seen as about more than mere nostalgia[7]— myth must take from existing elements of the culture, from the collectivity that created it, for it arises out of the culture and is not a graft of alien flesh.

The Third Reich consequently teemed with myths—a complex of mythologies integrated into a coherence. Figures from the past were conscripted in the cause of pan-Germanism and hyper-nationalism, such as the Prussian hero of the Napoleonic wars, General Field Marshal Gneisenau (who was in fact a liberal), or Frederick the Great, who once remarked that German was the language one spoke to one's horses and whose Prussian army contained seven regiments of soldiers who spoke Slavic languages (i.e. were *Untermenschen*).[8] Another tributary to the mighty sea of Nazi myth was the idea and legend of Prussia, the heroic state that had vanquished Austria to become hegemon of all Germandom and which had survived and matured in the face of great adversity and hostile adversaries. The ethos of old Prussia was something the Nazis claimed and caricatured, for central to it were ideas of discipline and superordinate loyalty to the state, expressed above all in terms of military service: the individual existed to serve the state, not the other way around. Be loyal and honest until your cold grave, these words of the Prussian poet Ludwig Hölty (1748–76) summoned the essence of ideal Prussianism. The Nazis turned Prussia into an anticipation of the Third Reich, a proto-Nazi state as in the crowd-choric singing at the beginning of the film *Kolberg*. It had in fact been nothing of the kind.

The medieval in particular was a source of myth reinforcement via aesthetic form and symbolic reference, and this attributed-Germanism of the medieval past represented a search for rootedness and authenticity. Thus the ubiquitous Gothic lettering was symbolic of continuity with the greatness of a Germany that had been, a Germany that had given birth to Gutenberg. Gothic script was routinely used as packaging, and hence a regime which made wonder weapons of destruction also spoke in medieval accents. Print therefore became ideological, with *Der Stürmer* and *Der Angriff*, for instance, purveying their respective vitriol in a typeface based on that which had been used in the Gutenberg Bible (Hitler eventually abolished the use of Gothic idiom in 1941 when it was discovered that Gothic script had been polluted by Hebraic writing).[9] The mythology reflected the underlying incoherence of Nazi ideology. But this was emotional logic, so internal contradictions were irrelevant. The posters, for example, transferred Germans to a magical realm away from the everyday. They melded the medieval and the modern, heroes and autobahns and ancient high-gabled townhouses, knights in armour, statistics and pictograms, futurism combined with the sham archaic. They celebrated a Technopolis; cars, roads and the machinery of war. Yet they were also anchored in a rural idiom where land was a source of meaning and virtue, and the soil was sanctified.

Folkloric

Most myth systems also contain folkloric elements, such as the idea of a cosmic conflict between good and evil, of devils and the diabolic, and the Nazis were no exception to this general rule. These elements merged with history-derived myths such as those of the Teutonic Knights, conquerors of the East and the Slavs, and ancient German myths such as that of King Frederick Barbarossa who sleeps with his knights beneath a mountain to await Germany's most terrible hour of need (the name of course was applied to the conquest of the USSR, Operation Barbarossa). Arnold Perris has suggested that:

> perhaps nationalism, like race, is a utopian myth of purification, and nationalist expressions of propaganda share commonalities of mythic structure: in Smetana's Blanik the hero sleeps in the halls, one day to re-awaken with the

nation. Sleeping, also, is Wagner's Kaiser Frederick Barbarossa, an anticipation of the Führer concept.[10]

The mythology of a leader as Hitler conceived it derived not from one source but from the accumulated lore and debris of civilisations. As well as the Messiah, there was the Nietzschean notion of the Superman, and the thaumaturgic (i.e. possessed of magical powers) monarchs of the middle ages,[11] although the Ministry of Propaganda drew the line at plans for a new Nordic religion centred on the Thingstätte, an open-air auditoria for rituals and plays.[12] The rituals and the mythological structure of Christianity could be plagiarised since they represented cultural commonalities. This was the deep structure upon which new myths could be based—the holy text (*Mein Kampf*), the hymn-like unison group choral singing, didacticism, ritual and the idea of consecration (the 'blood banner') or mystic transmission of a spiritual essence. And martyr myths were the very flavour and pith of the Nazi myth system; hence Goebbels searched eagerly for martyrs and found them, desperate men made heroic by the metamorphosis of Nazi martyrology.

Another source of Nazi myth was their claimed kinship with the classic world. In sculpture especially, the classic forms and styles and subject matter were slavishly emulated, though the countenances of these retrieved forms betray a neuroticism, a psychotic rage even, that is thoroughly modern. Such a connection was not merely cultural but racial. The beginning of Leni Riefenstahl's great film of the 1936 Games, *Olympia* (1938), establishes a patrimonial link between Germany and ancient Greece: 'the Reich was not only the present home of the Olympics, but the true repository for all the virtues of the ancient Greeks'.[13] Similarly, Dr Theodor Lewald, the president of the German Olympic Committee who was himself partly Jewish (and subsequently ousted), articulated the orthodox party view of Germany's relationship with classical antiquity, speaking of 'a real and spiritual bond between the German fatherland and the sacred places of Greece founded nearly 4000 years ago by Nordic immigrants'.[14] Hence the Nazis claimed ethnic as well as cultural derivation from Greece and Rome.[15]

Bettina Arnold reminds us that the Nazis had a venerable prototype to follow:

The first-century Roman historian Tacitus produced an essay titled 'On the origin and geography of Germany'. It is less a history or ethnography of the German tribes than a moral tract or political treatise. The essay was intended to contrast the debauched and degenerate Roman Empire with the virtuous German people, who embodied the uncorrupted morals of old Rome. Objective reporting was not the goal of Tacitus's Germania; the manipulation of the facts was considered justified if it had the desired effect of contrasting past Roman glory with present Roman decline. Ironically, this particular piece of historical propaganda was eventually appropriated by a machine notorious for its use and abuse of the past for political, imperialist, and racialist purposes: the Third Reich.[16]

Beyond that classical world lay the Teutonic pre-historical one. There were the German primitives who summoned 'a unique German-pagan pre-history whose heroic tradition was broken by Rome and Christian influences', and the work of Wagner similarly sought to forge national symbols based on a romantic representation of a barbaric-heroic Teutonic past.[17] Under the Reich, history and archaeology were essentially myth-making disciplines, the task of which was to justify the present by rearranging the past. As Himmler said:

> the one and only thing that matters to us, and the thing these people are paid for by the state, is to have ideas of history that strengthen our people in their necessary national pride. In all this troublesome business we are only interested in one thing—to project into the dim and distant past the picture of our nation as we envisage it for the future. Every bit of Tacitus in his Germania is tendentious stuff. Our teaching of German origins has depended for centuries on a falsification. We are entitled to impose one of our own at any time.[18]

One site excavated by the SS Ahnenerbe, an organisation set up to investigate the archaeological and cultural origins of the Aryan race, was depicted in the literature as a symbol of the nation's unity and the splendours of its past. But there was actually no evidence of any German occupation of the site, let alone a temple, even though the Ahnenerbe chose to believe that solar worshippers had once gathered there.[19]

Nationalist

Another perennial function of myths was to flatter the vanities of German nationhood and ethno-chauvinism, to celebrate the self-gratifying idea of a unique people. Moreover, since Germans were not just a national but a pan-national grouping, Europe's roving tribe, they needed an identity that was portable and not merely located in a geographic territory. Myth supplied this. R.J.W. Evans speaks of 'an itinerant urge that marked out Germans as Europe's greatest internal migrants until their steps were gradually re-directed in modern times towards the New World' (the Transylvanian Saxons, for example).[20] East Prussia, that 'far-flung realm of Germandom', was conquered by the Teutonic Knights nearly eight centuries ago. Hence Germany's origins were partially Slavic, and as German-speaking communities straddled a number of countries throughout Europe, this necessitated strong identity-defining myths. This '*Drang nach Osten*', the drive eastward, was a feature of German history and the source of mythologies, as with the naming of the great victory of 1914 as the Battle of 'Tannenberg' after the battle of 1410.[21] In the nineteenth century, this confetti of Teutonic communities began to be endowed with a new and supranationalist meaning: 'In consequence the continuum of German settlement from west to east began to be imagined as a single community, "from the (river) Maas as far as the (river) Memel" as the (nowadays suppressed) first verse of the Deutschlandlied, the future German anthem, written in 1841, proclaimed.'[22]

Hitler was an expert, indeed brilliant, publicist and orator. But his ideas were the philosophic clutter of the past, from theories of German exceptionalism and hegemony which had been elaborated since the dawn of the nineteenth century, including Fichte's 'Addresses to the German Nation' (1807–8). As mentioned in Chapter One, Fichte advocated the idea of a special mission for Germany, and his address should be seen as a polemic against the rationalist constitutional state and Western political thought more generally, with only Germans represented as original thinkers. The claim was that German culture was unique but also uniquely vulnerable, and that alien contamination was an existential threat.[23] In a similar vein, Friedrich Jahn's *German Nationhood* (1810) portrayed a future Greater Germany which would include Denmark and a new capital, Teutonia. He also suggested an education constructed around 'popularised national history, on a language purified of all foreign words, on physical labour and military sports, on the glorification of national symbols and heroes'.[24] In many ways this clearly anticipates, over a century before, what the Nazis were to do, and illuminates their extensive ideological ancestry. Adam Müller, another early nineteenth-century polemical nationalist, predicted that 'the great confederation of European nations will one day be a reality and, as sure as I am alive, will fly the German flag ...' What really mattered, polemicists claimed, was not the individual but the nation to which the individual was bound in a mystical national community.[25] Von Treitschke envisioned an all-powerful state superseding the constraints of law and morality, in fact the expression of 'Divine will as it exists on Earth', whose citizens exist to obey; Germany was to emerge transformed into a monocultural Lutheran state.[26] Nietzsche's works, such as *The Will to Power* and *Thus Spake Zarathustra*, were grossly distorted by the Nazis who claimed the philosopher as a spiritual ancestor, pillaging his slogans for the ultra-nationalist cause.[27]

Such hubristic spasms reached their apogee in the nation–race narcissism of the Reich. As Wells, the Nazi propaganda theorist, once proclaimed: 'we are in fact the most schooled and the best taught nation on earth'.[28] One article by G. Stark provided a revealing reading list for the party faithful, including: Dr Joseph Goebbels, *The Little ABC of National Socialism*; Dr Rosikat, *The Destruction of Farmers*; Herwig Hartner, *Eroticism and Race*; Henry Ford, *The International Jew* (in two volumes); Miloftonsky, *The Blood Thirst of Bolshevism*; Fetz, *World Annihilation Through Jehovah's Witnesses*; and Karl Heise, 'Freemasonry and World War' (a journal article).[29] The focus of these works was on inducing paranoia, and the enemies were not only the Jews.

Academe

Academics were also a significant source of regime mythology because they bestowed intellectual credibility. More than mere dignity or legitimacy, they offered truth through the claimed validation of scientific empiricism and method.

The academe consequently played an important role in fomenting Teutomania. Swathes of academe were too harmless, too recherché to trouble Nazis. Academic journals were permitted a minimal degree of latitude because of their trivial impact, which meant that a journal could question such rarefied aspects of Nazi theology as the idea of Charles the Great as the Saxons' heir as claimed by the party's chief ideologue and pseudo-mystic Alfred Rosenberg.[30] Statistically, of 337 articles published in one journal between 1933 and 1943, 101 were pro-Nazi, 195 were neutral and forty-one were anti-Nazi.[31] But substantial areas could be integrated into the race chauvinist discourse (i.e. propaganda), and the function of academe therefore was myth-building and myth-sustaining, as for example with the perversion of biology into a scientific basis for racialism (academic studies of literature and history were also important sources of mythology).[32] Bogus institutes for racial and pre-historical research were created which searched for the origins of the Aryan race, and there was also an institute for research into the Jewish question. There was also a polemic directed against theoretical physics.[33] The distortion of empirically based culture and the perversion of science were important propaganda objectives. Hitler termed nuclear physics 'Jewish science' and great scientific luminaries were labelled 'White Jews' (their error, according to Richard Grunberger, was to critique the rejection of theoretical physics pioneered by an anti-Semitic Nobel Prize-winner who postulated the existence of a mystical entity called 'German Physics').[34]

Academe thus played an important role in creating the supposedly objective 'evidence' that helped to convince a more tutored and more sceptical modern German public, and academics were therefore dragged into the vortex of public myth-making and became complicit in their manufacture. The illusions of scientism were cast over essentially political and propagandist processes, lending the patina of veracity to ideological lunacies with the authority of library and laboratory. The aim was not to investigate a proposition or a hypothesis but to begin with the acceptance of its truth and then to find the supporting evidence. Academe helped to elevate the Nazi idea above the gutter and the street brawl; its aura, its dignities of truth-seeking and scholarship, the accrued equity of centuries, lent to an infernal creed what it most craved, namely credibility and specifically a scientific basis. In the Reich, the function of academe was simply to 'prove' that the myths were true. Conformity was achieved by expulsion (i.e. sacking deviants) and propulsion (i.e. funding the work of sympathisers).[35]

As Arnold has argued, archaeology in particular became the colony of Nazi charlatans and a manufactory of myth,[36] with the discovery of 'German' archaeological materials being used as evidence that a territory was Germanic as per Gustaf Kossinna's concept of *Kulturkreis* (culture circles), where ethnic regional identity could be inferred from excavated artefacts.[37] After assuming power, the Nazis created eight new chairs in pre-history, as well as museums, open-air museums and institutes such as Bonn's Institute for Pre-History. There was also a series of popular journals on the subject of German history including *The Message* and the Ahnenerbe's *Germanic Heritage*, in addition to a number of films such as *Threatened by the Steam Plough, Germany's Bronze Age, The Flames of Prehistory* and *On the Trail of the Eastern Germans*. The Reich's intellectual contribution here was a perpetual endowment, showing how Nazi obsessions had a permanent impact on the formation of scholarship and specifically early German history, and that is a legacy of their myth-making. As Arnold points out, Germanic prehistoric archaeology remains a relatively recent discipline, the emergence of which resulted from Nazi patronage. Roman archaeologists were considered anti-German. Nazism could also appropriate the genetic as well as cultural heritage of the classical era where necessary, as was the case with a 1941 archaeological expedition to Greece which claimed to have found new evidence of the migration to Greece during Neolithic times.[38] The Führer himself was classically inclined (it is surprising that Hitler had such obvious contempt for early Germanic civilisation): 'now Himmler is starting to dig up these villages of mud huts and enthusing over every potsherd and stone axe he finds. ... We should really do our best to keep quiet about this past.'[39]

The Anti-Types—Bolshevism and Democracy

An important part of the mythological realm of Nazi Germany was the creation of a collective psychosis, or chimaera of injustice. There was the need for scapegoats, for a rationale to explain past German failure and to offer a reason to hope for a better future once the problem had been taken care of. The sense of an existential threat was fomented, and as Gonen notes, a succession of crises means that people tend to 'prefer a leap of faith to rational understanding of their predicament'.[40] Enemies were created. Posters featured cartoon figures of such foes—Catholic parties, socialists—being in some way crushed by something giant, a huge Aryan, a massive swastika and so forth.[41] Most especially, there was the inflation of the 'Jewish-Bolshevik', a hybridised monster representing an existential threat to the continued life of the *Volk*. The virtue of stereotype is that it gives flesh and blood to ideological abstractions. The Nazi images of Jews are crude phantasmagoria and it is difficult to believe that anyone at any level of intelligence took them seriously, yet the images do not ask for belief. Rather, the viewer is invited to share in a fantasy, a co-produced hallucination of enmity. Le Bon had noted that the perception of the crowd is essentially binary in that it has no sense of comparative merit or nuance, for things are turned by the metamorphosis of crowd psychology into absolutes of truth or falsehood.[42] Everything is simple and everything is extreme in their perception.

It was Hitler's particular skill and insight to recognise the function of enemies in the manufacture of solidarity. Such enemies did not have to be 'real' in any authentic sense as they could always be fabricated. This has been described as 'a major act of political imagination on Hitler's part'.[43] It had the happy consequence of uniting many of those on the centre and the right and even some from the left of the political spectrum round common internal or external threats. In other words, the Third Reich was inspired by problems which were imaginary as well as real, and the superlative ability of Adolf Hitler to 'sell the right myths'.[44] The fabrication of enmity is inherently reductive; a complex, fluid and febrile world can be elided into a simple conspiracy emanating from a single source. A subtle construction of enemies would never have succeeded; simplicity was everything. Hence good propaganda, as the Nazis understood, needs an enemy, and the function of such propaganda is reductivist in that it aims to airbrush out all nuance. The enemy was a caricature, luminous and wicked, but it also resonated—enmity must surface people's inner murmurings, becoming a 'co-production'.

It was a worldview teeming with internal and external enemies that had to be slain, and which were energised via the concept of an existential threat, that is to say, what was at stake was the future of the tribal community. This fabrication of enmity was redefined and refreshed through the fear of extinction. Le Bon in particular had believed in the regressive nature of crowds:

> [Man] may be a cultivated individual; in a crowd he is a barbarian—that is, a creature acting by instinct. He possesses the spontaneity, the violence, the ferocity, and also the enthusiasm and heroism of primitive beings, whom he further tends to resemble by the facility with which he allows himself to be impressed by words and images.[45]

This logic applies to all group activities such as juries and assemblies. Thus:

> taken separately, the men of the [French Revolutionary] Convention were enlightened citizens of peaceful habits. United in a crowd, they did not hesitate to give their adhesion to the most savage proposals, to guillotine individuals most clearly innocent, and, contrary to their interests, to renounce their inviolability and to decimate themselves.

The delusional world of the Third Reich found expression in its serial creation of enemies—Slavs, Poles, Judeo-Bolsheviks, Anglo-Americans and in general anyone who opposed the Nazi *Weltanschauung* (worldview). Part of this was inversion. The Nazis would often project their own sins, such as the compulsive greed of the Nazi Party and its officials, on to others, or twist the truth so that the Second World War became an anti-imperialist war in Nazi propaganda. This worked because it contained truths, despite it not being 'truth' (i.e. the incipient US global hegemony excoriated by Nazi propagandists). But such hegemony was a consequence, and not a cause, of American involvement in the Second World War. And in a similar vein the Nazis cast their role in the conflict as anti-capitalist. This was another of their 'truths'—British society was indeed class ridden and American capitalism had victims; both countries had enabled the rise of outrageously crass and amoral people who had become astonishingly rich.

Bolsheviks

A mythologised enemy cannot be ambivalent or vague, but must be crudely cruel and murderous, and preferably an existential threat. The Bolshevist could be both—painted in lurid colours, with some foundation in proof; truths that lay unburied amid the boundless morass of Nazi lies. Therefore, from the myth of Bolshevism was derived a unanimity of purpose via the construction of a common and universal threat: solidarity via an ideological anti-type that stood for the universal not the national. In *Athenian Myths and Institutions* the scholar W. Blake Tyrrell examines how myth-makers provide a binary perspective, evoking both an ideal to be strived for and a warning, describing those forces of nihilism which could tear the social fabric.[46] A myth is an edited image of the social ideal and an example of what happens when that ideal is forgotten or denigrated. Yet there really was a Communist threat, whose assertion was credible because it was a half-truth and not merely a phantom summoned by the vitriolic pens of Goebbels's agitprop. For the German bourgeois, Communism was a distinct possibility. In July 1931, the diarist Victor Klemperer wrote: 'is Hitler going to follow, or communism?'[47] Eventually the combined number of Reichstag seats of the two left 'Marxist' parties came to exceed those of the Nazis: 'for many middle-class Germans, this [was] a terrifyingly effective performance that threatened the prospect of the Communist revolution in the not too distant future'.[48]

The burning of the Reichstag was the incendiary backdrop to the commencement of Nazi rule in Germany. These flames were really the funeral pyre of democracy itself, and, indeed, the rule of law. The fire was used to justify implementing the Reichstag Fire Decree, a coercive piece of legislation which was 'launched amidst a barrage of propaganda in which Göring and the Nazi leadership painted a ghastly picture of an imminent "German Bolshevik Revolution" accompanied by outrageous atrocities of every kind. The propaganda had its effect.'[49] An atmosphere of palpable terror infected the ensuing elections, with the strategic positioning of police suggesting vulnerability to attack. Communists were supposedly 'preparing a bloodbath'; Göring said they were poisoning public kitchens, kidnapping innocent civilians and stockpiling explosives.[50]

But it should also be remembered that Bolshevism was a competitor to the Nazi worldview since it promulgated an alternative vision of humanity's future, one which negated the idea of the nation, race and heritage— and this made it truly hateful to Nazis. A type can only be defined and refreshed by an anti-type. The strategic aim was to draw workers away from the Communists. Hence Bolshevism, its Jews and commissars, could be caricatured, but not the deluded worker who had to be won back for the Reich. The film *SA Mann Brand* (1933), for instance, which is about the Nazi son of a Communist who leaves home, initially portrays the Communists in a sensitive light (the leader of the commune in the film only gradually becomes a destructive individual).[51] Similarly, in *Hans Westmar* (1933)'s juxtaposition of Communists—the Moscow-oriented boss and the cowardly Jewish petty official—there is also a decent idealist who is the target of Nazi evangelism, and as the storm troopers march past, illuminated by torchlight, his fist is shown opening into the Nazi salute.[52]

Yet Communism was also feared for reasons other than its ability to compete with Nazism. As well as being the competitor brand and the rival religion, the other suitor for the impassioned soul of the German worker, it also offered a coherence theory of truth, a structured totality that was the prism through which all economic, cultural and political realities could be interpreted and integrated. Hence the following entry in Goebbels's diary on 8 May 1943:

> the states based on a worldview have one advantage over the bourgeois states. They stand on a clear spiritual foundation. This worked to great advantage until the beginning of the campaign in the east. Then we met an opponent who also represented a worldview, even if it was false.[53]

The proletariat, Marx had said, has no fatherland: it was the achievement of the Third Reich to prove him wrong.

The concept of Bolshevism in Nazi propaganda was not static but evolutionary, with new meanings packed in over time. Fear of Communism was grafted on to other elements of Nazi ideology so that Bolshevism became a more nuanced concept in that it acquired associations of race, crusade and so forth, and the notion of the Bolshevik–Jewish conspiracy consequently provided 'a potent ideological metaphor for what the regime stood for and against'.[54] The effect was to externalise the internal anti-Communist psychosis of the early Nazi years—the Communist menace now lay without, having been defeated within, as depicted, for example, in the films *For the Rights of Man* (1934), *White Slaves* (1936) and *Frisians in Peril* (1935).[55] There was a recurrence of the anti-Russian, anti-Bolshevik film after 1941, as for example in the film *GPU* (1942), where a White Russian girl seeks to avenge the deaths of her parents by joining the Russian secret police (the GPU) to hunt their murderers.[56]

Thus war with Russia enabled the re-assertion of the old ideological nostrum, Jewish Bolshevism, and Goebbels publicly observed in 1941 that 'National Socialism started as a movement in the struggle against Bolshevism.'[57] War with Russia was the externalisation of the internal struggle that had given them birth and meaning and sustenance. To Goebbels, Germans were 'reverting to the principles that first impelled them—the struggle against plutocracy and Bolshevism'.[58] The public were offered an idea of preventive war, the attack as a war of defence that forestalled a Soviet invasion. The true measure of the homicidal nihilism of a steroidal ethno-nationalist credo that made its enemy not only a political but also a race criminal, that elided ideology with race, is embodied in the statistics: Germans took 5 million Soviet prisoners—fewer than 2 million survived the war;[59] 3.1 million Russian soldiers were in fact to die in German captivity.[60]

Propaganda often, though not always, has a transient relationship with the truth. Yet a relationship exists nevertheless; thus the film portrait of the GPU villain who executes members of an innocent family is presented as typical of the international Jewish-Bolshevik conspiracy.[61] This was made credible because Red as well as White Russians had committed atrocities in the Civil War.[62] To be successful as propaganda, myth must have intuitive plausibility: myth, Schöpflin argues, 'cannot be constructed purely out of false material; it has to have some relationship with the memory of the collectivity that has fashioned it ... for a myth to be effective in organising and mobilising opinion, it must ... resonate. The myth that fails to elicit response is alien or inappropriate.'[63] As a result, *GPU* is not an exercise in truth or falsehood, and that is exactly how the Nazis wished it to be; Nazi propaganda was always fictionalised but it was seldom pure fiction.

In the Bolshevists the Nazis could also see the reflection of their own demented and perverse fundamentalism, thereby providing a further incentive to demonise them, and there were indeed common links between the two movements. There were the Baltic Germans like Rosenberg who had direct experience of the Russian Revolution, or others who had been prisoners of war of the Russians and witnessed the same events, such as Roland Freisler, the notorious president of the People's Court who had been imprisoned for five years in Siberia before escaping in 1920.[64] Many Germans had also experienced domestic Communism in power during the Räterepublik, the communist rule of Munich in 1919.[65] Hence Bolshevism in Nazi propaganda was a mixture of fabricated and real elements. It was equated with murder, with degeneracy physical and social, and above all with an international anti-culture, not rooted in the nation, and that is to say it is the antithesis of blood. For Germans, then, revolution had been a personal experience, especially for the ex-militiamen or Freikorps at or after the end of the First World War—Red Munich, the Spartacists, the Wilhelmshaven and Kiel naval mutinies, the oratory of Rosa Luxemburg and Karl Liebknecht; and then, the later Weimar-era battles in the Berlin streets, the forebodings of a Communist Germany: the right had no absolute monopoly of political murder. There had even been a short-lived red revolt in working-class areas of Berlin led by mutinous sailors in November 1918, and a few deaths, but the revolution did not last for more than a few days.[66] Thus, unlike the British, the Germans had direct exposure to Communism, and the possibility of a Communist takeover was hardly unimaginable.

The early Hitler exploited this with evocations of Communist savagery, and this visceral anti-Communism resonated with target groups. Hitler claimed the aim of Nazism was to exterminate the Communist worldview, and 'incomparable, brilliantly orchestrated propaganda and information organization' would be used to achieve this.[67] In this anti-Bolshevism they were hardly alone; Churchill himself had described Bolshevism as a 'philosophy of hatred and death ...'[68] In the 1930s, British paranoia about Bolshevism, combined with admiration for Germany, was consequently a common if not general or frequent sentiment. Thus the editor of *The Aeroplane*, a popular British magazine, saw Germany as 'the first line of defence of Western civilisation against Eastern barbarism' and the German people as 'cheerful and contented'.[69]

Documentary and film helped foment anti-Bolshevism, as for example *Forest of Katyn* (1943) about the Russian massacre of the Polish reserve-officer corps. Documentary is the purest form of propaganda since it is the least disguised, posing as fact, not fiction, and therefore makes the case more explicitly than, say, a costume drama. Another documentary, *Struggle Against the World Enemy*, ostensibly about the Condor Legion in the Spanish Civil War, features the arrival of Moses Rosenberg, the first Soviet ambassador to Red Spain. He is the deviant, cosmopolitan adversary, and the International Brigades are composed of the detritus of the human race, being used to pulverise (decent) Spain.[70] It is a Manichaean order—noble Fascist and brutal Bolshevik (the documentary was withdrawn because of the Molotov pact).

Then there were the movies. The film *Hitler Youth Quex* is based on a novel of the same name, about a real case, a youth killed by Communists as he distributed Nazi Party literature;[71] for myth-entrepreneur Goebbels, it was the opportunity he needed for a grand funeral and a fresh, innocent youth martyr.[72] The film is constructed around three geographic axes— woodland, fairground and park bench—which are both physical and symbolic locations: the natural wood, the land of disciplined patriotic youth; the fairground, the place of cosmopolitan debauchery and the Communist anti-culture; the park bench, a no-man's-land, a sedentary locus of verbal exchange where the rivalry between two competing political brands, and two ideologies at war, is negotiated. Heini's (Quex's) conversion is visually prompted, the contrast between Hitler Youth and the decadence and emotional incontinence of the Communists is both aesthetic and political. The Nazis defined themselves via their obverse.

Yet *Hitler Youth Quex* embodies the ambivalence: Communists are damaged folk comrades who could be healed, but they are also brutal, treacherous agents of an alien faith and its foreign sponsor. The famous park bench scene between Heini, his Communist father and the Hitler Youth leader embodies this conflict. The film brings together conservative images and left-wing impulses;[73] and that it represents in some manner a quintessence of the European Fascist idea is a useful way of explaining its power. Audiences numbered well over 20 million through the years.[74] The bench scene goes in fact to the emotional core of the Nazi argument, that is to say the privileging of nation, a racial concept, above all else. The father represents the international, the Hitler Youth leader, the national. But 'International' is an abstract concept, something external, the National is here, the soil on which the feet are planted. The father's perspective is made to look unreal, a dreamy, ephemeral ideal, not rooted in our turf: and polluted by Russia. The Hitler Youth leader dominates Heini's father, politely but remorselessly, in an interrogation that condenses an entire worldview: he asks where he was born, what city, what country: 'In Germany, that's right! ... in our Germany!'[75]

The film is a masterpiece of emotional political propaganda, and Jay Baird has eloquently evoked the cinematic death of Heini in the final scene, triggered by 'the sharp double whistle of the communists' (this is their alarm system) that rings out: the Communists 'swarm into the darkened streets, and a horrifying expression of fear crosses Heini's face'.[76] He runs through the silent carnival site, the homicidal mob in hot pursuit, hiding in a tent stuffed with the props of the funfair trade. The denouement is expected, inevitable but still shocking: 'an ungodly shriek pierces the ugly Berlin dawn, as the drunken, unsightly Moscow hit men carry out their evil deed'.[77] This is a powerful symbol; Bolshevik barbarity would not baulk 'even at the murder of a proletarian boy from drab, industrial north Berlin'.[78] There is an added piquancy in the death taking place in the fairground, conventionally a place of childhood fantasy, which now turns into murderous terror. The ending of the film is forced, with the youth artfully dying in his comrade's arms and muttering words about the flag marching on. The boy's spirit strides on in some parallel world, inspiring those who still toil in this one: death as transcendence is Nazi make-believe. The macabre nature of the ending had been enhanced by the fairground horses and all the other panoply of a fair. The fairground had been the symbolic centre of *Hitler Youth Quex*: the focus of the violence, degeneracy and licence which the coming Reich would pulverise out of existence. Weimar was an idea and an anti-type, a realm of putrefaction that awaited sanitisation: 'this film evokes the atmospheric urban venues of Weimar and revisits working class spaces: narrow apartments, smoky pubs, joyless streets'.[79]

Slavic Beast

The imagined enemies the Nazis mythologised comprised a creed (Communism), but they also included a local 'race' (Germany's Slav neighbours) and a global one (Jews). Hitler once told his guests that 'if I try to gauge my work, I must consider, first of all, that I have contributed, in a world that had forgotten the notion, to the triumph of the idea of the primacy of race'.[80] For Nazis, race was a critical element in enmity, as the fight was never just national but ethno-national, even with the Americans. *Cadets* (1939), an anti-Russian film set during the Seven Years' War in 1760, chronicles the noble resistance of Prussian officer cadets against the Russian brute.[81] In *Homecoming* (1941), a film about the persecution of ethnic Germans and their salvation by the Reich, Marie, a schoolteacher, dreams of going into a shop where 'they will not be speaking Yiddish or Polish, but German'.[82] She says: 'not only do we live a German life, we die a German death'—a classic statement of the people and homeland theme, *Volk und Heimat*;[83] hence the myth of the brutal Slav was both incentivising and self-justificatory. Similar racial themes also feature in *Campaign in Poland*, which is a documentary celebration of the destruction of a hated enemy as well as a rhapsody about the German air force.[84]

Hitler's Reichstag speech of 1 September 1939 elaborated on this theme of the mistreatment of Germans at the hands of the Slavs—again the minority psychosis—with the idea of the Slav gradually becoming inseparable from the image of the German minorities persecuted by them in Nazi propaganda. Hitler exploited the idea of Germans as a wronged and persecuted race both before and after assuming power, while, paradoxically, expressing the German desire for hegemony; an underclass transformed into the overclass. The Russian people were depicted as welcoming their German saviours, as in the film *The Soviet Paradise* (1942) about the menace of Communism and the horrors it had wrought in Russia.[85] According to *Signal*, Russia was a squalid country, a fitting domain for the *Untermenschen*, whose population was 'a human current whose mass invades the streets'. The same article celebrated the beneficial effects of the German raj, including the churches which had reopened, thereby enabling the priests to escape the return of their 'Soviet torturers'.[86] Its photographers revealed Russian people rejoicing at the lightness of their new yoke and happy to come and labour in Germany, while imagery of enemy prisoners was also orchestrated for the camera (with bread being distributed, for example).[87]

The horrors of murderous Bolshevism were even pressed upon Germany's enemies via the use of tactical battlefield weapon propaganda (psychological artillery). Poles, for instance, were told they would 'come away alive from the Bolshevik paradise', but that the English intended to throw them 'into the hell of Casino'.[88] Other pieces of propaganda directed at the Poles depicted a Russian flag with the question 'Is this your country's flag?', or sought to capitalise on the Katyn massacre: '12,000 Polish officers, the bloom of Polish youth, Poland's pride, were murdered by bandits from the Kremlin ...'[89]

Weimar

As well as races, creeds and nations, the target of polemic also included the predecessor regime, Weimar, the mythology of which conveniently defined the Nazis by embodying everything that they were not.

Weimar and the problem of liberal democracy

The German experience of the Weimar Republic encapsulates some of the problems of liberal democracy and the antagonisms it generates. It was a system many Germans detested: as Richard Evans argues, voters 'were not really looking to anything very concrete from the Nazi party in 1930. They were, instead, protesting against the failure of the Weimar Republic.'[90] There was a perception of universal decay; what has become a survivable feature of life in modern market democracies was shocking to Germans of that era: the gay scene, criminality, drugs, pornography, financial scandal, sex criminals (crime virtually doubled in some categories from 1927 to 1932).[91] Thus Stanley McClatchie's *Look to Germany* (a hagiography of the new Reich with 300 photographs) included an image titled 'In Berlin's formerly notorious "El Dorado", a night-club for Lesbian women and feminine men PROHIBITED in the Third Reich.'[92]

The construction of the anti-type was indeed created out of a race, Jews, and a political ideology, Communism; but it was also created out of a historical period, that of Weimar. The imagined Weimar of the Nazi was everything the Reich was not—cosmopolitan, tentative and experimental: a society that believed in nothing and tolerated everything, and one which was apparently prostrate before its conquerors, the confiscators of German turf. But Weimar was also a symbol or an image of the failures of democracy—the failure to build a national consensus, the multiplicity of parties and the timeserving mediocrities leading them. Hatred of Weimar was ultimately a hatred of democracy and compromise. What the Nazis sought to offer was a historical narrative of rebirth, a 'decay–regeneration metaphor'.[93] 'Weimar' was a vivid mythology of Nazi manufacture, but again the properties of the myth had some light foundation in reality from which the Nazis were able to derive a superficial credibility. To the Nazis, Weimar represented a gross failure of the patriotic nerve and it also incorporated the other myths—myths of the national past, myths of terrorism, myths of the era of struggle and of the Nazi past specifically. It was above all a regime manned by traitors, by those who had made a craven peace with the Allies. The persuasiveness of any myth resides in its ability to express complexity in simple form, often via narrative and a dramaturgy of heroes and villains; thus the German General Staff fabrication of 1918, the myth of the 'stab in the back', was generally if not universally accepted in Germany. Indeed, without the backdrop of this myth the rise of Nazism would be inexplicable.[94]

The Nazis turned Weimar into a myth of antithesis, a parable of every 'horror' they opposed. Weimar was both the negation of the Reich and the legitimation of the Reich via the scale of its imagined excesses. There is an objective Weimar and the Weimar of Nazi mass media, the latter of which was a crude and deceitful caricature of what had been. Weimar was portrayed as a Bolshevised, Judaised landscape of the imagination and a protracted assault on every decent German value. The English-language *Look to Germany* purported to show 'typical contrasts: the former Marxist-Jewish Berlin Chief of Police, Grzesinski, the new National Socialist Chief of Police Count Helldorf.'[95] From disorder to order, from abstraction to clarity: in every way the Nazi type was defined by the Weimar anti-type; Weimar was gutless, a protracted epistle of surrender to the pressures of carnality and foreignness and subversion. The contaminated and the sanitised: Nazism was returning Germans to some purified original state. Indicatively, the producer of the propaganda film *Pour le Mérite* (1938):

> delighted in employing every negative stereotype about the hated Weimar Republic. He presented it as a world where business and money are key, where criminals and prostitutes, stock market racketeers and manipulators, parasitic Jews and wire pullers have all joined hands with corrupt politicians. The Knights of the Air are totally alienated in this world of corruption, materialism, and hedonism.[96]

In Nazi film Weimar was both the past civic order and the justification for the Nazi state. It became a metaphor where torpid flesh sought enervation in every vice, where fine Germans wandered as strangers in their *Heimat* (homeland). Over this pestilential realm was cast the shadow of the Communist. Thus in *Hans Westmar* the Weimar Republic was positively dripping with degeneracy: a black jazz band plays a version of the 'Watch on the Rhine'.[97]

Yet the Reich was degenerate on a scale that Weimar never achieved or even imagined. As Hugh-Trevor Roper argues:

> When a staid German general compared Göring to Elagabalus, he was not exaggerating. In the absolutism, the opulence and the degeneracy of the middle Roman empire we can perhaps find the best parallel to the high noonday of the Nazi Reich. There, in the severe pages of Gibbon, we read of characters apparently wielding gigantic authority who, on closer examination, are found to be the pliant creatures of concubines and catamites, of eunuchs and freedmen; and here too we see the elite of the Thousand Year Reich as a set of flatulent clowns, swayed by purely random influences. Even Mussolini was embarrassed, but then Mussolini had, after all, like Goebbels, a Latin mind; he could never be at home among those cavorting Nibelungs.[98]

However, like the elites of many regimes, the Nazis actually believed their own myths, so that the Second World War came to replicate for them the experience they had already undergone in the era of struggle when they had fought the Communists in the streets and the Weimar government in the courts. European statesmen resembled the German conservatives they had beguiled and deluded. The fight with Russia was but the actuality of a dress rehearsal once performed on German streets in the fight with the German Communists. As John Lukacs observes:

> what [Hitler] saw then [i.e. following the Soviet invasion] (and he had agreed with Joseph Goebbels when the latter had said something like this in April) was that this is but a repetition, on a larger scale, of the struggle that he had fought and won in Germany, which had brought him to power. He and his National Socialists were bound to win the struggle, even though they had started out as a minority, because they and their ideas were more determined and stronger than those of their opponents.[99]

Pour le Mérite

All ideological utopias need their obverse to gain self-definition, and in this sense the illusion and mythology of Weimar was a gift. *Pour le Mérite* is clearly an important film in this regard because it captures not only the ideology but the heart of the emotional concept—that is, the First World War experience as the defining perspective. In the film a heroic group of fighter pilots find themselves strangers in their native land. Baird describes a vignette in the film that:

> contrasts the hero with the collected menagerie of Weimar business and demi-monde circles gathered at a Berlin nightclub ... with the orchestra bellowing its tunes in the tingle tangle of the glittering club, a thoroughly offensive crowd of parvenu businessmen in tuxedos and the women of the night rollick and cavort over champagne and caviar. Nausea wells up in the soul of the protagonist ... he is simply unable to close a lucrative business transaction.[100]

He argues further that 'good from the nobility of comradeship is juxta-posed to the forces of evil, embodied in Marxists, defeatists, pacifists, war shirkers and profiteers, traitorous intellectuals and hysterical women in political leadership roles'. He sees the film as both a parable and a metaphor, 'a military and political biography from World War One and a cultural state-ment of decline, suffering and resurrection that paralleled the career and cultural outlook of the front soldier Adolf Hitler. Hitler himself attended the Berlin premier in 1938.'[101] The film reflects the world of the ex-soldier, an internal exile in a world he did not understand and where he could not suc-ceed because his skills and values were irrelevant. But after the coming of the Reich the old leader receives command of the squadron again—resurrection. The film fades out with a close-up of a radiant *Pour le Mérite* medal, the high-est gallantry award in the old imperial German army.[102]

Anti-Type: Unfit and Impure

Social Darwinism

Hitler once remarked that Europe 'is not a geographic entity, it's a racial entity'.[103] According to Hitler, the Aryan was 'the Prometheus of mankind, out of whose bright forehead springs the divine spark of genius at all times ...'[104] The Nazis believed they had discovered the source of history, and that they offered a universal and primordial explanation.[105] Such a distortion of intellectual theory was sourced from academe. Thus Friedrich Max Müller, Taylor Chair of modern languages at Oxford (1854) and latterly professor of Sanskrit, studied the Indo-European linguistic stratum and its evolution and proposed a simplified term for the concept, 'Aryan'. His was a theory of language, not race; he was incensed when others started using it as a racial concept since this was an illicit transference.[106] The translation of a linguistic concept into a biological one is both irrational and illogical. Yet by the twentieth century, the notion of an 'Aryan race' was well established even in the English-speaking world. Again, Charles Darwin's ideas on natural selection conceived successful (i.e. surviving) species as specialist adapters, evolving towards a particularist niche. This was never meant to have an extra-zoological import, and its applications to human society via the Social Darwinism of Herbert Spencer is thus another example of illicit conceptual transfer. Indeed, it is nonsensical. Yet the Nazis took these intellectual streams, combined them and polluted them. The great ideologues of race were the Comte de Gobineau and H.S Chamberlain, and Gobineau's *Essay on the Inequality of the Races of Man* was published in a number of volumes between 1853 and 1855.[107] Gobineau was the rhapsodist of white supremacy and the primacy of race, while Chamberlain's *Foundations of the Nineteenth Century* (1899) conceives history as a race struggle where the 'creative culture' Aryans were menaced by inferiors; such fantasies were re-packaged in Rosenberg's *Mythus*.[108] Hence a misapplication of nineteenth-century science fashioned the most dangerous of the twentieth century's myths.

Another source was the German romantic tradition. For Klemperer, the contemporary diarist and later rhetorical theorist, the origin of the Nazi idea was clear:

> I am convinced there is a close affinity between Nazism and German Romanticism. I believe that the one was the inevitable result of the other ... All the distinctive features of National Socialism are present in Romanticism in embryonic form: the dethronement of reason, the canonisation of man, the glorification of the idea of power, of the predator, of the blonde beast.[109]

These formative influences on the young Hitler and subsequently on Hess, Himmler and others were strong: 'They sanctified instinctual bigotry with the liturgies of scientism.'[110]

Social Darwinism, a reductivist or primitive version of which was really the theoretic underpinning of Nazism, was also fuelled by junk nineteenth-century pseudo-science and philosophic charlatanry, including Ludwig Woltman (1871–1907)'s extreme racial Social Darwinism.[111] In Bracher's words, these theories 'had one common theme: a declaration of war on all those moral values stressing compassion, tolerance, and the protection and welfare of the individual'.[112] Hitler attributed his Social Darwinism to the experiences of the First World War, for this is what the trenches had taught him. In *Mein Kampf* he wrote that:

> It was with feelings of pure idealism that I set out for the front in 1914. Then I saw men falling around me in thousands. Thus I learnt that life is a cruel struggle, and has no other object that the preservation of the species. The individual can disappear, provided there are other men to replace him.[113]

Hitler's private secretary Martin Bormann similarly recorded him as saying:

> the earth continues to go round, whether it's the man who kills the tiger or the tiger eats the man. The stronger asserts his will, it's the law of nature. The world doesn't change; its laws are eternal ... men dispossess one another, and one perceives that, at the end of it all, it is always the stronger who triumphs.[114] ... and it is all in the natural order of things—for it makes for the survival of the fittest.[115]

Social Darwinism also underpinned Hitler's antagonism to Christianity: 'the law of selection justifies this incessant struggle, by allowing the survival of the fittest. Christianity is a rebellion against natural law, a protest against nature. Taken to its logical extreme Christianity would mean the systematic cultivation of human failure.'[116]

The Social Darwinist message was reinforced by the *Kulturfilms*, the Nazi documentaries about the natural world (a 'strategy of distraction') in which humanity's struggle with nature was a recurrent theme. Thus, according to one journalist, the documentary film, *The Struggle for the Himalayas* (1937), was 'a general German symbol of the will to overcome all difficulties of life in order to reach the light'.[117] The Nazi anti-types were the feeble-bodied and the chronically sick, the mentally ill and the racially contaminated. In this they caricatured in a particularly crude and brutal way the Social Darwinism derived from Herbert Spencer; what others had left implicit they made explicit, the doctrine and operational policy of a nation state. In a contribution to the book *Sport and State* (1934), Hitler notes that 'our absolute ideal for the future would be a human being of radiant mind and magnificent body'.[118] But the glorious type presupposes the inglorious anti-type, the *Übermensch* steps on the *Untermensch*. The day of the invasion of Poland was the day Hitler issued orders to exterminate the incurably ill (50,000 Germans were subsequently murdered as part of this programme). This was of course never admitted but swathed in verbiage and virtue-words; euthanasia institutions boasted such titles as the 'Charitable Foundation for the Transportation of the Sick' and the 'Charitable Foundation for Institutional Care'.[119]

The euthanasia campaign remained a secret until it was exposed and condemned by a Roman Catholic prelate. Bishop Galen's famous sermon of 3 August 1941 publicised details of the campaign and the scale of the subterfuge behind it, such as the fake death notices and the public illusion that these were natural deaths (the programme was halted by command of the Führer on 24 August 1941).[120] The psychopathology of Nazi race propaganda was constructed around the rhetoric of disease—terms like 'diseased genes', 'healthy blood', 'mental illness' and 'hereditable disease'.[121] Central to this rhetoric was the concept of blood, which is a metaphor for racial and cultural and spiritual essence, but one which is tragically easy to contaminate, and thereby lose. The propaganda provided a long list of the ills that affect us when 'blood' is corrupted—insanity, schizophrenia and so on—always with the words 'diseases' and 'congenital abnormalities'. 'Blood' was corrupted above all by copulation with the physically imperfect or with the various breeds of *Untermensch*.

A statistical neverland buttressed the case for the defence of 'blood'. Bogus statistics calibrated the number of Germans with genetic mental deficiencies, epilepsy or feeble minds in order to claim soaring numbers of the unfit over the previous fifty years (by sixfold, apparently). In *You and Your People* (1940), a Nazi propaganda primer aimed at children, for example, the numerous descendants of 'a single alcoholic woman born in 1810' were said to have cost the state about '5 million marks altogether, which had to be paid by healthy and sometimes very valuable people'.[122] Statistics were manufactured and presented as scientific fact in order to foment crisis, that is to say, the artificial fabrication of political and social problems where none existed. The same publication refers to an 'army of the mentally ill' and lists the astonishing costs of looking after 'a child who is an idiot'.[123] Various other works give the reader a recitation of the laws to protect genetic inheritance, such as the law 'For the Protection of the Genetic Health of the German People' (1935).[124] But, significantly, the methods (castration, sterilisation, outlaw marriage) were defended on the grounds that they only applied to the very worst cases and that the medical treatments involved were safe and caused no harm: 'it is more humane to prevent great misery than to pity the unfortunates and later burden the People's Community with their care'.[125] Sterilisation was the kindly response: '"Humanity" is not ignored in these cases. One not only leaves the ill alive, but cares for and protects them. Sterilisation is safe and harmless.'[126] Here we see a familiar Nazi advocacy trick, where the project is presented as non-invasive. In practice it became organised murder, yet the defence was one of humanity. The law 'For the Prevention of Genetically Diseased Offspring' (1933) was even likened to a natural law since in nature 'weak creatures are eliminated and this is called natural selection'.[127] And this connects directly with its obverse, the Nazi celebration of physical perfection. Thus while Riefenstahl 'sat at an editing table reworking the sublime physiques from the Berlin games, the afflicted physiognomy of the sick and mentally ill victims confronted viewers in German cinemas. Nazism's ideals of physical strength and beauty were inextricably bound to its disdain for the degenerate, diseased, and disabled bodies.'[128] Goebbels's film propaganda stressed the thriving of the fittest. In one such film:

> scientists are shown filming an experiment in which two stag beetles are fighting each other. The laboratory technician expresses some doubts about what she sees. 'It is a shame really', she says to her Professor, to catch these beautiful, strong animals for a fight between life and death. And to think back in the forest they could have had a quiet life. But my dear, the Professor tells her, there is no such thing as a quiet life anywhere in nature ... They all live in a constant struggle, in the course of which the weak perish.[129]

Space and race were the twin aspects of Nazi ideology. National myths can embody purely rhetorical truths, such as the American myth of national benevolence, representing a kind of idealised national self. But nations may also view their myths more literally, as objective truths even, and then they become dangerous. The Nazi faith in the objective existence of an ancient Aryan race is one of these.[130] Space and race, in the view of Fest, were 'the only more or less fixed structural elements' in the Nazi worldview.[131]

Yet the Nazis denied race narcissism. Writing in 1937, for instance, the Nazi propagandist Fritz Bennecke argued: 'some see racial arrogance and intolerance [in Nazi Germany]. That is absolutely false.'[132] The Nazis claimed they rejected racial mixing out of pity for the young: the child-victim would be 'an unhappy, restless creature' as well as a 'victim of natural contempt'.[133] The analogy was really with the species rather than a race;

Bennecke for example claimed that the racial differences were not value distinctions 'but rather differences in kind'. Hence race became a kind of primordial essence: 'the goal of racial hygiene is to secure recognition for the racial nature of our people in all areas of life'.[134] Racial mixing was consequently seen as the most heinous of crimes, a sin against the essence, that is, blood: 'remember the black disgrace on the Rhine!' (i.e. the fiction that French colonial soldiers had raped German women).[135] Thus *You and Your People* expresses horror that in the French army 'it can happen the black officers command whites'.[136] Children were exhorted to reproduce, since this would perpetuate the race of Germandom. Families were a pious duty to the *Volk*, the transmission of an unbroken link down 100 generations: *You and Your People* even calculates that any given child would have over 2 million German ancestors if they traced their ancestry back to 1340.[137] Race was everything, the key Nazi idea and the lynchpin of their thinking. One could not be a Nazi without being a serious racialist; otherwise the entire ideology made no sense since race consciousness was its foundation, the substructure on which everything else was built.

Social Darwinism, as distinct from biological or evolutionary Darwinism, is clearly a myth in the sense that no one 'race' (if such a category can be said to exist) is 'fitter' than another. However, within this myth system, ideological contradiction and inconsistency was never a problem. The Nazi propagandist manipulated a world of feeling, not analysis, so he was able to deplore racialism in order to achieve a particular rhetorical effect. Such was Nazi humbuggery: thus under the heading 'Poverty and Destitution in a World Empire', one propaganda article speaks of the British Empire's importation of 'negro slaves' 'unhampered by a civilised conscience', of poverty and exploitation.[138] Hitler argued that:

> National Socialism is not a cultic movement, but rather exclusively the racial knowledge of a mature ethnic political doctrine. It is no mystic cult, but rather the care and leadership of the people determined by blood. We therefore have no cultic spaces, but rather only people's halls, no cultic spaces but rather meeting and marching places. We have not mystic groves, but rather the sports grounds and sports fields.[139]

For Nazis the war was also a race war: not just against Slavs, Judaised Saxons or Jews but also against the miscegenated armies of the colonial powers and their native troops. Commentaries in the German media frequently drew attention to this fact: for instance, one article refers to 'thousands of French prisoners, an assortment of the coloured races of the earth' walking along the roadside, complete with a colour image of French Asian troops to reinforce the message.[140] Hence there were two wars, the first being the war of the Allied media, of documentaries and newsreels, Hollywood and Elstree, from which non-whites have been edited out, and the second a Nazi media war where non-whites are omnipresent.

The Third Reich represented an appeal to solidarity, one which began at a very young age. In *The German National Catechism* (1934), a book aimed at explaining Nazism to school children, readers are told that 'once you have come to see your people in this way, in an enormously complicated, yet unified, network of millions related by blood, you will never be able to consider yourself an isolated individual again'.[141] The book goes on to enumerate the characteristics of the Nordic race, including courage, bravery, creative ability, desire and loyalty.[142] The book was not intended simply as a text to be read, but as an elaboration of a religion to be cherished: it is written in an unctuous pseudo-sacerdotal tone celebrating the core tribal values, with expressions like 'path to salvation'. Here and elsewhere, 'blood' means more than race in that it evokes notions of inherited culture, ancestry and ties to the land; it connects to ancient peoples and is a kind of life essence that is also metaphoric and metaphysical. There was therefore a juxtaposition of 'blood' against reason; irrational instinct was reinforced by an un-interrogated faith in synthesised heritage and imagined folk tradition.[143]

Purity and perfection

The underlying myths of the Nazi regime were essentially utopian. The Nazi mythology invoked a condition of solidarity and social community, a regression to some kind of native authenticity and above all the salvation of the race from racial pollution. In this nirvana, the man or woman was cared for and valued as long as they conformed; all individualism was bleached out, and a race of 'sunny' (that word), standardised people produced. Other-hatred was a necessary stage in this progression towards a perfect world, or at least a perfect world for Germans: behind the ranting, the visceral loathing, the neo-pornographic depictions of assorted enemies, lies, in fact, a longing for paradise. A myth of a 'pure' race necessarily implies the impurity of other races, and therefore pamphlets with titles like 'Keep Your Blood Pure' abounded in Nazi Germany,[144] with threats to this mythologised purity being attributed particularly to the (forcibly immigrant) foreign workers as well as the Jews. The illicit connection between personal health and the health of the *Volk* was a much-exhausted analogy. Parallel to this was an extraordinary interest in personal hygiene, in which creams and cosmetics were a constant refrain of the Nazi advertising industry: thus jackbooted and Nivea-creamed, the Reich marched towards mid-century. This notion of hygiene was translated wholesale to society. The Nazi promise was not just of the nation re-energised but of an entirely new kind of civic order.

In the view of Klemperer, Gobineau's *Essay on the Inequality of Human Races* (1853–5, four volumes) provided 'all the ingredients required by the Third Reich, for its philosophical justification and its policies. All subsequent Nazi consolidation and application of this teaching invariably goes back to him. He alone is or appears to be the person responsible for conceiving this bloody doctrine.'[145] Indeed, Alexis de Tocqueville, who was highly critical of Gobineau, had warned that the latter's ideas would prove particularly dangerous in a country like Germany: 'alone in Europe, the Germans possess the particular talent of becoming impassioned with what they take as abstract truths without considering their practical consequences'.[146] Hence this pseudo-biological doctrine of aggressive and exclusionary racialism found a receptive audience in Germany, and Hitler developed it further and in even more dangerous directions. As Klemperer notes, it was not Hitler's division of mankind into races that was original, but rather that he completely discarded the term 'mankind' and instead favoured the notion of independent races.[147] The Nazis' assertion of the superiority of blood derived from their neurosis as well as their race narcissism, which largely stemmed from their sense of insecurity at not being what they so aggressively proclaimed. In the view of William Shirer, a US journalist who was based in Germany, the result of the official race doctrine was quite ludicrous, involving as it did the falsification of history and the teaching of racial 'science' in universities: he refers to one university where the rector was a storm trooper and another institute which offered no fewer than twenty-five newly created courses in racist pedagogy.[148]

The Anti-Type: Jews

Hitler and the phenomenon of Hitlerism was a response to a contemporary cultural climate. It did not originate this: a large section of the German political and economic elite was already anti-Semitic. The Thule Society, an upper-class nationalist society that was influential in early twentieth-century Germany, for instance, had helped supercharge the anti-Semitic atmosphere prevailing in the Munich of 1919 by issuing a torrent of documents spouting venom towards the Jews.[149] Anti-Semitic riots occurred in ten universities in 1931 alone.[150] Nor was this a nineteenth- or twentieth-century phenomenon, as the roots of German (and indeed European) anti-Semitism dug deep into ancient soil. In 1492, for instance, twenty-seven Jews had been burned alive in the German town of Sternberg for desecrating the host, and thirty-nine were burned and two beheaded for the same crime in 1510 in Berlin.[151]

Pseudo-intellectualism: the anti-Semitic rhetorical debris of the nineteenth century

While all European countries (and specifically Poland, France and Russia) experienced anti-Semitism in the nineteenth and twentieth centuries, it was the embrace of biological notions of race and contamination that distinguished the German discourse and precipitated a new and more virulent anti-Semitism. The race myth was largely bequeathed to the Nazis via the ideas of nineteenth-century pseudo-intellectuals. But there were also artistic sources, pre-eminently Wagner, who declaimed his antagonism towards the Jews in the essay *World Jewry in Music* (1869). This new hostility was legitimated by the previous nationalist and Christian anti-Semitism, but of course went much further.[152] For the historian Heinrich von Treitschke, the Jews, liberal and cosmopolitan, represented the antithesis to his Lutheran Culture State and should be seen as an 'element of national decomposition'.[153] Theodor Fritsch, a nineteenth-century anti-Semitic German polemicist, originally published his *Handbook of the Jewish Question* in 1888, yet its popularity was such that by 1933 it had reached its fortieth edition.[154]

Some of the anti-Semitism prevailing in Germany arose from an imagined pre-modern German: the fluidity and the tentativeness of modern life with its urbanisation, proletarianism, immigration, commercialisation, internationalisation and secularisation could all be blamed on the Jews.[155] The German polymath and orientalist Paul de Lagarde claimed that the German middle-class was suffering from Jewish market manipulation and he contrasted 'Jewish' high finance with the true productivity of German industry and agriculture. As well as being influenced by these ideas, the youthful Hitler was also deeply impressed by the work of Gottfried Feder on the menace of Jewish high finance.[156] Thus on one occasion Hitler remarked that 'the essential cause of the stability of our currency was to be sought for in concentration camps'.[157]

Yet as the nineteenth century neared its end, the essentialist nature of the German anti-Semitic discourse changed from the traditional canon to something much more sinister, a new and appalling fiction. It is the attribution of a biological basis to racial difference which licenses genocide and the possibility of genocide. The transformation of religious anti-Semitism into political and biological anti-Semitism was embodied in the writings of other nineteenth-century German anti-Semitic provocateurs such as Wilhelm Marr and Eugen Dühring,[158] and it was in their work, as well as in similar polemics, that the first calls for the destruction of Jewry were made.[159]

There was also a parallel stratum of populist anti-Semitism, the rough urban cousin to the intellectual, that is to say the incendiary, Tractarianism offered at newspaper stalls that promulgated an image of Jews as criminals and usurers.[160] This movement began to have political consequences as hostility to Jews found public political expression. There were early anti-Semitic parties such as the League of Anti-Semites, which was founded in 1879, and in 1887 the first independent anti-Semitic candidate was elected to the parliament.[161]

There is no question that Hitler believed that the Jews really were an existential threat, and that there was little time left to save the *Volk*. There was thus always an apocalyptic tone to Hitler's ravings, and this also gave a sense of urgency to a regime which believed itself to be defending a race and a folk culture that faced imminent extinction. The biggest threat to this culture gradually evolved into a hyphenated entity, the Jew-Bolshevik, an amalgam of the race and political credo that represented the obverse of all the Nazis believed. All enemies were ultimately Jewish. Klemperer claimed that what distinguished the Nazis from other forms of Fascism was 'a concept of race; reduced only to anti-semitism, and also fired exclusively by it. Thus Bolshevism turns into Jewish Bolshevist, the French are beniggered and bejewed, the English the lost tribe of Israel.'[162] And as far as Hitler himself was concerned, Jesus was not Jewish. In Hitler's words: 'Galilee was a colony where the Romans had probably installed Gallic legionaries, and it's certain that Jesus was not a Jew ... For the Galilean's object was to liberate his country from Jewish oppression. He set himself against Jewish capitalism, and that's why the Jews liquidated him.'[163]

The anti-Semitic theme had always been present in Nazi proselytisation. For example, Nazi posters from 1924 featured the fat top-hatted Jew sitting on the shoulders of a muscular worker. There was a clear similarity between these poster images and those associated with left-wing movements:[164] race was simply substituted for class while the Jews were endowed with the signature of the overclass, almost as if anti-Semitism had become simply a variant, or parallel, class struggle. There was, therefore, the imagined Jew of Nazi propaganda, a sluice gate into which all their fears, frustrations and loathing were poured, and a distillation of their own traits. Hitler claimed his aggression was responsive to international Jews, and thus propaganda inverted the actual relation. The Final Solution, when viewed though the Nazi perspective or worldview, was 'a necessary campaign of retaliation' within the context of the Second World War. Similarly, Goebbels once wrote that 'if in a dark hour war should one day break out in Europe, this cry must resound over the whole part of the earth. The Jews are guilty!'[165]

However, Nazi anti-Semitism was dynamic rather than static; it did not begin and end with a coherent anti-Semitic ideology in 1933. Instead, Nazi anti-Semitism evolved over time and became increasingly radical as it did so.[166] This is clearly reflected in the films produced by the regime, in which anti-Semitism was a marginal theme until the end of the 1930s. Films like *Robert and Bertram* and *Linen from Ireland* marked the onset of a new policy of overt antagonism that would subsequently continue in other films such as *Carl Peters* (1941), with its depiction of a Jewish civil servant who was antipathetic to German colonial aspirations.[167] A primer in anti-Semitic training was even available in Braille, and there was also an anti-Semitic medical journal.[168]

The problem for the Nazis was that many things the Jews were derided for were objective talismans of superiority, such as their presence in academia and their prominence as physicists. In other words, the myth was driven by envy of superiors as well as by contempt for the imagined inferior. Jews could not simply be dismissed as ghetto artisans given their relationship to higher learning and European high culture. This would present a major conceptual problem for any putative master race seeking to make itself feel superior to a superior people. Jews accounted for 12 per cent of all German professors and a quarter of Germany's Nobel Prize-winners.[169] Part of the Nazis' antagonism to the Jews arose from a misunderstanding of the sophistication of a modern economy, insofar as the service economy, where Jews were employed, was not viewed as 'real' work. Those employed in the service/professional sector were by definition parasitic as far as the Nazis were concerned and this was a perspective which clearly appealed to the petit bourgeois base of the Nazi party. Moreover, once it is accepted that the service sector is exclusively parasitic, then it follows that Jews were a destructive force. In explaining why the Nazis sought to fight against the 'Jewish race', one propaganda article states that that the Jew is not 'a creative spirit, [but is] rather a destructive spirit'. The article's author, Werner May, ponders why 'there are no Jewish construction workers in Germany'.[170] His definition of creativity is inevitably outrageously narrow, with May stating that 'nearly all the [world's] major inventions were made by Aryans'[171] (conveniently ignoring the role of Jews in such disciplines as nuclear physics). The focus of other Nazi propaganda material, such as *Stürmer*, was also on Jewish professionals, with one typical article showing a couple visiting a Jewish lawyer; a year later they are thin and poor while he is now fat and rich.[172] Another *Stürmer* article (published on 21 January 1938) even went so far as to demand the death penalty for Jews who slept with non-Jews.[173]

Principal accusations

Four principal depictions of the Jew were used in anti-Semitic Nazi propaganda, and it is these which served as the foundation for the entire incendiary superstructure of the Reich: (1) the physical caricature of Jews as monstrous; (2) a stereotype of the Jewish mask (see below); (3) the association of Jews with notions of dirt and uncleanliness; and (4) the misrepresentations of Jewish belief as a foundation for mythmaking.

The principal mythologies of Nazi anti-Semitism also included laziness.[174] This alleged Jewish character trait was not in fact part of the traditional anti-Semitic canon and consequently demonstrates the inherent plasticity of myths and their potential for sculpting fresh layers of falsehood. Hence Jews were supposedly workshy, as depicted in one of the *Stürmer* children's stories (*The Parable of the Drones*): 'they laze away the whole day. The only thing they do is eat! Yes, and how!'[175]

Then there was mastery of disguise, one of the constituent elements in this imaginary Jewish persona. In films such as the *Rothschilds at Waterloo* or *Jud Süss* the Jew was shown as being capable of counterfeiting the persona of a civilised gentleman, though cinemagoers were constantly reminded that this was a mere façade (a theme also explored in Goebbels's essay on Jewish mimicry (1941)).[176] In *Jud Süss*, for instance, Süss removes his distinctive Jewish dress early on and is re-created as an urbane lawyer; when Dorothea asks him where he feels most at home, his response is 'everywhere', to which she asks, 'have you no home then?'[177] In the film's final scene, set in a court, he drops the mask and Süss reverts to a Jewish prototype—speaking in Yiddish dialect, for example.[178] Similarly, in *The Rothschilds*, the procession of Jewish agents circulating gold are successively regressed until they ultimately appear in Middle Eastern folk costume. The idea was that the Nazis were revealing a conspiracy, as with the claim that there were so few Jews visible in leadership roles in Russia because that country had cunningly hid them from its people. One Nazi volume, *Jews in the USA* (of which nearly half a million copies were published), attempted to reveal mimicry by visual juxtaposition, with contrasting images of New York's governor during an election campaign and on the election night, exposing him as a smiling 'orthodox Jew' among other Jews.[179] It was this notion of Jewish camouflage and subterfuge that lay behind the imposition of the Star of David insignia, which meant that Jews could no longer self-conceal in order to work mischief.[180]

The Jews were also accused of avarice, with one indicative propaganda article boldly claiming that 'Money is the God of the Jews'. There were of course a large number of great Jewish capitalists, and it was not difficult for the Nazis to find candidates out of the global menagerie of capitalist leadership who could be surfaced as outstandingly base representatives of the genre. Thus a whole series of pictures were offered in Nazi propaganda of 'prototypes of the exploit-the-system types' who would not be able to exist in the 'new Europe', such as Sir Basil Zaharoff, who was alleged to have 'financed the seventeen revolutions in Greece between 1910 and 1930',[181] or another financier, 'the son of a rabbi', who was said to have delivered inferior aeroplanes to the Austrian air force in the Great War, thereby 'sending hundreds of gallant airmen to their death'.[182] Even the battlefield was not immunised from anti-Semitism. The leaflet bombardment of Allied forces at Cassino included one piece that featured a 'Jew' in black tie, a naked woman on his lap, reading a paper with the red star brand. A bottle of champagne is clearly visible.[183]

A further myth was that of Jewish ubiquity, of a Teutonic living space and economy swamped with Jews. *The German National Catechism*, for instance, claimed that 'the number of people in Germany with Jewish blood was estimated in 1935 at two million'.[184] The same book also exaggerated the dimensions of Jewish professional domination, with claims that they constituted 34.3 per cent of independent bankers (the decimal point implies scientific accuracy but the phrase it qualifies—'independent bankers'—is inherently vague).[185] The press, likewise, was described as 'the centre of the anti-German spirit', with the assertion that 124 out of a total of 177 newspaper editors were Jewish.[186] As often with Nazi propaganda there was a thin thread of truth here amid the great garbage tip of lies: Jews were indeed prominent bankers and they also had some representation among the Bolshevik leadership. Neither of these facts is particularly surprising given the ancient Christian ban on usury combined with the original quar-

antining of many public professions such as army/civil service, while identification with Bolshevism partly resulted, among other things, from Tsar
Nicholas's terrible pogrom (there was one Jewish member of the Soviet
Politburo in the 1930s and by 1939 only 10 per cent of the Central Committee were Jewish).[187]

As was the case with other targets, in their propaganda assault on the
Jews the Nazis adopted a particularised methodology of persuasion. This
methodology involved a case-history approach of allegedly true stories;
false stories with a thin sliver of truth which, as a result, raise the credibility of the whole; the manufacture of statistics to appease the demand of a
culture ostensibly based on scientific rationalism and empiricism; and the
device of projection, or the attribution of Nazi characteristics on to the very
people they sought to demonise so that the caricature face of the enemy
was really that of the Nazis themselves. This was combined with the creation of an assertion-based myth system which was non-falsifiable because
the myth was always self-confirmatory: thus there is no evidence for
Jewish concealment because Jews are so good at concealing the evidence of
their concealment.

The Nazis consequently sustained an assortment of methodologies to
perpetuate their myths:

– *Fantasy.* Nazi images and assertions did not ask for belief. Rather, the
  viewer was invited to share in a fantasy, a co-produced hallucination of
  enmity, as with the idea of Jewish monstrosity. The Jew was simply a
  goblin from a fairy-tale for the Nazis, a representative of what lurks for
  mankind in the dark Teutonic wood. For *Jud Süss*, the director secretly
  imported 120 Jews from the Lublin ghetto in Poland to perform in order
  to lend the film some 'authenticity'; in other words, the way to achieve a
  'Jewish' look was to trawl among those still surviving in the portal to
  genocide.[188] The Jew was also presented as the devil incarnate, with one
  propaganda article claiming that Jews were 'the devil in human form',
  while little children were taught 'to get rid of the Jewish Devil'.[189]

– *Doublethink.* The Jew combined two targets for the Nazis, namely communism and capitalism, and was, paradoxically, a representative of both.
  This was doublethink as Orwell defined it (i.e. the ability to hold two
  contradictory ideas simultaneously).

– *Case History.* Vivid stories persuade more effectively than statistics. In
  Nazi Germany tales abounded of elderly women who had lost their life
  savings or farmers who had lost their livelihood. A sense of imminent

danger and universal victimhood was also articulated via readers' letters in the newspapers.[190]

– *Statistics*. Hyperbolic statistical claims were made about Jewish dominance of the global economy. In the United States, for example, the Nazis claimed that Jews owned 97 per cent of the newspapers.[191]

– *Non-Falsifiability*. The removal of Chamberlain's Jewish secretary of state for war, Leslie Hore-Belisha, for instance, was explained in a German press directive as a manoeuvre to conceal the extent of Jewish influence. The Nazi alone, in other words, had the gift of insight.[192]

– *Projection*. Gonen views the demonisation of the Jews in Germany as a classic case of projection in which the Nazis attributed their own pathologies to their enemies, inflating into an existential threat, for example, Kaufman's 'plan' for the sterilisation of all Germandom; hence the Germans arrogated to themselves in fiction a fight for survival which they had inflicted on the Jews in fact.

– *Resurrection of Ancient Myths*. Nazi propaganda involved the mobilisation of ancient myths which were often medieval in origin. A new myth system was consequently fashioned out of the old: myth can therefore be seen as dynamic, absorbing new elements and being perpetually recreated. In the documentary *The Eternal Jew* the imagery could sustain the thesis simply because any people filmed starving to death, and dwelling in the borderlands of ethnic extinction, would look as the Jews filmed in the Warsaw ghetto looked. The title of the documentary surfaced a medieval fiction, the legend of the Wandering Jew (Ahasuerus) who derided Christ on his journey to Calvary. In this ancient lie Ahasuerus was thus condemned by divine vengeance to the most terrible punishment: immortality itself, never to die, forever to roam the pitiless face of the earth, unforgiven, unforgotten, glimpsed here and there down all the generations until the Second Coming. The myth of ritual child murder was also resurrected, as for example in one of *Stürmer*'s children's stories where the Jew asks a young boy and girl to follow him, but the boy soon realises the man's true and monstrous identity (*The Experience of Hans and Elsa with a Strange Man*): 'You are a Jew, he cries, and, seizing his sister, runs off as fast as his legs will carry. At the corner of the street he meets a policeman ...'[193] The hint here is of paedophilia or even worse: the little Nazi boy embodies sham-heroic Nazi virtues in childlike form.

- *Shared Illusion.* Thus there was the role of shared fantasy, an assault on the consciousness with propositions too risible to be taken seriously at the rational level (i.e. seepage, where ideas creep below cognitive defences). This was the case with the creation of the myth, the alleged Kaufman sterilisation plan (above) 'revealed' in a 1941 pamphlet by Wolfgang Diewerge and which was claimed to be 'background music' to Allied foreign policy.[194]

- *Distortion of Practice and Ritual.* Ritual killing was a source of more myths, with Jews represented as sadists who relished inflicting pain on other creatures. One propaganda article contained images from the 1939 Vienna fish market, for example, where, readers were told, Jews turned up to watch the killing of fish; another image was entitled 'Joy in Murder'.[195] Sacred texts were another source of wilful misrepresentation.[196]

- *Exaggeration of Physical Characteristics.* If the Jews were to be made a different race, then they needed to be made to look like one. A differentiated people need attributed distinctiveness and outsize physical characteristics, and with Nazi propaganda they received these to the extent of becoming not merely a different race but a different species. Thus in one children's story from *Stürmer, How to Tell a Jew,* 'Little Carl' reaches for the pointer: 'one can most easily tell the Jew by his nose, the Jewish six, their noses go upwards not downwards'. Fabricated, universal characteristics were also enumerated: the Jews are 'small with short legs, often bow-legged, slumping forehead, curly hair like a Negro's, large ears'. A 'smiling blonde lad' explains to a sceptical classmate that 'one can recognize a Jew from his movement and behaviour ...' Social ostracism is implicit in these images: 'Just look at these guys! The lice infested beards! The filthy, protruding ears.'

The Utility of Anti-Semite Mythology

The myths of the Jews had a utilitarian function in Nazi Germany. They explained, simplified and condensed a complex world; they motivated action and they facilitated solidarity. In particular:

- *Explanation/Justification.* The function of the Jews in Nazi propaganda was to provide for a universal and comprehensive explanation of all that had gone wrong in the life of the *Volk,* from defeat in the First World War onwards. Jews were to blame for everything, while conversely the Aryan

German was to blame for nothing. For Klemperer, the Jew was the most important person in the Hitler state, folk history's scapegoat, a plausible adversary: 'had the Führer really achieved his aim of exterminating all the Jews, he would have had to invent new ones, because without the Jewish devil ... without the swarthy Jew there would never have been the radiant figure of the Nordic Teuton'.[197] Indeed, Hitler in fact remarked that 'if the Jew did not exist we would have had to invent him. A visible enemy, not just an invisible enemy, is what is needed here.'[198] This was secular absolution for the Nazis—the Jews were made the focus of all the evil in the human race, the vessels into which our original sin was poured.

– *Solidarity.* The anti-type in Nazi propaganda defined the type; they articulated a virtue by manufacturing its opposite. The very creation of social solidarity in the Reich was achieved by the creation of a common enemy, a menacing antagonist who threatened the group with extinction. If such an enemy did not exist then it could be fabricated. It was Hitler's particular skill and insight to recognise the function of enemies in the manufacture of solidarity. In other words, the Third Reich was inspired by problems which were imaginary as well as real, and the superlative ability of Adolf Hitler to 'sell the right myths'.[199] The construction of enmity is inherently reductive: a complex, fluid and mysterious world can be elided into a simple conspiracy from a single source. A nuanced construction of enemies would never have succeeded; simplicity was everything.

– *Existential Threat.* What Hitler offered to Germany was the notion of an existential threat. In other words he was self-cast as a prophet, a messenger of doom, and this latter fate could only be avoided if the right action was taken.[200] Hence on 1 January 1940, in his annual New Year address, Hitler spoke of the Jewish plan to liquidate Germans: 'the Jewish capitalist world enemy that confronts us has only one goal: to exterminate Germany and the German people'.[201] This notion informed Hitler's oratory and gave his public persona its unique authority and dynamically charged performance. As Gonen points out, there was 'a messianic end of days and timeless quality of this shaping battle that Hitler prophesied in *Mein Kampf;* it was not clear that the Aryans would win and in particular that the Jews might actually succeed in their world historical mission'.[202] Hitler believed all this as an article of faith: this being the belief, all the rest followed. This drama had no possible end but extinction—it depended for its momentum on continuous provocation; that is to say, the bunker in Berlin became the only possible terminus when such a messianic mission had failed in its task. Jewry was seen as the quasi-invisible driving force of history. In the words of Ernst Gombrich, 'what is characteristic of Nazi propaganda is less a lie than the imposition of a paranoiac pattern on world events'.[203]

The Jews were depicted as being all-powerful throughout the world, with propaganda emphasising the Jewish origins of New York's Mayor La Guardia, for instance (who was in fact only half-Jewish),[204] while other luminaries of politics and commerce, such as J.P. Morgan, Jimmy Durante and Roosevelt, were casually lifted on to the roster of Semites without any evidence at all.[205] Indeed, in the case of the Nazis, anti-Semitism is descriptively inadequate: a better phrase would be an apocalyptic anti-Semitism. Gonen claims that the publication of the 'Protocols of the Elders of Zion' in Germany represented a critical combination of means and ends, and that it was the coexistence of the Protocols with the theorising of Le Bon that created such a combustible mix in Germany.[206]

- *The Ultimate Enemy*. In Nazi propaganda the Second World War was the final struggle to save European civilisation. One propaganda article states, 'now ... we recognize our old enemy, world Jewry. After being defeated within Germany, it is now embodied in Anglo-Saxon plutocracy and Bolshevik state capitalism and tries to attain its goal from abroad'; the paradox is explained by the assertion that 'plutocracy and Bolshevism have one master, the Jews!'[207] The Nazis were seeking to repeat their internal victory on a global scale, and hence the invasion of the USSR was presented as 'a return to orthodoxy'. But there was a sense in which all the enemies of the Third Reich were in fact Jewish: what the Nazis had supplied was 'an almost mono-dimensional/mono-causal view of recent historical events'.[208] Marxist and plutocrat were alternate masks of the same vengeful phenomenon.[209] Under this light, the attack on the Soviet Union and the Holocaust were alternative responses to the same perceived disease, in that the war against the Allies and against the Jews were the same thing. Hitler claimed that politically the war 'presented itself in the main as a conflict between Germany and England, but ideologically it was a battle between National Socialism and Jews'.[210] This was the way in which all the propaganda against Germany's enemies was integrated via the provision of one final ultimate enemy, and, in consequence, it was therefore comparatively easy to absorb the United States into the Nazi discourse of enmity. Indicatively, Hitler's diatribe to the Reichstag on 11 December 1941 explained that 'once again, as in the year

1915 ... [the United States] will be incited by the Jewish President and his completely Jewish entourage to go to war without any reason ...'[211]

Hitler asserted that nearly all the leaders of Communist Russia were Jews: 'overly refined, parasitic world intellectuals'.[212] Jews had also corrupted the United States, as for example in the film industry where 'prostitution, immorality and crime are depicted as acts of heroism'—Roosevelt was 'the grand Rabbi, Roosevelt' and 'the head of Zionism' (all of these allegations were made via the Athens transmitter).[213] Moreover, there is no question that Hitler believed fanatically in his construction and we should reject 'any lingering tendency to see Hitler's expressions as mere overblown propaganda': for Hitler 'the Jew is baser, fiercer. more diabolical than Streicher depicted him'.[214] There is no evidence that the top Nazis and Hitler did this out of cynicism, and contemporary observers thought they actually believed their own 'paranoid logic'. Klemperer would write in 1944: 'however much I resisted it, *the Jew* is in every respect the centre of the language of the Third Reich, indeed of its whole view of the epoch';[215] he recognised that anti-Semitism goes beyond prejudice into an entire explanatory framework for history.[216] Race was also Germany's ambassador, to be evangelised in conquered lands as a new and up-to-date way of thinking about identity: thus 'in August 1941 the German authorities in the occupied Netherlands decreed that every Dutch cinema should include *The Eternal Jew* in its programme during the following six-month period. And so the film became at the same time a prelude to the Holocaust, a propagandist's excuse for it, and a perverted documentary-format record of its early stages.'[217] The Middle East was another export target audience for Nazi race propaganda. Germany's radio station in Athens, VFA, urged listeners to write down names and details of Jews so that 'they may be wiped out at the earliest opportunity'.[218] The Nazis' propaganda state even sponsored a jazz band: 'Charlie and his Orchestra' crooned anti-Semitic versions of Fred Astaire and also American jazz.[219] In the newly conquered Russian city of Kharkov, grotesquely anti-Semitic posters leered from broken buildings,[220] and similarly, in the Middle East, German radio urged its listeners to 'kill the Jews before they kill you' and alleged that Jews were 'planning to violate your women, to kill your children and destroy you'.[221]

But the literature was also anti-capitalist, claiming speculators dominate the world 'rather than the law of labour and of blood': again the direct translation of Nazi concepts (such as their obsession with global plutocracy), and their assumption that these would also prevail elsewhere. Even the Allied armies and publics were targets for Nazi race hate propaganda.

Hence 'News in Brief', a German news sheet dropped over Italy, had titles like 'England's Jews Pile Up Profits'.[222] A leaflet claimed, for example, that the 'American Jew Baruch' had given orders to 'Butcher Harris' to kill German civilians indiscriminately;[223] in other words, the Royal Air Force accepted its orders from a New York financier.

The Anti-Type: The English Class Enemy

Nazi propaganda was consequently based on a bestiary of hyphenated entities such as the Jewish-Bolshevik and Anglo-Saxon plutocracy, all painted in luminous colours. In private, Hitler claimed that 'the Englishman can only respect someone who has first knocked him out. The memory of 1918 must be obliterated.'[224]

Nazi Anglophobia had several components, one of which was the idea that the British were masters of duplicity, the mavens of insidious cunning, and while the Nazis initially had an ambivalent attitude towards Britain, based on the idea of racial solidarity, this fractured as the Second World War progressed. Indeed, early in the life of the regime, Britain had been the respected adversary in films such as the *Riders of German East Africa* (1934).[225] But this changed dramatically during the war, when the representations of Britons in many German films were so outrageously exaggerated that few in Germany actually took them seriously.[226] These films include: *The Heart of The Queen* (1940), about the life of Mary Queen of Scots; *The Fox of Glenarvon* (1940); and *My Life for Ireland* (1941), in which the British are portrayed as oppressors.[227] Nazi propaganda also came to excoriate British arrogance and perfidy in songs like 'Bombs over England', and short films such as *Soldiers of Tomorrow* (1941).

Dr Ernst Lewalter's essay in *Signal*, 'The Road to Dunkirk', is a caricature but not a fib ('Britain reached Dunkirk on the well-worn tracks of tradition'):[228] a picture of the world of the 1930s as it appeared to outsiders. Nazi propaganda was always believable and never true, an interesting paradox; a truth but not the truth. The essay is set on a hot June afternoon in London during Ascot and the Season: 'heat-waves rise from the sea of houses and rob the sun's rays of their wholesome effect. We are standing in the stifling, sooty hall of Waterloo station waiting for a train.'[229] Then the drama starts:

suddenly two trains arrive at the same instant, one on either side of the platform. An invisible hand opens all the doors as though with a single turn of the wrist, and immediately two streams of men begin to merge into one another and pour from the platforms out into the main hall of the station—two very different groups indeed: one train emits a dark stream of workers—dirty, sweaty, tired and dejected—the other a bright stream of gay gentlemen, with light, measured step, in grey cut-aways and grey top hats, white spats, small silver-knobbed walking sticks in their hands, their monocles dangling from ribbons, flowers in their buttonholes.

The author opines that such a rigid social structure would be unable to 'compete with the onset of a young world. Germany has rearranged its forces in a revolutionary process.'

The Nazis again used a distinctive formula in their disparagement of the British:

– *Projection.* As a matter of course, their methodology was a projection of their crimes and procedures of criminality on to their enemies, although it is unclear whether this was a conscious tactic or a perverse form of self-knowledge. For example, an illustrated pamphlet (written in Dutch and presumably aimed at the occupied Netherlands) excoriates Britain's counterinsurgency methods in the Boer War (1899–1902).[230] It is illustrated with period drawings of a woman surrounded by a pile of twelve naked child corpses; Joseph Chamberlain tormented by ghosts; British soldiers laughing at the dead and dying prisoners; hostage women and a child bound to an armoured train as the soldiers hide inside; six prisoners hanging from a gibbet as the British march away having done their deed of darkness. The film *Ohm Krüger* (1941), which has been recognised as 'perhaps the most impressive propaganda film made during the Third Reich', contains similar themes.[231] Krüger, the lead character, is a textbook Nazi patriarch—avuncular, the leader of a proto-nation bonded to the land, honest and brave; a Hitler surrogate and fatherland symbol—while Churchill is presented in the film as a bulldog-besotted concentration camp commandant who shoots starving women, and Queen Victoria is shown as 'a whisky sodden crone, lurching and slurred of speech'.[232] The prince of Wales, meanwhile, is depicted as obese and lecherous,[233] whereas Kitchener is a sadist. Krüger's Oxford-educated son becomes an Anglophobe only when a British soldier attacks his wife: 'he becomes the martyr for the Boer cause, hanged by the British on a hill that looks like Golgotha ... "I died for the fatherland", he says.'[234] The Nazi talent for attributing their crimes on to their enemies, for asserting moral superiority, for wrapping their murderous ambitions in the cloak of sanctimony, is nowhere better illustrated than here. Similarly, with the voice at the end of *Baptism of Fire*:

what have you to say now, Mr Chamberlain? Here you will find conclusive evidence of the catastrophe you brought about in the Polish capital ... All this is your work, yours is the guilt, and you will have to answer for it one day at the last judgement. And remember one thing: this is what happens when the German Luftwaffe strikes. They will also know how to strike at the guiltiest of the guilty.[235]

Göring then speaks before a song of the German air force is played: 'we sit here in judgement, an empire is crumbling ... Bombs on England! Bombs, bombs, bombs on England!'[236]

– *Existential Threat.* Britain and its ally America came to represent an existential and not just a military threat to Germany in Nazi propaganda, in that they proposed the physical extinction of Germandom in a bizarre parody of the actual extinction of the Jews. According to this interpretation, Britain had attacked the German race and not just its political system. The juvenility of the Nazi critique of England asked not for belief but faith. In a similar fantastical vein, Britain was now merely an adjunct of the Soviet Union.

– *Pseudo-History.* Nazi pseudo-intellectuals speculated on the historical and cultural origins of the Anglo-Judaic alliance: 'the Jews saw themselves as the chosen people ... and in consequence of this flourishing tradition the English regarded themselves as the chosen people of the world'.[237] This belief in being chosen was the basis of Britain's world rule and therefore of a world empire. As Walter Schellenberg argued:

> the rise of puritanism brought about a revival of Jewish influence in England, and Cromwell recognized the similarity of the English scheme for world domination and the Jewish one. Cromwell was convinced his people were the chosen ones and this set the foundations of the Anglo-Jewish Alliance. The relationship between the Jews and the English was reinforced by an old tale that the English people were one of the lost tribes of Israel, a myth which still has supporters in England and is deliberately propagated by the Jews.[238]

Both anglo-capitalism/puritanism and Judaism, in the words of the Nazis, were 'religiously articulated egoism ... [both] rest on the idea of a chosen people. Among Jews and the English, political superiority and unscrupulousness are grounded in this kind of religion.'[239]

– *Judaisation.* The Nazis maintained that the English upper-class had been Judaised. Thus Hitler argued in private, 'it's a queer business, how England slipped into the war. The man who managed it was Churchill, that puppet of the Jewry that pulls the strings.'[240] Goebbels claimed that the English were the 'Jews among the Aryans':[241] the English character was a 'melange of brutality, mendacity, sham piety and sanctimonious godliness'.[242] Nazi propaganda spoke of 'the Jew in the city and the Jew in the Kremlin'.[243] The nature of the enmity, and the stereotypes, were not therefore defined *ab initio*. Rather, they were changeable over time in light of the political situation and the fortunes and experiences of war. Thus *The Rothschilds*, which blends anti-Semitism with Anglophobia, was structurally altered after its initial release, and then re-launched. Anglophobic propaganda became more hyperbolic as the German military succeeded (over eight films between 1940 and 1943), and the idea of Aryan Jews now replaced that of cruel colonialists, while SD reports noted that cinemagoers wanted even more 'British lying lords etc.'[244]

The new entity, Judaised Anglo-Saxon plutocracy, is an example of the Nazis' ideological incontinence. In *The Rothschilds*, the immigrant Rothschild manipulates share prices by deceiving the Stock Exchange about the outcome of the Battle of Waterloo; his instrument is rumour and the explicit message is that brave men die while a Jew is making money. The end of the film is a classic of the genre: for the chancellor of the exchequer, Rothschild sketches the branches of Rothschild Bank on a map of Europe and the pattern forms a Star of David. The final image is the Star superimposed on a map of England. It is part of a trinity—with *The Eternal Jew* and *Jed Süss*—made in 1940 as prologue to and surrogate indicator of the Holocaust. In this Judaised England, the Jews dominated the arts and public media, 'along with the faculties of the universities in Cambridge, London, and Birmingham'; Nazis spoke of the 'inner jewification of English politics'.[245] The Judaisation of the English elite and establishment, both through the participation of Jews themselves and also through the Judaising impact of the Puritan heritage, is a particularly fascinating myth. The tone of the Gestapo handbook to Britain by SS General Schellenberg can be accurately suggested by such lines as 'Baron Southwood of Fernhurst, formerly Julius Salter Elias ... Lord Rosebery, a half Jew ...'[246] The England of Nazi propaganda was seething with Jews and Freemasons who seemed to control much that went on. Jews are shown in the handbook as dominating business and media in England, and Schellenberg's aim was to unmask prominent Jews in banking and so on, naming them all from Lord Reading, a former viceroy of India, onwards. Particular attention was devoted to Jews in press, radio and film. The handbook also offers discourses on the story of Jews in medieval England. England is furthermore the country of Freemasonry, and the general argues that Freemasonry arose here and was exported to the continent—its historical significance 'is the advancement of Jewish emancipation in Europe'.[247]

- *Social Caricature.* There were the English, and then there was the illusionary England of Nazi media. Goebbels proclaimed and perhaps even believed curiously feudal ideas about England, writing in his diaries: 'I write a leading article for *Das Reich*, unmasking the English lords.'[248] The Nazis were enthusiastic participants in England's class war; anatomising the degradations of the English class system and a culture divided between the polarities of a Dickensian underclass, seeking to survive in seething and filthy tenements, and a ruling class desensitised by its inherited privileges—a very long way from George Orwell's England as a family with the wrong members in charge. The images embellished in German media were from another century, not just another era—little boy workers sleeping curled up (from a mid-nineteenth-century engraving) or similarly a London tenement room crowded with children and despairing parents. But, according to Bormann (1941), 'Germany's appearance on the scene' was a 'disaster' for the English elite.[249] W.J. West even asserts that the genesis of the Beveridge Commission lay in the incendiary polemics of 'Lord Haw-Haw'.[250]

- *Social Menace.* Then there was the global perfidy of the English plutocracy; the top-hatted English capitalist with a monocle, pipe, silver cane, wing collar and orchid might equally have come from Bolshevik propaganda.[251] This portrait was not without nuance, for the English masses were innocent of the oppressions wrought by this craven elite, and so Goebbels made a distinction between them.

- *Comparisons with the Reich.* Invidious comparisons were made between new Nazi institutions and old English ones. Propaganda magazine *Der Schulungsbrief* (1942) contrasts an Adolf Hitler School in Germany with images of Eton and Harrow youth: the young Nazis are smiling and happy, touching each other in comradely fashion and musing thoughtfully over a game of chess.[252] *Wir Fahren Gegen Engeland* offers the usual symbols of English class idiosyncrasy (such as the picture of Etonians, here with gas mask canisters).[253] *Der Schulungsbrief* gives a two-page montage of iconic representations of enemy culture: Soviet peasants; English ladies at a party dressed as eighteenth-century grandes dames; a young 'English Lord' and 'servant' (that is to say a boy attending a hunt and being given a drink); the image of starving Russian children and then Hollywood partygoers quaffing champagne (allegedly these are 'Hebrews'); a Florida mansion viewed from the air and girls surrounded by a mass of oranges; and an impoverished village on the Eastern Front.[254] The inference is that this is what the German soldier is fighting against, the combined perversities of capitalism and Communism, an imagistic litany of symbols both of deprivation and excess. Only in Nazi Germany has a mature and technically based culture attained real balance and social harmony.

The Nazis consistently failed to understand the British. Hence in the eyes of SS General Schellenberg, the Boy Scouts were a sinister and insidious threat.[255] The Boy Scout movement's central headquarters was in London:

in the so-called International Bureau which until recently has been managed by a half Jew, Mr Martin, who was simultaneously the head of the passport office ... Although the individual Boy Scout organisations are ostensibly almost entirely devoted to pre-military youth education, the Boy Scout movement is a disguised instrument of power for British cultural propaganda, and an excellent source of information for the British intelligence service. Lord Baden Powell was run as an agent against Germany during the last war. The dissolution of the Austrian Boy Scout movement ...[256]

Thus propaganda even distorted an SS manual—there is no objectivity here, only fantasy.

Moreover, in Germany there was still an excess of the kind of myopia/ hubris characterised by the Kaiser when he dismissed the British army as 'contemptible' on the outbreak of the First World War. An article by Benno Wundshammer (1940) about an attack on the 'the burning capital of a dying empire' naturally presents the British enemy as incompetent: 'as is so often the case, the enemy flak is wild and ineffective'.[257] There is a sense in the article of crass triumphalism, self-deceitful and other-deceitful, unreal, and of the enemy's competence and tenacity being underestimated via the two-dimensional heroics and rhetorics of disdain; slogans and clichéd scenarios are strung together like a comic book: 'my job was to sit in my fine Messerschmitt and to see to it that as many English as possible were shot down'; and the enemy are pusillanimous: 'the Tommies broke off and looked for safety'.[258] The German was always presented as the technological superior ('But my plane was faster'), and the enemy is always vanquished—'The Tommy was done for.' A pilot of a reconnaissance mission is quoted as saying: 'Wherever one looked, Tommies were falling. Everywhere British planes were chased by Germans ... The British bomber fell like a rock, leaving a cloud of smoke as it plunged into the water ... every few minutes we shot down another Tommy.' Again the pejoratives: 'the old lady Spitfire was in my sights ... as I dispatched the Spitfire, my comrades in the rear had done the same to the other one ...' In the end they break away from the enemy only 'slowly', fearful that the 'dogs' would bite to the last. Yet there was always a latent regard for these leasors of a global empire; the SS noted that 'even Britons are only human and make blunders', apparently without irony.[259] But the Britons were ultimately regarded as ruthless. Their Secret Service, for example, was said to make use of 'means which can hardly be distinguished from those of a common criminal,' an interesting comment coming from the SS.[260]

Types: Adolf Hitler

The German leadership was imagined and popularly conceived in propaganda 'as existing in some extra-terrestrial dimension of its own since Bismarck, such as the glory besotted Kaiser, [or] Hindenburg's larger-than-life image'.[261] The image of the great man in German history who rescues Germany—Bismarck, Frederick the Great, Kaiser Frederick Barbarossa—was incorporated into the Hitler myth. The ideology of the Fascist insofar as he had one was total loyalty to the supreme leader; Fascism was simply what the leader said it was on any given day. The leader consequently had to be built up by the propaganda as superhuman, or more specifically in the Fascist case as an extraordinary ordinary man, in order to sustain the faith the Nazis demanded. Hitler was the messiah, with the first and most important construct in the Hitler myth being the idea that he was the saviour and chosen one. But like any dramatic role the Hitler act was not static: it was his evolving interpretation of what Germans were looking for.

The first element of the Hitler myth was of a simple First World War soldier. He was an everyman, his act a synthesis: one of the people but also an inspired seer, a visionary who could see beyond the nimbus of confusion that wraps human affairs. He was the super-patriot, the austere, ascetic bachelor leader with Germany as his bride, self-sacrificing, the artist who had left his easel. In this act of people's Kaiser there were also elements of Cincinnatus, the leader who led the Roman Republic in its hour of need and then returned to his plough. Hitler was medium and mystic and maven; a prince walking among men, but also a prince of the people. This offered a completeness of myth system and also a fluidity—new elements could always be added, and thus he was the greatest diplomatist since Metternich, dazzling a proud and stupefied Reich, and a supreme warlord, a military genius who transcended even Napoleon and Alexander. Yet the myth had a flaw in that it had to be sustained by the continuous production of success, and as a result success had to be continuously produced. Beyond this, Hitler came to believe in it, and there is an inherent blasphemy in the myth, given that it accorded god-qualities to a man. Thus an actor playing a role became that role; the myth became the script.

Was Adolf Hitler an anti-Nazi?

The oracle–orator–mountaintop philosopher, the Hitler of Nazi propaganda, existed far above the tribulations and shadowlands of the German everyday. Part of the illusion was of Hitler as first citizen. The belief was long perpetuated that Hitler was ignorant of the darkest aspects of Nazism.[262] An image of an honourable Führer was created, one who was civic and civil. Some could even see in Hitler a defender of Christianity against the Nazi fundamentalists and as someone who would save Germany from the Communists (according to one German bishop).[263] Central to this was the growing public discrimination between Hitler and the party he embodied. In Kershaw's words, 'Hitler's popularity develop[ed] unaccompanied by a rise in party popularity and to an extent at the expense of it. The Hitler myth served an important compensatory function in the Third Reich.'[264] The public had created an imagined Führer, one unaware of the abuses committed by underlings in his name:

> contrary to any rational understanding of how a dictatorial party works, people believed in a Führer without sin, presiding over an army of little Hitlers of whom they were fully prepared to think the worst ... Likewise, and contrary to all evidence, Hitler was regarded as a relatively moderate figure, restraining the excesses of party radicals, a mistake sometimes made by Western statesmen. But there was more going on than this suggests.[265]

The fact that Hitler could be seen as representing an ostensibly moderate wing of his party was a deliberate part of the methodology of illusion.[266] Hence this illusion was not accidental, as in the case of more naive or imagistically inept regimes, but was entirely deliberate. Via propaganda Goebbels created a human Hitler who loved children, and children in fact became a critical component of the Hitler myth insofar as they lent an aura of benevolence to the figure of the Führer (indeed, as Kershaw reminds us, children were as omnipresent in Nazi propaganda 'as the statuesque SS men').[267] Thus the receipt of a delegation of children was an integral part of the formula.[268] It was an iterative process, in that Hitler was as much the creation of the masses as self-created: they saw in him what they wished to see. At one level, he was a harbinger of what we have known to know as celebrity culture.

Alongside their coverage of film stars, for instance, women's magazines would also show pictures of Hitler laughing while speaking on the telephone, or the children and wives of the other Nazi leaders.[269]

One aspect of this illusion was Hitler's preternatural ability to play multiple roles. He was a consummate actor of parts as occasion and evolution of image dictated. Against a backdrop rich with chauvinist symbolism, Hitler could graduate from immortality to adorable mortality. As Baird writes in his analysis of a documentary on the reburial of the Munich martyrs:

> as the camera focuses on the Führer's face, the braziers belch forth their black oily smoke, which presents a marked contrast to the beauty of the white marble. Muffled drums in shifting cadence reinforce the element of drama. The effect of the whole conveys the sense that one is witnessing an event of world historic importance. At the conclusion, the regime is seen wearing a human face; Hitler becomes a veritable Prince of compassion, greeting the survivors individually. In one particularly suggestive scene, he comforts a young girl who is in tears, gently stroking her face, and touches the shoulder of a grieving widow.[270]

The other stratum in Hitler's image projection was that of military genius, something propaganda was already anticipating before the war began.[271] Hitler can consequently be seen as playing a medley of different acting parts: street fighter and anti-Communist activist, statesman, father of his people, entrepreneur of a new political idea and, finally and ultimately, conquering general-hero.

The mythology of the leader was elaborated indirectly in Nazi propaganda. In order to internalise the Hitler myth, Germans had to absorb it obliquely as well as through the obvious, surface hagiographies of newsreel, newspaper and photojournalism. This method would postpone the point of satiety and refresh key concepts. The chosen method for this was the film biography of great Germans—such as Friedrich Schiller, William Tell, Rudolf Diesel and Otto von Bismarck—men who were prime movers in their fields. These great Germans, significantly, not only straddled war and politics but also included industrialists, scientists and writers as well as princes, all of whom converge on a number of superlative characteristics, and specifically romantic rebellion. These are individuals who rejected timorous conventions and the parochial mediocrities who surrounded them, who paid homage not to some titular head but to a quasi-mystical idea of state and nation. They were men set apart, handmaidens of fate, through whose tortured souls alone does the human race, and the German race in particular, progress. All of these men were anticipations of Hitler as well as versions of him; he was their fulfilment. The key to this model of charismatic governance was not the leader's competence but a more mystical idea. In other words, Hitler represented an idea of possibility, of future fulfilment, rather than the actual conditions Germans had found themselves in since the start of his regime. Critical aspects of the idea of Hitler were: one, the loneliness and burden of the high office; two, that he was motivated by patriotism alone, the mission to save Germany; three, that he was supremely lucky and by inference subject to some sort of providential protection; four, as patriarch; five, as fellow human, both close and remote, loving nature, simple flowers, children; and six, as the austere self-disciplinarian.[272]

The 'Hitler cult' was precisely that: a cult with a deeply quixotic world-view, elaborate rituals for its ideological parish and a demented vision articulated by a weirdly charismatic leader. But it was not a cult in the usual sense of a small group, for this was a great nation, not a tribe of desert zealots. The difference therefore lay in the number of believers, the eccentricity of the worldview, the magnificence of the rituals and the out-size charisma of the chosen one and the messianic incendiarism of his vision. In the words of one German soldier: 'our Führer is the most unique man in history. I believe unreservedly in him and in his movement. He is my religion.'[273] The language of the Reich was indeed religious. Thus *Song of the Faithful*, a book of Hitler Youth poems, was festooned with words like saviour and spirit; newly married couples in Nazi Germany would even receive a copy of *Mein Kampf*.[274] There were Hitler household shrines and Hitler squares and streets.[275] The oath of loyalty to Hitler—'I swear to you, Führer ...'—reinforced the myth: 'the task was to instil the Hitler myth deeply into the hearts of the faithful'.[276]

Types: Leader

Like everything the Reich stood for, the advent of the leader was vividly anticipated by a long canon of literary polemic. In a book published in 1920, Oswald Spengler called for a 'barbaric caesarism' as the path of the future, and a book actually called *The Third Reich* was written by Arthur Moeller in 1923.[277] Literary figures like the poet Stefan George praised the anti-democratic, elitist, combat-and-leader ideology: 'It was a vast backdrop of exalted prophecies founded on a vague, irrational mysticism that became concrete only in their criticism of the West and in the arrogant vilification of the democratic present.'[278]

Idea of Leader

The Third Reich was founded on the leader principle, and it is this which governed the organisational culture of Nazism. But there was a more general interest in leadership per se that thrived in such a society; the principle was something that had to be replicated at every level and was a constant theme of the propaganda. Many films, for example, functioned as training manuals in how to be a leader, and Nazi books, pamphlets and magazines were all replete with heroic homilies. Just as today the airport departure lounge school of management guru literature purports to tell us how to lead, so then did the popular cultural product of the Nazis. Films educated in dominance and initiative, as for example Gneisenau in *Kolberg*, but also Moltke (during the Battle of Sedan) in *Bismarck*: explicitly, a fussy, risk averse, older military style is contrasted with the thrusting techno-centricity of the new. These men are prototype officers. They are focused, scientific, brave, commandeering, but they are not in fact cruel, since cruelty was not the regime's publicly articulated self-concept. This fascination with leadership style, with the idea and ideal of the leader, functioned at all levels of the Third Reich: the leader could emerge in anything from a pack of Hitler Youth to a detachment of German Labour Front road diggers. The programme was not just about ideology; Germans would lead not by being some kind of automaton delivering orders in a rasping voice but via an admixture of rigour, conceptual thinking, human warmth, bravery and utter dedication to the nation.

Single Man

Thus an aspect of the mythology/psychopathology of Nazism, and indeed of Fascism in general, was the attribution of qualities to a single man who became more than the embodiment of the nation, in that he was the embodiment of its consciousness. But this dependence on the idea of a single man also speaks of a wish to regress to some childlike state of dependence. Hitler, and the steroidal patriarchy he represented, was the creation of collective insecurities or a kind of mass hallucination. He represents a warning about the immense danger of charisma. He was, in fact, if not an earthly god at least one who was blessed with some of the ascribed attributes of deity. The genius of Hitler was widely believed; faith in his judgement a matter of certainty. The leader ideal was promulgated indirectly via entertainment, with the Führer concept finding its endorsement in the story of Frederick the Great, who was the ultimate Hitler surrogate. For example, in *The Old King and the Young King* (1935), the king forswears 'salons teeming with gamblers ... He situates himself in a world of straight lines, uniformed masses and unquestioned allegiances, joining the masculine space of the parade ground of the state, assuming its language.'[279]

In a similar vein, in the film *Der grosse König* (1942), Habsburgs and Hohenzollerns vie for the leadership of Germandom. But the Habsburgs tolerate multi-ethnicity, a fickle enemy, and, importantly, lack the idea of duty. The film reflects the official values and preoccupations of the Third Reich in the mid-war period—it 'reads' the public mood and replies to it. Frederick loses the first battle, leading to a popular defeatism against which only the will of the great leader, the Führer surrogate, succeeds. He ignores the universal advice to surrender (including advice from his generals), and his brother denounces his militarism. There are public murmurs about wishing the king dead and a scene where the Bürgmeister complains about the cost of the war: this reflects contemporary popular anger towards the continuity of the Second World War. Then there is the ignominy of retreat: the Bernberg, a Prussian regiment, actually runs away in battle and their colonel shoots himself in front of his soldiers out of pure shame. Frederick, numb, incredulous, orders the men to march to drum and fife, the same beats continuously repeated, their stripes to be torn off, a ritual humiliation. The price of absolute obedience is evoked via the Sergeant Treskow subplot: at the Battle of Torgau (1760) an officer carrying a critical message is shot; Treskow sees the Austrians approach and tells the bugler to call the cavalry into action (but without orders being issued). This saves the day, yet Frederick orders him bound to a wheel for his disobedience before eventually promoting him. His putative desertion both attempts to capture the mood of disloyalty and rhetorically replies to it. The message is that you must, must remain loyal. Treskow's later redemption is in battle when he is killed carrying the colours. Frederick addresses his lifeless body.

In the early battlefield scene Sergeant Treskow's wife (the ubiquitous Christina Soderbaum) unwittingly expresses her anger about the king to Frederick without recognising who he really is. Nor does Frederick then reveal himself (the gods walk among the people); his despair is explicit. When she later comes to plead for her husband, Frederick observes her through his window and grasps the story: the leader, the Führer, is omniscient. His subsequent welcoming back of the disgraced Bernberg regiment similarly reveals an iron will mellowed by humanity; and his love of culture draws indirect comparisons with Hitler, as in the scene of his dream of flute-playing at Sanssouci. But duty to the state transcends all other loyalties. Hence Frederick will not leave battle to see his dying nephew, and his gilded carriage returns empty to the Berlin victory celebration. Prussian austerity ultimately saves his life when the Austrian agent tries to poison him (his factotum eats the spurned delicacies, and dies). Thus the nature of Frederick's power is not so much that of inherited authority as charismatic authority in Weber's sense.

Types: Altruist

During the war, German forces were self-presented by their own media as decently behaved and selectively chivalrous. While magazines and film glorified the war, audiences were always reminded that the German forces remained essentially human. In one *Signal* magazine account, readers were told that the Germans had taken a 'nest of resistance' by 'assault at the point of the bayonet'. The enemy was 'taken prisoner and disarmed', with no mention of anyone being killed.[280] The unprovoked attacks on smaller European countries were argued away as justified by context.

Ethos: The Illusion of Altruism

The Nazis also made use of the myth of self-sacrificial altruism, an attributed characteristic of the *Volk* which the regime sought to mobilise; they not only took credit for this but also used it as part of their broader construction of social solidarity. This social mythology was an aspect of the illusion and it transcended 'mere' manipulation. It meant the substitution of complete fiction for fact, creating a perceptual construct which was invented *ab initio* and which people were invited to buy into. A regime for which there was literally no moral boundary, for which any bearer of hostility, however muted, was a target to be destroyed, was able to swathe itself in the language of ethical exhortation and moral imperative. This effect was a great part of the illusory world the Third Reich represented. It is sometimes imagined that the Fascist appeal lay in brutality and hatred, and these things were certainly visible. But it consisted more largely in the appeal to ideals of duty, self-sacrifice and other-devotion. This, the use of good for evil, was the regime's greatest and most perverse achievement. Indeed, Le Bon had observed that a crowd (not just a physical crowd, but mass publics) can be high-minded:

> personal interest is very rarely a powerful motive force with crowds, whilst it is almost the exclusive motive of the conduct of the isolated individual. It is assur-

edly not self-interest that has guided crowds in so many wars ... Even a scoundrel can become moral in a crowd and this 'moralising of the individual by the crowd' is frequent; crowds are often prudish despite being composed of coarser elements of society.[281]

Nazi Germany was a theatre of altruistic appeals to the civic imperative, exhortations to do good work, a constant evocation of duty and other-regarding action. To many ordinary Germans it must have seemed like a vast benevolent society. This perspective on Nazi German illusions, far from being inconsistent with the appalling horrors we are so familiar with, is both concomitant with and in many ways a necessary preamble to them. In other words, an altruistic appeal on this scale was ultimately an appeal for social solidarity. But the aim of social solidarity was also achieved in equal measure via the construction of external and internal enemies. They were actually part of the same process: the hideous cruelty of Nazism and the extraordinary feats of dedication were all composites of the same phenomena. While Winter Relief, for example (see Chapter Five) had a practical purpose, its real aim was propaganda and the achievement of solidarity and the recognition of mutual interdependency (via a racial equality) of all in the *Volk*. The collections for Winter Relief were in-your-face and ubiquitous, and similarly the so-called Pot (*Eintopf*) Sunday. In fact, some of the generic appeals of Nazism, for example to women, were also made via altruistic ideas. The persuasion of women focused on the endorsement of selfless action for their husbands and families: for Nazis, the German woman was supposed to be an altruist and nothing else, and many women heard this message.

According to Nazi media the inherent altruism of the Reich also extended to the way in which the enemy was treated. A 1943 *Adler* article, for instance, presents a drawing of a U-boat shooting down a British plane which crashes into the sea—the British pilot has climbed on to the fuselage and the article suggests that the U-boat will save him; Germans, as imagined here, are not only humane to each other but humane to the enemy as well.[282] Photographic images feature a sinking ship in the Battle of the Atlantic; a non-swimming crewman clings to its side 'until he is rescued'. *Wir Fahren Gegen Engeland* shows, similarly, the sinking of the British aircraft carrier *Courageous*, with the German U-boat picking up survivors.[283] The humanitarian presence is always there. Thus it would be a mistake to imagine that all the propagandists ever dealt in was the coinage of race-narcissism and overweening militarism. 'Altruism' gave the regime a more subtle public face, one that could seem on occasion human and even kind, a mask for the realities which were even then being implemented or planned for the future. People's best, as well as their basest, instincts were being used to persuade them. Thus one poster for the Winter Relief campaign translates as 'no one shall go hungry, no one shall go cold' and shows the classic image of the poor woman of European tradition wearing a black shawl and covering a child with a dark cloak. She looks like an image from Dickens.[284]

German culture also afforded the image of the enlightened folk-oriented businessman who sought to deploy his great wealth on behalf of the broader community. This was an idealised type represented in Germany by such figures as Alfred Krupp, who said of his workers: 'they must be able to earn in work, the maximum that an industry can offer—or we must abandon an industry which starves its workers',[285] or the physicist Ernst Abbe, who co-founded the Zeiss Optical Works: 'he gave his fortune to the enterprise, creating an endowment and introduced social measures and good wages—profits were to benefit the whole undertaking'.[286] This is undoubtedly an admirable sentiment, one which few would decry, but these in fact represent Nazi propagandists' iconic alternative to their images of corrupt Anglo-American capitalists. It was part of the enigma of the Third Reich, the moral paradox it poses before the bar of history, and of the questions which its very emergence raise about the nature of our humanity (questions which have not and cannot be answered): that Nazism appealed, among other things, to the finest instincts of human nature in order to deprave; in order, in fact, to bring into being a criminal imperium so murderous that the roll-call of its victims would fill a large European country.

The war was inevitably presented as an epic of altruism on the part of the German forces. Winkelnkemper's technique was to list various representative German types and functions and record the heroism of each one in the attack on Cologne (1942): the mason, the painter, the seventy-year-old roofer, the twelve-year-old girl, the pregnant mother who gave birth and was miraculously saved, mothers who rescued their babies, the young worker who was a block leader and fought through the smoke and fumes to rescue trapped women and children.[287] As for Hitler Youth, 'after hours of work, it sometimes took an order from a political leader before they were willing to stop'. Then there were the noble observers in their watch-towers: 'in one case, the observers remained at their post even though the roof all around them was in flames. Only an order from their superior made them leave their observation post at the last minute.' There was also the heroism of 'a physically handicapped man' who 'succeeded in saving a large apartment building, on the roof of which a fire had broken out'.[288] He extinguished an incendiary bomb. All these citizens were chronicles of utter courage and dedication to the lives of others—admirable virtues whose authenticity transcends the Nazi Party's bombastic rhetoric.

Solidarity

Another part of the psychology of Hitlerism must lie in its satisfaction of drives and needs ignored by civil society, and in particular its ability to minister tenderly to the psychological wounds of German's defeated First World War veterans. What the Nazis offered was a panacea, a lenitive to conditions of economic depression, and more generally a sedative for those alienated by restless modern society's lack of fixedness or sanction of custom, its voracious interrogation of tradition, heritage social norms and values. Nazism was the antidote for the culturally dispossessed. It appealed to many needs frustrated in the anonymity of urban-suburban mass consumerism (which they both excoriated and exploited) and democracy. Theirs was a world framed in absolutist terms, an absence of introspection, and which embodied a rejection of the tentativeness found in Weimar and democracy. Such an ethos saved mental labour and provided the template against which all other evidence could be interpreted.

But if there was one central idea that dominated Nazi propaganda culture, a constant ideological imperative, it was solidarity. This was the essence of *Volksgemeinschaft*, or national community (see below). In this notion of solidarity lay all the other ideas of Nazism. The focus was overwhelmingly on cohesion of the group. To be cohesive, a group has to have an identity of purpose and a perceived commonality of origin—at least to gain the extreme cohesion the Nazis cultivated. This stress on bonds of social community was therefore used to mitigate the created climate of surveillance and subservience. The individual was no longer alone in the world but a member of the group with which he was united by ties of blood, of inherited folk wisdom, culture and history, and by antagonism to all that threatened these things—for to gain total solidarity, a menacing enemy who threatens the group with extinction is truly needed; and if such an enemy does not exist, then it can be fabricated, as indeed it was. The creation of the pseudo-folk culture, the idea of the community, even things like the focus on the overseas Germans and the unity of all Germandom, were all aspects of this enterprise. Nazism offered the modernist man, rootless in an amorphous and fluid urban environment, a regression to the warm, febrile tribal family.

In film after film, documentary after documentary, book after book, the interdependency of individuals was constantly stressed. Nazi propaganda consistently emphasised reliance on friends, fellow soldiers and neighbours, and highlighted how help was always generously given when needed. It was not dependence but interdependence which Nazi propaganda most prized. Thus the posters also proclaimed the idea of 'folk community': their appeal was to solidarity, and this emphasis, while certainly an assault on individualism, also made the intrusive authoritarianism of the regime more palatable. For example, a poster for the German Labour Service captioned 'We Build Body and Soul' features two men, one with his arm around the other and looking into his eyes, a shovel over his back. They are both bare-chested and seem very young indeed, their sinuous musculature recorded by the artist, every contour crafted, the background vague and out of focus.[289] Such imagined comradeship, and the wholesomeness of community work, were powerful values which more individualistic societies had lost. This tender comradely embrace made the cultural system liveable for a great many Germans.

Today, an era of diversity and inclusion connects us also with the world of the Nazis by showing us their opposite image. They are the historical causation that made us liberal. In essence, Nazism represents all that goes wrong when the bonds of solidarity are over-stressed in a regression to tribalism (today, however, pundit and politician still search for that elusive thread of community; we have, they claim, forgotten social cohesion in the pursuit of individual and subcultural self-legitimation). Then there is the visceral emotional charge of the Fascist appeal. Fascism has been described as 'socialism of the soldier', and it arouses a hyper-solidarity, a fraternal excess perhaps, which would be unintelligible to civilians. It recreated in civic society the deep cohesion of military life, and the appeal was to that which the civil world had denied them, namely the romantic bonhomie of the trenches. During the war itself a key theme was the unity of Home and Front, as with the poster 'You Are the Front!', which featured a blacksmith foregrounding a massive image of a soldier staring mystically into the middle distance.[290] The soldier is sketched in light watercolours, almost as if he were formed of the steam arising from the blacksmith's anvil, while the blacksmith is bathed in perspiration covering his athletic frame. The aim was to elevate the everyday, to conscript everybody into the sacred ethos of fighting; and (again a familiar message) to stress the interdependency of soldier and civilian in a symbiotic relationship.

Civic Altruism

In Nazi propaganda, and particularly in the posters, there was a great stress on civic altruism and sacrifice, a Reich more credible because the less expected. Hitler did indeed stress idealism again and again. As one observer said, Nazi propaganda indicates 'what people sincerely hope to be true ... totalitarianism is not only hell, but also the dream of paradise'.[291] Arendt pointed out that the popularity of totalitarianism is the consequence of illusion, not ignorance, nor brainwashing: it was self-positioned as something virtuous.[292] The Nazi Party itself was always the supreme exponent of civic altruism, always proclaiming itself to be above reproach: as one propagandist wrote, 'wherever bombs fell or flames broke out, political leaders were there to care for the wounded, to rescue those buried in the rubble ...'[293]

At least some of the institutions of the Nazi state were in themselves propaganda and they left a deep impression on many influential foreigners. The British ambassador, Sir Nevile Henderson, was much taken with the labour corps:

> To my own countrymen I would, for instance, particularly recommend the labour camps. Between the age of 17 and 19 every German boy, rich or poor, the son of a Labourer or of a former reigning prince, is obliged to spend six months in a Labour camp, building roads, draining marshland, felling trees, or doing whatever other manual labour may be required in his area. In my humble opinion these camps serve none but useful purposes. In them not only are there no class distinctions, but there is, on the contrary, an opportunity for better understanding between the classes. Therein one learns the pleasure of hard work and the dignity of labour as well as the benefits of discipline; moreover, they vastly improve the physique of the nation.[294]

He asserted that National Socialism was a revolution just like the French Revolution and that 'it would be foolish to assume either that there is nothing to learn from it, or that it will vanish in all its forms from this earth "unwept, un-honoured, and unsung"'.[295] He also observed the moral fervour of some of the Nazi state's promulgators:

> Others have described with greater authority and competence the utility and beneficial nature of many of the institutions, such as, among others, the Strength Through Joy movement, developed by the 'socialist' rather than the 'national' part of National Socialism. I do not propose to comment here thereon. But it would be utterly unjust not to realise that great numbers of those who adhered to and worked for Hitler and the Nazi regime were honest idealists, whose sole aim was to serve Germany, to improve the lot of her people, and to add to their happiness. Hitler himself may well have been such an idealist at the start.

He lists the senior Nazis he held in high regard, and comments for example that 'Germany owes much to the astounding organising ability of men like Field Marshal Göring, Dr Frick, the Minister of the Interior, Dr Todt ... most of us would have been proud to do for our country what these and others like them did for theirs.'[296]

Types: Hero

A myth is above all else a story. It both makes visible and condenses, summoning the key elements of a belief system and embodying them in narrative form. Its fables offer a human interest yield which mere advocacy or education could never achieve. According to Tyrrell, heroes are pre-eminent in the myth-world. They represent those behaviours which are the most deeply admired and culturally endorsed. Crowds, according to Le Bon, create heroes and villains, and the original legend is transformed over time and place: 'it is not even necessary that heroes should be separated from us by centuries for their legend to be transformed by the imagination of the crowd'.[297] This directly informed the work of Goebbels and his synthetic creation of martyrs.

Time and again, the Nazi media celebrated the austere warrior, one who was bold and selfless even to the point of sacrificing his own life, and the pseudo-courageous also coloured much of the Third Reich product, including its texts, its films and its arts. Thus *Titanic* (1943) offers a heroic German ship's officer juxtaposed with the villainous, vainglorious president of the White Star Line whose culpability the German tries to expose.[298] There was therefore a serial creation of idealised role models throughout the media. Nazi Germany was, in fact, one gigantic military training manual. *Heroes of the Luftwaffe*, for example, is a celebration of standard heroes of the type that all totalitarian regimes produce: two-dimensional paragons.[299] The airman-hero of the biography is a farmer's son who 'wanted to take off his uniform after the war to become a farmer on his own land'. Virtue in Nazi ideology was derived from the soil and therefore the idea of a warrior longing to return and farm the land is not an unusual one in Nazi propaganda. The biography is festooned with buzzwords such as 'enthusiastic'. The hyperbolic exploits of this valorous aeronaut include shooting down eighty-five enemy planes and setting a Soviet gunboat ablaze. The text is enlightened with celebratory drawings of the actions which generated for this leader of men the Knight's Cross with Oak Leaves.[300] German fighters are endowed with moral and physical qualities: 'the pluck and daring, the firmness, toughness and strength of duty and will with which the German fliers carried on the glorious battle was unprecedented ... His damaged motor could hardly splutter, but he still made a round before landing to announce his aerial victory.'[301] 'Sham-heroic' is a term which condenses and judges a great deal of the Nazi media.

In Nazi propaganda, physical courage was often underpinned by moral nobility, as for example in one film where a German pilot is seen withholding his fire when the machine guns of his English enemy become jammed.[302] Men such as these were portrayed as knights in a new era of chivalry. As far as Germany was concerned, they represented the highest embodiment of the nation's offensive spirit: they were utterly courageous yet capable of self-sacrificial humanity, even though this was not reciprocated by their enemies.

The idea of transfiguration through martial death, of joining a kind of spectral army of fallen heroes, was a constant image throughout this time. Military leadership could not be detached from ideas of supreme bravery, and popular narratives constantly embroidered the concept of the heroic. In another piece of propaganda, the film *Fighter Squadron Lutzow*, a dying pilot is shown saving his crew: there is little visible bloodshed, only 'the ... consecration of a fine young German'. Thus, as Herzstein writes, 'an apolitical war film managed to support and convey Nazi ideological views in three crucial areas: social egalitarianism in a common struggle, the cause of Germans in other countries, and heroic death as transfiguration'.[303]

In this and other ways Nazism was hardly unique, even if it remorselessly pursued the theme; the 'hero' is an example of a cultural universal, something venerated by all communities. It can also be seen—however long the conceptual journey—as a version of the 'greater love hath no man than this ...' of Jesus Christ. To be heroic is to discharge the ultimate and highest obligation of being human. That the Nazis seized on this as a building block of the propaganda and the ideology—it is hard to distinguish between them—is not surprising since it lent to the Nazi cause the Christian ideal of self-abnegation. Unlike civil life, war presents many opportunities for selfless devotion to the common good, even to the point of death, so that participation in war can appear to be a form of the sacerdotal. This was typical of the Nazis. They would mobilise generic elements in human civilisation, its deepest stirrings and honour codes, in the service of infamy. Heroism can, moreover, only exist in relation to extreme risks, and such risks are seldom available in civil life. Death is the most significant risk and all heroism is a dance with death, courting it, evading it, a species of coquetry where the extinction of life is not merely a possible but a probable outcome. As a result, the Nazi project acquired intense narrative properties: breath-taking action/resolution, the storytelling values of suspense and excitement, the ending of which could never be less than satisfactory because even if the hero died, the great ideal gained more life by his death. Nazism's fantasy factory was a highly organised way of creating hero myths. In this mechanistic way it had vulgarised the courage of the warrior by manufacturing facsimiles via a formal managerial system. A conveyor belt heroism; hero-making as industrial process.

Types: Soldier

The Nazis adopted a similar approach and used similar themes in their portrayal of soldiers more generally. Here as elsewhere the Nazis hijacked something common to all communities, in this case the honour of the fighting man which is a source of deep civic and tribal pride in nations throughout the world. None of this was unique to Nazi Germany. What was different was, again, the steroidal excess with which they endowed the idea. Militarism was not just a culture but a cult, and this cult stained the fabric of all social, civic and cultural life. By the later 1930s, for example, the Propaganda Ministry was harvesting a crop of military films such as *Pour le Mérite* (1938) and *Patrioten* (1937), *Menschen ohne Vaterland* (1937) and *Kameraden auf See* (1938).[304] Radio programmes were sometimes produced as joint products by the army and the Hitler Youth.[305] A military culture is different from a culture where militarism is a significant property, as with, say, the old European imperial powers, and ideas like discipline, self-sacrifice and duty are civic ideals too.[306] Such an ethos provided a superordinate social bond to counter class and region-driven tendencies to fragmentation. Moreover, Germany was only sixty years old in 1930. It had no founding principle or charter, and it consequently absorbed the ethos of its conqueror, the Kingdom of Prussia, which thus gave a raison d'être, a meaning and an integrity to Europe's newest great power. Soldierliness was the edited essence of the cultural ideal—the source of its inspiration, and a way of rising above the pursuit of trade, of feeling superior. The example of Hindenburg will suffice, for part of his appeal was that he seemed the very embodiment of those ideals. It is easy to see how military ideals could be confused with the most cherished moral values and indeed to some extent they did represent those values. Such a culture was a source then of the highest societal strengths, but also of vulnerability. Insular chauvinism and the latent violence it invokes need wars to sustain them, and therefore enemies, and the creation of enemies. As Rutherford remarks:

> the image of the sweaty, battle begrimed soldier leaning on his Mauser in the doorway of the smashed, burning house, is hardly one that most people would care to have staring down from over the mantelpiece, but in a society so uncompromisingly militaristic it was the accepted alternative to birds in-flight or lubricated monks sipping port around the refectory table.[307]

This theme was taken so seriously by the Nazis that they even had a range of tanks, guns, horses and anti-tank weapons at the Potsdam Army School (Kriegsschule) which could be set up for artists to reproduce battle scenes faithfully.[308]

Military life is a ritualised realm. Since dying was a part of soldiering it had to be made both accessible and enviable. Much of the Nazi propaganda product was devoted to that end. It sought to make death in war glorious because how otherwise could men be made to contemplate with equanimity their own extinction? But this was not an easy thing to do given the closeness, the emotional bonds, of the military as a family. Death rituals consequently assumed great importance in the Reich.[309] Hence at Nuremberg (*Triumph of the Will*) the names of the First World War battlefields were all read out: Tannenberg, Verdun, the Somme and Langemarck; the standards solemnly lowered as the bands play that most sonorous funereal dirge, 'I Had A Comrade'.

The need was to invest German deaths with meaning without the solace of spiritual or existential justification. This could not be Christian, at least at the official level, given that this was privately and, less ostentatiously, publicly, an anti-Christian regime which could not subscribe to the idea of a hell, a purgatory, a heaven. The Nazis struggled with this contradiction and suggested some notion of eternal life within the *Volk*, a rhetorical idea but also an irrational one. Mysticism without a religion must present a certain intellectual challenge. They therefore wrote and acted as if this were a truth and not a contrived propaganda fiction, as if the insubstantial shadows of their rhetorical contrivances had, somehow, somewhere, a tangible reality in some other dimension. Since these intimations were not governed by the kinds of revealed truth claimed by religion, the synthetic nature of the contrivance was laid bare. This was a 'belief' that could not actually ever sustain a true belief; it was intellectually risible, the surfaces of religiosity without the essence.

For Baird, the death of a Nazi was not tragic but glorious, a celebration of national rebirth: 'in its most radical form, a cult of heroism can unleash the daemonic in man, calling for the annihilation of the antihero'.[310] Death cultism was also necessary because of the high blood sacrifices that Hitler would demand, and to make them possible death had to be elevated into a new form of life. Hence the great funerals of Nazi Germany, with their marches and their rituals and their symbolism; there was certainly a corporate paradigm—wreaths, the final salutation, the orchestra playing Siegfried's Funeral March (as at the burial of SA Chief Lutze, May 1943, the occasion of one of Hitler's last great funeral addresses).[311] Other great funerals in Berlin included Heydrich's and Rommel's. As Baird points out, National Socialist ideology 'was based on the principle that life is but a preparation for noble death for Hitler'. All of this was sentimentalised. Mawkish poems and letters 'were not viewed as demonstrating weakness but strength—to steel the warrior for the brutality of combat'.[312] Even before Rommel's death, everything was already organised, including his grand funeral and its star billing in the newsreels.[313]

Death was presented in Nazi propaganda as the ultimate life form. Thus in one film an officer reflects on the letter written by the mother of a fallen youth: 'a true Prussian mother feels pride and fulfilment about how her son had had the privilege of dying a heroic death … one does not think about their death, but instead about what they have died for, and remembers them like the Young Gods that they are'.[314] Similarly, in *Kolberg*, the words and actions of the various characters communicate the idea that dying in war is a blessing.[315] In another film, German prisoners are torpedoed by their own side; lest this confuse the audience, a dying German sailor murmurs, 'it is beautiful and honourable to die for the fatherland'.[316] Bravery, unflinching, is a constant motif in such films as *Cossacks*, which recounts the heroism of Prussian officer cadets during the Seven Years' War. For Hitler war should be a semi-permanent state. As a convinced Social Darwinist he felt war was the only way of maintaining the vigour of the race: 'for the good of the German people, we must wish for a war every 15 or 20 years. An army whose sole purpose is to preserve peace leads only to playing at soldiers—compare Sweden and Switzerland. Or else it constitutes a revolutionary danger to its own country.'[317] He speaks of driving Asia back behind the Urals: 'A permanent state of war on the Eastern front will help to form a sound race of men, and will prevent us from relaxing into the softness of a Europe thrown back upon itself.'[318]

Types: Martyr

Martyrology is not unique to Christian cultures, but it has a special place within them. Christian history has been calibrated by a long procession of martyrs from its very inception. As I have argued elsewhere, deaths and martyrdom have always been fecund sources of myth-making. Christ was the ultimate martyr, and all martyrdom consequently has the tincture of divinity.[319] For Goebbels, propaganda value was maximised when embodied in the martyrdom of a vividly evoked human personality, as with the mythology created around the death of Hitler Youth Herbert Norkus and his elevation to the martyr's pantheon in the film *Hitler Youth Quex*.[320] There were many other examples too, such as the dying youth in *S.A. Mann Brand* who proclaims: 'I go now to the Führer.'[321] And hence 'when Goebbels smelt the blood of a possible martyr, objective truth meant little to him. He has each martyr die with a tranquil smile of the lips, a believer until the end.'[322] According to Adorno, people could be indoctrinated into an 'irrational enthusiasm for death',[323] and all regimes have subsisted to a greater or lesser extent on a diet of myths. None has managed to do without them. The significance of the Nazi regime, however, was that it understood and internalised this at the intellectual level and deliberately sought to create myths in a highly self-aware way. Burleigh gives an example of Goebbels completely inventing the story of a Nazi martyr in all of its properties—the taxi with its gang of reds inflamed with bloodlust, the pale, dead Nazi who had been beaten to death, the mourning wife.[324] Nazism was a manufactory of martyrs; they were important because they had sustained the ultimate test, namely that of the surrender of life itself. Apart from Schlageter, a genuine—and pre-Nazi—martyr, the Nazi ones such as Horst Wessel were fictionalised but never fiction; the smaller truth sustained the greater lie. Their numbers over the years—five in 1928, seventeen in 1930, forty-three in 1931, eighty-four in 1932[325]—were not nearly as huge as the propaganda implied.

The Munich Martyrs had been re-interred in a great ceremony in November 1935 (see Chapter Five), their new home a gleaming marmoreal palace, the Temple of Honour, whose grandiloquent excess well complemented Third Reich standards in vulgar ostentation. Thus through the smoke of oil-burning pylons the hearses advanced, the music changing for each station of the cross;[326] 'even the tempo of the march was regulated by a telephone communication system placed in buildings along the parade route'. The exhumed dead were re-dedicated in bronze sarcophagi.[327] Hitler 'moved from casket to casket, greeting each comrade individually', and the entire Reich was incorporated in this event—via radio, but also via the other death-watch ceremonies.[328] At the end, 'Gauleiter Wagner began the final roll-call, a ceremony borrowed from Mussolini's fascist repertoire. As Wagner called off names from the list of the dead fighters the Hitler Youth responded with "here" in unison.'[329] Myth-entrepreneur Goebbels seized his opportunity with the murder of his protégé Horst Wessel (Goebbels had sent him to study the Viennese Nazi youth movement).[330] He offered an image of an idealist who 'would rescue his girlfriend from a life of prostitution and sacrificed himself out of missionary zeal to the cause of the Fatherland'.[331] This became part of the late-Weimar propaganda battle in which there was mythology and counter-mythology. The KPD Central Committee, for instance, responded to this by claiming that Wessel was nothing but a degenerate pimp, and the Communists created a propaganda campaign to depict his death as irrelevant since it was part of an underworld dispute.[332] In other words, the meaning of Wessel's death was posthumously 'spun' by both totalitarian rivals. At the extravagant funeral (with a violent backdrop of the Red Front fighters), Goebbels 'praised Wessel in terms that deliberately recalled Christ's sacrifice for humankind'.[333] Wessel was now a secular religious cult, with the song he had written becoming the party's official anthem, something which says much about the elemental role violence played in the Nazi pursuit of power.[334] Martyrdom was not simply a process of creation but of management as the inviolability of the myth had to be protected. Thus Goebbels only licensed ceremonies for the anniversary of Horst Wessel's death in order to prevent the commemorations becoming cliché-kitsch.[335] The film *Hans Westmar* entirely sanitised the manner of Westmar's (Horst Wessel's) life and death by presenting him as a virile university student who was idealistic and anxious about class divisions.[336]

Key Concepts of the Third Reich

Culture Nation

In contrast to the ephemera of the mass media, art was considered more meaningful to the Nazis. It was of radical importance for Germans' self-concept that they represented a higher cultural order than other races and other countries, yet the criteria were entirely self-referential and therefore incestuous. 'Culture' in the Reich only really meant German culture or the classical world which was its progenitor. Culture therefore became part of the ethno-nationalist discourse (i.e. propaganda), and the accumulated gatherings of centuries of German culture were shoehorned into this perspective.

There was, for example, the retro-Nazification of the greats of German literature, music and arts such as Friedrich Schiller. Rank mediocrities were also elevated to the cultural pantheon. In many ways 'culture' meant the antithesis of what it would mean today. Nazism was an anti-culture in that its motive force was not just exclusivity, but excision, the banishment of all that was not of the creed, whether hostile or merely neutral.

Hence the Nazi idea of culture shrivelled the concept to the extent that it came to be about the rigid definition and preservation of identity. Based on their fear of the modern, fear in fact of the very idea of interpretation, the Nazis demanded dogmatism in the arts, not suggestion. What they meant by culture was ossified classicism. Although they did accept certain elements of the high culture of the rest of Europe, they excluded anything ever produced by a Jew, and everything modernist in any art form was absolute anathema. The first holocaust was the holocaust of literature, especially the distinctive Jewish cultural contribution, a preamble to the real thing. The ceremonial book burnings of May 1933 took place in the presence of capped and gowned academics and students in order to lend them a sense of cultural gravitas, with the squares of university towns chosen as the place of conflagration.[337] This was in turn followed by the Nazi attack on visual art in 1938 (the Exhibition of Degenerate Art was almost a kind of concentration camp for paintings).

The integuments of German superiority covered everything from social solidarity to the arts, an alternative paradigm for the Aryan (i.e. non-serf) part of the human race to follow. The need was to differentiate German culture from Anglo-Saxon nations, which had a debased culture (i.e. market economies), or from 'plutocracy'. Germany was supposed to transcend the vulgarities of the marketplace. 'Culture' was just a different way of talking about things Nazis held dear, such as patriotism, heritage, identity and the general superiorities of Germandom. To the Nazis culture meant more than operas and orchestras: it was the spiritual essence of race. It was a constituent element in German 'blood' and therefore of the psychology of racism. As it was impossible to have a race without a culture, this therefore became a source of racial superiority. Culture was also patrimonial, a way of establishing a Nazi link with the classical past through the replication of architectural and sculptural forms. 'Culture' (*Kultur*) was simply part of the vernacular, the argot of the Third Reich, something everyone paid lip-service to.

Culture could fire the soul; music, drama, literature—in their various voices they could speak in a way no political tract could ever manage. As sophisticated propagandists, the Nazis understood this well insofar as they realised that culture addresses the emotions and gains conviction without the need for rational argument. Conviction won at the intellectual level can later be lost at the intellectual level in line with the emergence of new arguments and new evidence. But belief founded not on persuasion but ignition, illuminated by cadences and rolling notes, a catharsis, awaking the spirit such that the new dawn is greeted in a delirium of emotional exhaustion: belief thus formed is resilient, even deathless. Hitler was right: the arts stimulate, they offer escapist fantasy and therefore their wartime continuity must be permitted. Hitler pontificated on art extensively. Culture was so important that even as leader of the German Reich in a global war he could still find time to talk about it. The continuity of the cultural system, theatres and so forth, was a source of fierce pride, and attempts to increase the price of theatre and opera tickets were sabotaged by Hitler himself. As Spotts has argued, 'portrayals of [Hitler] as someone who cynically used the arts merely for their value as ideological propaganda therefore misunderstood him as much as those which made him out a nihilistic revolutionary with no aim except power for himself and as an end in itself'.[338] Culture was a reason for which the Nazis fought, an idea of possession, of uniqueness. Fear of its extinction was a part of the broader construction of the existential threat. A threat had to destroy something of incalculable value to be a threat. If the culture was not valued, nor would the threat be feared. *Victory in the West* 's organ-playing soldier (Chapter Two) had saved his group, allowing them to escape since the French fired at the sound of the organ. The dying man is 'transfigured, blazing faith in his eyes and German culture in his heart'.[339]

Yet the Nazis had a rival from another quarter, indeed another continent: the perennially alluring blandishments of American culture, and this they feared, for America represented cultural competition and offered an alternative way of being to the austere pieties and organised visceral hatreds of the Third Reich. An article in the SS journal admitted that the United States represented 'competition to National Socialism's racial worldview in the struggle for youth, in the struggle for the future of humanity'.[340] It also used the phrase 'American century', arguing that one should not underestimate the danger of Americanism, or its seductive power. After the First World War, it went on, 'a significant part of our youth too fell under the appeal of Americanism, waving their limbs in the Shimmy and the Charleston because there was nothing else to do'.[341] However, under the Reich, the German youth was apparently impervious to the American anti-culture:

'Certainly there is no danger that our young boys and girls will fall into sexual frenzy while listening to some Jewish lout blowing on a saxophone. One can introduce them to the high priests of the American jitterbug with no worries at all. At most they will laugh.' Yet 'the American lad feels his "freedom" restricted by such behaviour. He wants to keep the hot music spinning on the record player ... It is nice to be able to dismiss all criticism of too hearty enjoyment of life with the claim that one is defending human rights against Nazi brutality.'[342]

Volksgemeinschaft—National Community

The new retro-revolutionaries celebrated organic rather than materialist thinking and folk community rather than class. Hence, according to Bracher, the left-wing view of Nazism as a socio-economic phenomenon missed the point: a propaganda appeal to nationalist sentiment 'brought into play attractions and ties which promised an integration beyond the manifold immediate interests'.[343] The appeal of National Socialism lay not in it being a middle-class interest group but a movement capable of unifying varied and antagonistic groups, one which offered a cohesive force across heterogeneous interests, considerations and emotions. In addition to his preoccupation with race, for instance, Hitler would often also pontificate on the class system, as for example when he remarked on the fact that only an officer could win the Pour le Mérite in the First World War and that it was 'quite exceptional' for a merely middle-class officer to receive such an award.[344]

It has been observed that the idea of people's community is at once egalitarian and exclusive, and in that ostensible contradiction lies its success as a formulary and an explanation for the Nazis' effectiveness. The Nazi emphasis on social solidarity had real impact, with extreme nationalism and the cult of Hitler following at some distance.[345] But such a highly cohesive group, founded in reciprocal obligation, was a catastrophe for outsiders who were thereby stripped of humanity. Ideas of nativeness, the thirst for that which is elemental, are concepts—or more properly sentiments—that have had other manifestations and sustained left-wing/radical chic as well as right-wing articulations in the twentieth century. The idea of a homogenous mass community based on shared commonalities—race, class, education—had different guises and forms, and at their worst provided an alibi for genocide. The decision to eliminate Jews was madness, but no more so than the Khmer Rouge's attempt to eliminate everyone who could read or write, or Joseph Stalin randomly running through a telephone directory to indicate arbitrary candidates for liquidation.[346]

The Nazis embodied the hysteria of ethno-nationalism and to some observers it seemed to permeate nearly everything. There were new styles of social address such as 'Your German-born worship'. Klemperer complains that even cat lovers' magazines got in on the act, proclaiming the superiority of the 'German cat'. Thus one cat magazine was rebranded *The German Feline* (Klemperer was prohibited from writing for it).[347] However, the idea of a primordial race-nation essence, to be defended at all costs against its putative contaminants, was a flexible one and even exportable, or so they pretended, to other nation-folk groups, including the Arabs: 'One day, Arab youth, you will face the question of your nation's essence just as we have.'[348] Ethno-nationalism remains a powerful idea today. North Korea, for example, inherited a Japanese-trained cadre of propagandists who stressed not the material superiority of Communism but the nativeness/authenticity of a North Korean state that, unlike its southern rival, evolved uncontaminated by the alien, the Western.[349] This is clearly a variant of ethno-nationalism and explains the resilience of this museum-piece state. Nazis did not have an exclusive patent on some of these ideas. In the same epoch Gandhi with his spinning wheel, de Valera with his land of saints and scholars, even António Salazar with his anathema on Coca-Cola all represented ostensibly contradictory creeds that nevertheless embodied the same core idiom of a return to an aboriginal state; an idea of regression to the land and production at its very first and primal stage.

But the Nazis were a mass of contradictions and if we seek a logic or coherence in their ideology we search in vain. As Paxton observes, 'Fascists often cursed faceless cities and materialist secularism, and exalted an agrarian utopia free from the rootlessness, conflict and immorality of urban life. Yet fascist leaders adored their fast cars and planes, and spread their message by dazzlingly up-to-date techniques of propaganda and stagecraft.'[350] If there was a rationale it was a marketing/persuasion rationale, not a coherent weave of thought. The merit of this was clear in a polity hitherto divided by region, class, history and religion, divisions superficially resolved through the proclamation of a unitary culture founded on commonalities of ancestry which were elevated into mystical essence. The creation of an alternative to socialism and communism had to be made intelligible and attractive, and the art of doing so lay in making people feel special, that the Nazi 'product' had something over the brotherhood of man. So Germans were part, not of the proletariat, but the *Volk*;

not ordinary, but special; not equality, but superiority, was the crux of the Nazi message. Its essential offer was a vista of faces upon which to look down; for those lower in the existing class hierarchy—and Germany, like all European countries, had an entrenched class system—this was an appealing notion.

One aspect of this folk community with its blood and soil myths was rejection, at least at the rhetorical level, of capitalism, and fulmination against plutocracy. Thus *Hans Westmar*:

> And that's where we must be—with the people. We can no longer live in ivory towers. We must join our hands in battle with the workers. There can't be classes anymore. We are workers, too, workers of the mind, and our place now is next to those who work with their hands.[351]

The anti-capitalist credo was a part of the anti-Semitism as well; the Jew was capitalist and Bolshevist, with both antitheses being captured in that name. Moreover, since capitalism was the ideology of the Anglo-American enemy, 'plutocracy' was a super-myth that integrated other, subaltern, myths. Thus *Signal* complained of the menace of the Anglo-Saxon orchestration of the global market and the need for protection 'against competition in those world markets dominated by Great Britain with cheap nigger and coolie Labour'.[352] The article's authors claim that 'Britain prevents Europe from having a united front, Germany is part of that Europe and Europe can only be healthy if the best [i.e. Germany] is healthy.' Thus Nazism anticipates current debates and represents a critique, albeit a deviant one, of the ethic of neo-liberalism and the phenomenon of globalisation, both of which continue to be attacked for reasons similar to those adumbrated by the Nazis. The Nazis had a talent for seizing the fault lines in the political and economic condition, for capturing the essence of people's discontentment and, with brutal resolve, exploiting them with the ceaseless battering of an obsessive-compulsive disorder. Thus European peasants were now safe under German hegemony, 'no longer dependent on the fluctuations of the Anglo-Saxon world markets'.[353] But, as Bracher explains, we should interpret bourgeois anti-capitalism not as a manifestation of socialism but as a cry for protection against the threat of big business.[354] Goebbels was convinced of the propaganda advantages of this stance: the line on plutocracy, he said in his diaries, is 'my best weapon against England',[355] to which he adds, 'the anti-plutocratic aspects of the fight will be singled out for particular attention'. On another occasion he notes that 'London is launching massive attacks on us again. But our results on plutocracy are giving the English something to think about.'[356] In prac-

tice, Nazi attitudes to capitalism were more ambivalent, and the antagonism flourished largely at the level of propaganda. Paxton, for example,
sees the Nazis' anti-capitalism as a power-pursuit tactic, to be dropped on
the assumption of power: 'what fascists objected to in capitalism was not
its exploitation but its materialism, its indifference to the nation, its inability to stir ourselves ... more deeply, fascists rejected the notion that economic forces are the prime movers of history'.[357]

Blood and Soil/Heimat

Nazism was an urban movement posing as a rural one, and this resonated
with people because disconnection from the land was still a recent folk
memory in Germany, given its late industrialisation. The function of the
rural was purely to provide mythological and rhetorical properties to the
Nazi propaganda product. It was also part of the pseudo-mystical structuring of Nazi consciousness. Walther Darré was the Nazi prophet of agriculture and also the author of such works as *The Peasantry as the Life Force of
the Nordic Race* (1929) and *New Nobility from Blood and Soil* (1930).[358] In this
as in much else, the Nazis tapped into universal human yearnings for
belonging and perverted them; the theoretic antithesis, a society of atom-
ised, self-sufficient human beings, is unacceptable, even if it is scarcely
improbable. The locus of our being is a piece of physical territory, a fixed
and immutable and ancestral place—this was an idea of immense sentimental value. This then is the meaning of *Heimat*: according to Rentschler, it
was a place, a feeling: 'the physical space, a province of the zeitgeist; at
once something inordinately rich and something irretrievably lost'.[359]

The Nazi idea of the nation transcended the merely conservative and patriotic. It was a revolutionary, blood-based, absolutist idea.[360] This was a theme
in *The Prodigal Son*, a film about a German émigré, Tonio, who is lost amid
the polyglot anonymity of the United States—a land without an authentic
culture, bereft of the comfort blanket of folk ritual. The film tries to contrast
'the natural plenitude of the mountains with the spiritual poverty of the
metropolis', and the United States is depicted as the 'realm of inhuman tempo
and brutal competition': when Tonio cannot find work, for instance, the
humiliation is emphasised by the smiling black man next to him who gets the
job instead.[361] Tonio returns to his village for the winter solstice celebration
and assumes his place as the Sun King, the master of ceremonies, while
Tyrolean villagers resurrect ancient powers in nocturnal rites with bonfires
and torches.[362] This was only one of a number of such films about homesick-

ness and the return to the fatherland, with *A Man Must Return to Germany* (1934), *The Kaiser of California* (1936), *Shoulder Arms* (1939), *Enemies* (1940) and *Homecoming* (1941) among the many other examples.[363]

'Blood and soil' was a dominant theme in Nazi art, a matter perhaps of indirect rather than direct allusion. For example, a portrait of a peasant woman by Adolf Wissel which was displayed at the Great German Art Exhibition of 1938 is an exaggeration of the real that transcends photography in its capture of the private topography of this woman's face, the lines, the wistful expression, the heavy headscarf; the big arms and etched hands denote toil.[364] She is dressed entirely in black and white. According to the ethos of blood and soil, virtue would derive from the land and the people of the land, since they were the least corroded by metropolitan decadence, and the purest bearers of the blood of the race. Numerous films celebrated the doctrine of blood and soil such as *Phantom Rider* (1934), *The Girl from the Marshland Farm* (1935), *Ferry Boat Woman Maria* (1936), *An Enemy of the People* (1937), *The Journey to Tilsit* (1939), *Immensée* (1943) and *The Great Sacrifice* (1944).[365] Nazi propaganda had a sense-making function insofar as it enabled people to interpret the world around them, and Nazi literature focused on the idea of the eternal chain that links past and future generations, and the (apparent) internal (pseudo-) consistency of National Socialist thought offered a comprehensive explanation to Germans of who they were and where they were going.[366] Indeed, in the 'lyrical' documentary *The Eternal Forest* (1936), the German race is portrayed as an eternal forest that is constantly renewed.[367]

There is explanatory value in the fact that Germans were never just one people within one static national border. That border was fluid through history. For example, the town of Luckau (Brandenburg), just east of Berlin, currently burnishes the fact of its ancient membership of the Kingdom of Hungary (Vlad the Impaler's image is on prominent display). Germanic communities in fact existed throughout the old Europe in countries including France, Italy, Romania, Russia, Poland, Croatia and the Baltic states; the Germans were a pan-European tribe who once were themselves Europe's racial minority.

Lebensraum

West European notions of statehood were opposed by an antithetical idea, the cultural and ethnic nation as conceived by German nationalist thinkers. Such a notion of nationhood was not fixed in geography but in heritage and hostility to national boundaries. It 'denied full sovereignty to others within the old supra-national realm'.[368] Hitler was merely faithful to this antiquated template: 'In any case, my demands are not exorbitant. I'm only interested, when all is said, in territories where Germans had lived before'.[369] He also remarked that the areas reached by the German forces during the war were those areas that had retained the memory of a Germanic presence,[370] and that, in Crimea, fifty years ago, 'nearly half the soil was still in German hands'.[371]

The idea of living space had been popularised by Hans Grimm's best-selling book *Nation Without Space* (1926).[372] The ideology of *Lebensraum* was made acceptable by the contempt race-theory generated for the original possessors of the soil. The Slavs, Hitler claimed, were a mass of born slaves who needed a master. This idea was sustained by colonialist fantasies lifted from the annals of British imperialism: 'like the English, we shall rule this empire with a handful of men'. Hitler's model was the British in India, and thus 'of what India was for England, the territories of Russia will be for us ...'.[373] Indeed, Hitler once told Lord Halifax that his favourite film, *Lives of a Bengal Lancer* (1935), was compulsory viewing for the SS, as 'this was how a superior race must behave'.[374] What the analogy ignored was any sense of how British government had survived in India via the operation of strategic coalitions. The Nazi, of course, would not conceal his contempt for the subject people but advertise it. As Hitler once remarked, 'we will supply the Ukrainians with scarves, glass beads and everything that colonial peoples like'.[375]

Utopia

Idealism

The psychology of Nazism was intimately linked to ideas of perfection, in fact to notions (if not of an earthly paradise) of the perfectibility of human society. It is not surprising that Nazism emerged in an era of revolutionary technological innovation: flight, sound and colour film, radio, television, powerful cars, rocket power and jet propulsion had all made or were making their appearance. It was an illicit, but at the same time comprehensible, inference that civic society could be remade in the image of the machine, that the metaphor of the machine should penetrate civic and social discourse to the extent that it could actively usurp it. This is a case therefore not of having been usurped by automata as in some science fiction parallel universe, degenerating from the human to the humanoid, but of in fact re-organising human consciousness. The Nazi promise was not just of the nation aroused but of an entire new kind of society.

Here too was an illusion which all forms of fundamentalism hold in common: the demanded regression to the purity of ancient dogmas or the assumption of rule by self-appointed saints, the idea of editing compromise out of life. The longing was for a pre-lapsarian era and the retrieval of some essence which the intervening period had contaminated. Yet by rejecting the ambiguity of modern life, fundamentalisms ultimately eject essential elements of what it is to be human. This is something propagandists understand intuitively because the presence of an undisclosed utopia is behind much of propaganda in general, including the blandishments of the consumer advertising industry.

Technopolis

The Nazis were a self-consciously modernist movement which claimed that its idiom was the idea of the future, of the coming man. As such, they used technology in every conceivable way as both an object and a medium of propaganda. The aim was to create sensations of the cutting edge, of technical ingenuity mobilised for the purposes of the state, and beyond that of Germany as the crucible of the modern; the first jet-plane flight, under the auspices of Hans von Ohain in 1939, took place in the Third Reich, for example. Civic life had long celebrated such miracles of technology as the *Autobahn* motorway, imagery and instrumentality compounded. Stanley McClatchie's *Look to Germany* (1937) is both a hagiography and an encyclopaedia;[376] it reveals a new age, not just a renewed country, which readers were exhorted to explore with every artifice of sophistry, for example in its image of an alleged 'Telephone-Television'. The imagery of the technology was blended with ancestral reference: ruins, thatched huts and rockets, the Cyclotron, flying wings, four-engined jet bombers and superfast submarines next to images of stocky peasants in costume. Nazis thus sought to create a technopolis, as is evident in everything from the big railway gun (Schwerer Gustav) tormenting Sevastopol in 1942 (see Chapters Two and Five) to the ability to fly four-engined jet spy planes (the Arado Blitz) so high up that there was no need for them to carry any weaponry; nothing could reach them.

The technology itself did not possess a mere utility function alone, but had expressive meaning. It was both symbolic of the modernity of the regime and of its innovativeness and supremacy. The long stream of major technological marvels attested to this. Other nations may have possessed cutting-edge pieces of technology, but whatever they had the Nazis had in larger sorts or more plentiful numbers. Modernity, that sense of being at the experimental edge that was so special to Nazis, was evoked above all by the magic of the *Autobahn*, with its promissory note to the German masses of speed and a world of mobility on offer. Yet it was in the realm of new weaponry and its symbolic construction that Nazism really excelled, for weapons such as the V2 were the first of their kind. For the Nazis and many Germans these weapons seemed to validate their belief in their own superiority. However, the 'miracle weapons' that were the last propaganda hurrah of the Third Reich were militarily useless, and while an exploded V2 could destroy 150 homes both the V1 and V2 could only be targeted imprecisely at large areas. But what mattered to the Nazis was the terror imagery. It is not surprising that representation of the Nazis has been a recurrent theme in science fiction media. The comic magazines were on to something; this is not accidental: as cyborgs with ancient accents, as a default programme of the modern consciousness—however we conceptualise the Nazis, they saw themselves as not mere modernists, but futurists. They were enacting a kind of society which rested in every conceivable sense on science and technology, from the machines used to propel its military aggression to the foundation doctrine of race theory, which would promote an efficient and scientific base for civil society and its future reproduction.

Conclusions

Myths were not unique to the Nazis. The nation itself is a myth system of sorts and mythologies are critical to social cohesion. A myth is an account that society tells to itself about itself, a story that illuminates the values to be conveyed to cadet generations. For Schöpflin, culture itself may be defined as 'a system of collectively held notions, beliefs, premises, ideas, dispositions, and understandings, to which myth gives a structure'.[377] Under the Third Reich, part of this was indeed the appeal of the regressive, a summons to the primary tribal identifiers. The power of myth resides in its gift of simple comprehensive explanations that resolve the ambiguities of a complex world and facilitate interpretation. Al-Qaeda, for example, offers its targets the myth of the global conspiracy against Islam. Such a comprehensive perspective seems to illuminate and reconcile the mass of contradictory signals: to answer perplexity and the contrarian flows of information. It is this coherent integrating perspective which lay behind the power of Hitler's apocalyptic anti-Semitism, since it offered a universal explanatory framework for everything, to the extent that all of Germany's ills could be blamed on the Jews.

Thus the Nazis recognised the value of myths. But their real insight was into their manufacturability, a recognition that myths were not merely hereditable, like heirlooms. As I have argued elsewhere, this 'myth entrepreneurship' is the insightful seizure of material from a mass of cultural properties. Serious propagandists like the Nazis will always think through their myths very carefully, because a myth has an inherent plasticity that can be re-cast for modern purposes.[378] Much Nazi propaganda sustained a utopian myth. It preached the superiority of the Aryan race, and the exclusivist claim to humanity of unadulterated German civilisation, via the fabrication of a blameworthy group: the all-pervasive threat of inferior Semite blood that is barely human. Their myth system offered a version of utopian thinking; a journey, then, progressive or regressive, to some uncompromised master copy. The Reich was not the only utopian paradise conceived by man that became a morgue, or a butcher's yard. Mankind would be more perfect, capable of realising a paradise on earth—since there was no heaven. The contrast was between the essential vagueness of what was promised, and the terrible tangibility of what was delivered: when Churchill referred to 'the lights of perverted science', he could scarcely have understood the full import of those words in advance of the post-war revelations. The Nazis aimed to destroy Christian values and replace them with race and Social Darwinist ideology. Hence the new liturgical year and in general a quest to undermine religion by creating this mystical and secular parody, with its celebration of heroic death; the nation as necropolis where the dead watch the living.

5

SYMBOLISM

A LANGUAGE THAT LIES DEEPER THAN LANGUAGE

We don't want lower bread prices, we don't want higher bread prices, we don't want unchanged bread crisis—we want National Socialist bread prices!

NSDAP Speaker

Introduction

For any regime, political success or failure lies in the ability to master the manipulation of symbols. The reasons for this are partly to do with the apoliticality of most people and, perhaps, the cognitive miserliness of nearly all of us: we are simply not prepared to read substantive arguments like those contained in party manifestos. The failure of the Weimar Republic was a failure to arouse the nationalist imagination, to assuage the vainglorious dream.[1]

The Third Reich was a fabricator of symbols, and the experience of the Third Reich was guided and structured by symbolism. The Nazis possessed an intuitive insight into the symbol-mindedness of human beings. Jesse Delia argues that the strategy the Nazis adopted was based on symbolism and on the idea that symbols are key to effective communication and persuasion—what Leon Mayhew (1997) describes as a 'rhetoric of presentation'.[2] The Nazis recognised the essentially emotive nature of successful mass communication. Their appeal exploited a distinct group of emotions—

fear, pride and loathing—and they invested in the symbols designed to trigger them. As I have written elsewhere:

> Since symbols are a shorthand, they conserve mental effort, but the explanation for their unique power lies deeper than this, that is to say an understanding is first emotional and only latterly rational: we feel before we think. Thus symbolism alone can suffice, bereft of the support scaffolding of argument/reason ...[3]

As a result, the presentation of symbols can stand in place of argument, and the response they evoke is visceral and emotional. Indeed, to speak of a propaganda devoid of symbolism is really to speak of some other phenomenon, because a propaganda bereft of symbol-structures would not be intelligible as propaganda.[4] Nazism's symbols asked not for reason but for faith.

Everything that Hitler did was charged with symbolism, and it is through symbols that we remember leaders and the regimes they lead.[5] We 'read' history through its symbols and it is difficult to separate what is history from what is symbol. Anything can become politically symbolic if the right context is found, and, therefore, anyone can briefly become a politician if the core definition of that role is the authorship of symbolism.[6] All political failure is ultimately a failure in persuasion, and in persuasion the right symbolisation strategy is essential.

Ubiquity of Symbolism

The Reich abounded with symbolic functions, as can be seen in projects ranging from the mass development of seaside holiday flats (still existing) at the Prora beach resort, a Nazi Butlins, or the German pavilion at the Paris exhibition (a kind of super-stretched Roman temple), to the airship *Hindenburg* or ocean liners such as the *Robert Ley*. The Nazis set out to create symbols that captured the desired public mood of initiative and dynamism. Allen, for example, describes their formulaic methods of town renewal, a kind of 'place branding' in fact, including the inscriptions now affixed to significant town buildings. Quite why the Nazis had such a well-developed understanding of symbolism is an open question, yet part of the answer must be Hitler's own awareness of the importance of symbols. For resort to symbols was a way of aestheticising the regime as well as instrumentalising it: they had both a decorative and a pragmatic purpose. All of the Nazis' symbols were public signs of the new, more mobile and ultimately more exciting way of life. Nazi institutions, for example, invariably had a symbolic component, such as the PR-savvy concentration camp, Theresienstadt, an idealised world of sunny inmates pursuing sports and cultural pursuits. Moreover, these symbols of Nazism were not refracted through the prism of Auschwitz, as they are today. They were fresh, sanitised, ostensibly not evil at all. In the Reich, daily life itself could seem to be an enacted symbol, for example the tin thrust smilingly in your face by a member of the German Maidens' League collecting for Winter Relief, her hair done in the politically correct 'Gretchen' locks.[7] This was the kind of iconic representation of the regime and its values present at the everyday and domestic level. Symbolism was even a strategy in the power struggles between the paladins, as with Goebbels's decision to close Göring's favourite restaurant, Horcher's, as an egalitarian PR gesture.

Hitler's personal diktat ordained the symbolic realm in its entirety, including art policy; he would inspect condemned art, and dismissed all of the entries for the original House of German Art Exhibition, for example.[8] Thus Hitler intervened directly in all decisions about symbolism, whether art or architecture, or the symbolism of war, even when the ostensible purpose was mere functionalism. Indeed, he could sometimes end up designing the show himself, as was the case with his design for a counterpart to the French Maginot Line, including pill boxes and bunkers, along Germany's western border with the aim of frustrating the powerful French army in a future war.[9]

In practice, Hitler's preoccupation with symbolic values had a catastrophic effect on the German ability to fight the Second World War, as revenge is not only irrelevant as a military objective but it also serves to divert resources away from the pursuit of victory. It was this obsession with revenge that led Hitler to demand that the ME262 jet be used as a bomber (i.e. to kill civilians—a propaganda objective, not a military one) and not as a fighter, and in February 1943 he even went so far as to decree that every new fighter jet should also function as a fighter-bomber. When he saw one new fighter jet, his first question was: 'can this aircraft carry bombs?'[10] A concession was eventually made whereby one in every twenty would be a fighter, but even in the Reich there was what management scientists call 'authority leakage', and Hitler was long ignored and had to re-assert his demand: 'the bomber was what I wanted, none of you thought of that'.[11] Hugh Morgan and John Weal conclude: 'Many machines which, had they been available a full year earlier, could have cost the allied air force dear, were now destroyed on the ground, in assembly halls or awaiting delivery to beleaguered and fuel starved units.'[12]

Hence under the Reich the instruments of war had a symbolic as well as functional purpose. Indeed, symbolism was part of their function. For example, the three naval guns of the Batterie Lindemann, south of Sangatte on the Atlantic Wall, were a paradigm of über-modernist aesthetic, visually beautiful with their mighty canon and surround of diminishing concrete circles guarded by the taut German sentries of so many war films.[13] German propaganda also contained imagery of Hitler surveying the 1,330-ton railway gun Schwerer Gustav (see Chapter Two), which was crewed by 2,000 men; each of its rounds weighed nearly 7 tons.[14] Was this necessary, was it useful and how far was the function partly symbolic? The triumph of symbolic over utilitarian values was also well evidenced in the later war, as for example in the so-called 'weapons of desperation', such as the Bachem Ba 349 Natter, the world's first design for a fighter capable of taking off (via rocket) and landing (via parachute) vertically, essentially making it a 'manned surface-to-air missile'.[15] Then there was the symbolism of the V1. In 1944, Harald Jansen hailed this new device 'which day and night thunders down with fiery blows on the city on the Thames'.[16] The British 'had pleasant dreams of having only 100 yards to go, when suddenly they hit a new wall. At first they were blinded, poking around looking for a way to eliminate the problem. Overnight the invasion leadership had a second front—the V1 front.'[17]

Symbols had multiple other functions too, constituting a way of being all things to all men, eluding close scrutiny, and above all requesting blind faith, not rational analysis. Symbols resonate. Their meaning is powerful but it is also imprecise and they convey different shades of meaning to different groups. For a party like the Nazis, which was bent on wooing not merely diverse but actively antagonistic groupings, symbols with their open texture, their plasticity of meaning, were a gift. They gave structure to a perplexing world.[18] More generally, it is as if Hitler had managed to tap into some primordial symbol system of special signification to the human psyche. For it is not just the fact that symbolism was placed centre stage in the self-presentation of Nazism, but the particular choice of those particularised symbols, everything from the SS lightning rune to the stylisation of the eagle. In concept and execution, then, the symbol strategy worked its peculiar magic in furthering the ends of the Hitler regime.

Symbolism was the language through which the regime expressed itself. The Hamburg war memorial, for example, was changed after the Nazi assumption of power to substitute a rampant eagle for its earlier form, a weeping mother holding a child.[19] In Nazi imagery individuals were only ever symbolic of a social function. When individuals were depicted in Nazi propaganda, they tended to be shown as the 'worker intimately bound to a machine' or the 'soldier wedded to his arms' (Ulrich Kurowski),[20] while in

Nazi film individuals were simply a numerical constituent of the broader *Volksgemeinschaft*.[21] Nazi symbolism was not just a matter of images, logos and the choreographed, flame-lit rituals of public events. Symbolism penetrated everything and everything was interrogated for its symbolic possibilities: every surface, every event—quite simply, symbolism was the default mode of Nazi methodology. In this lay a source of Nazism's demise, for the decision to make an inflexible stand at Stalingrad, a fight to the finish, began the process of German defeat; so it was not mere strategy alone but the resonances of a name (i.e. the symbolism) that over-determined the decision.

The Nazi world was a symbolically constituted world whose medium was primarily visual and whose language was symbolism. A photograph was therefore neither a mere record of an event, nor a capture of a newsworthy item, but was framed and carefully constructed so as to optimise meaning via the arrangement of symbolic properties. The Nazi propaganda photograph of bombers over the Parthenon, for instance, was not just a picture of planes in flight against a scenic backdrop: rather it sought to convey an associative message, the pictographic reinforcement of a culturally territorial claim, that Nazi Germany was the rightful heir to classic civilisation (a claim constantly asserted by other representations of classic idiom in ritual and aesthetics).[22] Thus a photograph of Hitler energetically digging served an important symbolic function, but it was also about more than this; the Führer is shown bayonetting the soil with a real vigour and an expression of bull-necked delight,[23] and the image clearly seeks to symbolise the soul of the regime. The vehicles for this were not only the newsreels but also the illustrated press. Hence, for example, an *Illustrierter Beobachter* issue, 'Hitler in Prague' (1939), was dominated by a huge picture of Hitler looking out of the window over the city itself;[24] the other images were of Hitler in grand buildings with his generals, the 'decision shots' and the 'visionary-expressive' views of him. The generals are of course omnipresent, but we notice the dramaturgy of composition—in so many of the photographs they are looking at maps, standing beneath the enormous chandeliers; it is a symbolic narrative of power and dominion. The paper is telling a story, not a random record of events but rather a highway to meaning with its framing devices and the visual construction of the moment. Later we are back in Berlin and nocturnal imagery of its grandeur, with crowds and searchlights scorching the night sky; we are returned, satisfyingly, to our imperial home. A photo-picture as opposed to an artwork is supposed to be 'real', not interpretive or a created entity but a capture of truth as it happened, the veracity of the pictorial record. Nazi pictography did indeed capture a version of truth, but it was Nazism's truth: it seemed to be an authentic record of the world but was really an authentic record of the world as the Nazis wished it to be.

Impact of Symbolism

The argument then is that the Reich was impactful because it was symbolic, and that a Third Reich without the calibration of its symbols would simply be unimaginable. This is because the Reich did not primarily offer an argument but a call to faith, and symbols and their presentation were the most effective way of doing this. Symbols spoke to the apolitical mass in a newly mediatised and comparatively recently industrialised polity. The Nazis sought to create a new kind of politics, a 'politics as feeling', in which trivial lives found meaning,[25] such that it was 'not absurd to salute a spade with a spade', as Aldous Huxley once wrote,[26] since the new symbolic order was so pervasive (and apparently extinguished all sense of irony).

That the stress on symbolism had consequences both then and now cannot be denied. The symbols spoke of immense power of course, but did they deceive their creators? The very success of the symbols obscured strategic vulnerability in the regime, for example much of the army transport remained horse-drawn. The imagery of Blitzkrieg, the powerful cutting-edge engineered by massed ranks of tanks and dive bombers and mobile troops (the Panzer concept), hid significant weaknesses. Other curious deficiencies included the lack of a large surface fleet (yet what ships—*Bismarck*, *Tirpitz*, *Gneisenau*); the absence of any operational aircraft carrier (Britain had around thirteen), and the paucity of large four-engine long-distance bombers. All of these things the Allies came to possess in quantity.

The pursuit of the imagery drove the action, but it also created a myopia, one which still deceives writers on military history, documentary makers and popularisers of various sorts. Thus, to Germans and a fearful world, the symbols of military strength meant that Germany was militarily strong. 'Blitzkrieg' was a persuasive military concept which helped the Nazis win the first instalment of the Second World War, the conquest of most of Europe, and most of European Russia, but the necessary integuments of a long military campaign—the equipment, the tactics—were missing. It was not all 'mere' symbolism—the Tiger tank attests to that—but symbols were the necessary adjunct to everything. This was a universe which teemed with symbols, in fact a sensory assault: wherever Germans looked, they saw symbols of the Reich. Often these were symbols of comradeship, for

German lives were now state property, but the state was after all the sum of their race comrades. Nevertheless it all amounted to de-individuation, the aspiration to supply two-dimensional individuals for a two-dimensional world. *Triumph of the Will* attests to this: it is a rhapsody to the editing of human possibility, the reduction of personality to a small number of typologies; it condenses, not expands. Yet there was also the construction of a private and domestic realm, achieved through public presentation of the symbols of modernity, materialism and global entertainment. This symbolism too was quite deliberate, for it was recognised that there was a need to create a refuge from politicisation and the latent criminality of life in the Third Reich.

Function of Symbolism

Hitler had an intuitive appreciation of the role of symbolism in structuring the lives of ordinary folk and giving them meaning: it was part of his skill. The Reich learnt its imagistic grammar from its tutor, Adolf Hitler. Every use of the hail and hand represented affirmation and interconnectivity: it related the identity of ordinary Germans to the absolutist social values of the regime. The symbolism of the corporate ritual, the German Greeting, was a way of proclaiming the state's sovereignty over its subjects in a kind of neo-Roman style. One louche sometime-member of the Führer's court, the Harvard graduate 'Putzi' Hanfstaengl, claimed in fact to be the author of the 'Sieg Heil' salutation and to have based it on the Harvard football cheer.[27] The psychological impact of this and other methodologies can never be overstated—they enlisted the power of repetition and conditioning. Symbols also delineated hierarchies and rival groups, with a uniform for every function and every functionary in a uniform; symbolic methodologies were ways of getting people to internalise the values, to think that there was a coercive solution for all problems.

The symbolism the Nazis used was a way to telegraph the values of the regime indirectly. For example, a cover of *Die Woche* (1933), at the start of the life of the Reich, featured a colour drawing of a young blonde mountaineer on the top of a mountain with his ice axe: symbolism.[28] Nothing has to be said. Soft inference is everything and the shouting can be left to other formats. A message can only take root if it is conveyed in many diverse ways, subtle as well as crude. Symbols are condensed meaning; they are the anti-circumlocution, summative and pictorial, visually evoking what would take many words to describe, an immensely economic form of persuasion.

A brand, for example, is a symbol. As such, they are a form of very direct speech, one that is accessible to the uneducated and the principal means of communicating with them. For Mary Douglas, 'symbols are the only means of communication. They are the only means of expressing value; the main instruments of thought, the only regulators of experience.'[29] Symbols were also a substitute for action. People could believe in the perfectibility of society via the offer of its symbols—cruises, cars, social equality, powerful armed forces. Yet social deficits, such as the perpetuity of a stratified society, did not dissolve. It was often difficult in the Nazi world to separate truth from the symbolic representations/distortions of that truth, as symbols were so inextricably confused with everything that nothing had an objective existence.

Symbols trigger mood and feeling and they avoid specificity. They resonate and elude analysis and interrogation, and people can construct from them the kind of world that they want. There was 'no immutable fascist style', with Fascists in Europe generally embracing anything from female suffrage to the avant-garde.[30] Hence a symbolic strategy was invaluable to the Nazis who tried to be, if not all things to all men, then many things to many men. This reliance on symbols is explained by Nazism's appeal in the same breath to diverse populations, to very different target segments who would not ordinarily find themselves within the same political church: its supporters ranged from ex-Communists, socialists, proletarians, conservative nationalists and romantic nationalists to Catholics and many others besides. The coalition base of Nazi support comprised people who were not social or political equals, so that what was offered, both at the level of policy and imagery, had no logical coherence or design. Only symbolism could keep this extraordinary leviathan together, to give it at least a pretence of co-ordination and rationale. As Richard Evans relates,

> the Nazi party had established itself with startling suddenness in September 1930 as a catch-all party of social protest, appealing to a greater or lesser degree to virtually every social group in the land ... the vagueness of the Nazi programme, its symbolic mixture of old and new, its eclectic, often inconsistent character, to a large extent allowed people to read into it what they wanted to and edit out anything they might have found disturbing [such as the thuggery, for example].[31]

Fascism itself was not a coherent ideology but was riven with internal contradictions which the geometries of the parade ground might conceal,[32] for their aim was to integrate diverse factions into one single grouping.[33]

The inconsistencies and the plain old lunacies could be mystified, placed beyond common perception, by the dazzling illumination of symbolism.

For even Nazism rested to a degree on a strategic coalition, the continuity of which depended on its various memberships getting something tangible from the Nazi state, or at least thinking they did. There were Nazis of course, but following in their wake were a vast caravanserai of compliant others and those non-Nazis who had thrown in their lot with the new regime. These fellow travellers and new converts were even a source of regime leadership (e.g. Ribbentrop) as well as supporters. The pressure for clarity, for self-definition of the issues, was difficult to assuage given that the Nazis represented an extreme coalition.[34] Sometimes the Reich possessed the symbols alone without any of the evoked reality; for example, the symbols of traditional institutional autonomy. Thus the Reich Association of the German Press, VDP, was given the appearance of a self-governing guild. It was in fact an agency of coercion and control.[35] Such symbols also performed the necessary function of reassurance via suggested continuities with the German civic past, for example the retention of first the substance, then the mere shell, of the bourgeois press. Indeed, as Oren J. Hale points out, at the end of 1934 the press in Germany was by no means dominated by the Nazi Party, with barely 25 per cent of daily newspapers being produced by party-owned publishing houses.[36] This illusion of normality was cultivated for several years. Even its termination was concealed by the facade of custom: the extinction of the traditional German bourgeois press was accomplished via a pseudo-legal subterfuge, the Amann ordinances of April 1935 (Max Amann was Reich press leader and Hitler's former sergeant in the First World War).[37]

Form: Symbolic Politics

The grand diplomatic triumph was one aspect of the Nazis' symbolism: high risk, high reward, but a stratagem of finite limits, which was something the regime never recognised. They were an ideological end in themselves, certainly—to destroy Versailles and go beyond that to the chauvinist ideal of a Greater Germany, the imperium of the Reich. But diplomatic triumphs also functioned as a propaganda stratagem to stimulate euphoria, the sense of being in an outsize world where all dreams came true and wherein all crazy longings were made real.

Diplomacy

Diplomacy was symbolic theatre. As Spotts observes, 'diplomatic coups de main were flourished on Sundays as foreign governments dozed ... stimulating double press coverage'.[38] For example, the abrogation of the limits on German armaments carried the strongest symbolic charge—a public and popular obliteration of the Treaty of Versailles, a 'gala of frenzied nationalism'.[39] As was common with Hitlerite foreign policy triumphs, its symbolism was magnified by happy coincidence with a Nazi memorial event, for it was announced before the day of the Commemoration of the Fallen.[40] The symbolism of merging diplomatic triumphs with symbolic dates enabled the Reich to score regular, costless triumphs, such as the re-militarisation of the Rhineland in 1936, the reintroduction of conscription in 1935 and the Anschluss of 1938. In a totalitarian state the domestic media could of course be centrally structured and controlled; after the Anschluss Hitler personally ordained the response by summoning 400 media people to discuss how the event should be presented.[41]

Referenda

It should be remembered that there was also an element of symbolic democracy located in the five 'referenda' Hitler ordained before the Second World War. The fiction Hitler publicly created was not of an omniscient dictator but something much more than this: the mystical, self-cast seer of the public will. Nor was this fantasy, as in many ways it represented a proximate truth. The referenda were part of this symbolism, part of a new concept of acclamatory democracy, offering the symbols of affirmation, as also were the massed rallies where supporters could go and act out rituals of loyalty. According to Rutherford, participation in such rallies was used by the regime as a substitute for real involvement in policy-making: 'Goebbels would often suggest that the measures his government was implementing were simply the expression of public demands which had been detected in some way by speakers as they addressed them on mass occasions.'[42]

Symbolic Socialism

The Nazis had attacked indulgence and conspicuous consumption during their rise to power, and they always affirmed the socialist part of their identity, but almost always at the imagistic and rhetorical level. The symbolic red of the socialist was one of the colours of the swastika and the colour bled from Nazi posters, while socialism was a component of the brand name and the acronym Nazi. But the real socialists—Major Röhm, Gregor Strasser—had been murdered in 1934. Socialism now resided, however, in symbolic forms via the Strength Through Joy organisation. The socialist idea was not of course entirely empty of content. The Hitler Youth, for example, involved genuine class mixing in what had been a highly stratified society, and it was this kind of classlessness which was celebrated in cultural products like the film *Hitler Youth Quex*. How socialist therefore were the National Socialists? The short answer is very national and seldom socialist. But rhetorical socialism had immense value in the rise to power and in sustaining working-class support, as for example when declaiming against the iniquities of class enemies such as 'old reaction', a favourite Nazi straw man. Hitler well understood the symbolism of class antagonism, and once remarked that the Kaiser had only received a labour delegation on a single occasion.[43] Part of the Nazis' symbolic socialism involved plagiarising the imagery and iconography of the left, the melodies of their songs, and the stylisation techniques of the Weimar proletarian film (*Hitler Youth Quex*), as with the cry of the film *SA-Mann Brand*: 'everyone has to have a job and bread'.[44]

Total War

Total War itself was a symbolically charged strategy. Fashion magazines and luxury shops such as jewellers, as well as nightclubs, professional sporting events and smart restaurants, were closed, and even riding in the Tiergarten was forbidden; the restaurants were later re-opened with solidarity-enhancing field-kitchen menus.[45] Members of German royal families were to resign their commissions; corrupt aristocrats, the regime implied, were sabotaging the state.[46] Goebbels demanded mass mobilisation, yet the symbolism was almost more important, for example removing the copper cladding over the Brandenburg Gate as an image of austerity, and there was even a campaign against fashion since women would please 'victorious homecoming soldiers just as much in patches'; but Hitler astutely intervened when rumours multiplied about a banning of the permanent wave, leading Goebbels to proclaim that 'there is no need for a woman to make herself ugly'.[47]

Sources: History, Tradition

The sourcing of the symbols was not accidental but derived from the imagistic granary of German history, culture and tradition, the rituals of the Christian religion, and the German Middle Ages with its signature pitched roof (the flat roof was Middle Eastern and therefore Jewish, so that even blocks of flats had to have pitched roofs).[48] This had the special gift of making Nazi symbols look at once both new and familiar. They represented both a cherishing of the past and a greeting of the future. The Nazis were also competent at refurbishing old, even ancient, symbols and endowing them with fresh meaning. Symbolism is not invariably static; it is also dynamic, and the great leader will be a symbolic entrepreneur; symbols can be created but also re-created or retrieved from the past and given new meanings, as was the case with the swastika, for example, in the almost surreal vistas of massed swastikas in *Triumph of the Will*.[49] The swastika symbol itself originated in the Indus civilisation two and a half millennia ago, and Hitler ordained it as the national flag in 1919 (though this did not happen until Hindenburg died).[50]

Yet the tradition plagiarised could also be of recent vintage, for the swastika had also emerged in the early twentieth century as a symbol of the political right, and it was permeated with ideological and anti-Semitic significance.[51] All Nazi symbolism was therefore anchored symbolism. It condensed into its meaning symbolic resonances forged long ago in other spheres. It evoked the power of religion, it enlisted the pride of military tradition and it connected the Reich to great historic epochs in German history. Icons of the ancien régime who were still alive could also be conscripted as a source of legitimacy, such as Hindenburg, but also such old regime personalities as Field Marshal August von Mackensen and 'Auwi', Crown Prince August Wilhelm. Imagery could also make associative transfers with the monarchical epoch. Hence the colours of the swastika were the colours of the imperial flag, and the war banner was the iron cross on swastika flag,[52] while the aesthetic of SS uniforms was loosely derived from that of the black-coated 'death's head' (*Totenkopf*) hussars in which Mackensen had served.

Classical sources

Beyond this, symbolism connected Germany to that ancient, classical world to which the Reich claimed ancestral fealty, that it was in fact the true evolution of the classic tradition. In private Hitler claimed that 'the fascist movement is a spontaneous return to the traditions of ancient Rome'.[53] Nazi symbolism was evocative of great historical imperiums such as those of Alexander, Caesar or Napoleon. Pastiche reminiscence abounded—the Roman idiom-flaming plinths at Nuremberg, the Roman salute. This is the imagery of power in the Western canon; it intimidates, but it also invites.

Nazi culture and its symbols can be seen as the sordid fruit of the European classical tradition, gimcrack Romanism, in its architecture, salutes, torches and especially the classical sources for its sculptural celebrants such as Arno Breker.

High culture sources?

The symbolism of high culture was important to the Nazis, not least because they had a leader addicted to opera: 'when I hear the word culture I reach for my revolver'; this dictum, which is wrongly attributed to Julius Streicher and even to Göring, is actually a line from a contemporary German play, Hanns Johst's *Schlageter*. But no senior Nazi would have dared to articulate such sentiments, as even the coarsest of them tried to claim intellectual membership of the so-called 'culture nation'. Hitler made an annual cultural speech at the Nuremberg rally.[54] This meant a lot to the Nazis in their conflict with America, the anti-culture, or with the Eastern hordes of *Untermenschen*. Germany, with its philosophy and music, its palatial opera houses in every town, would stand against them in reproach. They aspired to symbols of intellectual class, as with Goebbels's founding of a *Times*-like newspaper, *The Reich*, at the beginning of the Second World War. It sought a 'thoughtful' approach to Nazism, narrated international affairs from a Nazi perspective and was an incubator of some distinguished post-war journalists. The symbols of tradition were everywhere, and not only in the claims to the heritage of high culture but also those of a common folk community embedded in the soil of Germany, as with the symbolism of the folk parade in *Triumph of the Will*. The past was a constant present in Nazi Germany.

Christian tradition as source

Nazism was a faith, with a text, a messiah, hymns, rituals, a priesthood and episcopacy, sacred groves, holy symbols and an exalted pseudo-language. It offered the classic properties of cultism, that is, an in-group and out-group fortified by the creation and sustenance of euphoria. The exploitation of Christian imagery in an anti-Christian cause was irrational but instrumental, since this was the cultural background all Germans shared. The Nazis intuitively understood man's unique religiosity while perverting it; symbols were not plagiarised from religion directly (and therefore blasphemously), but indirectly—old forms were retained in the service of not merely a new but a contrarian message. Thus by invoking symbols derived from Christian tradition, the Nazis suggested the authority of that tradition without directly appealing to it. For this was also an attempt at displacing religion by capturing the sense of its symbols in pursuit of a secular order. The mythologies, symbol structures and rhetorical idioms of Christianity were applied to the political realm and invested with political meaning while still retaining something of their magical aura; something of the mystical carried over.

Hitler understood this process well, having been both altar boy and acolyte. He once recalled how he would 'intoxicate' himself 'with the solemn splendour of the brilliant church festivals'.[55] Recognising this capacity for transferability was an act of supreme political entrepreneurship on Hitler's part, as for example with the Nazis' secularising of the Netherland Thanksgiving prayer.[56] Artists might exploit Christian imagery in very obvious ways. One picture in particular, entitled 'In the Beginning was the Word' (see Chapter Four), draws heavily from Christian iconography to the extent of having a star-like swastika lighting the sky. Klemperer describes in detail the pseudo-sacerdotalism of the blood banner which carried some kind of spiritual essence and would consecrate through its touch.[57] Hitler 'acted as a priestly medium transmitting the magical *fluidum* of the old sacred symbol through his body to the new ones'.[58] The key device was the existence of political holy days, in effect, which leavened the mundane routine of the year. These were: 30 January, Seizure of Power; 24 February, Foundation Day of NSDAP; 16 March, Day of Remembrance; 20 April, Hitler's Birthday; 1 May, People's Day of Unity; and 21 June, Midsummer Day (mass meetings, policy statements).[59] There was also the party rally at Nuremberg and the October Festival of the Harvest. However, the sacerdotal calendar was dominated by the essential blasphemy of parodying the Easter myth with a Nazi secular version—the mummeries of 9 November, when The March would be enacted, ending with The Martyrdoms. But the messiah was alive to consecrate the sarcophagi of the dead and address their heroic spirits. Thus 'the drama of 9 November became a station in the Germanic passion, featuring parallels to Golgotha, the Crucifixion, the Resurrection and the Return'.[60] Baird describes how each station in the Munich passion concluded with the affirmation 'Germany we believe in you.' The rites were broadcast live; on 9 November 1933 Germans awoke to the song 'Wake Up, You German Land! You Have Slept Long Enough'.[61] The procession passed by blazing biers: 'belching black smoke, they added an altogether pagan aura to the macabre death ritual'.[62]

Symbolic Mediums

Nazi Germany was self-articulated through symbols. But it spoke and elucidated its key meanings through a public theatre that was crude and ostentatious and cruel, both actually and symbolically. The aim was to indicate with utter clarity to everyone what the new ideals, the integuments, of the new anti-culture were. The Nazis took great trouble to do this and these events were a key part of its governing methodology. Only in the case of the Berlin Games did they demonstrate sensitivity to international opinion; otherwise it did not really appear to count. The violence was neither random nor anarchic, but merely gave the feeling of being so—Fascist thuggery transmitted a calibrated set of coded 'messages'.[63] The regime revealed its nastiness in such a public way because fear and coercion were part of the Nazi product. As Paxton argues, 'the legitimation of violence against a demonised internal enemy brings us close to the heart of fascism'.[64] There were the great episodes of public political violence, whose symbolism was unambiguous: the Night of the Long Knives and Kristallnacht. Both were explanatory in nature—the regime would not hesitate to unleash murderous violence against any imaginary threat or ideological foe. The very lack of an attempt at concealment was itself a symbol. Röhm and his fellow 'conspirators' were freely announced as having been extra-judicially murdered, while the ransacking of Jewish premises was an act of extrovert and public criminality. Kristallnacht was antithetical to German norms, and regressive even beyond arbitrary feudal authority styles (it was dressed up as a popular act of protest against the vom Rath killing). It continued the pattern of the illegality/criminality associated with the regime, as if the Nazis were deliberately spitting in the face of bourgeois pieties of tidiness, order, bureaucracy, legalism—a violation of the very German culture they claimed to honour.

Then there were the symbolic exhibitions in which the regime would create some massive public happening, a luminous extravaganza which would celebrate some ideological building-block of Nazism. On one level there is a large gulf between an exhibition, something edifying and polite, and the cascade of remorseless violence the Nazis unleashed on the streets. But in fact they were two sides of the same coin, both authored by the same controlling regime: the one actually violent, the other representing not physical but cultural violence. The Exhibition of Degenerate Art in Munich was one such symbol, excoriating the nihilism and un-Germanism of all forms of abstract and interpretive art; the regime went well beyond public aesthetics here, demanding ownership of private taste as well as public space. As to the question of Germany's international image, Germany emerged much diminished by these events, shrunken in international esteem and—much, much more—feared.

Symbolic Mediums: Expositions

The book burnings

In May 1933, 20,000 books were publicly burned (see Chapters One and Four). The fires had started, and leading the Berlin incinerations (including work of eminences like Sigmund Freud) was a professor of political pedagogy: Erich Kästner, the author of *Emil and the Detectives* (1929), actually watched the flames consume his own books.[65] The imagery and the symbolism derived from this was powerful and a permanent repository of our idea of the Third Reich—the crowds of students, their faces illuminated by the flames, the shakos of the storm troopers; the piles of literature fed the conflagrations, great bonfires of erudite paper, for anything which was non-Nazi, not merely left-wing, was potentially 'subversive'. The notion was that people should be licensed only to think in the same way and be creative along the same tram-lines; behind this ultimately lay a terror of modernity. Its symbolic value was as a rejection of mind, of intellectualism, and the enthronement of intoler-ance as a way of life. It was expressive of a murderous inner being—we kill ideas, then people, and the methodologies of Torquemada and the Spanish Inquisition were disinterred from their tombs.

This turning back of the clock exposed the fallacy of the idea of progress as linear (the so-called 'Whig view of history'), for now humanity could regress, in central aspects of society, to a more primitive archetype. This was a harbinger of a new mode of governance, the Nazi cultivation of mobs, apparently spontaneous outbreaks of popular violence against what the regime had vilified, which were in fact highly controlled—Goebbels had praised the burnings on national radio.[66] Symbolic violence anticipates actual violence, and the symbolic events functioned as a way of dispelling all ambiguity. Their representational value was immense in conveying the idea that pluralism would not be tolerated.

Exhibition of Degenerate Art

The Nazi approach to modern art was initially tentative but later congealed into a more nihilistic approach towards the end of the 1930s. Since all mod-ern art was seen as Jewish, the attack on modern art was also a part of the attack on the Jews, and hence art in the Reich was laden with symbolic meaning.[67] Art was a branch of politics, pure and simple; there was no independent aesthetic realm that was free of politics. The antagonism to 'Judaised' modernist art was part of a larger thesis on 'degeneracy' that tapped into popular conservatism and its visceral response to the artistic manifestations of modernity, where indeed Germany had in many senses been a world leader. Much of this 'modernity' was in fact an abstracted or caricatural reaction to the experience of the First World War, in which many of Germany's artists had fought. These included George Grosz, who offered grotesque visions of Berlin, a netherworld of nightclubs and prostitutes. This was a representation of Weimar as the Nazis remembered and hated it, a symbol of the decay of democracy.

The oddness of Nazism's art convulsions draws comparisons with Stalin and the Zhdanov decrees, and this recognition of the potency of art is impressive in a way. Both the Nazi and Soviet regimes found awe in its power, but what they wanted from art was declamation, not interpretation. Nazis were not unanimous in their allergic reaction. Goebbels was a secret admirer of modernism; Baldur von Schirach, as Gauleiter of Vienna, even held a reverential modern art exhibition during the war, 'Junge Kunst Im Deutschen Reich'.[68] However, the war on art represented a radical extension of the idea of what is political. 'Degenerate' was a label applied not just to perverse and exaggerated caricatures of human form or the evocations of the neon-lit, remorseless hedonism of Berlin's demi-monde, but all kinds of abstract and interpretive art, anything in fact that did not embrace hyper-literalism and whose subject matter could be viewed as less than patriotic, or passively critical. The Exhibition of Degenerate Art reversed the normal idea of an exhibition, which is to showcase the best, or the most representative, or elucidate a positive theme; this on the contrary was cultural assassination, the aim being to lop off the cultural membrane of much of the late nineteenth and especially the twentieth century's aesthetic discourse. Again the point was to make the regime's values unambiguous via a symbolism so stark and crude that even the dullest-witted member of the *Volk*, and, of course, the rest of the world, would get the message. Nazis turned art into a freak show.

The 1937 Munich Exhibition of Degenerate Art circulated throughout Germany and was well publicised via radio and newsreel. The cartoonist Mjölnir (Hans Schweitzer) was made Reich deputy for artistic conception; this is actually like a ghastly joke—he was a cartoonist, after all.[69] In the end the anathema on degenerate art also concluded with flames, as some of the paintings were actually burned at Berlin's central fire station.[70] Again Nazism can be seen here as representing a shrinkage of human possibility, but this invasion of the idea of freedom transcended what Germans could publicly say to what could be displayed, what could be privately expressed, on canvas. Beyond this was the loss of the idea of interpretation. Abstract and expressionist art forms are capable of multiple readings, since their meaning is negotiated: a Grosz image can sustain an authoritarian interpretation and be seen as a critique of the demi-monde and its license, or the reverse. Indeed, one leading artist who found himself in the exhibition, Emil Nolde, was also a loyal, convinced party supporter.[71] This symbolised something more, namely that the state did not just want your acquiescence, your public apoliticality. To say that we can only paint—even in private—according to a certain aesthetic dogma (a mandate the exhibition essentially imposed)—limits all creative expression, even where it has no overt political content, to the rigid formularies of the state. By inference, the state ordains what we can and cannot feel. There was in fact more to come, for music was next. In 1938, the Exhibition of Degenerate Art was followed by a 'Degenerate Music' show in Düsseldorf, where Jewish composers were ridiculed along with others who based their rhythms on jazz or conformed to the twelve-tone scale.[72] In specially erected cubicles the scandalised Nazi music-lover could seek gratification of their prejudices: 'visitors could choose from some seventy condemned recordings, including the works of modern composers such as Berg, Paul Hindemith, or Arnold Schoenberg, and Kurt Weill'.[73]

Paris Exposition

The symbolism looked outward as well as inward, such as the German Pavilion at the Paris Exposition of 1937, which was another regime setpiece, a massive rectangular building facing down the Soviet Pavilion. This was one of the great images to emerge from the 1930s, and one often used to express the conflicts of that decade: the much-parodied male and female worker brandishing a scythe atop the Soviet Pavilion versus the elongated classicism of the Nazi Pavilion. The German structure was surmounted by its mighty eagle, the traditional icon of the German nation and, in its stylised format, the brand-logo of the new state. Here was Nazi symbolism in an international context, confronting its ideological adversary face to face, that same Bolshevik enemy the storm troopers had fought in the early days. The symbolism of both sites 'spoke': they were public advertisements for the rival credos and their national sponsors in a neutral international setting. The celebration of proletarian fundamentalism confronted a steroidal Roman temple.

The Paris Pavilion was an exemplum of Nazi public packaging and of the way Nazism used architecture as propaganda, in that it framed the Nazi image in a classic past. The simplicity of its stylisation, its high formality and rejection of abstraction represented a banishment of modernism, whose style and evoked set of values were by this stage in history scarcely novel (going beyond the young Frank Lloyd Wright at the turn of the century, to nineteenth-century figures like Charles Rennie Mackintosh). It was regressive, a rejection of everything that the aesthetic of the twentieth century had done and said. Its simple white lines gleaming in the Paris sun self-proclaimed the new order's cultural embassy to the world in a foreign place, and not just any foreign place but Paris, spiritual home of revolution and progenitor of Liberté, Égalité, Fraternité. This took place amid the low murmurs and distant flashes of the awakening storm. While Paris exhibited, Spain fought, with European and American volunteers travelling there to 'do something' about Fascism. And the Spanish Republic presented an über-modern pavilion that remembered the styles of the modern masters like Le Corbusier—so the architecture spoke of the values of the regimes, symbolism in concrete, public sculptuary. A battle of dogmas transmuted into a battle of architectures and mirrored the actual, current, happening battle of the ideologies via proxy in the Spanish Civil War. It was an epic moment.

Aesthetic monumentalism

Public decoration, the Fascist theatre of monumentalism, was an important part of this symbolism. While talking about the new Chancellery, Hitler told one of his adjutants that 'when these gentlemen enter the Mosaic Hall they must immediately sense the whole sublime nature of the Greater German Reich. The long corridors will reduce my visitors to humility.'[74] The Reich Chancellery was a protracted essay in the language of intimidatory symbolism:

> Beyond the granite hall with its cupola there stretched a hall of mirrors lined with red marble modelled on that of Louis XIV at Versailles, except that at 146 m. it was a little under twice as long. The goal of the visitor was Hitler's study. Its proportions were just as generous: 27 metres by 14.5 m., and nearly 10 m. high. At one end a portrait of Bismarck hung over a massive fireplace, while on the white marble table rode a statue of Frederick the Great on horseback. The whole edifice cost just under 90 million marks. The wraps came off the new Palace on January 12 1939, Göring's birthday.[75]

In contrast, Hitler's mountain retreat, the Berghof on the Obersalzberg above Berchtesgaden in south-east Bavaria, was a study in monumentalist utility. It was a kind of reverse apartment block and was his residence for much of the period of the Third Reich: it had thirteen floors, of which only three were above ground.[76] Then there was the troglodyte gloom of the bunker in Berlin, which was below the Reich Chancellery. In fact, even the Nazi home, the domestic abode of the paladin, was symbolically charged, and petty bourgeois aesthetics were replaced by domestic monumentalism as tenure of power progressed.[77] Art and architecture were a synthesis under the Reich: part of a building's construction budget had to be spent on artwork, and artists received money from building funds.[78]

The 'toys' of dictators, as well as their homes, perhaps always fascinate because the dictator has unlimited power to self-imagine and indulge, and in Hitler's case the toys possessed intimidatory, celebratory and symbolic as well as utilitarian functions. For example, there was his mobile wartime HQ, the leader's special train, *Führersonderzug*, with its two Flakwagen and radio car with its radio and tele-printer; his private aircraft was a four-engine metal Focke-Wulf Condor with a range of 2,212 miles and a cruising speed of 208 mph.[79]

Symbolic Mediums: Art

Symbolism was more than just a medium for Nazi self-articulation. For the regime it was indeed 'a language that lies deeper than language', particularly important given that Nazism lacked intimacy, and its tone was public and declamatory. Moreover, the ambition was certainly totalitarian, the aim being to control all thought and feeling, and hence art lacked any real room for manoeuvre even if designed only for the private and domestic market. It had to be literal, and in this sense all art, even a landscape, was also propaganda since it had to be realistic or transcend the real. The subject matter had in ways implicit or explicit to be adulatory of the culture and of the regime. An artist could not present war as a tragedy, for example. A new re-ordering of artistic worth now placed the old German masters at its apex, and endowed the Austro-Bavarian landscape with aesthetic primacy.[80]

Symbolism played the major role in all of this. Images speak not just of themselves but of a larger universe of ideas, so paintings and statuary became vistas on to the thinking of the regime even when they were ostensibly apolitical. In fact, what would in other cultures have been apolitical, such as a nude statue, symbolised the epicentre of a worldview in the Reich (or, in their language, the mature ethnic consciousness of a folkish people). Nazi art was symbolic; it represented and typified and served as a condensed expression of the social ideology—its function then was unlike that of most art down the ages, which is to speak in a private voice. Adolf Wamper's relief, *Genius des Sieges*, for example, owes an obvious debt to classicism, and especially to Michelangelo's *David*. But there is none of the magisterial repose evident in the classics. This is hysterical; the dead man's face is calm, but his comrade's face is contorted with rage. What then does this mean, these scowling men and their muscles, pseudo-classic, naked, with swords, killing mythical beasts—in action, in repose? Nudity was the medium of classical antiquity, but it also symbolises the different functions of genders in a gender-defined world, and it is, in a sense, a way of unveiling the pure essence of the race. For these nudes were not real portraits of real people; they were idealised types and the nudes are public essays in utopian typology. Thus an American journalist spoke of 'ideological nudity ... all the news stands displayed books and magazines filled with pictures of nude men and women ...' The painter Adolf Ziegler was even described as the 'Reich Master of Pubic Hair'![81] The genders have very different symbolic meanings: the male symbolises the principle of utility (warriorness and physical labour), the female signifies fecundity (and domesticity). The foregrounded woman is sometimes a mass of shapeless flesh, the desexualised Nazi female nude; you never get under the skin, there is no musculature. The preoccupation is with male physical fitness and its symbolic expression: muscle was a key signifier in art of the Third Reich; muscle was political. Muscle replaced thought and character as the dominant ideal; it was the insignia of physical labour, and the promise of aggression. It represented a physical path that had already been exercised, and a physical potential yet to be unleashed. The symbols of race and national chauvinism, of race conceit, were everywhere in the Third Reich.

Ideology can often only be inferred through the symbolism inherent in the choice of subject matter rather than articulated in any more explicit way. But because it was symbolically constructed, all Nazi art was also a public art. The sculptures, and the paintings, de-individuate by portraying exemplars of human physical perfection. Shapes are frozen in time and there is a sense of arrested movement—the postures ritualistic, the expressions self-aware—because these individuals are symbolic, bearers of function and of explicit status within the hierarchy of the folk community. Often the canvases were self-conscious reproductions of the painterly style of the sixteenth-century Italian Renaissance, with a studied Italian neoclassic background: the Nazis favoured romantic rural landscapes with their rivers, hills, forests, hay gathering with oxen, and skies. The point of such painting was really somewhat obscure, except to say that it was symbolic, the self-conscious reworking of an old tradition and thus the essence of reactionary. Why do badly what had been done so well centuries ago? This is moribund, art enacted in the prison cell of the mind. The core of Nazi art, then, was really repro. The 'renaissance' idiom was in itself highly symbolic, connecting the contemporary German aesthetic to an imagined past of folk culture and artistic greatness that pre-dated the degeneracy of modernism and cosmopolitanism.

Symbolic Mediums: Public Violence

Night of the Long Knives

Luchino Visconti's notorious version of this event in the film *The Damned* (1969) represents a metaphoric rather than actual truth; the SA men were mostly shot later in prison, but these deaths were not hidden; the regime boasted about it. The scale of the extra-judicial killing was so extreme—at least seventy deaths—and so antithetical to German custom that its acceptance by the bulk of Germans must be regarded as a triumph of propaganda. The deaths in 1934 were of course not merely those of the restless SA leadership cadre most closely associated with Röhm (although Hitler took some persuading to agree to the execution of Röhm himself). Also murdered were others from the previous regime, including two ex-generals, Ferdinand von Bredow and the former Chancellor General Kurt von Schleicher (along with his wife). Von Papen—also a former chancellor—was more fortunate. Yet the army, to its perpetual discredit, was prepared to accept the murder of two of its own. The leader of Catholic Action was also killed. The military and religious establishment was silent (Field Marshal Werner von Blomberg had accepted the purge because the SA would thus no longer threaten the army).

The Night of the Long Knives had other functions too—to remove people whom Hitler had been persuaded represented a threat to his authority, and to reassure a terrified army, standing at little more than 100,000 men, that the massive SA would not now replace it. The event also reveals the extent of bourgeois horror of this plebeian, thuggish 'brown army', a fear so great they either forgave or simply averted their gaze from mass murder as a solution. This amounted to a public announcement that the regime had ceased to be constructed on a legal basis. The Night of the Long Knives was thus another concoction of the great Nazi illusion, and in that lexicon of irrationality, that imperium of unreason, it deserves special mention. The great 'spin' was to project it as a moral crusade when, as Burleigh points out, the motives were entirely political.[82] A homosexual plot, then, against the very heart of the Reich: Sopade (the SPD organisation in exile in Prague) analysts noted the utility of this appeal to bourgeois morality, which was an effective mask 'disguising the essentially political nature of what actually happened'.[83] In Burleigh's words, Hitler would appear as 'the avenging agent of popular indignation and justice—except that he was not a monarch, but a self-consciously ordinary man, who could articulate the anxieties and desires of his ordinary countrymen in words which made them laugh and cry, switching from coarse diatribes to the most flighty rhetoric'.[84] The public were ignorant of the internal narrative.

Nuremberg Laws

Under the 'Nuremberg Laws', so called because they were promulgated at the 1935 party rally, Jews were excluded from the army and civil service and from marrying 'Aryans'. It was not so much a declaration of second-class citizenship as of non-citizenship, and a major step towards making Germany *judenrein*, for what Jew would want to remain in such a state? The laws were an enunciation of the race ideology—'blood' was now the basis of the state, a gesture of contempt for all the world and international public opinion. They were thus symbolic as well as juridical. Jews now became a non-group in their own country, murmuring ghosts in the twilight of their people, tenants of a spectral realm. This was a proclamation of non-identity; this confiscation of civic personhood gave a licence to groups and people, public and private, to further degrade them.

Kristallnacht

Kristallnacht (1938) saw the trashing of Jewish businesses and 100 synagogues destroyed.[85] Again the regime chose the symbolic elements: the people who were the exclusive objects of attack, Jews and no one else; the kinds of properties that were attacked (shops, temples); and the very symbolic signature of the attack, the smashing of shop windows. Much political violence, including war, focuses the attack on identifiable and specific targets that are deeply symbolic and whose defilement pleasures the partisans of a cause. Indeed, Michael Blain concludes that 'human violence is not the fall into latent animality but rather an extreme expression of our symbol mindedness'.[86]

As with the Night of the Long Knives, the inference was that the regime understood exactly what it was doing on Kristallnacht, drawing a clear line of division between this and constitutional nationalism and bourgeois legalism, and it fingered the Jews as the regime's greatest enemy and candidates for psychotic violence. Previously the regime had many enemies—Communists, plutocracy, old reaction; the merit of Kristallnacht was that it condensed this previous range of enemies into just one. To symbolise this intent, Goebbels chose the occasion of the murder of a German diplomat as the *casus belli* (see Chapter One). For Jews this terror was a nightmare and an early step in the Golgotha of their people. But the terrorist message was not for Jews alone. It was a warning, and a regime unmasking, for all Germans. It was also the preface to genocide. The indifference to international opinion, indeed the contempt for it, is manifest in the choice of an image-rich event, unlike the Night of the Long Knives where murder took place in prison yards. But smouldering synagogues and the faces of the SA contorted with imbecilic rage, the fumes and the acrid smell of burning in the night air, the daubed slogans of '*Jude verrecke*' and Stars of David; the masses of broken windows beneath the Jewish store names; the legions of the bloodied and the beaten—these were a visible public theatre to be seen, discussed and photographed by the international press. This was an advertisement of a peculiar kind whose content and meaning could not be misinterpreted even by the simplest soul or most naive observer. Nazi propaganda could be self-concealing or even on occasion subtle, but when the need for portrayal was in savage primary colours, the regime rose, or rather descended, to the occasion. The provocation of international opinion was thus another aspect, the judgement, of a changing world, one which saw the tentative beginnings of anti-racialism, as with the black American Marian Anderson's singing 'My Country 'tis of Thee' before the Lincoln Memorial and a crowd of 75,000 on Easter Sunday 1939.

This symbolism was so clearly the symbolism of the bully, and it helped endow the Reich with that public persona. The strong terrorising the weak and defenceless, expressed via beatings, graffiti and broken glass, was a symbol that would be globally recognised irrespective of culture. It was a violation of every innate, universal sense of human fairness and decency. The Nazis began on the streets as an organised gang, but the astonishing thing for the world, and indeed many Germans, was that they never outgrew their street-incubator, but governed as the urban terrorists they had once been. It was too a symbol that Europe's self-styled culture nation, and the capital, even, of European science and technology, could revert to the inflammatory sectarian passions of its remote ancestors. The very idea of progress was challenged: was there then no onward march of civilisation but rather a system of circuits and regressions? It was of course appalling anti-propaganda for the regime, but that is to assume that what the regime wanted was influence or respect. It did not. It wanted, at this stage, towards the end of the 1930s, to be feared. Moreover, it wanted to demonstrate to the world that the old ways—the ways of due process, the constraints of both legality and democracy—were now defunct. It was a new order.

Symbolic Mediums: Public Spectacles

Pageantry was not an occasional resource of the Third Reich but an integral part of its symbolic methodology both at the local and national level, as Allen reveals in his study of the town of Northeim,[87] and was something Germans were acculturated to, as with the traditional Corpus Christi processions. This was a way of solving those problems at the symbolic level that could not be solved at the political level. Pageantry also acted as a diversion: it could dissolve the functional and ethical limitations of a regime that was corrupt as well as harsh; the elaboration of the symbol system constituted a face mask with which to hide something about a regime which went beyond the traditions of the autocratic tyrant and into the far shores of nihilism. These image-managed events, starting with Potsdam, were a way of answering the question of legitimacy and were a preamble to Hitler's methodology of governance via symbolic theatre.

Potsdam

The role of Hindenburg as president was as secular monarch of Germany, the Kaiser substitute. But he also stood for an ethos and a history. He was the victor of Tannenberg and along with Ludendorff the supreme military titan of the First World War. He was the embodiment of much that the Germans valued most, the German ideal self (an integrity only slightly tainted by a tax matter), nobility and unflinching resolution, high patriotism: the ethic of the old world. Hitler, in other words, received the apostolic succession of German kaiserdom and he was legitimated as heir to the throne.

After Hitler had been made chancellor there was a torch-lit parade through Berlin and then a formal ceremony at Potsdam with that famous handshake between the marshal and the corporal, the president and the new chancellor. The inauguration of the Third Reich in the Garrison Church at Potsdam was the apogee of Hitlerism's theatre of symbolism. In Kershaw's words it was a masterpiece of suggestive propaganda, with Hindenburg blessing Hitler and the new Germany: henceforth Hindenburg was incorporated into the Nazi mythology until his death.[88] Beyond the political opportunism of exploiting the symbol of Hindenburg, these images created the ideal Nazi blend of Prussianism and militarism. In other words a bricolage which is entirely without any other coherence, the imagistic synthesis of heritage, modernity and the ideological supremacy of the Nazi party in power. It was a travelogue festooned with ripe symbolism, Hitler for example descending into the vaults to offer homage at the tomb of King Frederick the Great; this was expert impression-management, the idea that these new people were the authentic heirs of Prussian tradition and venerated it. Hitler would describe this day as the marriage between the symbols of the old greatness and the new strength.[89] The aim was to endow the leader of what was formerly a movement of street thugs, and a foreigner (until 1932 an Austrian citizen), with respectability.

Since the Garrison Church at Potsdam was an ecclesiastical building, there was of course an implicit public request that God would bless the Reich. And such a church, where Bach had played—it was the spiritual heart of the old Prussia and the symbol, more than any other, of its virtues and its military glory. Within, a baroque high altar with soaring columns and complex lines, as much theatre set for an opera as tabernacle of the Lord, commanded the centre of an auditorium decorated with militarist images, the panoplies of arms and so forth which were incongruous in a place of religion. It is significant that, though damaged from bombing in the Second World War, the structure survived, but in an epic of ideological spite was torn down by the East German regime in 1968. This was because of the meaning the Nazis had invested in the building. They had made it the locus of the start of their state, of its commencement ritual. The fate of this church was ever symbolic, as eloquent today by its absence as by its former presence.

Spectacles: Re-burial of Munich Martyrs and ceremonies of 9 November

Nazi Germany was never more alive than when remembering the dead. To die was the ultimate affirmation of loyalty and it was important that death was given transcendent meaning and dignity via a ritual.[90] The Reich loved to stage-manage the theatrical funeral of a grandee and to celebrate a whole constellation of martyrs: in Baird's words, 'the Führer was never more at home than when communing with the souls of the dead'.[91] The intimations of an afterlife for heroes were ever present, but it was the empty shell and not the living substance of religion that Germans were left with. Thus, as Heini lays dying in *Hitler Youth Quex*, his eyes blaze with ethereal joy, phantom youth legions march through clouds and into eternity, to a rousing chorus of their anthem. It was Catholicism without Christianity, according to Grunberger; it confronted the 'total lack of transcendence by means of ever larger infusions of ritual'.[92]

The re-enactment of the 9 November March became the great event of the Nazi liturgical year, beginning in November of 1933 with a ritual of dedication. The route of the march represented 'stations of the cross' with musical orchestration adapted for each stage of the progression.[93] On arriving, Hitler performed the rites appropriate for a priest-king:

> thereupon Hitler descended the steps of the Feldherrnhalle and proceeded with the ceremony. To the accompaniment of muffled drums, he approached the memorial, followed by his most intimate paladins. Deeply moved, he listened as the crowd sang the Horst Wessel song ... Hitler gazed at the Monument and saluted the wooden cross that had been placed directly across the street on the walls of the Residenz.[94]

Several years later, the 'Martyrs' of 9 November were re-buried (in November 1935, see Chapter Four), and Baird has lucidly evoked the gilded weight of invented ritual. Thus on 8 November 'an identical deathwatch was in place throughout the night at four hundred points in the Reich, at all those places where National Socialists had been murdered by "Reds or reactionaries"'. That night, horse drawn carriages took their mortal remains to the Feldherrnhalle. SA men with torches lit the parade route, where the glorious dead, both comrade and ancestor, watch over the living. Four hundred oil-burning pylons framed the journey, on each one the gold-embossed name of a fallen hero. The next day, 9 November, the men reassembled for the march to the Temple of Honour, the site of the re-interment. The new Temple was in itself a symbolic realm, 'cast in marble, surrounded by columns, and open to the air, the temple incorporated his ideal that true art should express political ideology'.[95] Hitler had proclaimed 'because they did not survive to see this Reich, we are going to make certain that this Reich sees them ... Because for us they are not dead. These temples are no mausoleums, but instead an "Eternal Guard". Here they stand guard for Germany ...' The idea was of the fallen of November being resurrected and taking their positions as eternal guards, according to the official script: 'At the precise moment when Hitler reached a pylon, the name of a hero was called out on a sound system that transmitted the proceedings to the city of Munich and to the national radio hookup.' The high drama of these resonantly symbolic moments was captured in perpetuity by the watchful media (and accessible today in cyberspace).

The meaning of 9 November was celebrated in the documentary *For Us*.[96] The remembrance of 9 November was to become an annual event in the Nazi sacerdotal calendar; the survivors were led by the human principal in the drama, the Führer, and the principal artefact, the blood flag itself. Its transfiguration was 'from flag to Holy shroud and it was employed for liturgical use on occasions of great importance as well'.[97] Thus the reburial itself, and the rituals of 9 November, were drenched in Christian imagery—martyrs, disciples, high priest, death and resurrection; the route itself was a Golgotha. Nazis 'did' synthetic-sacerdotal with apparent conviction, a parody of Christian symbolism and a plagiarism from it. But unlike in Christian mythology, the material objects and human-divine subject were visible by their presence, rather than being imagined by their absence. The November re-enactment of the Munich putsch was thus 'a silent march of survivors and invocation of the stations of the cross but this time led by the savior'.[98] Nazism was indeed a secular religion, one which included many millenarian, apocalyptic, gnostic and Manichaean elements.[99]

Symbolic Mediums: Design

House style

A cacophony of symbols was used to create the synthetic dignity of the great Nazi set-piece occasions: bands, the glint of steel, the flashing of medals, the massed columns in perfect order, the scowling of the leadership cadre and the lone walks through serried ranks to place a wreath, make an address, plant a medal. But above all were the torches, since ceremonies at night were more mystical and evoked darker and more primitive emotions. One is reminded of the remark of Sir Nevile Henderson that these were not normal men; more in fact like condottiere or medieval robber-barons in remote castle fastnesses. But there were also the public symbols, everything from the monumentalist architecture of Troost or Speer to the powerful Mercedes which was the omnipresent symbol of the leadership cadre.

The party colours were an important part of symbolism. The violent red of poster and banner tore into consciousness, but it also functioned as a self-conscious provocation of the left. As Burleigh observes:

since Nazi propaganda was both professional and reactive, when red became inopportune, to a party casting its net wider, they duly opted for a plurality of colours. In their respect for imagery and flexibility these people were very modern ... [they were therefore] cunningly incorporating the imperial black and white into the overall scheme.[100]

It was not just the colour. As Rutherford reminds us, the vividness of tone also mattered—'the red of the brilliance of new spilt blood, the white of the same inflorescence/purity, the black, dense, without highlights'. Stories emerged of whole batches of posters being rejected after printing because the colours were thought to be too pallid. Hence 'the final result was a triad of colours, which, to those who like myself have been exposed to it, can never fail to reawaken memories of the flags, bunting, vistas of banners and standards. Their impact was extraordinary.'[101] The swastika was foregrounded against dull backgrounds in order to enhance it the more, for instance against the brown uniforms of storm troopers: these were violent physical symbols.[102] Hitler also had an instinctive understanding of the emotive power of symbols—flags, uniforms, standards and so on—and applied this to the way in which the party's iconography was conceptualised.[103] This included the swastika, the omnipotent symbol in which the Nazis invested so much, as Hitler himself recalls in *Mein Kampf*.[104] The swastika was hijacked from the Free Corps and earlier folkish sects and the particular stylisation was created by a party member who worked as a dentist. Hitler's contribution lay not in the idea but in his perception of its importance (i.e. his mastery of symbolism).[105] In Spott's words:

> He secured the adoption of the swastika and it was he who determined that it face right rather than left and who ordained its colours to such potent effect, he who chose the black, white (for the nationalist idea, according to Hitler) and (from the left) red. He sketched a party flag and discovered it has the effect of a burning torch.[106]

This technique of slanting the symbols at an angle to generate an aura of dynamism was developed during the Nazis' market rivalry with the Communists.[107]

Moreover, Hitler also designed a party badge and stationery, as well as the mast head of the party newspaper, all embossed with an eagle with a swastika in its talons, and he also created the standard that became the insignia of mass meetings.[108] He apparently worked out measurements and detail. The uniforms (such as the SS uniforms) were symbols at their most aesthetic and suggestive, presenting an image of men who, as Spotts writes, 'were not only supremely violent but also supremely beautiful'. Hitler also developed a repertory of oral symbols such as the Sieg Heil which had old German roots, and the Heil Hitler.[109] None of the other parties' symbols seemed to be as effective, and in a competitive political marketplace, this mattered:

> Neither the three arrows invented by the Social Democratic party as a counter symbol to the swastika, nor the Hammer groups created within the Democratic Militia (Reichsbanner), nor the establishment of an 'Iron Front' of the Reichsbanner and other auxiliary organisations of the Social Democratic party could help. They did not symbolise a vital and realistic policy. The leadership was unwilling to take risks ...[110]

Symbolic Mediums: Ritual

Vacuity of content

Unlike Marxism, Fascism offered little that was concrete enough to get hold of, so it supplied ritual in place of belief—or even ritual as belief.[111] For Nazis, the essence was mere loyalty rather than conviction. It was not necessarily a question of internalising what was a manufactured, self-contradictory, illogical and fluid ideology. What mattered was homage: unquestioning devotion to an absolute master. Ritual was not so much an outward expression of belief as a mode of producing it.[112] Ritual indeed may be defined as a kind of symbolism whose essence is repetition in a formulaic style, the symbolic representation of an inherited idea. Revolutionary regimes have thoroughly understood the need to create new rituals to replace those they have extinguished; revolutionary France, Stalinist Russia and Nazi Germany pilfered the semiological debris of ancient monarchies and the vapid ghosts of marginalised religions. As with much else, the Nazis both used and perverted such things. But no society was ever more ritually conscious than Nazi Germany. Hitler even owed at least part of his survival to a ritual that he created, that is, the soldier's personal oath of allegiance; in the later conspiracies many officers were reluctant to break their oath. This hold over the officer corps, achieved by a very public ritual, was just one example of how Hitler's power was buttressed by symbolic structures. The Nazis specialised in the creation of new ritual and recognised a civic and social vacuum that could be filled by the pursuit of common rituals—in this sense, Nazism can again be seen as one response to conditions of urban modernity. There were even new rituals of industrial life: sirens became fanfares, roll calls replaced clock in–clock out.[113] Allen describes how in the first months of the Nazi regime there was a major public ritual/celebration in the town of Northeim about every three weeks.[114]

Nazism ritualised the public space and the life of the citizen via a new civics which, ostensibly, embodied a replica of traditional moral nostrums, fealty to state, duty to neighbour and so forth. There were the rituals of Winter Relief (Chapter Four), for example, which serviced the regime's need for what Grunberger describes as 'permanent emotional mobilization'.[115] Its essentially bogus prospectus was manufactured by propaganda, with the associated 'Pot Sunday' idea of the family consuming an austere stew every month, the surplus to be given to Winter Relief to assist the indigent among the *Volk*; leading lights of the regime were naturally photographed smilingly consuming this thin gruel.[116] The aim was to create a superordinate social solidarity via ritual and symbolism. Ritual was for every day, it interpenetrated the fabric of ordinariness. And the new rituals were vivid, memorable: the Mothering Sunday crosses awarded, the garlands of life on childbirth homes; the celebrations of summer solstice—leaping through flames, fire speeches and so on. There were the great rituals of state, but also the infusion of state-worship ritual into private life as well. The ubiquitous 'German Greeting' had the happy effect of politicising the normal: 'one of the most potent forms of totalitarian conditioning'.[117] It punctuated almost every episode of social exchange and its impact as propaganda of reinforcement was profound. The display of the swastika flag was a part of this ritual of course, and Allen describes how in Northeim it now appeared everywhere, even hanging from the Lutheran church.[118]

Many, then and since, have come to view Nazi ritual through the perspective of anthropology and the associated realms of sorcery, relating it more to the elemental rites of tribal cultures than the organisational practices of modern techno-centric societies. Neumann, writing during the war itself, speaks of 'magical ceremonies', which the Nazis:

> celebrated on many occasions, reminiscent of the practices of primitive tribes. The annual induction of the Hitler youth into the party is the equivalent of primitive initiation rites. The words used at mass meetings carry in themselves means for changing nature and society. The touching of the blood flag of Munich and being touched by the leader are thaumaturgical practices.[119]

Thus the new storm trooper flags were baptised with the Blood Flag at Nuremberg, though the closer analogy is with confirmation, the passing on of a spiritual essence via the physical touch of a high priest. Hitler's role transcended that of mere political leadership, since this was one of those moments of deep ritual where he was transfigured into priest-king.

Symbolic Mediums: Nuremberg

Symbolism of site

Nuremberg was in a sense the consummation of everything within the Third Reich. Such was its symbolic importance that it became the target for one of Air Marshal Harris's thousand bomber raids, and the locus of the trial of the leadership cadre. The first thing to be explained about Nuremberg, however, is its choice as the site, for it was a medieval city, the quintessence of an old German aesthetic. The town itself, with its high-pitched roofs and half-timbering, was therefore a backdrop redolent of tradition and continuity, establishing what was for the Nazis a vital connection, the linkage between the modernism (uniforms, fighting machines and communications technology), and the ancestral nesting represented by the physical arena of the town itself.

A stage

In essence, Nuremberg was a political stage and nothing else. It existed to celebrate and showcase the political theatre and the associated ideologies. The classicism of Nuremberg's parade ground architecture self-consciously evoked Rome, the Coliseum and the Forum, the site of victorious legions' triumphs and the hails to Caesar. It was a modernistic reworking of the rituals of the Roman imperium; specifically, the great podium and gleaming columns that fronted the Zeppelin Field were a pastiche of the Altar of Pergamon. But Nuremberg was ultimately an auditorium, and its contextual detail, the architectural framework, constitutes, again, an exclusive language of symbolism. Geoffrey Cox (a young Rhodes scholar staying in Germany who recorded his impressions of the 1934 Nuremberg rally), recalled the massive metal swastika behind the speaker's platform, garlanded with red paper flowers, and the strapline 'All for Germany'.[120]

Loyalty symbol

What, then, was Nuremberg? It was in its entirety an exercise in symbolism and a serial process of symbolic episodes, but all subordinated to the one idea, that of loyalty to the supreme leader. For Nuremberg was a gigantic act of loyalty, a protracted affirmation and an epiphany, and for the participants an act of self-transcendence where the boundaries of human ego would dissolve in the merging with one great vital whole. It was a process of de-individuation.

The sacrament of the Blood Flag and the commemoration of martyrs

The rituals of the Blood Flag were the grandest and most elemental rituals of Nazi Germany and the sacrament of the Nuremberg rally. The myriad banners of the SA divisions were presented by their bearers and touched by the Blood Flag, held by the Führer himself. This was repeated every year. This magic was not only delivered on one single epic occasion, but had to be renewed annually to continue to have meaning.

Then there was the commemoration of martyrs where Hitler, Himmler of the SS and Viktor Lutze, Röhm's successor as head of the SA, walked down the massed ranks towards the flaming granite plinths while the bands played the soldier's lament, 'I Had A Comrade'. This funereal quality was an essential part of the Nuremberg experience which, collectively, offered a comprehensive odyssey around all of the human emotions, from mourning and ecstasy to pride and hope. The eloquence of this event was created as much by absence as presence, the ability of so many massed ranks to maintain a complete silence was an essential part of the stage management.

Mythologies

The most self-mythologised part of Nuremberg was the arrival of Hitler by plane, still a radical thing for a politician in any Western country to do. This is dwelt upon in *Triumph of the Will*, with a conscious reference to the Odin myth, the God who descends from the clouds, as Hitler did over Nuremberg. These rituals of Nuremberg connect quite specifically with the mythologies of Europe and in particular with those of Christianity. The Nazis always mined the collective historical, mythological and conceptual heritage of the German people; as a nationalist or hyper-nationalist credo it took the nation and the nation's culture as its exclusive focus and as the source of symbolism. But there is also a general sense in which the rituals of Nuremberg tapped into something more primordial and indeed shared by most cultures. Ideas of sacrificial death, of re-birth and resurrection, of commemorating the deaths of those who have given their lives to enable the community to continue being—these are the common stuff of ritual throughout many societies.

Internal mythologies

It was also a celebration and a retailing of the internal party mythologies, the battles with the reds and the reactionaries and the memorialisation of the dead from those fights. For remembrance of the dead was everywhere at Nuremberg. Nazis, who would turn all Europe into a vast necropolis, represented an ideology of death, and death cultism was a key part of all their ritual. It was further a symbolic way of healing the deep wounds after the cumulative horrors of death in the trenches and defeat in war, national humiliation in peace, hyperinflation and mass unemployment: the rituals were an unguent, a lenitive.

Modernist/medievalist

There was also the familiar Nazi package of modernist ideas articulated with traditional voices. The parade, for example, of farmers costumed in regional paraphernalia from throughout Germany's lands was a conscious affirmation of blood and soil tradition, and an appeal to the rural senti-ments of country people themselves and those many industrial workers who still had their roots in the country.

Integration

Nuremberg was also the place of affirmation for each one of the central social structures of the Nazi state, namely the storm troopers, the SS, the party, the labour battalions, the armed services and the Hitler Youth. Each one was hailed, its vitality and continuity affirmed: Nuremberg epitomised propaganda of integration (in Jacques Ellul's terms) via the symbols of inclusion. In *Triumph of the Will*, a surreally operatic sequence of song and speech has the workers, their faces constructed out of light and shadow, reply to the sonorous demand, 'Where do you come from?', each naming his region, thereby symbolically integrating all of the realms of the Reich. This sequence on the Zeppelin Field with the 52,000 Labour Front members is a ritualised celebration of solidarity, with elements both of a theatre and an open-air cathedral, with invocation and congregation responses. However, within this context a number of key ideas surfaced. One was geographic unity: this Germany had only been united for sixty-five years, and a Germanic folk-consciousness had to transcend and integrate the parish loyalties of myriad ancient principalities. Hence the liturgy, the ritualised verbal exchange: 'Where do you come from, comrade?—I come from Frisia. And you, comrade? From Bavaria. And you? From Kaiserstuhl. And you? From Pomerania ... From Köningsberg, Silesia, Baltic, Black Forest, Dresden, Danube, from the Rhine and from the Saar ... *One people, one Führer, one Reich!* (in unison).'[121]

Dignity of labour

Another principle of the liturgy is utility and the dignity of labour that underpins this. Work, mass amounts of it, was necessary for the physical renewal of Germany, and the status of the worker consequently had to be elevated both to celebrate his reconstructive role and as a bulwark against Bolshevism:

> *Today we are all workers together and we are working with iron.* With iron. *With mortar.* With mortar. *With sand.* With sand. *We are diking the North Sea ... We are building roads.* From village to village, from town to town. *We are providing new fields for the farmer.* Fields and forests, fields and bread—for Germany![122]

Moreover, this worker was a soldier too, and hence strenuous physical labour transmuted into battlefield pride, a moral and status equivalency was explicitly drawn between labourer and soldier: 'We did not stand in the trenches amidst the exploding grenades but nevertheless we are soldiers! ... From one end of Germany to the other. Everywhere, in the North, in the West, in the East, in the South, on the land, on the sea and in the air.'[123] Hence the noble status of a soldier was elasticated, and every muscle worker was now a soldier: 'You're not dead, you live in Germany!' To the massed ranks of spade-carrying workers the Führer would shout 'Hail my men!', symbolic socialism at its most manipulative and a microcosm of Hitler's ideal world—people as automata.

The Hitler act

Hitler's dress was entirely symbolic, its simplicity an important part of his self-production—the plain brown party shirt with the Iron Cross. While he could be more extravagantly costumed (for example in white tie at Bayreuth), this simplicity was deliberate, a contrast with the gaudy mannequins around him. There were strong symbolic elements as well to the core of the Hitler act, his speech. It was a gestural symphony, such as the pointing downward thrustfully; or the complex movements such as arms outstretched and head and eyes almost appearing to roll. In this he was acting not just as political leader but as priest-king, medium, tribune of the people, diviner of the public will: it needed a baroque performance. He was also of course father of the nation, and other symbols derived from this, the paternal signifier. But the Hitler speech never simply began: it was a process of seduction, progression, peroration. The pre-theatre to the speech was itself richly symbolic. According to Cox 'the storm trooper walked up and down the aisle spraying the sultry air with eau de cologne. Then a sudden blare of trumpets, and everyone was on his feet.'[124] Hitler would stride down the aisle and then the trumpets would play again and the uniformed bearer would come in with the Blood Flag, which was borne swiftly up the hall in the glare of arc lights. Then there were the SA standards three abreast, 'their storm trooper bearers hidden by the tasselled swastika banners'. The speeches did not begin straight away, for *Lohengrin* Act II was the prelude—'it was a mood music on a grand scale, preparing the audience's mind for higher things and deeper thoughts and at the same time throwing a cloak of respectability and legitimacy over whatever outrageous assertions or claims Hitler might make'.[125] And then a religious hush. The crowd, Cox observed, was core National Socialist: 'shopkeepers; small businessmen; clerks. Amongst them were many women.'

The Hitler speeches

Nuremberg was thus an auditorium of speeches. Many Nazi evangelists were in fact rhetorically underpowered, they were moribund speakers. This did not matter because of the stars of the show, Hitler, and to a lesser extent Goebbels. Nuremberg was a showcase for the Hitler speech. He made many of them, in day and night, and against the backdrop of various superlative visual effects—firing cannons, blazing torches, cathedrals of light, assembled uniformed cadres, khaki- and shako-clad SA men, Hitler Youth in baggy shorts. Hitler was not only therefore the object of reverence, the focus of adulation, but he was also the dramatic performer, the actor at the heart of his show. The tempo and character of his speeches varied very much and exploited a wide range of vocal and actorly mannerisms, the rhetoric and gestural symphony dictated by the point in the week when he was speaking, the time and the emotional climate, whether day or night, for example. No one speech, or physical performance, was ever a token of the other. They were instead a travelogue of Hitler's dramatic range, of the multiplicity of emotions he evoked and the various sources of charisma he deployed.

Mass culture

What was offered at Nuremberg was the communion of the masses with the messiah, the passing down of a mystical essence. But the experience was also cultural in a vulgar and massified sense of the word: there was music, choral singing and a vast glitzy theatre of fluttering flags and shimmering lights. The parallels with the latter-day rock concert have often been observed and are not in fact accidental. Nuremberg was a political event but it was also a mass cultural one. It anticipated in a very real sense the orchestrations of public euphoria which characterised the youth entertainment of the 1960s and their successor generations, albeit in their case at least ostensibly celebrating values of love and harmony rather than exclusivity and race narcissism. Oliver Thomson speaks of 'transcendence by means of herd intoxication': the rhythmic build up to the personal appearances of Goebbels and Hitler. He also quotes Aldous Huxley—'if exposed long enough to the tom-toms and the singing every one of our philosophers would end by capering and howling like savages'.[126]

The political meaning of geometry

Much of the remembered Nuremberg, the Nuremberg of popular imagining, centres on the orchestration of crowds. It is this ability to force the seething mass into abstract patterns, the perfect discipline of tens of thousands, which gives Nuremberg its peculiar resonance in cultural memory.[127] The name itself can function as a pejorative, so strong is its political legacy. The images themselves articulate the political ideology through a symbolic balletic, as in the march past of 100,000 members of the political leadership corps bearing 32,000 flags and banners.[128] Goebbels claimed that the power of arms was less than the power over our hearts.

But the symmetry had a political meaning: the idea that society, like machinery, can be engineered and turned into a powerful tool. So Nuremberg was a celebration of engineering, one which re-dedicated the citizen's relationship to the state not only as one of subordination but, beyond this, as a mechanical model of human civilisation. As Spotts relates, Goebbels 'made over one hundred thousand men stand motionless and at the snap of his fingers had them turn, march, sing, shout or raise their arms in the party salute ... never before was the relation of masters and slaves so consciously aestheticized'.[129] Private identities, voices all articulating different dreams and different opinions, were now defunct. In their place, like shining steel, emerged a new and victorious harmony, the elite and masses fusing together as powerful social machines. Such symmetries indeed were in themselves part of the propaganda, an articulation of the efficiency of the regime. Cox noted that as the legions passed Hitler he would respond theatrically:

> as the chromium plated metal standard carried by each detachment came abreast of him, Hitler would swing his right arm across his chest, then sweep it out in

the Nazi salute. At the same time his eyes would fix on the face of the men in the ranks with an intense, concentrated stare. He would then move his arm slowly to the right, following the standard, through an arc of about 15 degrees, and then cut it back abruptly to his side, hooking his right thumb into his belt until the next column approached. It was a skilfully designed movement, military and precise, which enabled him to alternate two or three minutes of saluting with a similar period of rests—without the rest appearing as slack or untidy.[130]

Militarisation

Nuremberg also symbolised the warrior. The bands, the marching soldiers, the officers with drawn swords, the charging cavalry, horse-drawn artillery, the mock battles and displays by machine-gunning teams, and the smiles of medalled, monocle-wearing generals, all testify to an army renewed and revived. The symbolism, though, goes beyond this; the nation itself has become an army, the political structures of democracy have been replaced by order-giving, by command and control. The army was at the heart of Nuremberg partly because it needed to be reassured of the centrality of its role in society, and for society to be reminded that it was now merely an extension of the army. So Nuremberg was a celebration of the militarisation of all civic relationships, of reductivism. What was ideologically permissible is strongly hinted at both by what was included in the rituals of Nuremberg but also by what was excluded. The sole sources of German tradition represented at Nuremberg were those of the peasants and those of the army. The only representatives of German society were the uniformed branches of the Third Reich: the army itself, the real army; and the stage army of storm troopers; but beyond this the various costumed functionaries of the police state.

Triumph of the Will: The 1934 Party Rally

In this film Hitler was using propaganda to conceal the memory of a serious political crisis. He had eliminated a major part of the leadership of the SA, the organisation that had captured and controlled the German street in his name, and had terrorised his enemies. He had liquidated Röhm, who, if the earlier imagery of *Victory of Faith*, Riefenstahl's subsequently suppressed film of the previous year's rally, is anything to go by, functioned as the regime's number two above Göring.

The film begins in the sky, in itself an announcement that we inhabit a purely symbolic realm. The visual construction of the 'triumph' is in fact largely symbolic since symbols are the building blocks of the narrative. Our tri-motor roams above the clouds and then descends into the white-grey oblivion to emerge in the air above Nuremberg with its gothicised congeries of spire, tower and battlement, its high-pitched roofs, for this is the landscape of tradition, heritage Germany. The music—the overture of Wagner's *Meistersinger*—merges into the Horst Wessel song. It is a rhapsody of rebirth. *Triumph of the Will* transmutes Nazi ideas into symmetrical forms, a 'dizzying symphony of flags', geometric patterns, tableaux vivants: there is a 'physiological marching in step that evolves, aesthetically transfigured, into the harmony between the Führer and people'.[131] Sontag declaimed that the film 'glorified subordination, celebrated blind obedience and heroicized death';[132] the idea of automaton-like obedience is captured and conveyed in the rigid geometries of the marching columns.

This film was technically ahead of its time. No expense was spared. To make the film, Riefenstahl used thirty cameras and four sound equipment trucks with 120 assistants, and her innovative methods incorporated wide angle photography and telescopic lenses.[133] Cox describes Riefenstahl as:

> very much in evidence on that overcast September morning ... She stood with her camera crews at the side, and on one occasion, when there was a pause in the parade, she appeared on the platform and took Hitler by the sleeve, drawing him to a point where she could get a better shot.[134]

Her technique was in particular the symbolic one of isolating Hitler in order to emphasise his separateness and the austere, romantic loneliness of the supreme leaderly role. Within the heaving throngs of humanity, he remains solitary. But Hitler is always presented in a carefully composed frame—often clouds and sky and the wild crowds; he was always placed, in other words, within a context that was symbolic, an interpretant that explains him further. There was also the visual methodology, juxtaposing action and reaction, capturing an image and then someone's emotional response to it (as if the two were linked in real time). Hence what was achieved in this chronicle was a form of what would later be called the hyper-real; an exercise in creating something that seems more real than real, the inauthenticity of its manufacture transformed into a lifelike event of overwhelming immediacy and visual power.

Conclusions

The Third Reich was an exercise in fantasy, and that fantasy was executed by symbolism. In making symbols the centre of its strategy, the Reich demonstrated an instinctual understanding of their power and of our tendency to interpret reality through them. Hoffmann cites the novelist Elias Canetti: 'from time immemorial men have fought with greater ferocity over symbols than over genuine interests'.[135] What often mattered was not content but imagistic charge, to create a public canvas alive with symbolic meanings. The Reich is remembered not only because of the enormities of what it did but also because of the ubiquity and resonance of its sign system. By creating the symbols of renewal and resurrection, the Nazis ministered to the deep shocks and insults and vicissitudes that fate had administered to Germans, and amplified public events by elaborating their significance. For Le Bon also, influence was immensely pictorial, and he argued that 'a crowd thinks the images, and the image itself immediately calls up a series of other images, having no logical connection with the first'.[136]

Hitler spoke through a rhetorical language, and acted via a symbolic one. The symbolism was a form of speech, a way of saying that the state was all-powerful both within the nation, domestically, and without, externally, via the intimidatory meanings it transmitted to foreign powers. This, then, early transcended a boundary: from fierce national pride to international self-aggrandisement.

6

RHETORIC

WORDS THAT THINK FOR YOU

No one is willing to die for the eight hour day.

Joseph Goebbels, 'Knowledge and Propaganda' speech, 9 January 1928

Look, there is the world's enemy, the destroyer of civilisations, the parasite among the peoples, the son of Chaos, the incarnation of evil, the ferment of decomposition, the daemon who brings about the degeneration of mankind.

Joseph Goebbels, 1937 Nuremberg rally

Introduction: The Language of the Third Reich and Victor Klemperer

The conquest of language was the foundation of everything else the Nazis did. The Third Reich was about the abuse of rhetoric, and to a lesser degree the use of rhetoric. Victor Klemperer, a professor at the Technical University of Dresden when the Nazis seized power, seized on this insight with astonishing clarity both in his brilliant dissection, the *Diaries*, and his magisterial book, *The Language of the Third Reich*.[1] The idea that linguistic strategies are the portal to totalitarian power and that control of the mind lies in the control of language, that words structure perception, that we see with and through words, stands as the pre-eminent idea of Orwell's *1984*. In this as in much else, the Nazis felt rather than theorised their way to the apprehension of a core truth of social control.

The Reich focused on the creation of a new vocabulary with language drawn from the world of machinery as well as from notions of ferocious dedication and hyper-heroism. There is a distinction between eloquence and rhetoric; the former may be depraved, or enlisted in the cause of depravity, but it is beautiful. Rhetoric, in contrast, is any premeditated linguistic strategy where the focus is ordinarily or primarily on verbal persuasion. It can be poetic, or it can be turgid—the term does not pre-judge the quality. The Nazis were seldom eloquent. Indeed, Hitler saw rhetorical value in the comparative clumsiness and circumlocutory struc-ture of the German language, erroneously claiming that German had no Latin in its vocabulary (unlike English), leading him to argue that 'Germans have to make up combinations of words and cumbersome as these can be, the language is often the more graphic for them.'[2] The Nazis used a distinct vocabulary to manufacture a reality that they recognised could be reshaped via the creation of new words, the perversion of old words and the inven-tion of phrases. Words which previously had no especially good connota-tions might now become virtue terms, such as the word 'fanatic', the highest term of approval in the Third Reich. Elsewhere I have argued that the power of criminal regimes arises from their abuse of rhetoric as well as their abuse of authority: persuasion and coercion are confederates, and the primary metaphor is seduction.[3] The Nazis' linguistic assault was actually an organised one, with predetermined words and phrases framed according to a template. One memo, for example, suggested that rhetoric should be used against Roosevelt in the Middle East, with propagandists being instructed to call the US president the 'Chief war culprit' or the 'lunatic in the White House'.[4]

Rhetoric is a highly parsimonious form of persuasion—a host of meanings are (economically) implied without being (verbosely) stated. Words are never neutral; they are association-rich. Through rhetoric we seek 'the engineering of consent', a phrase first coined by Edward Bernays in the 1920s and echoed by Noam Chomsky—the idea that public opinion is a commodity to be created, bought and sold. The judicious rhetorician must give the most compelling attention to selecting the right words and phrases, as the supreme art of the persuader is to make a label enter com-mon parlance so that whenever it is used it becomes an unself-conscious act of propaganda.[5] Rhetoric enlightens by explicitly or implicitly con-structing a coherent explanatory framework which works to clarify and simplify ambivalence and complexity.[6]

Rhetoric, in other words, provides illuminated signposts: 'Rhetoric pro-vides something for thought to get hold of, something concrete, an image, a scrap of language or feeling.'[7] The language of the Reich was designed to de-individuate. Its purpose was to create a homogeneous people, thinking, acting, believing similarly; the linguistic strategy was a masterstroke on the part of the propaganda directors. A new language would create a new people; restricting the meanings of language and focusing them restricts the domain of human personality and, critically, independence of thought. Klemperer speaks of the 'terrible uniformity' of the Third Reich symbol structure: 'anything which deviated in any way from the accepted pattern did not make it into the public domain ... all swam in the same brown sauce'. It was this 'absolute uniformity of the written language', he continues, which 'explained the homogeneity of the spoken language'.[8]

Colonisation of language

What especially astonished Klemperer was the ubiquity of Nazi expressions and the way in which they completely interpenetrated an ancient language and re-framed its terms of discourse, its inherited concepts and perspectives. He gives the example of a funeral oration in which the term 'Führer' was used to describe a community chairman, an 'embarrassing lapse of taste'.[9] Even the language of academe was colonised with Nazi uses. Klemperer speaks of specialist philological publications 'so replete with the jargon of the Third Reich that every page literally makes you want to be sick', such as 'science on a National Socialist footing' and so on.[10] Since this was a formula-driven approach to the re-invention of language—how could it be otherwise?—its familiar manifestation was the cliché: 'from all kinds of sources, educated and highly educated, come the same clichés and the same terms. A language of a clique became language of the people—even nurseries.' Klemperer concluded that 'some kind of fog has descended'.

Klemperer gives examples such as a Jewish lady who used Nazi language like 'radical changes', yet failed to see the subterfuge (she later disappeared into a concentration camp). He describes her reprimanding a pedantic schoolteacher when he points out that the Nazis have added these terms to their blood and soil, and had infected them with their filthy hands.[11] Another, Elsa, a Jew and a German patriot, says only 'fanatical Germans' can cleanse 'our' fatherland. She does not see the obvious.[12] Books published by the Jewish Book Club adopted the language of the victors with servility, using the characteristic forms of the Lingua Tertii Imperii (LTI)—the name Klemperer gives to the language of the Reich—such as the herding of people into the singular, as with 'the German Jew' and 'the German people'. Other examples of LTI terms include pariah, covert, autarchy, aggressive, attacking, call of the blood, ordained, injunction to act, half-Jew, of the people, advance guard, half-caste—'the LTI has slithered into the very core of the work'.[13] He describes an article in a Jewish publication about Jews who had settled in Burma: 'this is all blood and soil doctrine in a very explicit way'. A Jewish author's new novel shows how he has simply assimilated the language and concepts of the victor: 'you don't speak it with impunity, you breathe it in'. Klemperer even describes the appropriation of Nazi anti-Jewish expressions by Jews themselves. One man utters them so incessantly 'that he himself could probably no longer judge as to what extent he was ridiculing either the Führer or himself'.[14] This man was in the habit of never speaking to any member of his Jewish group without prefixing his name with the term 'Jew': the psychological process behind this may—it is speculation—be some bizarre re-working of Stockholm Syndrome. But the 'rose-tinted spectacles of us Jews earlier on' later precipitated a reverse reaction according to Klemperer—no longer believing in the imminent end of the war, against all the evidence, nor that Hitler must have magic powers.

Theory: Language that Thinks for You

Much propaganda may not be understood by the masses, they may be bored with it, and in Klemperer's view the most seminal influence was never formal propaganda: 'instead Nazism permeated the flesh and blood of the people through single words, idioms and sentence structures, which were imposed on them in a million repetitions and taken on board mechanically and unconsciously', and thus language came 'to dictate our spiritual being'.[15] If language were merely a vehicle for communication, there would be less interest in it, but, in the words of D. Umberson and K. Henderson (1992), 'language does more than merely express reality; it actively structures experience ... language and linguistic devices structure how we think about things'.[16] If language is power, then the ownership of language is the key to that power: 'language is not merely the vehicle for articulating our thoughts: it does in itself create meaning, an active agent for the creation of perception'.[17] Words thus do duty as sensitising concepts, such that if we have no word for something we are often actually blind to the existence of that phenomenon. And terms might be deliberately chosen to limit our vision—'language systems are a way of seeing but also of not seeing'.[18] For Klemperer in fact, the Nazi regime was a triumph of rhetoric alone—of the colonisation of the language with, in Schiller's phrase, 'words that think for you'; not of propaganda. Hence I have argued that the Reich promulgated a formulaic discourse which condensed elements of its ideology, thus making conventional persuasion less imperative, so that even enemies of the regime started to adapt its usages.[19] A.P. Foulkes (1983) also observed how language, a new rhetoric of the everyday, permeated the Nazi vocabulary and even that of non-Nazi opponents.[20]

Beyond Euclid, persuasion is all we have, and everything is ultimately persuasion. To control language is to control thought and the control of language is achieved by mastery of rhetoric. As Dr Goebbels observed, no one is willing to die for the eight-hour day:[21] it is for ideas and beliefs that people die, and it is rhetoric that animates us even to the extinction of life itself, our own and other people's. By controlling the language, we own the concepts through which people apprehend reality, and in owning the concepts we control the people far more thoroughly than through the apparatus of a police state. Language can restrict as well as expand perception. The linguistic strategy of the Third Reich represented a fundamental invasion of the human mind, an attempt, unique in history, to change human consciousness by changing the words and the language-derived concepts through which people think. It was the comprehensive nature of this invasion that helped Nazism to succeed, as virtually no branch of human activity was immunised from its rhetoric. There was little of the nature of an oasis of independent thought left. It is interesting to observe the speed with which this new lingua franca took hold and the flimsiness of the resistance to it.

Nor of course were contradictions ever a problem. Goebbels could describe Allied air raids as 'terror raids' with a straight face despite all the Nazis did to provoke this response: the destructions of the Rotterdam, of Warsaw, the infernos of London or Manchester and the devastation of Coventry (whence their new verb 'to coventryise'), to give just a few examples. So the air bombing also introduced the terrorist claim into German discourse; the boast was of German restraint in protecting civilians, in contrast to Allied ruthlessness.[22] Thus powerful rhetoric may toxify public discourse such that it succeeds in assassinating all counter-argument.[23]

Yet German was once Europe's great philosophic language, the language of Kant, Nietzsche and Schopenhauer, and as a language it was perhaps more capable of evolving philosophic and abstract ideas than any other. The ability to sustain intellectual volume was the heritage of the German language and it is this that the Third Reich tried to shrink, to degrade. It was ultimately about the diminution of human possibility. The language of the Third Reich was so insistent, so insidious in its ability to subvert pre-existing usages, that even the opposition to the Nazis, even Jews, began to use its phrases and coinages without any hint of irony. The aim, the will, was to subjugate the independent thinker. The language of the Reich could appear artless, even jejune, and certainly non-credible. But this was not really the point: effective rhetoric does not commit the error of confronting our rational judgement; rather it eludes critical analysis by offering propositions too ridiculous to be taken seriously.[24]

The Vocabulary of Dynamism

Nazi media specialised in the rhetoric of dynamism; their soldiers were forever alert, taut and eager. They were the physical enforcers of an idea and they negotiated manifold obstacles intelligently, energetically. There was no nuance to these portraits and the literary and pictographic renditions of them seem to owe more to the world of happy-face advertising, as they all have the two-dimensionality of actors in a consumerist drama. For example, in one article, *Signal* uses the rhetoric of momentum in describing the arrival of 'glider troops' in a 'ceaseless stream', while ammunition 'pours forth' from the ships.[25] A colour sequence of gun batteries was captioned: 'everywhere German soldiers guard, all batteries, even beyond the northern polar Circle, are fully manned and ready for the enemy'.[26]

The imagery in *Signal*'s photojournalist essays was of eagerness and focus, with descriptions of men scanning the horizon 'tirelessly', their attention 'still sharper' and so on; they 'thrust' through France, positions are 'overpowered', they 'demolish' several hundred enemy planes. It is a tribute to German supremacy, this 'lightning action' of the parachute troops and 'thundering' machines. A massive colour image of a mud-encrusted tank and SS men in black uniform is explained: 'Ten units, mobile, fast and hard-hitting, and directed by wireless from headquarters, attacked the enemy. This armoured machine paves the way to victory, flattening, crushing all obstacles and spitting destruction.'[27] *Signal* evoked the campaigns in Denmark and Norway in a similar way—'lightning expedition', 'too quick for the British invasion', 'the sudden roar of German fighter machines', 'like lightning'.[28] Then there was Tunis: 'it is of great importance that all of Europe should recognize the significance of the first combats raging in the North African desert under a blazing sun or in the inaccessible mountains of western Tunis'. There is the usual triumphalist oratory, a kind of rhetorical sanitary tissue, at once vivid, ephemeral and cheap: 'small but powerfully equipped Axis units' 'shattered the enemy's hopes', 'initiative' was 'in the hands of the Germans', 'fast bombers and dashing fighter squadrons', 'reinforcements flowed', 'small units with high firing power'. Phrases like 'an intrepid and indefatigable spirit' are formulaic, part of a literary 'paint by numbers'.[29] Such a style could easily be imitated, seemingly with absolute authenticity as in New York-published weekly newsletter *Facts in Review*.[30] Hence there was a Nazi rhetorical formula which excelled at the rhetoric of obliteration, as for example was the case with newspaper titles such as *The Attack* and *The Flame* and *The Storm* (called thus since in Streicher's words it would storm the red fortress).[31] There was a basic and universal Nazi rhetorical technique, involving the repetition of plain but dogmatic terms, with short, sharp, unadorned words like 'beat', 'bash', 'kill'.[32] *Stürmer* in particular was written to make it digestible to mass publics via simple sentences, a style mimicking vernacular speech. Hence sentences were brief, vocabulary primitive and themes repetitive, with the same medley of anti-Semitic points being continuously recycled.[33] The formula, according to Rutherford, 'was to keep a message sparse and stereotypical, but frequently repeated for reinforcement effects'.[34]

The Language of Contempt

Nazi propaganda also made use of the language of contempt, a language not of condescension but of extermination, as in the distinction between *Übermensch* and *Untermensch*. Language itself became judge and jury with terms such as beasts, devilish and butchers. In particular, the Nazi rhetoric of anti-Semitism was tedious as well as alarming; it offered no luminous phrase, no excitement, and its literary poverty was part of the generic problem of creativity in Nazi Germany. Mechanistic and crude phrases read like a Nazi propaganda crib—the same stock images, the same fallacies, the same libels; there was seldom the imagination even to invent new charges against the Jews. It impacted through sheer insistence and volume.[35] Gitlis offers examples of Nazi phrases such as reptiles and parasites, cancerous growth, vision of decay, microbes and insects, *bacillus judaicus*, cockroaches and rats,[36] as well as specific German terms such as subhuman (*Untermensch*), *untermenschlich*, non-human (*Unmensch*), *unmenschlich*, devil-man (*Satansmensch*), opposition-man (*Gegenmensch*) and anti-man (*Anti-mensch*).[37] The hyperbolic rhetoric of Nazi propaganda obsessively recycled stereotyped imagery of the blood-enemy: the 'November criminals', the 'red bosses', the 'Jewish wire-pullers', the 'red murder-pack'.[38] The

Nazis did not necessarily invent this rhetoric, as some was inherited from Germany's recent past, the civic landscape in the immediate aftermath of the First World War. In Evans's words, 'the whole language of politics in Munich after the overthrow of the Communist regime was permeated by nationalist slogans, anti-Semitic phrases, reactionary keywords that almost invited the rabid expression of counter-revolutionary sentiment'.[39]

The entire thrust of LTI was towards dehumanisation, and Klemperer gives numerous examples of this.[40] He describes a female Belsen warder who said she dealt on one day with sixteen 'Stück', that is to say, 'head' (as in head of cattle, say), and who talks of the 'utilisation of carcasses' (i.e. human corpses). He also refers to the use of the word 'liquidate', derivative of the language of commerce and a loan word, and an expression favoured in the Reich as it was a 'degree or two colder and more objective than its respective German equivalents'. When people were liquidated they were settled or terminated as if they were material assets. This is what Klemperer calls the objectification of the individual personality. But there was also a countervailing methodology of the personal, a rhetoric of inclusion; within the Nazi circle the personality was emphasised, and thus the military did not refer to soldiers as troops but as 'men', as in 'my man'. Hence there was the personalisation of all official communication, as in the use of 'I' when describing an action taking place rather than something happening 'at the office', since 'Nazism did not want to depersonalise those it regarded as human.'[41]

Disease metaphor

Any alternative to Nazism was described as a symptom of disease, with the Nazis making constant use of images of health and sickness. Thus a Gestapo expert might speak of sickness, healthy unity, organism, body politic, destructive selves. This kind of medical language is also a metaphor for how the Third Reich viewed itself: 'A biological theory of the police presented to the German people as rational.'[42] Anti-Semitism was, in Klemperer's view, the party's most effective means of propaganda. It was the core of the Nazi worldview and in every way the decisive factor. A representative example— because it encapsulates the principal rhetorical tropes—is a speech Goebbels delivered at the 1937 Nuremberg rally: 'look, there is the world's enemy, the destroyer of civilisations, the parasite among the peoples, the son of Chaos, the incarnation of evil, the ferment of decomposition, the daemon who brings about the degeneration of mankind'.[43] This sentence is a portmanteau of all the principal Nazi charges against the Jews—destructiveness, parasitism, diabolism, subversion, disease and ill-health.

Hitler and Goebbels would rarely use the word Jew without it being accompanied by an adjective like cunning, wily or deceitful, plus traditional terms of abuse relating to physical attributes such as long noses.[44] Similarly, a 1940 article from *Will and Way* reviewing *The Eternal Jew* ('a 2000-year rat migration') is merely a hyperbolic anti-Semitic diatribe, with every noxious stereotype on display.[45] In fact, the Nazis rarely had the resourcefulness to invent fresh forms of perfidy and new warrants. Thus the article employs words like disgust and loathing, criminal traits, eternal parasites, cheeky, dirty, bartering, sneaking, servility—the polemical lexicon of the Third Reich—and discourses on ritual slaughtering methods. It speaks of the 'insidious vulgarity of their methods, and the brutality and all-devouring hatred they exhibit when they reach their goal and control finance', and of 'filthy ghettos of the East, brutal greed', and inevitably at the end of the article 'one has a deep sense of salvation after seeing this film' (the Nazis would often pilfer the language of the sacerdotal in their rhetoric).

Klemperer relates how the Nazis also sought to de-Judaise personal names: Christ would become Krista and daughters would be given Teutonic names such as Heidrun; no German child could be called Sarah.[46] This implicated all names in all contexts, not just baptismal names: thus the opera *Judas Maccabeus* had a different cover name, with the original in tiny type. Publishers apologised for biblical names cropping up in classic English novels. Scientific terms and authorities were also de-Judaised: 'In the Physics Department, the name Einstein had to be hushed up. And the Hertz unit of frequency could also not be referred [to] by its Jewish name.'[47] Klemperer describes how anti-Semitic ideology saturated the language: new words arose, or old ones absorbed new meanings, or new combinations were formed, which rapidly ossified into stereotypes—'global Jews', 'international Jewry', and the distinction between Aryan and non-Aryan entered everything. A Jew without a Jewish-sounding name would be forced to add the prefix Israel or Sarah. Sexual relations between Jew and Aryan were referred to as racial defilement. The rhetoricised Jew, Klemperer says, is a hyphenated entity, the Jewish-Marxist, Jewish-chauvinist, Jewish-capitalist, Jewish-English, Jewish-American. Jews were the universal source of malice and malaise: in moments of high drama the term 'Judah' or even 'universal Judah' was chosen. Klemperer lists the core of the new racial vocabulary which was to saturate German discourse: '*artfremd*', alien, '*deutschblütig*', of German blood, '*niederrassig*', of inferior race, '*nordisch*', Nordic, '*Rassenschande*', racial defilement, '*prima organisiert*', fantastically well organised.[48] The word *Volk* was now a universal appellation: *Volksfest,*

Volksgenosse, Volksgemeinschaft, Volksnah, Volksfremd, Volksentstammt. Jews were 'parasitic', 'nomadic', 'bloodsuckers'; synagogues, in Streicher's words, were 'robbers' caves'.

But anti-Semites were also another market segment to be targeted by their own media—the publishing apparatus of Julius Streicher, Gauleiter of Franconia and proprietor of the *Stürmer*. Streicher was regarded as so grotesque that he was shunned by other members of the leadership cadre at Nuremberg; he specialised in such headlines as 'The Jew Sees Reason and Hangs Himself'. The Jew, according to Streicher, was a regressive entity of mixed blood: 'the Jew possesses the lust of the Negro, the craftiness of the Mongol and the criminal drives of all the races which have combined to produce his blood'.[49] This deformity of rhetoric was a necessary precondition for genocide via its construction of an existential threat; for example, the Nazis, as we have seen, medicalised the Jewish 'threat' by evoking it in the language of plague and disease. Two key notions were at work, the binary oppositions of: (1) purity–contamination, and (2) health–illness/putrefaction.

The rhetoric of anti-Semitism was a language for export as well as a domestic language. It could be used everywhere the Nazis went as a default mode of self-explanation, a public narrative, in France, in Eastern Europe, in Russia, and to sympathisers all over the globe. But it had a special home in the Middle East, in Vichy's colonies, among Palestinians and Egyptians, especially after the German landings. The Jews, naturally, were proclaimed in such diatribes as dominating Iran's government after the overthrow of a pro-Axis regime in May 1941. They were now 'looting the country' and 'flocking into' Syria. Palestinians were 'ruled by a reign of terror dominated by the brutal British and the dirty Jews'; Axis propaganda was remorseless about the original sin of Britain's admission of Jews to Palestine.[50] And it was exactly the same rhetoric, more perhaps like itself than even the domestic rhetoric, with the same steroidal hyperbole; lurid, crass and predictable, a linguistic cardboard cut-out taken from the Nazi template. Thus Palestine was 'swimming in a pool of blood'; the British violate[d] Arab holy places and spread famine and poverty; there were jeremiads about the ruthlessness of British imperialism in Iran and Egypt.[51] Murder was never far from the surface—'Arab mother, teach your baby to hate the British—there was much exploitation of Britain's alliance with Communism and descriptions of 'godless hordes', 'red hordes', 'locusts', 'river of blood'.[52]

Mechanics of Language

Metaphor and imagery

Metaphor was the vehicle for all this, as it is through metaphor and imagery that we can fracture existing paradigms of thought. One of the central properties of metaphors is their capacity for extensive elaboration, and the power of rhetoric resides principally in the power of metaphor. We are unable to forget a memorable image and the perspective it embodies: it lives and breathes in our consciousness no matter how far we seek to deny it oxygen.[53] The art of the rhetorician does not reason; instead it trespasses unbidden on our consciousness with images too luminous to be forgotten.[54]

Metaphor was one of the main rhetorical devices used by Hitler himself. As Blain points out, *Mein Kampf* is 'organised round a metaphor of a medical diagnosis and cure, the religious rite of guilt and redemption, and the drama of murder—revenge'.[55] Hitler's speeches and writings are convulsed by notions of health and sickness, purity and contamination. While the psychology of this is at one level quite clear, at another it becomes more difficult to interpret. For although sickness and disease metaphors were used as rhetoric, they also functioned as very real concerns: this is what he really believed, that 'an ideal state of health, which once existed, had been lost'.[56] Germans, in other words, inherited a toxic world; they were already contaminated and becoming more so. Central to this idea was the concept of blood and the magical qualities that Nazi ideology endowed it with,[57] the term thus condensing racial, biological, medical, religious, moral and murderous chains of association.[58] These were the key constructing metaphors through which the whole regime communicated its version of reality; ideas, like contamination, seeped into the psyche of the nation and became reflexive.

The machine metaphor was also a salient part of the linguistic strategy of the Third Reich. The Nazis used phrases like 'started up', 'overhauled', 'channelled', 'set up', 'back on track', 'working to their full capacity', 'organisation all round', 'used to capacity', 'well-adjusted steering'.[59] Thus the comparison of workers and administrators was with machines. Klemperer gives the example of the governor of Hamburg speaking of working 'like a motor which always runs at full tilt'.[60] This is taken further with an ending of the distinction between the image and the object of comparison, for example a quote from Goebbels: 'in the foreseeable future we will be running at full tilt again in a range of areas'; that is to say they have actually become machines so that machinery ceases to be just a comparison.[61]

Euphemism

Nazis required euphemism even to think, even to get through the working day: for euphemism was a way of blinding themselves, and those they led, to the truth of what they were doing. It bathed the horrific and the homicidal in a muted banality. Through euphemism language could de-toxify reality; through euphemism we purge the stains on our souls. Euphemism was not merely a method of persuasion but a way of coping, and hence it had enormous functional value. It was a way of endowing with ideological rectitude the inchoate and anarchic mass of death and destruction which mounted in steaming piles of rubble and corpses all over the lands of Europe. There were also euphemisms for torture; the Third Reich never called something unpleasant by its proper name but always found an alternative. No one, for example, was ever murdered by the Gestapo: they were always 'shot while trying to escape'. And custody was now 'protective', without the onerous necessity of the legal process.[62] The meaning of protective custody was turned on its head—the new double-think, the phrase became both their weapon and a euphemism. Klemperer refers to the 'mendacious euphemisms' which fed into the LTI. For example, daily death was a 'tragic misfortune'.[63] Civilians were not targeted by Germans, there were only 'military targets'. The Nazi Party never stole: private libraries were 'taken into safekeeping'. Dead soldiers were 'sunny' while they had lived. You were not imprisoned but sent away, and the verb 'to present oneself' acquired a horrible new meaning, as in 'to present oneself to the Gestapo'.[64] The expression 'gone away' carried with it 'a special meaning', and 'definitely belongs in the lexicon of the LTI, in the Jewish section'. Similarly, 'collect' meant to dispose of something unobtrusively, away from all processes; terrible consequences congeal behind the language of the everyday. Then there were the bureaucratic euphemisms: 'it will state the cause of death precisely, even with variations and an individual touch; it may say circumspectly "died of an inadequate cardiac muscle" ...'[65]

Extroversion—hyperbole

For Klemperer, Nazi language was a public and performative language, an extroverted language of the auditorium, and it therefore did not draw a distinction between the spoken and the written: 'rather, everything was oration, ... address, exhortation, invective'.[66] There was a semi-hysteria to a language fermented in an atmosphere of ecstatic paranoia. The Nazi state was a declamatory state, 'everything turned into proclamation as a matter of course'. In consequence this language lacked either an intimate or a sophisticated voice. LTI only ever gave expression to one side of human existence: 'every language able to assert itself really fulfils all human needs, it serves reason as well as emotion, it is communication and conversation; command and invocation. The LTI only serves the calls of invocation.'[67] There was thus no distinction in LTI between private and public spheres: 'everything remains oral and everything remains public'. The purpose of its self-originated status as a purely oratorical language was to de-individuate and create extras for a mass acclamatory state rather than citizens for a civic state: 'the sole purpose of the LTI [was] to strip every one of their individuality, to paralyse them as personalities, to make them into unthinking and docile cattle', and thus 'when it educate[d], it [taught] means of becoming fanatics and needs of mass suggestion'.[68] It was a language of obedience and serfdom.

Emotion

The language of the Third Reich was an anti-intellectual language. This was perhaps the most obvious thing about it, for it was distinguished by the fact that it dealt exclusively in the currency of intense emotion. It did not possess within the domain of its cognition abstract thought, intellectual nuance or even pragmatic application, but was entirely assertive, and the limitations of its intellectual scope were quite deliberate. The language carried with it hints of incipient violence such as the phrase 'to force into line'.[69] It was designed to exclude some thoughts as well as to include others. Klemperer observes how the word 'philosophy' had been replaced with 'worldview', *Weltanschauung*, 'someone who does not want to be persuaded but rather convinced'. The Nazi concept of *anschauen*, 'viewing something', was never an intellectual activity (while 'think' was actually the exact opposite): 'it denotes a wry way of seeing which discerns more than simply the surface of the given object, which in a strange way also grasps its essence, its soul'. Thought strives for clarity; magic takes place in semi-darkness. Populist speaking addresses the feelings not the mind, 'and it will cross the boundaries separating populism from demagoguery and mass seduction as soon as it moves from ceasing to challenge the intellect to deliberately shutting it off and stupefying it'.[70]

According to Neumann, grammar itself was re-structured to facilitate the assimilation of Nazi perspectives:

> the emphasis on magic has even changed the language. The noun tends to supersede the verb. Things happen—they are not done. Fate, providence, objective

natural forces produce things: German victories. The loss of man's active role in society is expressed by a language that negates activity and stresses the impersonality of the noun and of the 'it'.[71]

George Orwell once ascribed to totalitarian regimes the common feature that they 'substitute clinical abstractions for straightforward proper nouns and visceral verbs that refer directly to the violent and criminal acts committed'.[72] One technique, part of the reflexive methodology of the Reich's linguistic strategy, was the ironic inverted comma: it was an index of incredulity, indeed of contempt—'it questions the truth of that which is quoted',[73] part of the derisive, mocking way in which all that was not Nazi thought was stigmatised. Beyond this, it was also part of a confrontational literary method, one which is not entirely surprising in a movement that had risen from the streets and derived its manners from physical brawls: 'LTI loathes neutrality, always has to have an adversary and always has to confront that adversary.'[74]

Hyper-historicity

Klemperer speaks of a tendency towards more intensified forms of language, thus 'we are flying supplies' or 'we are freezing' (i.e. refrigerated vegetables). Devices for making speech more visceral alternated between the primordial, such as 'earth', and the medieval, such as 'Grail'. The jargon of the Third Reich also sentimentalised. Klemperer notes, for example, the use of the sentimental diminutive, such as Little Harold: 'the idea is to add a little sweetness and light to the heroic ballad-like name'. There was a hyper-historicity to Nazi rhetoric. Thus they raised 'everything to historical significance [*historisch*]. ... the Third Reich knows nothing but feast days ... views every day as historical, it is mortally ill from the lack of the everyday'.[75] This was a regime borne forth on a cascade of historic, histrionic and euphoric rhetoric; its characteristic was hyperbolic overdrive—Klemperer asked, 'but do they really feel so sure of themselves? There is also a good deal of hysteria in the government's words and deeds.' The language embedded a new and frenzied hyper-nationalism which permeated everyday discourse, as with the phrase 'With German best wishes.' Another rhetorical arena was the Soviet campaign, which gave the concept of Europe a new urgency as an entity that had to be protected from Bolshevism; during the campaign Goebbels warned of the danger that Europe would become a land of steppes.[76] A new language arose to make the point: 'unblockadable', 'economically self-sufficient Europe', 'honourable Continent' (betrayed by England), and conceptually therefore it became a 'fortress Europe'. Thus an exhibition was headlined: 'From the Vanguard of the Movement to the Defenders of Europe'.[77]

The use of words expressing hyper-historicity began to infuse the intellectual vocabulary of academic disciplines, including history itself: 'in 1935 for example, the entire prehistoric and early historic chronologies were officially renamed; the bronze and pre-Roman Iron Ages became the "early Germanic period", the Roman Iron Age the "Timex German period", the Migration period the "Late Germanic period", and everything from the Carolingians to the 13th century the "German middle ages"'.[78]

Sources of Rhetoric

Abbreviations

Abbreviations now became full words and there were a huge number of them. Abbreviations employ what are in effect creative contractions; the original word has some connection with what is expressed by its shrinkage, that is, the abbreviation. The abbreviations were often a technology derivative, with Klemperer describing how they would always appear with the emergence of new technologies or organisations.[79] This made them voguish and contemporary, the abridged language of a restless technocracy. Since new technologies were constantly emerging, so too were new abbreviations and therefore new linguistic entities: 'in line with its claim to totality, Nazism brings new technology and new organisation into everything'.[80] The abbreviation would become a word in its own right, part of a kind of telegraphic speech with its original source word forgotten, 'and if this process of visualizing could be achieved with recourse to Germanic traditions, by means of a runic sign, then so much the better'. Hence SA and SS were 'abbreviations that were so satisfied with themselves that in the end they were no longer abbreviations'; the new meaning obscured the original significance.[81] Klemperer gives the example of the SS rune, and in an essay worthy of Barthes analyses the symbol systems it evokes and how these multiple referents are yet shrunken into one symbol. SS was thus a masterpiece of condensed symbolism, summoning in its compression the idea of an electricity substation, a Nordic rune, lightning and the letters SS; for 'SS' is both an image and an abstract character—'it encroaches on the realm of painting, it is a pictogram, a return to the physicality of the hieroglyph. Within the LTI itself, the special jagged form of the letters S.S. represents the link between the visual language of the poster and language in the narrow sense.'[82] A sure sign of the demise of Nazi fervour was when the rune appeared less often in soldier death announcements.

Fluid

According to Klemperer, the LTI was a palimpsest, a polyglot verbal stew despite its loud proclamation of Teutonic soul; and he points out that there were even large numbers of Americanisms in the LTI. The new language was influenced by existing usages but it also suborned them—borrowing from military language but also corrupting it, for example. The word *Sturm* was a military term, but it was also applied to the newly militarised civic such as *Sturmtruppe* and later on to *Volkssturm*. During the war itself the sobriety of military announcements gradually yielded to Goebbels's propaganda style; the word 'fanatical' was applied first in a military dispatch about the Normandy landings.[83] Another technique was to appropriate the vocabulary of socialism and—like any propagandist—draw from the common cultural stock bank of languages, myths, forms and images. Thus Hitler 'concocted an insider discourse from cultural resources familiar to his German audience', and from religion in particular: Hitler's use of dramatic form represented a political perversion of the religious notion of the struggle of good against evil.[84]

The language of the Reich, being fundamentally a political-functional language, did not exist in any primal state of fixity but was fluid and malleable, changing according to context. The rhetoric was capable of flexibility and even progressiveness, thus the proscription of 'anti-Semitism' (Chapter Two)—the Nazi version of political correctness (contained in a periodical service directive of 13 June 1939).[85] As a thoroughly politicised language, it was also an ephemeral one, disposable. Earlier examples of their rhetoric rapidly disappeared, such as Blitzkrieg and other coinages from the sham-heroic early period. The phrase 'to organise' (e.g. Car mechanic: 'Didn't I organise that well?'), for example, subsequently became sullied after Stalingrad since it acquired suggestions of the black market.[86] What was excluded from this new language is as significant as what was included. Words were demoted as well as promoted; the process was a remembering and a forgetting. Thus terms like humanitarianism which 'might awake notions of old supranational Europe' were effectively proscribed. Phrases came and went, ascribable to particular historic epiphanies; so a Germany self-described as the 'power which imposes order' was an emanation of 'the late phase of the LTI' and was what Klemperer calls a 'euphemistic pretext for the use and abuse of power'.

Sacerdotal

The rhetoric of the Third Reich was filled with language taken from the Christian religion. The aim was transference, whereby the metaphysical embodied in scripture would migrate from the sacred to the secular realm. Specific individual expressions echoed those of Christ: 'sent to us by Providence'; 'we believe in him'; 'take leave of the false gods and render homage to him'. According to Klemperer, the fact that millions accepted Nazism as gospel emanated from its appropriation of the language of the Gospel. In funeral ceremonies there were the words 'you have risen again in the Third Reich', and there were phrases such as 'crusade', 'holy war', the 'Teutonic bible', 'Golgotha', 'pilgrimage'. There was thus something akin to Christian transcendence in all of this language of martyrdom and resurrection. Klemperer speaks of the 'smell of blood emanating from these expressions'. 'Eternal' was a Nazi favourite; it was 'the final rung in a long ladder of National Socialist numerical superlatives—but with this final rung heaven is reached'. The word 'martyrdom' was also used frequently: 'this whole National Socialist business [was] lifted from the political realm to that of religion by the use of the single word', while the idea of sanctity was conveyed through phrases like 'the consecration of an order of knights'.[87]

The abuse of neoreligious language reduced its power, shrinking such grand concepts as God, eternity, providence, life and death to the small change of linguistic currency.[88] Germany, according to Goebbels, had 'transformed into a single place of worship in which her advocate steps before the High Throne of the Almighty'.[89] The concomitant banality was an obvious consequence. Thus the obituary notice of a show-jumper read, 'another saddle is empty. He has followed his peers to the House', and the chairman of an East Berlin social club opined that dancers 'struggle for Germany's rebirth'.[90] Nazism inverted the moral language of its opponents so that words like 'duty', 'deliverance', 'mercy' and 'sacrifice' tripped off the tongues of people for whom such things were anathema. One of the functions of propaganda is to sow moral confusion,[91] and the replacement of a Christian moral order could be attained by the trick of deploying the same language but invested with different or even antithetical meanings. Hitler has even been accused of ecclesiastical plagiarism: Grunberger describes how one writer discovered a passage of sheer pastiche of texts from the Christian Gospel in one of Hitler's speeches.[92] Thus Hitler in 1934: 'the blood which they shed has become the baptismal water of the Third Reich'.[93] Klemperer describes the packaging of a Hitler speech on radio with phrases like 'in the thirteenth hour Adolf Hitler will visit the workers', that is, the language of the Gospel. Nothing comes after the Third Reich. Hitler called those who fell in the Feldherrnhalle 'my Apostles'—'there are sixteen, of course, he has to have four more than his predecessor'.[94]

Hitler did not allude to God but frequently invoked the concept of 'Providence'; implying he had a unique relationship to the godhead, as when 'fate' saved him after an assassination attempt.[95] One rhetorical climax paraphrased the last lines of the Protestant version of 'Our Father', ending with 'Amen'; Goebbels also describes Hitler ending a speech with 'Amen'—everybody is 'shaken and moved'—'when the Führer speaks it is like a religious service'.[96] Hitler remarked that his listeners gained the impression they were in the grip of a deep sense of prayer;[97] and Speer speaks of his speeches as being 'almost like the rites of the founding of a Church'.[98] His 1936 Nuremberg speech has been called a montage of biblical texts.[99] Klemperer mentions 'the radiant fog of religion surrounding his person', it is 'secular redemption soaked in pseudo-religious imagery'.[100] There were even possibilities of expressing a specifically Nazi turn of mind in National Socialist death announcements such as 'For Führer and Fatherland'. Even greater degrees of enthusiasm were possible—'He died in action for his Führer' or 'For his beloved Führer' (the Fatherland was not mentioned 'because Hitler embodies it'). Or even 'he fell believing in his Führer to the last', 'he died believing in Adolf Hitler to the last'.[101] Coded oppositionals were also used, as in 'only son died for the Fatherland'.[102]

Key Words and Concepts

So the Reich was, inter alia, a linguistic enterprise. One of the truly great rhetorical achievements of the Reich was to get its enemies to use its language. The real specialists on rhetoric were the Nazis themselves, who created an entire world of mirrors and fictions, and they achieved this by rhetoricising every aspect of their activities in order to distort perception. Thus we have as an example the slogan on the gates of Auschwitz, 'Work makes you free', in that context resembling a most ghastly joke. We have the *Jugendlager* at Ravensbrück, that is to say 'youth camp'; it was anything but, and was, in fact, the name of the extermination centre. The sloganeering radiated an inner banality, and shop-worn examples (some of them retrieved from tradition) were legion: 'Living Space'; 'Jew-Free'; 'Blood and Soil'; 'Strength through Joy'; 'One Folk, One Reich, One Führer'; 'New Order'. Even the Asiatic ally was incorporated into the ideology in phrases like 'removed the most important enemy bases in the Japanese living space'.[103]

Heroic

The language of the Reich was also the rhetoric of the hyper-heroic; men lived on an enlarged scale, a vivid stage wherein the factory worker or sub-urban male would transmute into a Siegfried-like warrior, blessed by ances-tral ghosts. Thus 'as soon as this concept was even touched upon, everything became blurred, and we were adrift once again in the fog of Nazis'.[104] What they really meant was sham-heroic: 'officially Nazism didn't recognize any kind of decent, real heroes'. The superficial neo-heroism of the Hitler Reich was captured in the phrase 'the glassy stare, which expresses a hard and thrusting determination coupled with the will to succeed'.[105]

Fanatical

According to Klemperer, the word fanatical denotes a 'threatening and repulsive quality', yet it was ubiquitous in the Reich, especially during the war as the situation deteriorated, an exemplar of the idea of 'language which writes and thinks for you', and thus 'for twelve years a sick and criminal state of mind was held to be the highest virtue'. This amounts not to giving this word a different meaning but of elevating that original and formerly degraded meaning:

> if someone replaces the words 'heroic' and 'virtuous' with 'fanatical' for long enough, he will come to believe that a fanatic really is a virtuous hero, and that no one can be a hero without fanaticism. The Third Reich did not invent the words 'fanatical' and 'fanaticism', it just changed their value and used them more in one day than other epochs used them in years.[106]

Thus the *Berliner Morgenpost* (5 October 1944) claims that 'fanaticism' has naturally 'grown'; Goebbels receives 'fanatic affirmation'; his mass meeting is characterised by a 'fanatical spirit of resistance'.[107]

Reich

Then there was the word itself, the word 'Reich'. Klemperer said it was not just decorative but had a serious function, to celebrate a state that was mystical and omnipotent: 'it implies that the state does not merely create order in this world, but that the next world is also taken care of'. It invoked the memory of the supra-national Holy Roman Empire, and hence the time-honoured and related word, Reich, was used to sanctify criminality. But Reich One and Reich Two had failed; their promise had only been brought to fruition, perfected, fulfilled, in the Third Reich, which was the apotheosis, the realisation of manifest historical destiny.

Physical training

Klemperer discusses Hitler's love of the expression 'physical training', which denotes the supremacy he attached to the physical over the intellectual because he had a 'fear of the thinking man'. The methodology was to turn terms of contumely into terms of praise, to drop some words, re-define others and elevate still further words from lexical obscurity: for example, Nazis introduced a rarely used word for belligerency into the common vocabulary. It all amounted to a re-imagining of the German language. Nazi rhetoric, with its use of short rhythmic and mnemonic phrases, echoed Hitler's own oratorical style based on years of labour in the great drinking halls of Munich.[108] So the phrases cascaded out—master race, living space, encirclement and the messianic notion of the Thousand-Year Reich; then there were the 'boo-hurrah' words, derivative of the bipolar universe of the Nazi ideology which recognised no shades of grey. Language could only function as an identity-definer, and thus something could only ever be good or bad—November Criminals, Jewish-Bolshevik, Jewry, plutocracy, heroic death, comrade—collectively, these formed a Nazi core identity.

Verbal formulations were often chosen for their evocativeness as political mood music, as in Hitler's invocation to the Hitler Youth to be 'swift as a greyhound, as tough as leather, and as hard as Krupp steel'. What does this really mean? The very essence of its design is imprecision, an avoidance of the particular. Discussing the rhetorical construction of a later and very different regime, David Bromwich (2008) commented, 'the mode of their non-meaning was the point ... these markers of unstated policy were float-ing metaphors with a low yield of fact. But they left an image of decisive-ness, with an insinuation of contempt for persons slower to pass from thought to action ...'[109] Exactly the same observation could apply to the language of the Third Reich, with its portentous-sounding phrases which convey feeling rather than content.[110] Some of the rhetoric was really in fact 'performative utterances' in J.L. Austin's sense, since the substance of their content was so indeterminate.[111] Nazi vocabulary drew from a stock set of words and phrases, which collectively evoked the totality of the worldview. But underpinning this rhetoric lay an ideology which answered all questions for its own resources. All ideologists ultimately seek a coherence theory of truth and a coherent integrating perspective; there is no loose change, no untidiness, it is a neat fit. Thus the confusions and messiness of a complex world can be coerced into a universal explanatory framework. And if concepts, the building blocks of the ideological system, carry the ghost of a cultural ancestry, it is done in order to pervert them; 'Work makes you free' is a specific invocation of Max Weber's Protestant ethic but it is also a perversion of it.

Such key organising concepts include, especially, *Heimat*, homeland, a richly laden term that has—very significantly—no precise English equivalent. It suggests ideas of rootedness, permanence, heritage, the home as a place of ancient spirits and the promise of repose and succour. But there is always something lost in translation—*Volk*, for example, are not just 'people', for the concept carries some notion akin to a tribe. Similarly, 'blood', the most fundamental concept in the Nazi vocabulary, evokes ancestry, kinship, ethnic purity. It means the mystical essence of the race, summoning not merely racial and genetic traits but cultural heritage also. The Nazis deliberately blended race and culture and in this word they become one. *Volksgemeinschaft*, folk community—compulsory donations were expressed as charity rather than tax, because one functioned not as a mere citizen but as something much deeper, a member of the national community. That is to say, such language invoked the conceptual/ideological structure underpinning it. '*Weltanschauung*'—the euphemism 'weltanschauung', which had emerged as a 'new' romantic word circa 1900, became a linguistic mainstay of LTI, engaging even 'the most uneducated member of petty bourgeois'.[112] Weltanschauung implied a vision of the mystical, the intuitive, and even of religious arousal. '*Virtue words*'—key Nazi concepts were also evoked as virtue words and phrases, such as folk, leader principle or master race.

Slogans

Slogans occupied centre stage in Nazi evangelism, since they encapsulated perspectives and telegraphed the key meanings that the party wanted people to absorb. There was a slogan of the day, and a slogan of the week, while every local municipal branch leader received the picture of the week.[113] Hitler's method was reductivist, shrinking ideas into slogans, and this was in itself a basis of the mass propaganda technique.[114] The same slogans were continuously recycled in the rise to power: 'Freedom and Bread', 'Against Marxism and Reaction'.[115] The slogans were always dynamic, and selectively brutal: 'Perish Judah', 'March with Us', 'Fight With Us', 'Join our Struggle', 'For Germany and Freedom', 'Onward—To Berlin', 'Forward, Over the Graves', 'The Infamy of Versailles', 'The Virus of Jewry', 'The Evil of Bolshevism', 'The Honour of the Race' (but 'The Call of Duty' and 'The Nobility of a Soldier's Death' came later).[116] During the war, even strategic activities themselves were serially branded, everything from Operation Barbarossa, the conquest of the USSR, relating of course to the mythological figure of Redbeard (Kaiser Frederick Barbarossa), or Operation Sea Lion, the putative conquest of Britain, or the infamous Night and Fog order during the invasion of the USSR. Hence war itself became a marketing operation, its strategic thrusts expressed in an (epigrammatic) marvel of condensed rhetoric, designed to inject drama, to summon some phantom of the Teutonic past or some idea at once mystical and murderous.

Later war slogans

The later war gave rise to a new set of civic requirements, and thus a new generation of slogans to stress the urgency, for example, of Total War, of working for the war effort and not listening to enemy radio propaganda, being aware of spies and so on. There was also a new rhetoric of anti-ter-rorism: the British plutocracy was described as launching attacks on Cologne in a collective spasm of criminal nihilism.[117] An image of British corpses next to their burning plane was captioned 'Terror Flight':[118] ven-geance gratified. For the campaign of 1942–3 Goebbels offered obedience: 'Führer, give us orders, we'll follow!' Phrases like 'Life or Death' were excessively morbid and he would substitute rhetorical uplift, for example 'For Freedom and Life'.[119] New slogans emerged such as 'Victory At Any Price', and they spoke about a Germany 'After the Victory', never 'after the war'.[120] The surfaces of daily life became tableaux for slogans, and by mid-war even a restaurant menu would hector diners: 'The soldier must often wait all day! Think about that, when you have to wait for a few minutes.'[121] People were becoming irritable, and these nostrums were part of Goebbels's (rather improbable) 'politeness' campaign.[122] Nostalgia was another marketing strategy, with the sentimental revival of song and slo-gan from the era of struggle. 'Victory in War', 'Bolshevik Chaos' and 'Hard

Times, Hard Work, Hard Hearts' festooned every conceivable mobile or retail front, walls, buses, trains, kiosks, shops:[123] an energised, politicised and vividly pictorialised public space.

Late war rhetoric and anti-rhetoric, the discourse of rationality

With the endgame arose an understated, plausible rhetoric. The Nazis constructed an edifice of rationality ('we enjoy the enormous advantage of short communication lines', we no longer have to deal with 'terrorists and partisans'); and a synthetic climate of false optimism: the 'coming victory is only a matter of endurance and winning time until new weapons and numerous new divisions are ready for offensive purposes and uses' (*Berliner Morgenpost*, 5 October 1944).[124] War weariness was nowhere to be found, with underwhelming formula phrases like 'stabilisation of the front' soothing by their very banality. There was the rhetoric of minimisation and mitigation; for Goebbels, 'Every building will be a fortress, should the enemy, who so far have succeeded in occupying only tiny pieces of German territory, occasionally succeed here or there in entering the fatherland's territory.'[125]

Conclusions

Perceptive observers particularly feared the vividness of Nazi rhetoric, 'doubtful that the dry prose of national governments could compete with the emotive poetry of the radical political movements on their own terrain'.[126] Nazism was principally about persuasion; there is a coercive residuum, but murderously so. The Soviet regime, by contrast, was primarily concerned with fear and its arbitrary application. Hitler—the 'expert scanner of the zeitgeist'[127]—knew that he could neither gain nor retain power primarily or even secondarily through coercion alone and there is no question that the Nazis' understanding of rhetoric, in fact their worship of the spoken and printed word, was a major explanation for their success. A less articulate, or articulated, party would never have succeeded as they did; in the twentieth century the worst ideas succeeded best because their sponsors had the best rhetoric and recognised intuitively the power of words to pierce the introversion of mankind.[128]

What distinguishes the language of the Third Reich is that it escaped the public domain to consume everything, including science. In the end, it was a linguistic structure that permitted the unthinkable to become thinkable: not merely clarity of reason, but common humanity, was negated through the rhetorical pollution of thought.[129] The kernel of Klemperer's perception, therefore, is that the propaganda triumph of the Third Reich was a linguistic strategy, and that everything else they did in terms of political evangelism was of secondary relevance. The Nazis understood the value of language, the importance of controlling it and how necessary this was to their rise and survival, and language is a weapon of thought control, the great theme of George Orwell's *1984*.[130] Rhetorical formulae such as the phrase 'living space' functioned via a kind of internal determinism, presenting something as the natural order of things, the situational given which cannot be negotiated. Language encapsulates a way of seeing that excludes other perspectives, other ways of seeing.

CONCLUSIONS

PROPAGANDA, THE LIGHT OF PERVERTED SCIENCE

But if we fail, then the whole world, including the United States, including all that we have known and cared for, will sink into the abyss of a new Dark Age, made more sinister, and perhaps more protracted, by the lights of perverted science.

Winston Churchill, House of Commons, 18 June 1940

It must indeed seem strange to offer a thesis which claims novelty value and significance when so much verbiage has been expended on the story of Hitler's rise to power and leadership of Germany into the Second World War. What, possibly, can there be to say about the matter that is genuinely new? The jaded observer may reasonably ask whether there is anything more to contribute on the subject; why another addition to this range of pyramids, another stone? Jane Caplan observed, citing Richard Evans, that by 2000 '37,000 publications had been devoted to the history of Nazi Germany, 12,000 of them added since 1995 alone'.[1]

The distinctive argument of the book remains: that Hitler was the prime mover in the propaganda regimen of the Third Reich, its editor and its first author, and this book places him at the centre of the propaganda process. Many historians perhaps unwittingly imply a propaganda order where Goebbels was the brilliant practitioner and dictator. This was never true except perhaps in the final year or so of the war. But Hitler was in no sense an innovator—the ideas were always second-hand and even the symbols themselves had a pre-existing life as nationalist icons or signs from earlier ideologies, or as images and rituals borrowed from the Italian Fascism of Benito Mussolini. Hitler's expertise was as a synthesiser, fashioning from the accumulated mass of forms and ideas, the historic debris and labyrinths and byways of the German mind, a modern and ravishing éclat articulated through deftly managed symbols and rituals.

Nazis understood the power of persuasion

The general premise of this book has been the idea that persuasion is the underlying mechanism behind great historical events, and persuasiveness is a common possession of event-making men and women. It was said of Pericles that 'a kind of persuasion played on his lips'. This remains a feature, or perhaps a curse, of our present age. Al-Qaeda, for example, often popularly imagined to be an organisation (although an unconventional one), can more properly be conceived as a kind of cyberspace advertising agency, and only if this is recognised does both the tenacity and the impact of al-Qaeda become intelligible. It does not command officer corps, or fighting legions; it exists only as a nexus of incitement.

Hitler possessed fateful insight into the rhetorically constructed nature of human actors and their persuasability, and it is this that makes him unique among historical performers. He recognised, as few others did, that persuasion in politics could never be merely one tool among others; not a political skill but the political skill. Nobody was born a Nazi; they became so by a process of argument, and the experience of the Reich makes this broader case for our persuasability: that the Reich tripped over one of the fundamental characteristics of our humanity. All regimes have employed persuasion, but no regime has ever turned persuasion into its governing philosophy. Yet the historical narrative since those days has taught us that the Third Reich was not merely an experiment but an anticipatory account. And a harbinger of what was to come, more tentatively, in the political world of the later twentieth and the twenty-first century; when the artifice of myth, symbol and rhetoric had become once again central to the activity of political struggle.

The strengths of Nazi propaganda

If we judge the Nazis' standard of propaganda and its appeal through the prism of *Der Stürmer*, or the three anti-Semitic films of 1940, we seriously misrepresent both its effectiveness and the credulity of its German targets. The assumption we often make is that the weight of the Nazi case—for what they offered, was in the end, an argument—represented an appeal to mere fanaticism and prejudice. Not so. Their critique of Anglo-Saxon capitalism and big business rang true then, and it does so today. More generally, their entire rejection of modernity illuminated the deficiencies in the condition of modernity such as the isolation of the individual, the fragmentation of community, the appeals to rationality alone as the basis for a civic order, and failure to engage the emotional or the mystical, or to discover symbolic and ritual forms to express our governing ideals. The great parades were one way of achieving this illusion of communality and social solidarity; rigid angularity, patterns of marching boots, were a balletic enactment of the values of the regime, insistent, organised, hard. In general also the Nazis were alive to the danger of materialism; hence the 'spiritual' protestations of Nazi propaganda. What they offered was the facsimile of a religion, mumbo-jumbo, an evocation of metaphysical concepts like eternity. They recognised above all the power of ritual and the necessity for it, the bankruptcy of a society founded on science and reason, equality and materialism, the yearning for a point of ignition, for transcendence.

The Nazis also knew that effective propaganda needs some inner core of plausibility to work, a recurrent theme of this text. The Communist menace, for example, the threatened extinction of the bourgeoisie (who in Germany were a huge group), could be made very credible; red scare was an easy thing to run—one did not need to be a Nazi to believe it. Thus concentration camps might become acceptable because so many of their early inmates were German Communists. The murderousness of Bolshevism was well understood by the German middle class, as was the belief that they were its targets; therefore an atmosphere of existential threat was easy to foment because there was an existential threat. If everything Hitler had ever said was lying, drivel and slander, or fantasy, then the Nazi Party would have got nowhere. But, no matter how hyperbolic the ranting, it was never entirely devoid of truth. The Germans had had a direct experience of Communism in the death throes of the First World War and also as prisoners of war in Russia. Their fears of it cannot therefore simply be dismissed as paranoia or McCarthyite hysteria.

But Hitler was, also, a practitioner of the classic politics as well as of a new kind of political art. He was a politician and did many of the things which politicians have always done, and thus the lack of a clear programme when running for election, the vagueness and indeterminacy of the Nazi promise, is hardly something unique to the Nazis; these are the standard practices of political parties in democracies. Nazis were almost entirely tactical.

The Nazis stand before the bar of history as representing a nullification (of every value), and a revelation (of humanity's infinite capacity for inhumanity). Yet it is their paradox that the core of the propaganda appeal was never thus, their adherents perceived the state perhaps as ruthless but seldom as perversely cruel, for it came clothed in the garb of self-righteousness. No regime was more sanctimonious than the Nazis, their humbug, their proclamations of morality or appeals to ideas of self-sacrifice. And at a certain level they were believed; their constant shrill assertions of civic decency, the invocations to social solidarity, could neutralise the peripheral vision of the dark side of the regime. The Nazis represented, in large and hyperactive form, a version of the politics of grievance, the mobilisation of an ostensible minority psychosis which has been so much of the grand political narrative since. Part of the pose was anti-plutocracy, a vibrant source of Nazi rhetoric—'world competition necessitates cooperation between European states to maintain their living standard', and so on. There was a very real sentimentality in all of this, an indulgence and indeed hysteria quite at variance with the implicit Nazi claim to be the bearers of the culture of old Prussia with its associated norms of austerity, restraint and emotional forbearance. The Reich was none of those things.

Another aim of the propaganda was intimidatory—to scare enemies, potential enemies and conquered people. The vistas of aggression evident in documentaries such as *Triumph of the Will* or newsreels were a form of speech to the international community, to arouse fear and respect by the presentation of a steroidal regime. But what is neglected in the analysis of Nazi propaganda is the attractiveness of menace: some people want to be part of something frightening, they identify with power. The imagery of latent violence and depravity in uniform which so repels most people today (as indeed it repelled many then) was also a recruiting device to the party, the SS and the SA, and a means of pulling in recruits, eventually from all of Europe.

Hitler also had an uncanny and almost preternatural understanding of the social condition of the class from which he was drawn, that is to say the lower middle class and its insecurities, its resentment of the privileged orders above it, and fear of ever returning to the proletarian morass from which it had with great difficulty arisen. For them Hitler was in fact an alter ego, and they were always the root of his support. Without them, Nazism would have been unimaginable. To their mass of craven resentments, and their aspiration to petty despotism, Hitler exerted an enormous appeal, while through their dedication, their robust practical skills, the Nazi Party before and during its tenure of power could implement both its propaganda and its control. What Hitler said resonated with these and other German listeners, and much of what he said was merely the conventional wisdom of the day, promulgated more forcefully and even nihilistically. And a part of the motivation too was the German sense of being a special people (an attitude certainly hubristic but perhaps not entirely irrational), with a manifest destiny in the East and a titular claim to the hegemony of Europe.

Psychology

The German in Nazi Germany was emphatically not a sieg-heiling automaton, contrary to popular image. Of the psychological concepts that might explain Nazi method, probably the repeated exposure effect encapsulates what they were really striving for and what they believed the essence of persuasion to be. Minds are crushed by the weight of repetition. A message, to be understood, to sink in, to be absorbed not just observed, must be repeated many times through different mediums and in different forms—yet remain the same message. In terms of advertising theory, the effect of such insistence is to frustrate counter-argument within the mind of the target individuals (or what one author in Germany called a blocking of the dams of doubtful criticism by 'sweeping them away on flights of emotion').[2] When repeated with sufficient force mere assertions become truths, and they appear in the end to invoke a pre-determinate destiny, one that is natural and right. While this is a reductivist theory of persuasion it is by no means a naive one. But it rests on an assumption of public apoliticality, and contempt for average intelligence and capacity of memory.

Another possible explanation would incorporate the theory of low-involvement learning,[3] whereby propaganda works via propositions, too facile to be taken seriously, that creep surreptitiously beneath the mind's cognitive defences.[4] Yet these can still influence us, as for example with the puffery and jingles of Ad-land. Indeed, Northrop Frye, the literary critic, compared advertising to the kind of nonsense syllables acquired as children.[5] We err in accepting Nazi propaganda at face value, for it is not necessarily the case that its targets themselves did. Messages, in other words, can also influence via both the cognitive periphery, and via their very implausibility. This most politicised of people produced the most ostensibly unpoliticised propaganda—entertainment garnished with heroism, maudlin sentimentality and domestic frippery, the decorous frivolity of musical and adventure and romance. Packaged thus, and appearing in this innocuous disguise, deviant ideas could be anchored, and blended with everyday values and attitudes.

The Reich also proceeded, probably unknowingly, through the notion of a binary consciousness in human perception, the tendency of the mind to sort out everything in bipolar terms, good and bad, hot and cold, black and white, as suggested by the neurologist Damasio. Perhaps this was originally a defence mechanism (instantaneous classification into threat or not, as a way of enabling survival in primitive conditions). Such a thesis might explain the success of the kind of negative propaganda they promulgated, how the rhetoric of extremes can actually persuade so many. There is of course a further impact, that is to say a tendency to believe one's own propaganda; for in an evangelical state such as this the targets are not only others, they are oneself. To propagandise actively is to engage in self-justificatory arguments that reinforce commitment: we see this with Goebbels, who had internalised the regime ideology to a remarkable degree, partly because by repeating it so often it had become reflexive. And in the end the Nazis were making propaganda only for themselves, for the elite. The regime sought its own immortality in celluloid (and in *Kolberg* this trend reached its apogee).

Failure of Weimar

The failure of the Weimar model of government lay in its rejection of propaganda as an instrument of governing, even though it possessed the means to propagate—ownership of a film company, for example, and ownership of radio. It precisely refused to do what Hitler precisely did, that is, to evangelise. But as a result the republic suffered from a 'sensory deficit so-called'—a 'lack of rituals and symbols objectifying and supporting the new political order', that absence, that 'poverty of symbolic self-representation' observed by contemporaries.[6] The republic, in the view of one critic, 'has been too sober and has had too little to offer the senses'.[7] Democratic parties pursued a rational model of persuasion; Weimar governments ran education courses and published a subscription journal, and in a sense they saw themselves as anti-propagandists: 'in the mass-political marketplace of ideas the forces of moderation were, so the argument ran, being completely out-advertised by the radical competition'.[8] In contrast the Nazis offered excitement rather than the pedantry of democratic discourse, and they were anti-rational in both credo and methodology: Hitler, speaking about the feelingness of the masses, averred that 'faith is harder to shake than knowledge', and that 'hate is more enduring than aversion'.[9] The monochrome pieties and circumlocutory peregrinations of the democratic parties, their constitutionalism and civic propriety, their rejection of histrionics and refusal to tell and sell, above all their impotence in the face of the collapse in employment, gave the Nazis an increasingly beguiling countenance. Their claim was of course to have replaced democracy by something deeper, more enduring, no longer bound by the ephemeral judgements of mass electorates but guided by a visionary leader. Dictatorship, people began to believe, could replace chatter with an assault on the problems that tormented them and, beyond this, to affix a lenitive or unguent to the tortured soul of the German race.

Nazi propaganda was both immensely crude and very subtle, stiflingly dull and brilliantly stimulating, and it eludes final categorisation. And yet there were Nazi propaganda failures as well. The regime's propaganda was generally disguised, as news, entertainment, documentary; the 'pure' propaganda was successful only when it was a medium of brevity and therefore would not exhaust the patience of the viewer. Yet within these pages we have recalled radical lapses in the popularity of Hitler and the Nazi party—the empty rally halls of late 1932 or the limited attention span which Germans accorded *Triumph of the Will*; the troubled reaction to the great military parade in 1938; the incidence in 1943 of people refusing to return the so-called 'German greeting'. How fragile, perhaps, the whole thing really was.

Thesis: events do not speak for themselves

The significance of propaganda can never be proven, but neither can it ever be dismissed. For example, the features of our social and civic landscape today represent the stamp of power but also the triumph of persuasion at some point in history, from women's rights and women's suffrage to laws protecting the environment. Yet the pressure for such things, the evangelism, did not originate internally with the traditional parties, but externally with advocacy groups. For what is perceived as normal or customary is manufactured and does not arise in nature. Belief systems and the social structures that express them may be hereditary, evolutionary or revolutionary, but they did not exist *ab initio*. Someone, somewhere, sometime, agitated for them. Social conventions are simply that, conventions; they are created, socially constructed.

In the end, the 1929 Wall Street Crash was indeed the assassin of peace in Europe, but the message still had to be articulated, the masses persuaded, the people convinced that the antidote lay with Hitler and not with some other pretender to the German throne. But events do not, or seldom, speak for themselves—they have to be interpreted, rhetorically amplified, and this is where the Nazi strategy of incendiary polemic becomes historically determinist. It was not inevitable that mass unemployment would collapse democracy; it was the democrats who were silent (Brüning's merely two radio addresses, for example) and the Nazis who were voluble. The critics of a perspective that places propaganda at the core of government, the organising principle of its political culture, would argue in response that the events did the talking and not the propaganda. This is a very defensible critique; but events have to be sold, the Anschluss for example (as with Hoffmann's photo-journalism) really must be made to appear the greatest happening in German history.[10] And that is an achievement of propaganda, not just the intrinsic dynamism of the incident. Moreover, the fabrication of these actualities themselves, the orchestration, surely arises from the same propaganda ideology—that everything was propaganda? Whether or not a thesis which places propaganda at the conceptual heart of the regime is contested or contestable, the point is surely that this is what the Nazis themselves believed, because it was their modus operandi; propaganda was a universal obsession in the Third Reich—of all the paladins, of government departments, of branches of the military. It was quite simply the methodology of government. Ultimately it is difficult to gauge the impact of the propaganda because it was ubiquitous and embossed on every surface. The Reich would be unthinkable without it. It would not have been the Reich. Therefore to debate its presence or absence and its weight relative to other factors can only ever be a theoretic and perhaps ultimately futile quest.

More generally it would appear as if Nazism, whose 'product' is a mixture of ideology and evangelism, tapped into some strange vulnerability in the human mind. According to Burleigh:

> sentimentality was arguably the most modern feature of National Socialism, in that by the turn of the millennium politics are permeated, if not by presentiment of survival-apocalypse, then by a cloying sentimentality from politicians hard to distinguish from preachers, and the wider culture of self-absorption, sincerity and victimhood. In this respect, Nazism was truly ahead of its time, beyond its remarkable fascination with technology. This was politics as feeling.[11]

This is one insight into the legacy of Nazism: that it was somehow able to delve the deep structures of modern consciousness long before anyone else had thought of this. It functions therefore as an anticipatory account of a world that came to be: the world of excess, of public emotion, the forging of the imagistic and symbolic into public narratives, politics as a meta-drama. In all of these things the Nazis were true originals, and it is only in our present time that we have come to recognise in Nazism a prototype.

NOTES

PREFACE

1. Nicholas J. O'Shaughnessy, *The Phenomenon of Political Marketing*, London and New York: Macmillan and St. Martin's Press, 1990.
2. *The Independent* blogs, 25 Feb. 2010.

INTRODUCTION

1. Richard Bernstein, 'The Insoluble Question', *New York Review of Books*, 3 Apr. 2014.
2. Corey Ross, *Media and the Making of Modern Germany*, Oxford: Oxford University Press, 2008.
3. Ibid.
4. Ibid.
5. Ibid.
6. There was even brand of tobacco known as 'Anti-Semit': see Louis L. Snyder, *Encyclopedia of the Third Reich*, New York: McGraw-Hill, 1976.
7. Ross, *Media*.
8. Theodore Kaufman, cited in Wolfgang Diewerge's pamphlet, 'The War Goal of World Plutocracy' ('Das Kriegsziel der Weltplutokratie'), Berlin: Zentral verlag der NSDAP, 1941. Calvin College German Propaganda Archive.
9. Laurence Rees, *The Nazis: A Warning From History* (documentary), London: BBC Worldwide, 1997.
10. Ibid.
11. Franz Neumann, *Behemoth: The Structure and Practice of National Socialism, 1933–44*, New York: Harper and Row, 1966.
12. Karl Bracher, *The German Dictatorship*, New York: Holt, Rinehart and Winston, 1970.
13. Ross, *Media*.
14. Ibid.
15. Ibid.

16. As has also been argued in a number of recent, insightful publications, such as Kevin Sharpe, *Selling the Tudor Monarchy*, New Haven and London: Yale University Press, 2009; and Greg Kennedy and Christopher Tuck, *British Propaganda and Wars of Empire*, Farnham: Ashgate, 2014.

17. Cited in Ross, *Media*.

18. Nicholas J. O'Shaughnessy and Paul Baines (eds), *Propaganda (Four Volumes of Key Readings)*, London: SAGE, 2012.

19. Nicholas J. O'Shaughnessy, *Politics and Propaganda: Weapons of Mass Seduction*, Manchester: Manchester University Press, 2004.

20. Ibid.

21. Ibid.

22. Ibid.

23. Ibid.

1. A NARRATIVE OF THIRD REICH PROPAGANDA (1920–39): IMAGINING THE REICH

1. Cited in Karl Bracher, *The German Dictatorship*, New York: Holt, Rinehart and Winston, 1970.

2. Ibid.

3. Baruch Gitlis, *Cinema of Hate*, Bnei Brak: Alfa Communication, 1996.

4. Ibid.

5. Bracher, *German Dictatorship*.

6. John Wheeler-Bennett, cited in Peter Vansittart, *Voices from the Great War* (2nd ed.), London: Pimlico, 1998.

7. David Welch, *Germany, Propaganda and Total War 1914–18*, London: Athlone, 2000.

8. Ibid.

9. Ibid.

10. Ibid.

11. Ibid.

12. Rodney Castleden, *The Concise Encyclopedia of History*, London: Parragon, 1994.

13. Ward Rutherford, *Hitler's Propaganda Machine*, London: Bison, 1978.

14. Welch, *Germany, Propaganda*.

15. Bracher, *German Dictatorship*.

16. Robert O. Paxton, *The Anatomy of Fascism*, London: Allen Lane, 2004.

17. Ian Kershaw, *The "Hitler Myth"*, Oxford: Oxford University Press, 1987.

18. Welch, *Germany, Propaganda*.

19. Ibid.

20. Paxton, *Anatomy*.

21. Joachim C. Fest, *Hitler*, London: Penguin, 2002.

22. Richard Evans, *The Coming of the Third Reich*, London: Penguin, 2005.

23. Ibid.

24. Frederic Spotts, *Hitler and the Power of Aesthetics*, New York: Overlook, 2004.

25. Fest, *Hitler*.

26. Ibid.
27. Rutherford, *Hitler's Propaganda*.
28. *Facts in Review*, 1940, Calvin College German Propaganda Archive.
29. Ibid.
30. Olivia Lang, 'Why has Germany Taken so Long to Pay Off its WW1 Debt?' BBC News Europe, 2 Oct. 2010, www.bbc.co.uk/news/world-europe-11442892, last accessed 22 Jan. 2016.
31. *Facts in Review*, 1940, Calvin College German Propaganda Archive.
32. *Signal*, 'The Peace Which Could Not Last', London: Bison Publishing, 1978.
33. Ibid.
34. R.J.W. Evans, 'In the Lost World of East Prussia', *New York Review of Books*, 12 July 2012.
35. Ibid.
36. Evans, *Coming*.
37. Ibid.
38. Bracher, *German Dictatorship*.
39. Ibid.
40. Ibid.
41. Ibid.
42. Evans, *Coming*.
43. Ibid.
44. Ibid.
45. Bracher, *German Dictatorship*.
46. Fest, *Hitler*.
47. Bracher, *German Dictatorship*.
48. Ibid.
49. Robert S. Wistrich, *Weekend in Munich: Art, Propaganda and Terror in the Third Reich*, London: Pavilion, 1995.
50. Guy Walters, *Berlin Games: How Hitler Stole the Olympic Dream*, London: John Murray, 2006.
51. Bracher, *German Dictatorship*.
52. Fest, *Hitler*.
53. Bracher, *German Dictatorship*.
53. Cited in Hilmar Hoffmann, *The Triumph of Propaganda: Film and National Socialism 1933–1945*, Oxford: Berghahn, 1995.
55. Fest, *Hitler*.
56. Ibid.
57. Ibid.
58. Cited in ibid.
59. Ibid.
60. Rutherford, *Hitler's Propaganda*.
61. Fest, *Hitler*.
62. Helmut Von Wilucki, 'Tested Methods of Propaganda', *Unser Wille Und Weg*, 2 (1932), Calvin College German Propaganda Archive.
63. Fest, *Hitler*.

64. Ibid.
65. Ibid.
66. Bracher, *German Dictatorship*.
67. Rutherford, *Hitler's Propaganda*.
68. Ibid.
69. Piers Brendon, *The Dark Valley: A Panorama of the 1930s*, London: Jonathan Cape, 2000.
70. Evans, *Coming*.
71. Helen Boak, 'Mobilising Women for Hitler', in Anthony McElligott and Tim Kirk (eds), *Working Towards the Führer*, Manchester: Manchester University Press, 2003.
72. Jay Y. Gonen, *The Roots of Nazi Psychology*, Lexington: University Press of Kentucky, 2000.
73. Ibid.
74. Paxton, *Anatomy*.
75. Ibid.
76. Brendon, *Dark Valley*.
77. Hoffmann, *Triumph*.
78. Kershaw, *Hitler Myth*.
79. Bracher, *German Dictatorship*.
80. Oren J. Hale, *The Captive Press in the Third Reich*, Princeton: Princeton University Press, 1964.
81. Bracher, *German Dictatorship*.
82. Ibid.
83. Ibid.
84. Brendon, *Dark Valley*.
85. Bracher, *German Dictatorship*.
86. John Weitz, *Hitler's Diplomat: Joachim von Ribbentrop*, London: Phoenix, 1997.
87. Corey Ross, *Media and the Making of Modern Germany*, Oxford: Oxford University Press, 2008.
88. Ibid.
89. Ibid.
90. Ibid.
91. Ibid.
92. Castleden, *World*.
93. Weitz, *Hitler's Diplomat*.
94. Kershaw, *Hitler Myth*.
95. Evans, *Coming*.
96. Ibid.
97. Bracher, *German Dictatorship*.
98. Brendon, *Dark Valley*.
99. W.S. Allen, *The Nazi Seizure of Power*, New York: Franklin Watts, 1984.
100. Kershaw, *Hitler Myth*.
101. Allen, *Nazi Seizure*.
102. Laurence Rees, *The Nazis: A Warning From History* (documentary), London: BBC Worldwide, 1997.

103. Fest, *Hitler*.
104. Kershaw, *Hitler Myth*.
105. Boak, 'Mobilising'.
106. Franz Neumann, *Behemoth: The Structure and Practice of National Socialism, 1933–44*, New York: Harper and Row, 1966.
107. Aristotle A. Kallis, *Nazi Propaganda and the Second World War*, Basingstoke: Palgrave Macmillan, 2000.
108. Allen, *Nazi Seizure*.
109. Richard Grunberger, *A Social History of the Third Reich*, London: Penguin, 1991.
110. Michael Burleigh, *The Third Reich: A New History*, New York: Hill and Wang, 2001.
111. Bracher, *German Dictatorship*.
112. Ibid.
113. Brendon, *Dark Valley*.
114. This was to prove a tactical error, however, since it alienated middle class voters. See Alan Bullock, *Hitler and Stalin: Parallel Lives*, London: Fontana Press, 1993.
115. Brendon, *Dark Valley*.
116. Ibid.
117. Ibid.
118. Weitz, *Hitler's Diplomat*.
119. Brendon, *Dark Valley*.
120. Wistrich, *Weekend*.
121. Hoffmann, *Triumph*.
122. Ibid.
123. Evans, *Coming*.
124. Fest, *Hitler*.
125. Kallis, *Nazi Propaganda*.
126. Evans, *Coming*.
127. Ross, *Media*.
128. Ibid.
129. Bracher, *German Dictatorship*.
130. Brendon, *Dark Valley*.
131. Kershaw, *Hitler Myth*.
132. Bullock, *Hitler and Stalin*.
133. Ibid.
134. Walters, *Berlin*.
135. Weitz, *Hitler's Diplomat*.
136. Walters, *Berlin*.
137. Evans, *Coming*.
138. Weitz, *Hitler's Diplomat*.
139. Walters, *Berlin*.
140. Evans, *Coming*.
141. Walters, *Berlin*.
142. Evans, *Coming*.

143. Randall L. Bytwerk, *Bending Spines: The Propagandas of Nazi Germany and the German Democratic Republic*, East Lansing: Michigan State University Press, 2004.
144. Evans, *Coming*.
145. Ibid.
146. Walters, *Berlin*.
147. Weitz, *Hitler's Diplomat*.
148. Brendon, *Dark Valley*.
149. Weitz, *Hitler's Diplomat*.
150. Ibid.
151. Walters, *Berlin*.
152. Brendon, *Dark Valley*.
153. Ibid.
154. Evans, *Coming*.
155. Ibid.
156. Castleden, *World*.
157. Hoffmann, *Triumph*.
158. Walters, *Berlin*.
159. Kallis, *Nazi Propaganda*.
160. Walters, *Berlin*.
161. Robert Edwin Herzstein, *The War That Hitler Won*, London: Hamish Hamilton, 1979.
162. Ross, *Media*.
163. Elizabeth Wiskemann, *Europe of the Dictators 1919–45*, London: Fontana, 1975.
164. Ibid.
165. Castleden, *World*.
166. Giles MacDonogh, *1938: Hitler's Gamble*, London: Constable, 2009.
167. Ibid.
168. Ibid.
169. Weitz, *Hitler's Diplomat*.
170. Ibid.
171. Kallis, *Nazi Propaganda*.
172. Allen, *Nazi Seizure*.
173. Bracher, *German Dictatorship*.
174. Ibid.
175. Eric Rentschler, *The Ministry of Illusion: Nazi Cinema and Its Afterlife*, Cambridge, MA: Harvard University Press, 1996.
176. Victor Klemperer, *I Shall Bear Witness: The Diaries of Victor Klemperer 1933–41*, London: Weidenfeld and Nicolson, 1998.
177. William Shirer, *The Rise and Fall of the Third Reich*, London: Pan, 1964.
178. Ibid.
179. *Berliner Illustrirter Zeitung*, 27 Apr. 1939.
180. Burleigh, *Third Reich*.
181. Castleden, *World*.
182. Wiskemann, *Europe*.

183. Louis L. Snyder, *Encyclopaedia of the Third Reich*, New York: McGraw-Hill, 1976.
184. Castleden, *World*.
185. Walters, *Berlin*.
186. Kershaw, *Hitler Myth*.
187. Walters, *Berlin*.
188. Wistrich, *Weekend*.
189. Neumann, *Behemoth*.
190. Robert Gellately, *Backing Hitler: Consent and Coercion in Nazi Germany*, New York: Oxford University Press, 2001.
191. Grunberger, *Social*.
192. Gellately, *Backing*.
193. Ibid.
194. Sir Nevile Henderson, *Failure of a Mission*, London: Hodder and Stoughton, 1940.
195. Albert Speer, *Inside the Third Reich*, London: Macmillan, 1970.
196. Herzstein, *War*.
197. Victor Klemperer, *The Language of the Third Reich*, London: Athlone, 2000.
198. Gellately, *Backing*.
199. Ibid.
200. Ibid.
201. Ibid.
202. Ibid.
203. Ibid.
204. Ibid.
205. Kallis, *Nazi Propaganda*.
206. Bytwerk, *Bending*.
207. Ibid.

2. A NARRATIVE OF THIRD REICH PROPAGANDA: ERSATZ VALHALLA (1939–45)

1. Ian Kershaw, *The "Hitler Myth"*, Oxford: Oxford University Press, 1987.
2. Corey Ross, *Media and the Making of Modern Germany*, Oxford: Oxford University Press, 2008.
3. Ibid.
4. Kershaw, *Hitler Myth*.
5. Ibid.
6. Ross, *Media*.
7. *Der Feldzug in Polen*, International Historic Films Chicago, 1985.
8. Roger Manvell, *Films and the Second World War*, London: J.M. Dent, 1974.
9. *Facts in Review*, 1940, Calvin College German Propaganda Archive.
10. Robert Edwin Herzstein, *The War that Hitler Won*, London: Hamish Hamilton, 1979.
11. Aristotle A. Kallis, *Nazi Propaganda and the Second World War*, Basingstoke: Palgrave Macmillan, 2000.

12. Ibid.
13. David Welch, *Propaganda and the German Cinema 1933–1945* (revised ed.), London: I.B. Tauris, 2007.
14. Kallis, *Nazi Propaganda.*
15. Alistair Horne, *To Lose A Battle*, London: Papermac, 1990.
16. Herzstein, *War.*
17. Goebbels, *Diaries*, 14 Dec. 1940.
18. Herzstein, *War.*
19. Goebbels, *Diaries*, 21 Oct. 1939.
20. Ibid., 9 Nov. 1939.
21. Ibid., 12 Nov. 1939.
22. Ibid., 2 Nov. 1939.
23. Ibid., 13 Oct. 1939.
24. Ibid., 17 Dec. 1939.
25. Ibid., 20 Nov. 1939.
26. Jay Baird, *To Die for Germany: Heroes in the Nazi Pantheon*, Bloomington: Indiana University Press, 1992.
27. Goebbels, *Diaries*, 31 Dec. 1940.
28. Herzstein, *War.*
29. Ibid.
30. Ibid.
31. Welch, *Propaganda and Cinema.*
32. Baird, *To Die.*
33. *Signal*, 'The Peace Which Could Not Last', London: Bison, 1976.
34. Ibid.
35. *Signal*, 'The Booty From 250 Wars ...' London: Bison, 1976.
36. Ibid.
37. Ibid.
38. Signal, 'Oran: The Gratitude of the "Comrade-in-Arms"', London: Bison, 1976.
39. Jeffrey Herf, *The Jewish Enemy*, Cambridge, MA: Belknap, 2006.
40. Ibid.
41. Ibid.
42. Ibid.
43. Kershaw, *Hitler Myth.*
44. Rodney Castleden, *The Concise Encyclopedia of History*, London: Parragon, 1994.
45. Baird, *To Die.*
46. Ibid.
47. *Signal*, 'Defenders of French Culture', London: Bison, 1976.
48. Baird, *To Die.*
49. Herzstein, *War.*
50. Kershaw, *Hitler Myth.*
51. NSDAP booklet, *You and Your People*, Munich: Deutscher Volksverlag, 1940, Calvin College German Propaganda Archive.
52. Herzstein, *War.*
53. Ibid.

54. Goebbels, *Diaries*, 2 Dec. 1939.
55. *Signal*, 'The Soldier with a Camera', London: Bison, 1976.
56. *Der grosse Sieg im Westen*, Munich: Deutscher Verlag Berlin, *c.* July 1940.
57. *Signal*, 'Soldier with a Camera'.
58. Ibid.
59. Ibid.
60. Joachim C. Fest, *Hitler*, London: Penguin, 2002.
61. *Signal*, 'Historical Hours Around Paris', London: Bison, 1976.
62. *Signal*, 'Soldier with a Camera'.
63. Ibid.
64. *Signal*, 'Above the Acropolis', London: Bison, 1976.
65. *NSDAP, Der grosse Sieg im Westen*.
66. *Facts in Review*, 1941, Calvin College German Propaganda Archive.
67. *Signal*, 'In the Cloud Covered Sky over England', London: Bison, 1976.
68. Ward Rutherford, *Hitler's Propaganda Machine*, London: Bison, 1978.
69. While the three great paladins, Göring, Goebbels and Hitler, were the supreme orators and wordsmiths of the Reich, it was Göring who made the direct threats; see ibid.
70. *Signal*, 'Striking the Balance', London: Bison, 1976.
71. *Signal*, 'How Britain was Repulsed', London: Bison, 1976.
72. Ibid.
73. *Signal*, 'The Booty from 250 Wars', London: Bison, 1976.
74. Herzstein, *War*.
75. *Signal*, 'Oslo April 9', London: Bison Publishing, 1976.
76. *Signal*, 'Thermopylae', London: Bison Publishing, 1976.
77. *Signal*, 'They Did Not Know Where They Were Going', London: Bison Publishing, 1976.
78. Ibid.
79. Fritz Sauckel, 'Introduction', *Europa Arbeitet in Deutschland*, Munich: Friedrich Didier, 1943, Calvin College German Propaganda Archive.
80. Ibid.
81. Mark Mazower, *Hitler's Empire*, London: Allen Lane, 2008.
82. *Adler*, 16 Dec. 1942.
83. Herzstein, *War*.
84. *Adler*, 8 Dec. 1942.
85. Ibid., 14 Sep. 1943.
86. Ibid., 6 Dec. 1942.
87. Ibid., 22 June 1943.
88. Ibid., 14 Sep. 1943.
89. Peter Adam, *The Arts of the Third Reich*, London: Thames & Hudson, 1992.
90. Not all heroes, however, were plaster saints, and this created real problems for the Nazi media machine. Captain Hans-Joachim Marseille, for instance, with his kill of over 120 enemy aircraft, chiefly over North Africa, was a genuine hero, but a hero for our time, not theirs, with his smiling, Hollywood looks and glint of amoral jollity. As a pleasure-seeking hedonist he sought solace in nightclubs

and female company. The cub of a dysfunctional family, with divorced parents, and a sister murdered by her jealous boyfriend, his inveterate nocturnal partying caused him to be disciplined for missing some raids during the Battle of Britain. See *Adler*, 29 Sep. 1942; Robert Tate, *Hans-Joachim Marseille*, Pennsylvania: Schiffer Publishing, 2008.

91. *Adler*, 27 Oct. 1942.
92. Harold Nicolson, *Diaries: The War Years 1939–45*, New York: Atheneum, 1967 (entry from 5 June 1941).
93. Colin Smith, *England's Last War Against France*, London: Weidenfeld and Nicolson, 2009.
94. *Signal*, 'Japan's Long Arm', London: Bison, 1976.
95. Ibid.
96. *Berlin, Rom, Tokio*, Aug. 1942.
97. *Signal*, 'Japan's Long Arm'.
98. Ibid.
99. Herf, *Jewish Enemy*.
100. Ibid.
101. Ibid.
102. Ibid.
103. Goebbels, *Diaries*, 14 July 1941.
104. Herf, *Jewish Enemy*.
105. Kallis, *Nazi Propaganda*.
106. Ibid.
107. Ibid.
108. Ibid.
109. *Die Wehrmacht*, 14 Jan. 1942.
110. *Adler*, 22 June 1943.
111. *Die Wehrmacht*, 29 July 1942.
112. Ibid.
113. Ibid., 7 Oct. 1942.
114. Ibid., 13 Aug. 1941.
115. Ibid., 29 July 1942.
116. Ibid., 13 Aug. 1941.
117. Ibid., 2 June 1943.
118. Ibid., 5 May 1943.
119. *Signal*, 'The Leader and his Reichmarshal', London: Bison, 1976.
120. *Adler*, 20 July 1943.
121. *Die Wehrmacht*, 7 Oct. 1942.
122. Ibid., 5 May 1943.
123. Ibid., 3 Dec. 1941.
124. Ibid., 5 May 1943.
125. Ibid., 2 June 1943.
126. *Adler*, 22 June 1943.
127. *Die Wehrmacht*, 7 Oct. 1942.
128. *Adler*, 29 Sep. 1942.

129. Jeffrey Herf, *Nazi Propaganda for the Arab World*, New Haven: Yale University Press, 2009.
130. Ibid.
131. Herf, *Jewish Enemy*.
132. Robert Gellately, *Backing Hitler: Consent and Coercion in Nazi Germany*, New York: Oxford University Press, 2001.
133. Michael Burleigh, *The Third Reich: A New History*, New York: Hill and Wang, 2001.
134. Herf, *Jewish Enemy*.
135. Kallis, *Nazi Propaganda*.
136. Herf, *Jewish Enemy*.
137. Welch, *Propaganda and Cinema*.
138. Ibid.
139. *Signal*, 'From Newfoundland to Cape Horn', London: Bison, 1976.
140. Ibid.
141. Herf, *Nazi Propaganda*.
142. Hans Otto Wesemann, 'The Kitschified Mass Soul: American War Advertisements', *Das Reich*, 31 Aug. 1944, pp. 5–6, Calvin College German Propaganda Archive.
143. Ibid.
144. Ibid.
145. Kallis, *Nazi Propaganda*.
146. *Signal*, Heinrich Hunke, 'Has The Big Businessman a Future?', London: Bison, 1976.
147. Kallis, *Nazi Propaganda*.
148. *Signal*, 'Roosevelt: Emperor of the World', London: Bison, 1976.
149. Baird, *To Die*.
150. Sauckel, *Europa*.
151. Antony Beevor, *Berlin: The Downfall 1945*, London: Penguin, 2002.
152. Goebbels, *Diaries*, 21 Oct. 1940.
153. Victor Klemperer, *The Language of the Third Reich*, London: Athlone, 2000.
154. Toni Winkelnkemper, *The Attack on Cologne*, Berlin: Franz Eher, 1942, Calvin College German Propaganda Archive.
155. Kallis, *Nazi Propaganda*.
156. Ibid.
157. Ibid.
158. Ibid.
159. Herzstein, *War*.
160. Ibid.
161. Ibid.
162. Kallis, *Nazi Propaganda*.
163. Antony Beevor, *Stalingrad*, London: Penguin, 1999.
164. Ibid.
165. Ibid.
166. Randall L. Bytwerk, *Bending Spines: The Propagandas of Nazi Germany and the*

German Democratic Republic, East Lansing: Michigan State University Press, 2004.

167. Burleigh, _Third Reich._
168. Ibid.
169. Albert Speer, _Inside the Third Reich_, London: Macmillan, 1970.
170. Bytwerk, _Bending._
171. Speer, _Inside._
172. Ibid.
173. Bytwerk, _Bending._
174. Beevor, _Stalingrad._
175. David Welch, '"Working towards the Führer": Charismatic Leadership and the Image of Adolf Hitler in Nazi Propaganda', in Anthony McElligott and Tim Kirk (eds), _Working Towards the Führer_, Manchester: Manchester University Press, 2003.
176. Ibid.
177. Ibid.
178. Kershaw, _Hitler Myth._
179. Beevor, _Berlin._
180. Hilmar Hoffman, _The Triumph of Propaganda_, Oxford: Berghahn, 1995.
181. Herzstein, _War._
182. Burleigh, _Third Reich._
183. Beevor, _Stalingrad._
184. Herzstein, _War._
185. Baird, _To Die._
186. Herzstein, _War._
187. Ibid.
188. Winkelnkemper, _Attack._
189. Herzstein, _War._
190. _Berliner Morgenpost_, 5 October 1944.
191. Elizabeth Sifton and Fritz Stern, 'The Tragedy of Dietrich Bonhoeffer and Hans von Dohnanyi', _New York Review of Books_, 25 Oct. 2012.
192. Herzstein, _War._
193. Ibid.
194. Ibid.
195. Kershaw, _Hitler Myth._
196. Kallis, _Nazi Propaganda._
197. Welch, _Propaganda and Cinema._
198. Kallis, _Nazi Propaganda._
199. Ibid.
200. Ibid.
201. Beevor, _Berlin._
202. Ibid.
203. Herzstein, _War._
204. Welch, 'Working'.
205. Herzstein, _War._

206. Ibid.
207. Beevor, *Berlin*.
208. Ibid.
209. Herzstein, *War*.
210. *Deutsche Wochenschau*, 22 Mar. 1945.
211. Ibid.
212. Speer, *Inside*.
213. Ibid.
214. Herzstein, *War*.
215. Freeman Dyson, 'Rocket Man', *New York Review of Books*, 17 Jan. 2008.
216. Herbert Friedman, 'The German V1 Rocket Campaign', www.psywarrior.com/ V1RocketLeaf.html, last accessed 25 January 2016.
217. Ibid.
218. Phillip Ziegler, *London at War 1939–45*, London: Mandarin, 1996.
219. Ibid.
220. Tony Iveson and Brian Milton, *Lancaster: The Biography*, London: Andre Deutsch, 2009.
221. Posters, Calvin College German Propaganda Archive.
222. Gary Hyland and Anton Gill, *Last Talons of the Eagle*, London: Headline, 1998.
223. Jeffrey Ethell and Alfred Price, *World War II Fighting Jets*, Shrewsbury: Airlife, 1994.
224. *Jane's All The World's Aircraft*, 1945.
225. Hyland and Gill, *Last*.
226. Ibid.
227. Anthony Pratkanis and Elliot Aronson, *Age of Propaganda*, New York: Henry Holt, 2001.
228. George Forty, *Germany at War*, London: Carlton, 2003.
229. Ibid.

3. TOWARDS A NAZI THEORY OF PERSUASION: THE PRIMAL SCREAM OF FASCISM

1. Hilmar Hoffmann, *The Triumph of Propaganda*, Oxford: Berghahn, 1996.
2. Karl Bracher, *The German Dictatorship*, New York: Holt, Rinehart and Winston, 1970.
3. Ibid.
4. W.J. West, *Truth Betrayed*, London: Gerald Duckworth, 1987.
5. Ibid.
6. Bracher, *German Dictatorship*.
7. Hoffmann, *Triumph*.
8. Corey Ross, *Media and the Making of Modern Germany*, Oxford: Oxford University Press, 2008.
9. Ibid.
10. Ward Rutherford, *Hitler's Propaganda Machine*, London: Bison, 1978.
11. Piers Brendon, *The Dark Valley*, London: Jonathan Cape, 2000.

12. Hoffmann, *Triumph*.
13. James J. Sheehan, 'Hello to Berlin', *New York Review of Books*, 8 Nov. 2012.
14. Dr Josef Wells, 'Political Propaganda as Moral Duty', *Unser Wille und Weg*, 6 (1936), Calvin College German Propaganda Archive.
15. Walther Schulze-Wechsungen, 'Political Propaganda', *Unser Wille und Weg*, 4 (1934), Calvin College German Propaganda Archive.
16. G. Stark, *Modern Political Propaganda*, Munich: Verlag Frz Eher Nachf, 1930, Calvin College German Propaganda Archive.
17. Bracher, *German Dicatorship*.
18. Ibid.
19. Ross, *Media*.
20. Roger Manvell, *Films and the Second World War*, London: J.M. Dent, 1974.
21. Aristotle A. Kallis, *Propaganda and the Second World War*, Basingstoke: Palgrave Macmillan, 2000.
22. Ibid.
23. Stark, *Modern*.
24. Schulze-Wechsungen, 'Political'.
25. Nicholas J. O'Shaughnessy, *Politics and Propaganda: Weapons of Mass Seduction*, Manchester: Manchester University Press, 2004.
26. Ibid.
27. Hoffmann, *Triumph*.
28. Jay Y. Gonen, *The Roots of Nazi Psychology*, Lexington: University Press of Kentucky, 2000.
29. Hoffmann, *Triumph*.
30. Schulze-Wechsungen, 'Political'.
31. Joachim C. Fest, *Hitler*, London: Penguin, 2002.
32. Schulze-Wechsungen, 'Political'.
33. Ibid.
34. Garth S. Jowett and Victoria O'Donnell (eds), *Propaganda and Persuasion*, London: SAGE, 2006.
35. Goebbels, *Diaries*, 29 Oct. 1940.
36. Baruch Gitlis, *Cinema of Hate*, Bnei Brak: Alpha Communication, 1996.
37. Ibid.
38. Ibid.
39. Neil Gregor, *How to Read Hitler*, London: Granta, 2005.
40. Joseph Goebbels, 'Children with their Hands Chopped off', Munich: NSDAP, 1941, Calvin College German Propaganda Archive.
41. Ibid.
42. Schulze-Wechsungen, 'Political'.
43. Leonard W. Doob, 'Goebbels's Principles of Propaganda', *Public Opinion Quarterly*, 14, 3 (1950).
44. R.B. Zajonc and H. Marcus, 'Affective and Cognitive Factors in Preferences', in Harold H. Kassarjian and Thomas S. Robertson (eds), *Perspectives in Consumer Behavior*, Englewood Cliffs, NJ: Prentice Hall, 1991.
45. Franz Neumann, *Behemoth: The Structure and Practice of National Socialism 1933–44*, New York: Harper and Row, 1966.

46. Ibid.
47. Stark, *Modern*.
48. Joseph Goebbels, *Unser Wille und Weg*, 1 (1931), Calvin College German Propaganda Archive.
49. Schulze-Wechsungen, 'Political'.
50. Oliver Thomson, *Easily Led: A History of Propaganda*, Stroud: Sutton Publishing, 1999.
51. Goebbels, *Diaries*, 7 Oct. 1940.
52. Ibid., 8 Oct. 1940.
53. Stark, *Modern*.
54. Randall L. Bytwerk, *Bending Spines: The Propagandas of Nazi Germany and the German Democratic Republic*, East Lansing: Michigan State University Press, 2004.
55. Robert Edwin Herzstein, *The War that Hitler Won*, London: Hamish Hamilton, 1979.
56. Jeffrey Herf, *The Jewish Enemy*, Cambridge, MA: Belknap, 2006.
57. Ibid.
58. Kallis, *Propaganda*.
59. David Culbert, 'Kolberg: The Goebbels Diaries and Poland's Kolobrzeg Today', in John Whiteclay Chambers and David Culbert (eds), *World War II, Film and History*, New York: Oxford University Press, 1996.
60. Ross, *Media*.
61. Bracher, *German Dictatorship*.
62. Eric Rentschler, *The Ministry of Illusion*, Cambridge, MA: Harvard University Press, 1996.
63. Hoffmann, *Triumph*.
64. Gitlis, *Cinema*.
65. Robert O. Paxton, *The Anatomy of Fascism*, London: Allen Lane, 2004.
66. Rentschler, *Ministry*.
67. Ross, *Media*.
68. Rentschler, *Ministry*.
69. Ibid.
70. Ibid.
71. Ross, *Media*.
72. Herzstein, *War*.
73. Gitlis, *Cinema*.
74. Ross, *Media*.
75. Ibid.
76. Ibid.
77. Ibid.
78. Kallis, *Propaganda*.
79. Ibid.
80. Ross, *Media*.
81. Ibid.
82. Ibid.

83. Stark, *Modern.*
84. Ross, *Media.*
85. Ibid.
86. Ross, *Media.*
87. Stark, *Modern.*
88. Ibid.
89. Wells, 'Political Propaganda'.
90. Schulze-Wechsungen, 'Political'.
91. Ibid.
92. Paxton, *Anatomy.*
93. Stark, *Modern.*
94. Schulze-Wechsungen, 'Political'.
95. Ibid.
96. Paxton, *Anatomy.*
97. Gustave Le Bon, *The Crowd*, n.p.: Filiquarian Publishing LLC, 2005.
98. Hoffmann, *Triumph.*
99. Frederic Spotts, *Hitler and the Power of Aesthetics*, New York: Overlook, 2004.
100. Ibid.
101. Goebbels's speech, Nuremberg rally 1927, Calvin College German Propaganda Archive.
102. David Welch, *Propaganda and the German Cinema 1933–1945* (revised ed.), London: I.B. Tauris, 2007.
103. Stanley Newcourt-Nowodworski, *Black Propaganda in the Second World War*, Stroud: Sutton, 2005.
104. Bracher, *German Dictatorship.*
105. Spotts, *Hitler.*
106. Rutherford, *Hitler's Propaganda.*
107. Hugh Trevor-Roper, *Hitler's Table Talk 1941–1944: Hitler's Conversations Recorded by Martin Bormann*, Oxford: Oxford University Press Oxford, 1988.
108. Fest, *Hitler.*
109. Paxton, *Anatomy.*
110. Goebbels, 1927.
111. Stark, *Modern.*
112. Paxton, *Anatomy.*
113. Ibid.
114. Cited in Ross, *Media.*
115. Ross, *Media.*
116. Ibid.
117. Ibid.
118. Bracher, *German Dictatorship.*
119. Neumann, *Behemoth.*
120. Wells, 'Propaganda'.
121. Franz J. Huber (ed.), *A Propaganda Primer*, Wels: Leitner & Co., 1942, Calvin College German Propaganda Archive.
122. Ibid.

123. Ibid.
124. *Unser Wille und Weg,* 1 (1931), Calvin College German Propaganda Archive.
125. Herzstein, *War.*
126. Lead article, *Unser Wille und Weg,* 1 (1931), Calvin College German Propaganda Archive.
127. Ibid.
128. Ibid.
129. Ibid.
130. Ibid.
131. Goebbels, 1927.
132. Joseph Goebbels, lead article, *Unser Wille und Weg,* 1 (1931), pp. 2–5.
133. Ibid.
134. Ibid.
135. Ibid.
136. Adolf Hitler, *Mein Kampf,* New York: Mariner/Houghton Miflin, 1999.
137. Bracher, *German Dictatorship.*
138. Ross, *Media.*
139. Hitler, *Mein Kampf.*
140. Ibid.
141. Fest, *Hitler.*
142. Herzstein, *War.*
143. Ross, *Media.*
144. Ibid.
145. Bracher, *German Dictatorship.*
146. Le Bon, *Crowd.*
147. Ross, *Media.*
148. Bracher, *German Dictatorship.*
149. Ibid.
150. Hoffmann, *Triumph.*
151. Spotts, *Hitler.*
152. Ibid.
153. Hitler, *Mein Kampf.*
154. Ibid.
155. Hans Thimme, *Weltkrieg ohne Waffen,* Stuttgart and Berlin: Cotta'sche Buchhandlung, 1932, Calvin College German Propaganda Archive.
156. Eugen Hadamovsky, *Propaganda and National Power,* Oldenburg: Gerhard Stalling, 1933, Calvin College German Propaganda Archive.
157. Peter Vansittart, *Voices from the Great War* (2nd ed.), London: Pimlico, 1998.
158. Ibid.
159. David Welch, *Germany, Propaganda and Total War 1914–18,* London: Athlone, 2000.
160. Ibid.
161. Ibid.
162. Ibid.
163. Ibid.
164. Ibid.

165. Goebbels, 'Children'.
166. Schulze-Wechsungen, 'Political'.
167. Goebbels, 'Children'.
168. Ibid.
169. Hoffmann, *Triumph*.
170. Vansittart, *Voices*.
171. Trevor-Roper, *Hitler's Table Talk* (conversation from 14–15 Sep. 1941).
172. Vansittart, *Voices*.
173. Goebbels, 'Children'.
174. Toni Winkelnkemper, *The Attack on Cologne*, Berlin: Franz Eher, 1942; Calvin College German Propaganda Archive.
175. Goebbels, 'Children'.
176. Ibid.
177. Ibid.
178. Ibid.
179. Ibid.
180. Paxton, *Anatomy*.
181. W.S. Allen, *The Nazi Seizure of Power*, New York: Franklin Watts, 1984.
182. Schulze-Wechsungen, 'Political'.
183. Guy Walters, *Berlin Games: How Hitler Stole the Olympic Dream*, London: John Murray, 2006.
184. Paxton, *Anatomy*.
185. Rentschler, *Ministry*.
186. Ian Kershaw, *The "Hitler Myth"*, Oxford: Oxford University Press, 1987.
187. Herzstein, *War*.
188. Bytwerk, *Bending*.
189. Kershaw, *Hitler Myth*.
190. Ibid.
191. Harold Nicolson, *Diaries: The War Years 1939–45*, New York: Atheneum, 1967 (entry from 29 May 1941).
192. Ross, *Media*.
193. Ibid.
194. Ibid.
195. Ibid.
196. Ibid.
197. Ibid.
198. Evans, *Coming*.
199. Ibid.
200. Ross, *Media*.
201. Manvell, *Films*.

4. MYTHOLOGIES: INVENTING THE THIRD REICH

1. Lisa Jardine, *Going Dutch: How England Plundered Holland's Glory*, London: HarperCollins, 2008.

2. George Schöpflin, 'The Functions of Myth and a Taxonomy of Myths', in Geoffrey Hosking and George Schöpflin (eds), *Myths and Nationhood*, New York: Routledge, 1997.

3. Gustave Le Bon, *The Crowd*, n.p.: Filiquarian Publishing LLC, 2005.

4. Mircea Eliade, *Images and Symbols*, Princeton, NJ: Princeton University Press, 1991.

5. Aristotle A. Kallis, *Propaganda and the Second World War*, Basingstoke: Palgrave Macmillan, 2000.

6. Schöpflin, 'Functions'.

7. Duncan Webster, *Looka Yonder! The Imaginary America of Populist Culture*, London: Routledge, 1988.

8. Giles MacDonogh, *1938: Hitler's Gamble*, London: Constable, 2009.

9. Ward Rutherford, *Hitler's Propaganda Machine*, London: Bison, 1978.

10. Arnold Perris, *Music as Propaganda: Art to Persuade, Art to Control*, Westport, CT: Greenwood, 1985.

11. David Welch, *Propaganda and The German Cinema 1933–1945* (2nd ed.), London: I.B. Tauris, 2007.

12. Bettina Arnold, 'The Past as Propaganda', *Archaeology* (July/Aug. 1992).

13. Guy Walters, *Berlin Games: How Hitler Stole the Olympic Dream*, London: John Murray, 2006.

14. Ibid.

15. Ibid.

16. Arnold, 'Past'.

17. Karl Bracher, *The German Dictatorship*, New York: Holt, Rinehart and Winston, 1970.

18. Arnold, 'Past'.

19. R.J.W. Evans, 'In the Lost World of East Prussia', *New York Review of Books*, 12 July 2012.

20. Ibid.

21. Ibid.

22. Ibid.

23. Bracher, *German Dictatorship*.

24. Ibid.

25. Ibid.

26. Baruch Gitlis, *Cinema of Hate: Nazi Film in the War against the Jews*, Bnei Brak: Alfa Communication, 1996.

27. Ibid.

28. Dr Josef Wells, 'Political Propaganda as Moral Duty', *Unser Wille Und Weg*, 6 (1936), Calvin College German Propaganda Archive.

29. G. Stark, *Modern Political Propaganda*, Munich: Verlag Frz Eher Nachf, 1930, Calvin College German Propaganda Archive.

30. Richard Grunberger, *A Social History of the Third Reich*, London: Penguin, 1991.

31. Ibid.

32. Ibid.

33. Ibid.

34. Ibid.

35. Ibid.

36. Arnold, 'Past'.

37. Ibid.

38. Ibid.

39. Ibid.

40. Jay Y. Gonen, *The Roots of Nazi Psychology*, Lexington: University Press of Kentucky, 2000.

41. Calvin College German Propaganda Archive, Posters 1920–33, no. 37.

42. Le Bon, *Crowd*.

43. Gonen, *Roots*.

44. Ibid.

45. Le Bon, *Crowd*.

46. W. Blake Tyrrell and Frieda S. Brown (eds), *Athenian Myths and Institutions*, New York: Oxford University Press, 1991.

47. Richard Evans, *The Coming of the Third Reich*, London: Penguin, 2005.

48. Ibid.

49. Ibid.

50. Ibid.

51. Ibid.

52. Gitlis, *Cinema*.

53. Randall L. Bytwerk, *Bending Spines: The Propagandas of Nazi Germany and the German Democratic Republic*, East Lansing: Michigan State University Press, 2004.

54. Kallis, *Propaganda*.

55. Welch, *Propaganda and Cinema*.

56. Roger Manvell, *Films and the Second World War*, London: J.M. Dent, 1974.

57. Goebbels, *Diaries*, 22 June 1941, cited in Jeffrey Herf, *The Jewish Enemy*, Cambridge, MA: Belknap, 2006.

58. Ibid.

59. Laurence Rees, *The Nazis: A Warning From History* (documentary), London: BBC Worldwide, 1997.

60. Tim Snyder, *New York Review of Books*, 21 June 2012.

61. Jay Baird, *To Die for Germany*, Bloomington: Indiana University Press, 1992.

62. George Leggett, *The Cheka: Lenin's Political Police*, New York: Oxford University Press, 1986.

63. Schöpflin, 'Functions'.

64. Louis L. Snyder, *Hitler's German Enemies*, London: Robert Hale, 1991.

65. Rees, *Nazis*.

66. John Weitz, *Hitler's Diplomat*, London: Phoenix, 1997.

67. Joachim Fest, *Hitler*, London: Penguin, 2002.

68. John Maynard Keynes, *Essays in Biography*, New York: Harcourt, Brace and Jovanovich, 1933.

69. Richard Griffiths, *Fellow Travellers of the Right*, Oxford: Oxford University Press, 1983.

70. Robert Edwin Herzstein, *The War that Hitler Won*, London: Hamish Hamilton, 1979.
71. Eric Rentschler, *The Ministry of Illusion*, Cambridge, MA: Harvard University Press, 1996.
72. Baird, *To Die*.
73. Rentschler, *Ministry*.
74. Baird, *To Die*.
75. Rentschler, *Ministry*.
76. Baird, *To Die*.
77. Ibid.
78. Ibid.
79. Ibid.
80. Hugh Trevor-Roper, *Hitler's Table Talk 1941–1944: Hitler's Conversations Recorded by Martin Bormann*, Oxford: Oxford University Press, 1988.
81. Manvell, *Films*.
82. Welch, *Propaganda and Cinema*.
83. Ibid.
84. Herzstein, *War*.
85. Welch, *Propaganda and Cinema*.
86. Sebastien Saur, 'The Soviet Union in *Signal*', *Histoire de Guerre*, 38 (July/Aug. 2003).
87. Ibid.
88. Peter Batty, *Paper War*, West New York, NJ: Mark Batty, 2005.
89. Ibid.
90. Evans, *Coming*.
91. Robert Gellately, *Backing Hitler: Consent and Coercion in Nazi Germany*, New York: Oxford University Press, 2001.
92. Stanley McClatchie, *Look to Germany*, Berlin: Heinrich Hoffmann, 1938.
93. Kallis, *Propaganda*.
94. Piers Brendon, *The Dark Valley*, London: Jonathan Cape, 2000.
95. McClatchie, *Look*.
96. Baird, *To Die*.
97. Ward, *Hitler's Propaganda*.
98. MacDonogh, *1938*.
99. John Lukacs, *Five Days in London: May 1940*, New Haven and London: Yale University Press, 2001.
100. Baird, *To Die*.
101. Ibid.
102. Ibid.
103. Trevor-Roper, *Hitler's Table Talk*, (conversation from Aug. 1941).
104. Robert S. Wistrich, *Weekend in Munich*, London: Pavilion, 1995.
105. Baird, *To Die*.
106. Louis L. Snyder, *Encyclopaedia of the Third Reich*, New York: McGraw-Hill, 1976.
107. Bracher, *German Dictatorship*.
108. Ibid.

109. Victor Klemperer, *The Language of the Third Reich*, London: Athlone, 2000.
110. Nicholas J. O'Shaughnessy, *Politics and Propaganda: Weapons of Mass Seduction*, Manchester: Manchester University Press, 2004. It is also an example of how the idea of 'blood' was a commonality of discourse in that pre-war world—the British Ambassador Nevile Henderson actually committed to paper his doubts about the racial purity of his Teutonic hosts. He speaks of 'the very considerable amount of Slav blood which flows in the German veins. The mixture is probably a bad one ...' See Sir Nevile Henderson, *Failure of a Mission*, London: Hodder and Stoughton, 1940. Hitler saw his movement as aiming 'scientifically to construct a doctrine that is nothing more than a homage to reason'. See Trevor-Roper, *Hitler's Table Talk*, (conversation from (conversation from 23 Sep. 1941).
111. Bracher, *German Dictatorship*.
112. Ibid.
113. *Mein Kampf*, 1999.
114. Trevor-Roper, *Hitler's Table Talk*, (conversation from 23 Sep. 1941).
115. Ibid., 13 Oct. 1941.
116. Ibid., 10 Oct. 1941.
117. Hilmar Hoffmann, *The Triumph of Propaganda*, Oxford: Berghahn, 1996.
118. Walters, *Berlin*.
119. Welch, *Propaganda and Cinema*.
120. Ibid.
121. See, e.g., Gitlis, *Cinema*.
122. NSDAP booklet, *You and Your People*, Munich: Deutscher Volksverlag, 1940, Calvin College German Propaganda Archive.
123. Fritz Bennecke, *On the German People and its Territory*, Munich: Franz Eher, 1937, Calvin College German Propaganda Archive.
124. NSDAP, *You and Your People*.
125. Bennecke, *On the German*.
126. NSDAP, *You and Your People*.
127. Ibid.
128. Rentschler, *Ministry*.
129. Rees, *Nazis*.
130. O'Shaughnessy, *Politics*.
131. Fest, *Hitler*.
132. Bennecke, *On the German*.
133. Ibid.
134. Ibid.
135. NSDAP, *You and Your People*.
136. Ibid.
137. Ibid.
138. Ibid.
139. Franz J. Huber, *A Propaganda Primer*, Wels: Leitner & Co., 1942, Calvin College German Propaganda Archive.
140. *Signal*, 'The First Coloured Photographs of the Great Battle in the West', London: Bison, 1976.

141. Werner May, *The German National Catchesism*, Munich: Franz Eher, 1937, Calvin College German Propaganda Archive.
142. Ibid.
143. O'Shaughnessy, *Politics*.
144. Herzstein, *War*.
145. Klemperer, *Language*.
146. Bracher, *German Dictatorship*.
147. Klemperer, *Language*.
148. William Shirer, *The Rise and Fall of the Third Reich*, London: Pan, 1964.
149. Bracher, *German Dictatorship*.
150. Grunberger, *Social*.
151. Gary Wills, 'Catholics and Jews: The Great Change', *New York Review of Books*, 21 Mar. 2013.
152. Bracher, *German Dictatorship*.
153. Gitlis, *Cinema*.
154. Evans, *Coming*.
155. Bracher, *German Dictatorship*.
156. Ibid.
157. Trevor-Roper, *Hitler's Table Talk*, (conversation from 15 Oct. 1941).
158. Bracher, *German Dictatorship*.
159. Gitlis, *Cinema*.
160. Ibid.
161. Bracher, *German Dictatorship*.
162. Klemperer, *Language*.
163. Trevor-Roper, *Hitler's Table Talk*, (conversation from 21 Oct. 1941).
164. Kallis, *Propaganda*.
165. Herf, *Jewish*.
166. Gitlis, *Cinema*.
167. Ibid.
168. Randall L. Bytwerk, *Julius Streicher*, New York: Cooper Square, 2001.
169. Grunberger, *Social*.
170. May, *German*.
171. Ibid.
172. Bytwerk, *Julius*.
173. MacDonogh, *1938*.
174. Bytwerk, *Julius*.
175. 'The Parable of the Drones', in Ernst Hiemer, *The Poodle-Pug-Dachshund-Pinscher*, Nuremberg: Der Stürmer-Buchverlag, 1940, Calvin College German Propaganda Archive.
176. *The Reich*, 20 July 1941.
177. Welch, *Propaganda and Cinema*.
178. Ibid.
179. Herf, *Jewish*.
180. Ibid.
181. *Signal*, Heinrich Hunke, 'Has the Big Businessman a Future?', London: Bison, 1976.

182. Ibid.
183. Batty, *Paper.*
184. May, *German.*
185. Ibid.
186. Ibid.
187. Herf, *Jewish.*
188. Welch, *Propaganda and Cinema.*
189. Ernst Hiemer, 'The Poisonous Mushroom' and 'How to Tell a Jew', in *Der Giftpilz,* Nuremberg: Stürmerverlag, 1938, Calvin College German Propaganda Archive.
190. Bytwerk, *Julius.*
191. Jeffrey Herf, *Nazi Propaganda for the Arab World,* New Haven: Yale University Press, 2009.
192. Herf, *Jewish.*
193. Ernst Hiemer, 'The Experience of Hans and Elsa with a Strange Man', in *Der Giftpilz,* London: Friends of Europe, 1938, Calvin College German Propaganda Archive.
194. Wolfgang Diewerge, *The War Goal of World Plutocracy,* Berlin: Zentralverlag der NSDAP, 1941, Calvin College German Propaganda Archive.
195. Bytwerk, *Julius.*
196. Ibid.
197. Klemperer, *Language.*
198. Fest, *Hitler.*
199. Ibid.
200. Ibid.
201. Herf, *Nazi Propaganda.*
202. Gonen, *Roots.*
203. Herf, *Jewish.*
204. Ibid.
205. Ibid.
206. Gonen, *Roots.*
207. Herf, *Jewish.*
208. Kallis, *Propaganda.*
209. Ibid.
210. Walters, *Berlin.*
211. Kallis, *Propaganda.*
212. Herf, *Jewish.*
213. Ibid.
214. Gonen, *Roots.*
215. Herf, *Jewish.*
216. Ibid.
217. Garth S. Jowett and Victoria O'Donnell (eds), *Propaganda and Persuasion,* London: SAGE, 2006.
218. Herf, *Nazi Propaganda.*
219. Nigel Farndale, *Haw-Haw: The Tragedy of William and Margaret Joyce,* London: Pan, 2006.

220. George Forty, *Germany at War*, London: Carlton, 2003.

221. Herf, *Nazi Propaganda*.

212. Herbert Friedman, 'The German V1 Rocket Leaflet Campaign', www.psywar-rior.com/V1RocketLeaf.html, last accessed 25 Jan. 2016.

223. Ibid.

224. Trevor-Roper, *Hitler's Table Talk*, (conversation from 22–3 July 1941).

225. Welch, *Propaganda and Cinema*.

226. Rutherford, *Hitler's Propaganda*.

227. Welch, *Propaganda and Cinema*.

228. *Signal*, Dr Ernst Lewalter, 'The Road to Dunkirk', *Signal*, London: Bison, 1976.

229. Ibid.

230. D. Wouters, 'Kruger, Klaagt Aan' (1941?) (no further detail printed).

231. Welch, *Propaganda and Cinema*.

232. Rutherford, *Hitler's Propaganda*.

233. Manvell, *Films*.

234. Ibid.

235. Ibid.

236. Ibid.

237. SS General Walter Schellenberg, *Invasion 1940*, London: St Ermin's, 2000.

238. Ibid.

239. Herf, *Jewish Enemy*.

240. Trevor-Roper, *Hitler's Table Talk*, (conversation from 18 Oct. 1941).

241. *Das Reich*, 16 June 1940.

242. Welch, *Propaganda and Cinema*.

243. Kallis, *Propaganda*.

244. Welch, *Propaganda and Cinema*.

245. Ibid.

246. Schellenberg, *Invasion*.

247. Ibid.

248. Goebbels, *Diaries*, 17 Dec. 1940.

249. Trevor-Roper, *Hitler's Table Talk*, (conversation from 22–3 July 1941).

250. In West's words, 'the roots of that battle were in the propaganda wars that raged over the radio beneath the smokescreen of Haw Haw counter propaganda and the efforts of the MOI, its anti-lie bureau and other departments all engaged in wartime equivalents of the prewar "conspiracy of silence"'. In West's view the propaganda of National Socialism and the socialist left were indistinguishable and perplexed people since both were anti-capitalist and sought revolutionary cures to social problems. His suggestion that the Beveridge Report, and the welfare state which evolved out of it, was a response to the content and persistence of the Nazi propaganda efforts is an extraordinary claim. W.J. West, *Truth Betrayed*, London: Gerald Duckworth, 1987.

251. *Signal*, Max Clauss, illustration to 'The False Path of Pan-Europe', London: Bison, 1976.

252. *Der Schulungsbrief*, 1942, Herausgeber: Der Reichsorganisationsleiter der NSDAP, 7/8 Folge, Berlin, 1X. Jahrgang Drittes Heft.

253. Franz Wynands, *Wir Fahren Gegen Engelland*, Deutscher Berlag Berlin (1940?).
254. *Schulungsbrief.*
255. Schellenberg, 'Invasion'.
256. Ibid.
257. Benno Wundshammer, 'Fighters Battle over London', in *Bombs Over England*, Munich: Zentralverlag der NSDAP, 1940, Calvin College German Propaganda Archive.
258. Ibid.
259. Schellenberg, 'Invasion'.
260. Ibid.
261. Grunberger, *Social.*
262. Ian Kershaw, *The "Hitler Myth"*, Oxford: Oxford University Press, 1987.
263. Ibid.
264. Ibid.
265. Ibid.
266. Ibid.
267. Ibid.
268. International Historic Films Inc., *Hitler's Fiftieth Birthday Parade*, Chicago, 2004.
269. Michael Burleigh, *The Third Reich: A New History*, New York: Hill and Wang, 2001.
270. Baird, *To Die.*
271. Kershaw, *Hitler Myth.*
272. Rutherford, *Hitler's Propaganda.*
273. Bytwerk, *Bending.*
274. Ibid.
275. Ibid.
276. Hoffmann, *Triumph.*
277. Bracher, *German Dictatorship.*
278. Ibid.
279. Rentschler, *Ministry.*
280. *Signal*, 'There Has Been A Shooting', London: Bison, 1976.
281. Le Bon, *Crowd.*
282. *Adler*, 20 July 1943.
283. Wynands, *Wir Fahren Gegen Engeland.*
284. Calvin College German Propaganda Archive, Posters 1933–9, no. 16.
285. Hunke, 'Has the Big Businessman a Future?'
286. Ibid.
287. Toni Winkelnkemper, *The Attack on Cologne*, Berlin: Franz Eher Berlin, 1942, Calvin College German Propaganda Archive.
288. Ibid.
289. Calvin College German Propaganda Archive, Posters 1933–9, no 36.
290. Calvin College German Propaganda Archive, Posters 1939–45, no 13.
291. Bytwerk, *Bending.*
292. Ibid.
293. Winkelnkemper, *Attack.*

294. Sir Nevile Henderson, *Failure of a Mission*, London: Hodder and Stoughton, 1940.
295. Ibid.
296. Ibid.
297. Le Bon, *Crowd*.
298. Manvell, *Films*.
299. Gerhard Koeppen, *Heroes of the Wehrmacht 1942–3*, Calvin College German Propaganda Archive.
300. Ibid.
301. NSDAP, 'Hunting Pirates in the Channel', 1940, Calvin College German Propaganda Archive.
302. Baird, *To Die*.
303. Herzstein, *War*.
304. Corey Ross, *Media and the Making of Modern Germany*, Oxford: Oxford University Press, 2008.
305. Ibid.
306. Although these values apply to many societies around the world, the case of the captain who took control of Köpenick (a suburb of Berlin) in 1906 on the basis of his uniform could only have happened in Germany.
307. Rutherford, *Hitler's Propaganda*.
308. Ibid.
309. Hitler, for example, remembers Langemarck in *Mein Kampf* and 'the myth of Langemarck became a basic component of the National Socialist propaganda repertoire' (it was where von Falkenhayn had sent the student battalions to their deaths at the hands of British regulars in 1914). Baird, *To Die*.
310. Ibid.
311. Herzstein, *War*.
312. Baird, *To Die*.
313. Herzstein, *War*.
314. Baird, *To Die*.
315. Peter Paret, 'Kolberg as Historical Film and Historical Document', in John Whiteclay Chambers and David Culbert (eds), *World War II, Film and History*, New York: Oxford University Press, 1996.
316. Herzstein, *War*.
317. Trevor-Roper, *Hitler's Table Talk*, (conversation from 19–20 Aug. 1941).
318. Ibid., 25 Sep. 1941.
319. O'Shaughnessy, *Politics*.
320. Z.A.B. Zeman, *Nazi Propaganda*, New York: Oxford University Press, 1964.
321. Hoffmann, *Triumph*.
322. Herzstein, *War*.
323. Hoffmann, *Triumph*.
324. Burleigh, *Third Reich*.
325. Ibid.
326. Baird, *To Die*.
327. Ibid.

328. Ibid.
329. Ibid.
330. Evans, *Coming*.
331. Ibid.
332. Ibid.
333. Ibid.
334. Ibid.
335. Baird, *To Die*.
336. Rutherford, *Hitler's Propaganda*.
337. Grunberger, *Social*.
338. Frederic Spotts, *Hitler and the Power of Aesthetics*, New York: Overlook, 2004.
339. Baird, *To Die*.
340. *Das Schwarze Korps*, 14 Mar. 1944, Calvin College German Propaganda Archive.
341. Ibid.
342. Ibid.
343. Bracher, *German Dictatorship*.
344. Trevor-Roper, *Hitler's Table Talk*, (conversation from 25–6 Sep. 1941).
345. Evans, *Coming*.
346. Simon Sebag-Montefiore, *Stalin: The Court of the Red Tsar*, London: Weidenfeld and Nicolson, 2003.
347. Klemperer, *Language*.
348. Herf, *Nazi Propaganda*.
349. Brian Reynolds Myers, *The Cleanest Race: How North Koreans See Themselves and Why it Matters*, Brooklyn: Melville House, 2010.
350. Robert O. Paxton, *The Anatomy of Fascism*, London: Allen Lane, 2004.
351. Baird, *To Die*.
352. *Signal*, 'The Peace Which Could Not Last', London: Bison, 1976.
353. Ibid.
354. Bracher, *German Dictatorship*.
355. Goebbels, *Diaries*, 23 Dec. 1939.
356. Ibid., 24 Dec. 1939.
357. Paxton, *Anatomy*.
358. Bracher, *German Dictatorship*.
359. Rentschler, *Ministry*.
360. Bracher, *German Dictatorship*.
361. Rentschler, *Ministry*.
362. Ibid.
363. Ibid.
364. Peter Adam, *The Arts of the Third Reich*, London: Thames & Hudson, 1992.
365. Welch, *Propaganda and Cinema*.
366. Bytwerk, *Bending*.
367. Manvell, *Films*.
368. Bracher, *German Dictatorship*.
369. Trevor-Roper, *Hitler's Table Talk*, (entry from Aug. 1941).
370. Ibid., 25 Sep. 1941.

371. Ibid., 5 Nov. 1941.
372. Bracher, *German Dictatorship*.
373. Trevor-Roper, *Hitler's Table Talk*, (conversation from Aug. 1941).
374. Andrew Roberts, *The Holy Fox*, London: Papermac, 1991.
375. Trevor-Roper, *Hitler's Table Talk*, (conversation from 14–15 Sep. 1941).
376. McClatchie, *Look*.
377. Schöpflin, 'Functions'.
378. O'Shaughnessy, *Politics*.

5. SYMBOLISM: A LANGUAGE THAT LIES DEEPER THAN LANGUAGE

1. Karl Bracher, *The German Dictatorship*, New York: Holt, Rinehart and Winston, 1970.
2. Jesse G. Delia, 'Rhetoric in the Nazi Mind', *Southern Communication Journal*, 37, 2 (1971).
3. Nicholas O'Shaughnessy, *Politics and Propaganda: Weapons of Mass Seduction*, Manchester: Manchester University Press, 2004.
4. Ibid.
5. Ibid.
6. Ibid.
7. See, e.g., Anthony Rhodes, *Propaganda, The Art of Persuasion: World War Two*, Broomall, PA: Chelsea House, 1993, p. 53.
8. Jonathan Petropoulos, *Art in the Third Reich*, Chapel Hill: University of North Carolina Press, 1996.
9. Giles MacDonogh, *1938: Hitler's Gamble*, London: Constable, 2009.
10. Hugh Morgan and John Weal, *German Jet Aces of World War 2*, London: Osprey, 1998.
11. Ibid.
12. Ibid.
13. See George Forty, *Germany at War*, London: Carlton, 2003, photograph on p. 174.
14. Ibid.
15. Jeffrey Ethell and Alfred Price, *World War II Fighting Jets*, Shrewsbury: Airlife, 1994.
16. Harald Jansen, 'First Results of the V1', *Das Reich*, 2 July 1944, p. 4, Calvin College German Propaganda Archive.
17. Ibid.
18. Nicholas J. O'Shaughnessy, *Politics and Propaganda: Weapons of Mass Seduction*, Manchester: Manchester University Press, 2004.
19. Richard A. Grunberger, *A Social History of the Third Reich*, London: Penguin, 1991.
20. Hilmar Hoffmann, *The Triumph of Propaganda*, Oxford: Berghahn, 1996.
21. Ibid.
22. *Signal*, 'Above the Acropolis', London: Bison, 1976.
23. *Die Woche*, 7 Oct. 1933.
24. *Illustrierter Beobachter*, 23 Mar. 1939.

25. Michael Burleigh, *The Third Reich: A New History*, New York: Hill and Wang, 2001.
26. Huxley, cited in ibid.
27. James Sheehan, 'Hello to Berlin', *New York Review of Books*, 8 Nov. 2012.
28. *Die Woche*, 7 Oct. 1933.
29. Mary Douglas, *Natural Symbols*, New York: Pantheon, 1982.
30. Robert O. Paxton, *The Anatomy of Fascism*, London: Allen Lane, 2004.
31. Richard Evans, *The Coming of the Third Reich*, London: Penguin, 2005.
32. Paxton, *Anatomy*.
33. Ibid.
34. Bracher, *German Dictatorship*.
35. Oren J. Hale, *The Captive Press in the Third Reich*, Princeton: Princeton University Press, 1964.
36. Ibid.
37. Ibid.
38. Frederic Spotts, *Hitler and the Power of Aesthetics*, New York: Overlook, 2004.
39. Ibid.
40. Ibid.
41. David Welch, *Propaganda and the German Cinema, 1933–1945* (revised ed.), London: I.B. Tauris, 2007.
42. Ward Rutherford, *Hitler's Propaganda Machine*, London: Bison, 1978.
43. Hugh Trevor-Roper, *Hitler's Table Talk 1941–1944: Hitler's Conversations Recorded by Martin Bormann*, Oxford: Oxford University Press Oxford, 1988; (conversation from 2 Aug. 1941).
44. Hoffmann, *Triumph*.
45. Antony Beevor, *Stalingrad*, London: Penguin, 1999.
46. Ibid.
47. Ibid.
48. Rutherford, *Hitler's Propaganda*.
49. O'Shaughnessy, *Politics*.
50. Hoffmann, *Triumph*.
51. Hoffmann, *Triumph*.
52. Ibid.
53. Trevor-Roper, *Hitler's Table Talk*, (conversation from 5 July 1941).
54. Petropoulos, *Art*.
55. Joachim C. Fest, *Hitler*, London: Penguin, 2002.
56. Hoffmann, *Triumph*.
57. Victor Klemperer, *The Language of the Third Reich*, London: Athlone, 2000.
58. Grunberger, *Social*.
59. Rutherford, *Hitler's Propaganda*.
60. Grunberger, *Social*.
61. Jay Baird, *To Die for Germany*, Bloomington: Indiana University Press, 1992.
62. Ibid.
63. Paxton, *Anatomy*.
64. Ibid.

65. Rutherford, *Hitler's Propaganda*.
66. Ibid.
67. Petropoulos, *Art*.
68. Ibid.
69. Ibid.
70. Ibid.
71. Ibid.
72. MacDonogh, *1938*.
73. Corey Ross, *Media and the Making of Modern Germany*, Oxford: Oxford University Press, 2008.
74. MacDonogh, *1938*.
75. Ibid.
76. Forty, *Germany*.
77. Petropoulos, *Art*.
78. Ibid.
79. Forty, *Germany*.
80. Petropoulos, *Art*.
81. Welch, *Propaganda and Cinema*; Solveig Grothe, 'Hitlers Pinselführer', *Spiegel Online*, 19 July 2012.
82. Burleigh, *Third Reich*.
83. Ian Kershaw, *The "Hitler Myth"*, Oxford: Oxford University Press, 1987.
84. Burleigh, *Third Reich*.
85. Jeffrey Herf, *The Jewish Enemy*, Cambridge, MA: Belknap, 2006.
86. Michael Blain, 'Fighting Words: What We Can Learn from Hitler's Hyperbole', *Symbolic Interaction*, 11, 2 (1988).
87. W. S. Allen, *The Nazi Seizure of Power*, New York: Franklin Watts, 1984.
88. Kershaw, *Hitler Myth*.
89. Spotts, *Hitler*.
90. Grunberger, *Social*.
91. Baird, *To Die*.
92. Grunberger, *Social*.
93. Baird, *To Die*.
94. Ibid.
95. Ibid.
96. Ibid.
97. Grunberger, *Social*.
98. Ibid.
99. Jay Y. Gonen, *The Roots of Nazi Psychology*, Lexington: University Press of Kentucky, 2000.
100. Burleigh, *Third Reich*.
101. Rutherford, *Hitler's Propaganda*.
102. Ibid.
103. Spotts, *Hitler*.
104. Burleigh, *Third Reich*.
105. Fest, *Hitler*.

106. Spotts, *Hitler*.
107. Rutherford, *Hitler's Propaganda*.
108. Spotts, *Hitler*.
109. Ibid.
110. Franz Neumann, *Behemoth: The Structure and Practice of National Socialism 1933–44*, New York: Harper and Row, 1966.
111. Spotts, *Hitler*.
112. Ibid.
113. Grunberger, *Social*.
114. Allen, *Nazi Seizure*.
115. Grunberger, *Social*.
116. Burleigh, *Third Reich*.
117. Grunberger, *Social*.
118. Allen, *Nazi Seizure*.
119. Neumann, *Behemoth*.
120. Geoffrey Cox, *Countdown to War*, London: William Kimber, 1988.
121. Welch, *Propaganda and Cinema*.
122. Leni Riefenstahl, *Triumph of the Will* (film), cited in ibid.
123. Ibid.
124. Cox, *Countdown*.
125. Ibid.
126. Oliver Thomson, *Easily Led: A History of Propaganda*, Stroud: Sutton, 1999.
127. Hoffmann, *Triumph*.
128. Grunberger, *Social*.
129. Spotts, *Hitler*.
130. Cox, *Countdown*.
131. Hoffmann, *Triumph*.
132. Ibid.
133. Welch, *Propaganda and Cinema*.
134. Cox, *Countdown*.
135. Hoffmann, *Triumph*.
136. Gustave Le Bon, *The Crowd*, n.p.: Filiquarian Publishing LLC, 2005.

6. RHETORIC: WORDS THAT THINK FOR YOU

1. Victor Klemperer, *The Language of the Third Reich*, London: Athlone, 2000.
2. Ward Rutherford, *Hitler's Propaganda Machine*, London: Bison, 1978.
3. Nicholas J. O'Shaughnessy, *Politics and Propaganda: Weapons of Mass Seduction*, Manchester: Manchester University Press, 2004.
4. Jeffrey Herf, *The Jewish Enemy*, Cambridge, MA: Belknap, 2006.
5. O'Shaughnessy, *Politics*.
6. Ibid.
7. Ibid. (citing Jeff Mason. *Philosophical Rhetoric*, London: Routledge, 1989).
8. Klemperer, *Language*.
9. Ibid.

10. Ibid.
11. Ibid.
12. Ibid.
13. Ibid.
14. Ibid.
15. Ibid.
16. Debra Umberson and Kristin Henderson, 'The Social Construction of Death in the Gulf War', *Omega: The Journal of Death and Dying*, 25, 1 (1992), pp. 1–5.
17. O'Shaughnessy, *Politics*.
18. Ibid.
19. Ibid.
20. A.P. Foulkes, *Literature and Propaganda*, London: Methuen, 1983.
21. Joseph Goebbels, 'Knowledge and Propaganda' speech, 9 Jan. 1928; Munich: Zentralverlag der NSDAP, 1934, pp. 28–52.
22. Aristotle A. Kallis, *Nazi Propaganda and the Second World War*, Basingstoke: Palgrave Macmillan, 2000.
23. O'Shaughnessy, *Politics*.
24. Ibid.
25. *Signal*, 'England's Plans Frustrated', London: Bison, 1976.
26. *Signal*, 'On Guard in the North', London: Bison, 1976.
27. *Signal*, 'Knights of Our Times', London: Bison, 1976.
28. *Signal*, 'Ten Hours Too Soon', London: Bison, 1976.
29. *Signal*, 'Tunis: Personages and Combats', London: Bison, 1976.
30. *Facts in Review*, 1940, Calvin College German Propaganda Archive.
31. Randall L. Bytwerk, *Julius Streicher*, New York: Cooper Square, 2001.
32. Oliver Thomson, *Easily Led: A History of Propaganda*, Stroud: Sutton, 1999.
33. Bytwerk, *Julius*.
34. Rutherford, *Hitler's Propaganda*.
35. Thomson, *Easily Led*.
36. Baruch Gitlis, *Cinema of Hate: Nazi Film in the War Against the Jews*, Bnei Brak: Alfa Communication, 1996.
37. Ibid.
38. Richard Evans, *The Coming of the Third Reich*, London: Penguin, 2005.
39. Ibid.
40. Klemperer, *Language*.
41. Ibid.
42. Robert Gellately, *Backing Hitler: Consent and Coercion in Nazi Germany*, New York: Oxford University Press, 2001.
43. M. Perry and F. Schweitzer, *Anti-Semitism: Myth and Hate from Antiquity to the Present*, New York: Palgrave Macmillan, 2002.
44. Klemperer, *Language*.
45. 'The Eternal Jew: The Film of a 2000-Year Rat Migration', *Unser Wille Und Weg*, 10 (1940), pp. 54–5, Calvin College German Propaganda Archive.
46. Klemperer, *Language*.
47. Ibid.

48. Ibid.
49. Bytwerk, *Julius*.
50. Herf, *Jewish Enemy*.
51. Ibid.
52. Ibid.
53. O'Shaughnessy, *Politics*.
54. Ibid.
55. Michael Blain, 'Fighting Words: What We Can Learn From Hitler's Hyperbole', *Symbolic Interaction*, 11 (1988).
56. Jay Y. Gonen, *The Roots of Nazi Psychology*, Lexington: University Press of Kentucky, 2000.
57. Ibid.
58. Blain, 'Fighting'.
59. Klemperer, *Language*.
60. Ibid.
61. Ibid.
62. Richard Grunberger, *A Social History of the Third Reich*, London: Penguin, 1991.
63. Klemperer, *Language*.
64. Ibid.
65. Ibid.
66. Ibid.
67. Ibid.
68. Ibid.
69. Ibid.
70. Ibid.
71. Franz Neumann, *Behemoth: The Structure and Practice of National Socialism, 1933–44*, New York: Harper and Row, 1966.
72. Herf, *Jewish Enemy*.
73. Klemperer, *Language*.
74. Ibid.
75. Ibid.
76. Ibid.
77. Ibid.
78. Bettina Arnold, 'Past as Propaganda', *Archaeology* (July/Aug. 1992).
79. Klemperer, *Language*.
80. Ibid.
81. Ibid.
82. Ibid.
83. Ibid.
84. Blain, 'Fighting'.
85. Herf, *Jewish Enemy*.
86. Klemperer, *Language*.
87. Ibid.
88. Grunberger, *Social.*
89. Ibid.

90. Ibid.
91. Ibid.
92. Ibid.
93. Max Domarus, *Hitler: Speeches and Proclamations, 1932–1945*, London: I.B. Tauris, 1990.
94. Victor Klemperer, *The Lesser Evil: The Diaries of Victor Klemperer 1945–59*, London: Phoenix, 2003.
95. Ian Kershaw, *The Hitler Myth*, Oxford: Oxford University Press, 1987.
96. Ibid.
97. Frederic Spotts, *Hitler and the Power of Aesthetics*, New York: Overlook, 2004.
98. Ibid.
99. Kershaw, *Hitler*.
100. Ibid.
101. Klemperer, *Language*.
102. Ibid.
103. *Signal*, 'Japan's Long Arm', London: Bison, 1976.
104. Klemperer, *Language*.
105. Ibid.
106. Ibid.
107. *Berliner Morgenpost*, 5 Oct. 1944, Calvin College German Propaganda Archive.
108. Thomson, *Easily Led.*
109. David Bromwich, 'Euphemism and American Violence', New York Review of Books, 3 Apr. 2008.
110. O'Shaughnessy, *Politics*.
111. Ibid.
112. Klemperer, *Language*.
113. Robert Edwin Herzstein, *The War that Hitler Won*, London: Hamish Hamilton, 1979.
114. Karl Bracher, *The German Dictatorship*, New York: Holt, Rinehart and Winston, 1970.
115. Herzstein, *War.*
116. Rutherford, *Hitler's Propaganda.*
117. Herzstein, *War.*
118. Ibid.
119. Ibid.
120. Ibid.
121. Ibid.
122. Ibid.
123. Ibid.
124. *Berliner Morgenpost*, 5 Oct. 1944.
125. Ibid.
126. Corey Ross, *Media and the Making of Modern Germany*, Oxford: Oxford University Press, 2008.
127. Gonen, *Roots.*
128. O'Shaughnessy, *Politics*.

129. Ibid.
130. Ibid.

CONCLUSIONS: PROPAGANDA, THE LIGHT OF PERVERTED SCIENCE

1. Jane Caplan, 'A Design For Life', *Times Literary Supplement*, 15 Sep. 2006 (review of Richard J. Evans, *The Third Reich in Power 1933–1939*, London: Allen Lane, 2006)
2. Ward Rutherford, *Hitler's Propaganda Machine*, London: Bison, 1978.
3. Michael Schudson, *Advertising: The Uneasy Persuasion*, New York: Basic, 1986.
4. Ibid.
5. Ibid.
6. Corey Ross, *Media and the Making of Modern Germany*, Oxford: Oxford University Press, 2008.
7. Ibid.
8. Ibid.
9. Hilmar Hoffmann, *The Triumph of Propaganda*, Oxford: Berghahn, 1996.
10. Heinrich Hoffmann, *Hitler in his Homeland*, Berlin: Zeitgeschichte verlag, 1938.
11. Michael Burleigh, *The Third Reich: A New History*, New York: Hill and Wang, 2001.

INDEX

INDEX

INDEX

INDEX

INDEX

INDEX

existential threats, 5, 23, 52, 57, 60, 62, 74, 124, 146, 148–56, 175–6, 180, 204, 281

Experience of Hans and Elsa with a Strange Man, The, 173

extermination camps, 5, 77, 217, 272

extraversion, 266–7

Fa 223 helicopter, 96

Fabian (Kästner), 33

Facts in Review, 22, 53–4, 57, 261

famine, 21–2, 58, 130

fanatic, 256, 273

fashion, 225

Fatherland Party, 18, 19–20, 24, 123

Feder, Gottfried, 20, 167

Feldherrnhalle, Munich, 241, 272

Feldzug in Polen, 62

Ferry Boat Woman Maria, 209

Fest, Joachim, 26, 163

Fichte, Johann, 17, 145

field-kitchens, 225

Fieseler Storch aircraft, 70, 74

Fighter Squadron Lutzow, 197

film, 4, 5, 27–8, 34, 43, 45–6, 57, 61, 69, 77–8, 82, 85, 86, 93, 106, 110–13, 123, 132, 133, 142, 143, 147, 151–9, 161, 162, 164–5, 169, 177, 178–81, 188, 189–90, 196, 197, 198, 200, 201, 204, 207–9, 263, 280, 284

First World War (1914–18), 2, 11, 16–23, 25, 28, 41–2, 54, 61, 63, 77, 92, 107, 117, 121–3, 125–30, 145, 153, 159, 161, 171, 174, 178, 183–4, 193, 199, 205, 231, 239, 248, 281

  1914 Battle of Tannenberg, 145, 199, 239

  1916 Battle of Verdun, 199; Battle of the Somme, 18, 199

  1917 Battle of Langemarck, 199

  1918 Treaty of Brest-Litovsk, 17; Operation Michael, 18; Armistice, 11, 25, 28, 41, 54, 63, 65, 92, 130, 157, 178, 261

Flakwagen, 234

Flames of Prehistory, The, 147

Florida, United States, 182

Flying Wing, 96, 211

Foch, Ferdinand, 28

Focke-Wulf Condor, 234

Folk Storm, *see Volkssturm*

folklore, 142–4, 184, 186, 193

For the Rights of Man, 151

For Us, 242

Ford, Henry, 146

Fordism, 78

foreign policy, 8, 29, 39, 40, 44, 51, 110, 223–4

Forest of Katyn, 153

Fortress Europe, 81, 269

Forum, Rome, 246

Foulkes, A.P., 259

Foundation Day, 228

Foundations of the Nineteenth Century (Chamberlain), 160

Fourteen Points (1918), 22

Fox of Glenarvon, The, 178

France, 16–17, 21, 23, 34, 37, 40, 52, 54, 57, 58, 59, 60–1, 63, 64, 66, 70, 71, 86, 96, 103, 129, 140, 164–5, 167–8, 209, 217, 232–3, 244, 260, 264

  1756–1763 Seven Years' War, 155

  1789–99 Revolution, 16, 123, 134, 195, 244

  1803–15 Napoleonic Wars, 3, 83, 86, 181

  1848 Revolution, 16, 17

  1870 Battle of Sedan, 188

  1914–18 First World War, 61

  1916 Battle of Verdun, 199; Battle of the Somme, 18, 199

  1917 Battle of Langemarck, 199

  1918 Armistice, 11, 25, 28, 41, 54, 63, 65, 92, 130, 157, 178, 261

  1919 Treaty of Versailles, 20–3, 25, 29, 32, 38, 40, 42, 45, 54, 61, 223, 224

  1920 occupation of Saar, 21, 22, 37

  1923 occupation of Ruhr, 21, 22, 24, 61; execution of Albert Schlageter, 61, 130, 201;

INDEX

INDEX

INDEX

reparations, 21, 22, 29, 39
Repeated Exposure Effect, 108
repetition, 107–10, 221
Request Concert, 112
resonance, 106–7
Resurrection, 228
Return, 62
revolution, 139–40
Revolutions of 1848, 16, 17
Reynaud, Paul, 60
Rheinisch-Westfalische Zeitung (RWZ), 34
rhetoric, 3, 11, 12, 21, 24, 41, 56, 60, 64, 255–78
  of contempt, 261–2
  declamatory, 41, 231, 266
  of dynamism, 260–1
  emotion, 267–8
  euphemism, 266
  extraversion, 266–7
  hyper-historicity, 268–9
  hyperbole, 3, 53, 57, 83, 95, 104, 114, 173, 181, 196, 261, 263, 264, 266–7
  of inclusion, 262
  key concepts, 272–5
  methaphor, 262–5
  of presentation, 215
  slogans, 34, 35, 49, 57, 80–1, 84, 85, 88, 90, 91, 101, 107, 116, 275–7
  sources, 269–72
  Virtue words, 275
Rhineland, Germany, 21, 39, 41, 100, 164, 224
Ribbentrop, Joachim von, 34, 52, 68, 78, 223
Riders of German East Africa, 178
Riefenstahl, Leni, 143, 163, 252
Ritter, Gerhard, 6
ritual, 11, 25, 27, 28, 31, 69, 87, 97, 143, 187, 189, 199–200, 208, 219, 221, 224, 244–5
ritual killing, 173–4
River Plate, Battle of the, (1939), 53
'Road to Dunkirk, The' (Lewalter), 178
Robert and Bertram, 77, 169

Robert Ley, 216
Robespierre, Maximilien, 123
Röhm, Ernst, 45, 48, 224, 229, 236, 252
Roman salute, 31, 37, 86, 132, 151, 226, 244, 245, 252, 285
Romania, 22, 83, 209
Romanticism, 16, 160
Rome, Ancient (753 BC–476 AD), 18, 39, 86, 143–4, 147, 158, 168, 184, 216, 226–7, 233, 246
Rome, Italy, 25, 246
Rommel, Erwin, 71, 200
Roosevelt, Franklin Delano, 59, 110, 256
Rosebery, Lord, *see* Primrose, Archibald
Rosenberg, Alfred, 10, 23, 146, 152, 160
Rosenberg, Moses, 153
Rosikat, Ernst, 146
Ross, Corey, viii, 7, 52, 111, 118, 134
Rothermere, Lord, *see* Harmsworth, Harold
Rothschilds, The, 78, 106, 170, 181
Rotterdam, Netherlands, 53, 63, 80, 259
Rouen, Normandy, 61
Royal Air Force (RAF), 65, 95, 178, 246
Ruhr, North Rhine-Westphalia, 21, 22, 24, 61
rumours, 10, 55–6, 89, 91–2, 93
runes, 218, 269–70
Russian Civil War (1917–22), 152
Russian Empire (1721–1917), 17, 123, 134, 145, 155, 167, 172, 209
Rutherford, Ward, 199, 224, 243, 261

SA (Sturmabteilung), 27, 32–3, 36, 37, 40, 43, 45, 112, 200, 236–7, 238, 245, 247, 248, 249–50, 252, 269, 282
SA Mann Brand, 78, 106, 151, 201, 225
Saarbrücken, Saarland, 39
Saarland, Germany, 21, 22, 37, 39
sacerdotal language, 271–2
Salazar, António, 206
salt, 55

INDEX

INDEX

Teutonic Knights, 142, 144

Teutonic people, 3, 17, 18, 60, 62, 81, 87, 122, 125, 142, 144, 145, 146, 175, 262, 270, 276

thaumaturgic monarchs, 143

Theresienstadt concentration camp, 103, 216–17

Thimme, Hans, 126

Thingstätte, 143

Third Reich, The (Moeller), 187

Thirty Years' War (1618–48), 48

Thomson, Oliver, 251

Threatened by the Steam Plough, 147

Thule Society, 24, 166

Thus Spake Zarathustra (Nietzsche), 145

Tiergarten, Berlin, 225

Tiger tanks, 220

Times, The, 126, 227

Tirpitz, 220

Titanic, 196

Tobruk, Libya, 71, 74, 76

de Tocqueville, Alexis, 166

Todt, Fritz, 196

Torgau, Battle of, (1760), 189

de Torquemada, Tomás, 230

Total War, 84–5, 225, 276

totalitarianism, 1, 9, 50, 52, 100, 195, 224, 234, 245, 268

Totenkopf, 226

Tractarianism, 3, 168

trade unions, 32, 33, 34

Transylvania, 144

Treaty of Brest-Litovsk (1918), 17

Treaty of Versailles (1919), 20–3, 25, 29, 32, 38, 40, 42, 45, 54, 61, 223, 224

Treblinka extermination camp, 77

von Treitschke, Heinrich, 145, 167

Trevor-Roper, Hugh, 63, 158

Trial before the People's Court, 90, 134

Triumph of the Will, 45–6, 134, 199, 221, 226, 227, 247, 248, 252–3, 282, 285

Troost, Paul Ludwig, 242

truth, 56–7, 59, 103–4, 106, 146, 147, 149–52, 163, 166, 171–2, 178, 199, 201, 219–20

Tunisia, 260

Turkey, 45

Tyrrell, William Blake, 150, 196

U-boats, 71, 191

UFA, 29, 34

Ukraine, 210

Umberson, Debra, 258

unemployment, 33, 40, 248, 286

United States, 3, 5, 7, 18, 22, 29, 35, 43, 50, 53, 59, 71, 72–3, 75, 77, 78–80, 85, 90, 92–3, 96, 110, 127, 129, 130, 140, 149, 163, 171, 173, 176–7, 182, 192, 204–5, 208, 227, 238, 256, 261

1918 Wilson issues Fourteen Points, 22

1929 Young Plan agreement, 29; Wall Street Crash, 29, 285

1939 Marian Anderson sings at Lincoln Memorial, 238

1941 Japanese attack on Pearl Harbor, 71, 72; Germany declares war, 71, 77

1942 fall of the Philippines to Japan, 71; sinking of SS *President Coolidge*, 75

1944 Battle for Cassino, 171

universities, 29, 32, 85, 113, 167, 181, 255

University of Cologne, 113

Untermenschen, 5, 74, 78, 88, 141, 156, 162, 227, 261

user-gratification, 133

utopianism, 1, 165, 210–13

V-1 and V-2 rockets, 95, 212, 218

de Valera, Éamon, 206

Valhalla, 87

van der Lubbe, Marinus, 45

Verdun, Battle of, (1916), 199

Versailles Treaty (1919), 20–3, 25, 29, 32, 38, 40, 42, 45, 54, 61, 223, 224

VFA, 177

INDEX